Middle School 3-2
중간고사 완벽대비

적중 100

영어 기출 문제집

중3

비상 | 김진완

Best Collection

구성과 특징

교과서의 주요 학습 내용을 중심으로 학습 영역별 특성에 맞춰 단계별로 다양한 학습 기회를 제공하여
단원별 학습능력 평가는 물론 중간 및 기말고사 시험 등에 완벽하게 대비할 수 있도록 내용을 구성

Words & Expressions

Step1 Key Words 단원별 핵심 단어 설명 및 풀이
Key Expression 단원별 핵심 숙어 및 관용어 설명
Word Power 반대 또는 비슷한 뜻 단어 배우기
English Dictionary 영어로 배우는 영어 단어

Step2 실력평가 단원별 수시평가 대비 주관식, 객관식 문제풀이

Step3 서술형 대비 학업성취도 및 수행능력평가 대비 서술형 문제풀이

Conversation

Step1 핵심 의사소통 소통에 필요한 주요 표현 방법 요약
핵심 Check 기본적인 표현 방법 및 활용능력 확인

Step2 대화문 익히기 교과서 대화문 심층 분석 및 확인

Step3 교과서 확인학습 빈칸 채우기를 통한 문장 완성 능력 확인

Step4 기본평가 시험대비 기초 학습 능력 평가

Step5 실력평가 단원별 수시평가 대비 주관식, 객관식 문제풀이

Step6 서술형 대비 학업성취도 및 수행능력평가 대비 서술형 문제풀이

Grammar

Step1 주요 문법 단원별 주요 문법 사항과 예문을 알기 쉽게 설명
핵심 Check 기본 문법사항에 대한 이해 여부 확인

Step2 기본평가 시험대비 기초 학습 능력 평가

Step3 실력평가 단원별 수시평가 대비 주관식, 객관식 문제풀이

Step4 서술형 대비 학업성취도 및 수행능력평가 대비 서술형 문제풀이

Reading

Step1 구문 분석 단원별로 제시된 문장에 대한 구문별 분석과 내용 설명
확인문제 문장에 대한 기본적인 이해와 인지능력 확인

Step2 확인학습A 빈칸 채우기를 통한 문장 완성 능력 확인

Step3 확인학습B 제시된 우리말을 영어로 완성하여 작문 능력 키우기

Step4 실력평가 단원별 수시평가 대비 주관식, 객관식 문제풀이

Step5 서술형 대비 학업성취도 및 수행능력평가 대비 서술형 문제풀이
교과서 구석구석 교과서에 나오는 기타 문장까지 완벽 학습

Composition

|영역별 핵심문제|
단어 및 어휘, 대화문, 문법, 독해 등 각 영역별 기출문제의 출제 유형을 분석하여 실전에 대비하고 연습할 수 있도록 문제를 배열

|단원별 예상문제|
기출문제를 분석한 후 새로운 시험 출제 경향을 더하여 새롭게 출제될 수 있는 문제를 포함하여 시험에 완벽하게 대비할 수 있도록 준비

|서술형 실전 및 창의사고력 문제|
학교 시험에서 점차 늘어나는 서술형 시험에 집중 대비하고 고득점을 취득하는데 만전을 기하기 위한 학습 코너

|단원별 모의고사|
영역별, 단계별 학습을 모두 마친 후 실전 연습을 위한 모의고사

교과서 파헤치기

- **단어Test1~3** 영어 단어 우리말 쓰기, 우리말을 영어 단어로 쓰기, 영영풀이에 해당하는 단어와 우리말 쓰기
- **대화문Test1~2** 대화문 빈칸 완성 및 전체 대화문 쓰기
- **본문Test1~5** 빈칸 완성, 우리말 쓰기, 문장 배열연습, 영어 작문하기 복습 등 단계별 반복 학습을 통해 교과서 지문에 대한 완벽한 습득
- **구석구석지문Test1~2** 지문 빈칸 완성 및 전문 영어로 쓰기

Lesson 5

Critical Minds

의사소통 기능

- 자세한 설명 요청하기

  A: Did you know that bats aren't blind?

  B: No. **Can you tell me more about** it?

  A: Some bats can see three times better than humans.

- 의견에 대한 이유 묻기

  A: Books of riddles are really useful for adults.

  B: **Why do you say so?**

  A: They help us think more creatively.

언어 형식

- 분사구문

  Let's look into some articles **thinking about the hidden motives**.

- so that ~ can ...

  They made up this fake article **so that** they **could** draw the readers' attention.

Words & Expressions

Key Words

- □ **admit** [ədmít] 동 인정하다, 자백하다
- □ **adult** [ədʌ́lt] 명 성인, 어른
- □ **argument** [ɑ́ːrgjumənt] 명 논쟁, 언쟁
- □ **awful** [ɔ́ːfəl] 형 끔찍한, 지독한
- □ **chemical** [kémikəl] 명 화학 물질
- □ **chest** [tʃest] 명 가슴, 흉부
- □ **citizen** [sítəzən] 명 시민
- □ **competitor** [kəmpétətər] 명 경쟁자, 경쟁 상대
- □ **condition** [kəndíʃən] 명 상태, 상황
- □ **confess** [kənfés] 동 고백하다, 인정하다
- □ **critical** [krítikəl] 형 위험한, 위독한
- □ **critically** [krítikəli] 부 비판적으로
- □ **criticize** [krítəsàiz] 동 비난하다
- □ **current** [kə́ːrənt] 형 현재의, 지금의
- □ **describe** [diskráib] 동 기술하다
- □ **disaster** [dizǽstər] 명 참사, 재난
- □ **escape** [iskéip] 동 달아나다, 탈출하다, 벗어나다
- □ **extremely** [ikstríːmli] 부 극도로, 극히
- □ **fake** [feik] 형 가짜의, 거짓의
- □ **formation** [fɔːrméiʃən] 명 형성
- □ **goldfish** [góuldfìʃ] 명 금붕어
- □ **harmful** [hɑ́ːrmfəl] 형 해로운, 유해한
- □ **height** [hait] 명 키, 신장
- □ **incident** [ínsədənt] 명 사건
- □ **injure** [índʒər] 동 부상을 입히다
- □ **judge** [dʒʌdʒ] 동 판단하다

- □ **loose** [luːs] 형 풀린, 헐거운
- □ **measure** [méʒər] 동 측정하다, 재다
- □ **mine** [main] 명 광산 동 채굴하다
- □ **mislead** [mìslíːd] 동 잘못 이끌다, 오해하게 하다
- □ **motive** [móutiv] 명 동기, 이유
- □ **muscle** [mʌ́sl] 명 근육
- □ **nevertheless** [nèvərðəlés] 부 그럼에도 불구하고
- □ **panic** [pǽnik] 동 겁에 질려 어쩔 줄 모르다
- □ **poem** [póuəm] 명 시, 운문
- □ **prove** [pruːv] 동 입증하다, 증명하다
- □ **public** [pʌ́blik] 명 대중, 일반 사람들
- □ **publish** [pʌ́bliʃ] 동 발행하다, 출판하다, 게재하다
- □ **recognize** [rékəgnàiz] 동 알아보다
- □ **reliable** [riláiəbl] 형 믿을 만한, 신뢰할 만한
- □ **riddle** [rídl] 부 수수께끼
- □ **seriously** [síəriəsli] 부 진지하게, 심각하게
- □ **shoot** [ʃuːt] 동 (총 등을) 쏘다
- □ **Slav** [slɑːv] 명 슬라브인
- □ **source** [sɔːrs] 명 출처, 자료
- □ **spell** [spel] 동 철자를 말하다[쓰다]
- □ **spot** [spɑt] 동 발견하다, 찾아내다
- □ **strengthen** [stréŋkθən] 동 강하게 하다, 더 튼튼하게 하다
- □ **support** [səpɔ́ːrt] 동 (사실임을) 입증하다, 뒷받침하다
- □ **temperature** [témpərətʃər] 명 온도, 기온, 체온
- □ **trust** [trʌst] 동 신뢰하다
- □ **wound** [wuːnd] 동 상처를 입히다

Key Expressions

- □ **according to** ~에 따르면
- □ **be related to** ~와 연관되다
- □ **be useful for** ~에게 유용하다
- □ **break down** ~을 부수다, ~을 무너뜨리다
- □ **catch a cold** 감기에 걸리다
- □ **draw one's attention to** ~의 관심을 …로 끌다
- □ **fall asleep** 잠들다
- □ **get caught -ing** ~하다가 걸리다
- □ **in that** ~라는 점에서, ~이기 때문에

- □ **look into** 조사하다, 들여다보다
- □ **lose weight** 몸무게를 줄이다
- □ **make up** 지어내다, 만들어 내다
- □ **on the loose** 잡히지 않은, 탈주 중인
- □ **search for** ~을 찾다
- □ **spend time -ing** ~하면서 시간을 보내다
- □ **think outside the box** 고정관념에서 벗어나다
- □ **What if** ~? 만약 ~라면 어떨까?

Word Power

※ 서로 비슷한 뜻을 가진 어휘

- □ **adult** 성인, 어른 – **grownup** 성인
- □ **awful** 끔찍한, 지독한 – **horrible** 끔찍한
- □ **current** 현재의, 지금의 – **present** 현재의
- □ **injure** 부상을 입히다 – **wound** 부상을 입히다

- □ **argument** 논쟁, 언쟁 – **debate** 토론
- □ **criticize** 비난하다 – **blame** 비난하다
- □ **describe** 기술하다 – **illustrate** 설명하다
- □ **spot** 발견하다, 찾아내다 – **detect** 찾아내다

※ 서로 반대의 뜻을 가진 어휘

- □ **competitor** 경쟁자 ↔ **helper** 조력자
- □ **fake** 가짜의, 거짓의 ↔ **true** 진실한
- □ **reliable** 믿을 만한 ↔ **unreliable** 믿을 수 없는
- □ **trust** 신뢰하다 ↔ **distrust** 불신하다

- □ **criticize** 비난하다 ↔ **compliment** 칭찬하다
- □ **harmful** 해로운, 유해한 ↔ **harmless** 무해한
- □ **strengthen** 강하게 하다 ↔ **weaken** 약하게 하다

※ 접두사 mis- [mis+어근]: 잘못된, 나쁜, 나쁘게

- □ **mis-**+**lead** = **mislead** (잘못 이끌다)
- □ **mis-**+**fortune** = **misfortune** (불행, 불운)
- □ **mis-**+**read** = **misread** (잘못 해석하다)
- □ **mis-**+**use** = **misuse** (오용, 오용하다)

- □ **mis-**+**take** = **mistake** (실수, 실수하다)
- □ **mis-**+**behavior** = **misbehavior** (나쁜 행실)
- □ **mis-**+**trust** = **mistrust** (불신하다)
- □ **mis-**+**understand** = **misunderstand** (오해하다)

※ 접미사 –ize [명사/형용사+ize = 동사]: ~으로 되다, ~이 되게 만들다, ~와 같아지게 하다

- □ **critic**+**-ize** = **criticize** (비판하다)
- □ **regular**+**-ize** = **regularize** (합법화하다)
- □ **fossil**+**-ize** = **fossilize** (화석화하다)
- □ **harmony**+**-ize** = **harmonize** (조화를 이루다)
- □ **moisture**+**-ize** = **moisturize** (촉촉하게 하다)

- □ **real**+**-ize** = **realize** (실현하다)
- □ **private**+**-ize** = **privatize** (민영화하다)
- □ **theory**+**-ize** = **theorize** (이론을 세우다)
- □ **memory**+**-ize** = **memorize** (암기하다)

English Dictionary

- □ **disaster** 참사, 재난
  → an event causing great harm, damage, or suffering
  해, 손상, 또는 고통을 초래하는 사건
- □ **citizen** 시민
  → a person who lives in a particular city
  특정 시에 살고 있는 사람
- □ **describe** 기술하다
  → to say or write what someone or something is like
  누군가 또는 무언가가 어떠한지 말하거나 쓰다
- □ **panic** 겁에 질려 어쩔 줄 모르다
  → to suddenly feel so worried that you cannot be reasonable
  너무 걱정이 되어서 이성적일 수 없다고 갑자기 느끼다

- □ **shoot** (총 등을) 쏘다
  → to fire a weapon
  무기를 발사하다
- □ **chest** 가슴, 흉부
  → the upper front part of the body of humans
  인간 신체의 상체 앞부분
- □ **spell** 철자를 말하다, 쓰다
  → to form words with the letters in the correct order
  문자를 가지고 알맞은 순서로 단어를 형성하다
- □ **source** 출처, 자료
  → a place, person, or thing from which something comes
  그것으로부터 무언가가 나오는 장소, 사람 또는 사물

서답형

01 다음 짝지어진 단어의 관계가 같도록 빈칸에 알맞은 말을 쓰시오.

harmless : harmful = trust : _____

02 다음 영영풀이가 가리키는 것을 고르시오.

an event causing great harm, damage, or suffering

① riddle   ② formation   ③ source
④ disaster   ⑤ temperature

중요

03 다음 문장의 빈칸에 공통으로 들어갈 말을 고르시오.

• You can _____ me all the time.
• Don't _____ what people are saying about me.
• If you put your _____ in me, I'll do my best.
• I have complete _____ in John.

① trust   ② judge   ③ spot
④ chest   ⑤ disaster

중요

04 다음 중 밑줄 친 부분의 뜻풀이가 바르지 <u>않은</u> 것은?

① They were caught at the airport because they had <u>fake</u> passports. (가짜의, 거짓의)
② Do you know geese fly in a V <u>formation</u>? (대형)
③ She wants to keep <u>goldfish</u> at home as pets. (금붕어)
④ He <u>injured</u> his back and legs on the mountain. (부상을 입히다)
⑤ My uncle found gold in a <u>mine</u> and became rich. (나의 것)

05 다음 주어진 문장의 밑줄 친 judge와 <u>다른</u> 의미로 쓰인 것은?

Judging by her last letter, they are having a wonderful time.

① As far as I can <u>judge</u>, all of them are to blame.
② To <u>judge</u> from what he said, he was very disappointed.
③ Schools should not be <u>judged</u> only on exam results.
④ Their concert was <u>judged</u> to have been a great success.
⑤ Considering the results, I think the <u>judge</u> was too generous.

서답형

06 다음 우리말과 일치하도록 주어진 단어를 모두 배열하여 완성하시오.

(1) 그는 팔에 상처를 입었었다.
(wounded / in / had / been / the / he / arm)
➡ _____

(2) 그녀가 또 거짓말을 했으므로 나는 그녀를 더 이상 신뢰할 수 없다.
(trust / I / she / her / anymore / again / lied / can't / because)
➡ _____

(3) 기온이 오늘 40도까지 올랐다.
(to / the / today / went / temperature / forty / up)
➡ _____

01 다음 짝지어진 단어의 관계가 같도록 빈칸에 알맞은 말을 쓰시오.

> regular : regularize = real : _____

 02 다음 우리말에 맞게 빈칸에 알맞은 말을 쓰시오.

(1) 나는 2,000명의 경쟁자들과 마라톤을 했다.
➡ I ran a marathon with 2,000 _____.

(2) 그 환자는 심각한 상태였다.
➡ The patient was in serious _____.

(3) 마침내, 그들은 경찰에게 모든 것을 고백했다.
➡ Finally, they _____ everything to the police.

(4) 그의 아버지는 위독한 상태이다.
➡ His father is in a _____ condition.

03 다음 문장의 빈칸에 들어갈 말을 〈보기〉에서 골라 쓰시오.

> ── 보기 ──
> catch a cold / got caught / on the loose /
> search for / think outside the box

(1) The prisoner escaped from jail, and he is still _____.

(2) We started to _____ to make something new.

(3) You can _____ a good hotel on this website.

(4) Be careful not to _____.

(5) One of my classmates _____ cheating.

04 다음 우리말에 맞게 주어진 단어를 사용하여 영작하시오.

(1) 너는 그 식당이 극도로 시끄럽다고 생각하지 않니? (loud, don't)
➡ _____

(2) 설탕을 너무 많이 먹는 것은 너의 치아에 해롭다. (too, for)
➡ _____

(3) 그는 내 여동생과 거의 같은 키이다. (as, the same)
➡ _____

05 다음 주어진 우리말과 일치하도록 주어진 단어를 모두 배열하여 완성하시오.

(1) 그녀는 그녀가 실수했다는 것을 인정했다.
(that / she / had / she / admitted / mistakes / made)
➡ _____

(2) 나는 어제 내 남자 친구와 논쟁을 했다.
(my boyfriend / I / with / yesterday / an argument / had)
➡ _____

(3) 어른들은 입장료를 내야 하지만, 아이들은 무료로 입장한다.
(should / adults / fee / but / an / in / children / get / pay / entrance / free)
➡ _____
_____

Conversation

1 자세한 설명 요청하기

> **A: Did you know that bats aren't blind?** 박쥐가 눈이 안 보이는 것이 아니라는 알고 있었니?
>
> **B: No. Can you tell me more about it?** 아니. 그걸 더 설명해 줄래?
>
> **A: Some bats can see three times better than humans.** 어떤 박쥐는 인간보다 3배 더 잘 볼 수 있어.

■ 상대방이 말하는 내용을 잘 모르거나 상대방이 사용한 단어의 뜻을 몰라서 추가적인 설명을 요청할 때는 'Can you tell me more about it?(그걸 좀 더 설명해 줄래?)'이라고 하거나, 'What does that mean?(그것이 무슨 뜻입니까?)', 'What do you mean by that?(그것이 무슨 뜻이니?)'이라고 한다.

■ 상대방에게 설명을 요청할 때는 '설명하다, 말하다'의 의미를 가지는 동사 explain, tell이나 give information, be specific 등의 표현을 사용하여 'Could you explain the meaning of it?', 'Could you tell me more about them?' 등의 표현을 사용하기도 한다. Could 대신 Would, Can, Will 등을 사용할 수 있고, 'Do you mind if I ask you to explain ~?'이라고 말할 수도 있다.

■ 상대방의 말을 알아듣지 못했을 때는 'I'm not following you.(잘 못 알아듣겠습니다.)', 'I don't get it.(제대로 이해를 못하겠어요.)' 등의 표현을 사용하여 상대방이 다시 설명을 하도록 요청할 수도 있다.

자세한 설명 요청하기

- Can you tell me more about it? 그걸 좀 더 설명해 줄래?
- Could you give me more information? 좀 더 정보를 주시겠습니까?
- Can you explain more in detail? 좀 더 자세히 설명해 주시겠습니까?
- Could you be more specific? 좀 더 구체적으로 말해 주시겠습니까?
- What do you mean by that? 그게 무슨 말이야?
- Could you explain what it means? 그게 무엇을 의미하는지 설명해 주시겠습니까?

핵심 Check

1. 주어진 문장에 이어지도록 적절한 순서로 배열하시오.

> w: I think I caught a cold because I didn't dress warmly yesterday.
>
> (A) Really? Can you tell me more about it?
>
> (B) The article said that people catch colds because of viruses.
>
> (C) Well, I've read an article saying that you don't catch a cold because your body temperature is low.

➡ _____

② 의견에 대한 이유 묻기

> A: Books of riddles are really useful for adults. 수수께끼 책이 어른들에게는 매우 유용해.
>
> B: Why do you say so? 왜 그렇게 말하니?
>
> A: They help us think more creatively. 그것들이 더 창의적으로 생각하게 도와주니까.

■ 상대방이 왜 그렇게 말하는지, 혹은 왜 그렇게 생각하는지 등에 대해 이유를 물을 때는 의문사 why를 써서 'Why do you say so?(왜 그렇게 말하니?)' 또는 'Why do you think so?(왜 그렇게 생각하니?)'처럼 물어본다.

■ why 대신 의문사 what을 사용해서 '무엇이 ~하도록 만들었느냐?'의 의미로 'What makes you+동사원형 ~?'의 형태를 사용할 수 있다. 'What makes you say that?(무엇 때문에 그렇게 말하니?)' 또는 'What makes you think so?(무엇 때문에 그렇게 생각하니?)'처럼 'What makes you ~?'로 이유를 물어볼 때 'what'은 '무엇'이라고 해석할 수도 있지만 '왜'라고 해석하기도 한다.

■ 의문사로 시작하는 이유를 묻는 말 앞에 'Can you tell me'나 'I'd like to know', 'I wonder' 등을 붙여, 간접의문문의 형식으로 좀 더 격식을 갖춰 물어볼 수도 있다. 이유를 말할 때에는 문장 앞에 'I think'나 'In my opinion' 등을 덧붙일 수도 있다.

이유 묻기

- Why do you say/think so? 왜 그렇게 말하니/생각하니?
- What makes you say so? 왜 그렇게 말하니?
- What makes you think so? 무엇 때문에 그렇게 생각하니?
- Why is that? 왜 그렇지?
- Can you tell me (the reason) why ~? ~ 한 이유를 설명해 주겠니?

이유 말하기

- I did it because ~. ~ 때문에 그렇게 했어요.
- (Because) ~. 왜냐하면 ~ 때문이야.
- That's because ~. 그것은 ~ 때문입니다.
- Because of ~. ~ 때문이야.

핵심 Check

2. 다음 대화의 밑줄 친 문장과 같은 의미의 문장을 주어진 단어로 시작하여 쓰시오.

> W: I think children write better poems than adults.
>
> M: <u>Why do you say so?</u>
>
> W: They're really honest about their feelings and much more creative than adults.

➡ What _____?

Listen and Talk 1 B

W: I read an article ❶saying ❷that Napoleon was actually ❸fairly tall.

M: Oh, really? ❹Can you tell me more about it?

W: ❺According to the article, a French doctor wrote down Napoleon's height according to the French measuring system, not the English one.

M: What was the difference?

W: At that time, an inch in France was longer than an inch in England. So, Napoleon was actually about 168 cm tall, ❻which was not that short in those times.

W: 나폴레옹이 실제로 키가 꽤 컸다고 하는 기사를 읽었어.

M: 오, 정말? 그것에 대해 더 말해 줄 수 있니?

W: 기사에 따르면 한 프랑스 의사가 영국식이 아닌 프랑스식 측정법으로 나폴레옹의 키를 기록했다는 거야.

M: 차이가 뭐였니?

W: 그 당시에 프랑스에서의 1인치가 영국에서의 1인치보다 더 길었어. 그래서 나폴레옹은 사실 168cm 정도였는데, 그것이 그 시대에는 그렇게 작은 키가 아니었어.

❶ 현재분사로 an article을 수식한다. ❷ 접속사 that으로 명사절을 이끈다. ❸ fairly: 꽤

❹ 상대방이 말하는 내용을 잘 모르거나 상대방이 사용한 단어의 뜻을 몰라서 추가적인 설명을 요청할 때 사용하는 표현으로 'What does that mean?'이나 'What do you mean by that?'으로 바꾸어 표현할 수 있다.

❺ according to: ~에 따르면

❻ 관계대명사의 계속적인 용법으로 that으로 바꾸어 쓸 수 없다.

Check(√) True or False

(1) An inch in England was shorter than the one in France.   T ☐ F ☐

(2) Napoleon was actually not that short in those times.   T ☐ F ☐

Listen and Talk 2 B

M: Hey, Sandy. Do you think I should buy this drink? It is said that it can help me ❶lose weight.

W: Let me read the label more closely. Hmm, it looks ❷a bit strange to me, David.

M: ❸Why do you say so?

W: There ❹isn't enough information about what's in the drink.

M: Oh, you're right.

W: Also, it doesn't tell you how much you have to drink to lose weight.

M: 안녕, Sandy. 너는 내가 이 음료를 사야 한다고 생각해? 내가 살을 빼는 것을 도와줄 수 있다고 적혀 있어.

W: 라벨을 더 자세히 읽어 볼게. 음, 내가 보기에 좀 이상해, David.

M: 왜 그렇게 생각해?

W: 음료 안에 무엇이 들었는지에 대한 충분한 정보가 없어.

M: 오, 네 말이 맞아.

W: 게다가, 체중을 감량하려면 얼마나 마셔야 하는지도 나와 있지 않아.

❶ lose weight: 살이 빠지다 ❷ a bit: 약간, 조금

❸ 상대방이 왜 그렇게 말하는지, 혹은 왜 그렇게 생각하는지 등에 대해 이유를 물을 때 쓰는 표현으로 'Why do you think so?' 등으로 바꾸어 표현할 수 있다.

❹ 'there is+단수 명사', 'there are+복수 명사': ~가 있다

Check(√) True or False

(3) David is wondering whether he should buy the drink or not.   T ☐ F ☐

(4) Sandy advised David to buy the drink to lose weight.   T ☐ F ☐

Listen and Talk 1 A-1

W: I think I ❶caught a cold ❷because I didn't dress warmly yesterday.

M: Well, I've read an article saying that you don't catch a cold because your body ❸ temperature is low.

W: Really? Can you tell me more about it?

M: The article said that people catch colds ❷ because of viruses.

❶ catch a cold: 감기에 걸리다 ❷ 'because+주어+동사', 'because of+명사(구)' ❸ temperature: 온도

 Listen and Talk 1 A-2

W: I usually drink ❶a glass of warm milk before I go to bed, but it doesn't ❷help me fall asleep.

M: I saw a show on TV, and a doctor said that a glass of warm milk doesn't actually help you fall asleep.

W: Oh, it doesn't? Can you tell me more about it?

M: Milk has special ❸chemicals ❹that make people sleepy. But the amount in a glass is ❺too small to have any effect.

❶ a glass of ～: 한 잔의 ～ ❷ help는 준사역동사로 목적격보어로 to부정사나 원형부정사(fall)가 이어진다. ❸ chemical: 화학물질 ❹ 관계대명사로 'which'로 바꾸어 쓸 수 있다. ❺ too ～ to ...: 너무 ～해서 …할 수 없다

 Listen and Talk 2 A-1

W: What are you reading, John?

M: I'm reading a book of ❶riddles.

W: Riddles? Aren't ❷they for children?

M: Actually, no. Books of riddles are really useful for adults.

W: Really? ❸Why do you say so?

M: ❷They help us think more creatively. We need to ❹think outside the box to find the answers.

❶ riddle: 수수께끼 ❷ they는 riddles를 가리킨다. ❸ 'What makes you think so?' 또는 'Why is that?' 등으로 바꾸어 표현할 수 있다. ❹ think outside the box: 고정관념에서 벗어나다

 Communication

W: There are so many pieces of information we call "facts" that are ❶completely wrong.

M: Why do you say so?

W: I read a book, and there were a lot of examples of these facts ❷that are wrong.

M: Like what?

W: Well, most people think ❸goldfish are not smart. But, goldfish are actually smart.

M: Really? Can you tell me more about ❹that?

W: They can ❺recognize their owners.

M: Oh, I didn't know that.

❶ completely: 완전히 ❷ 관계대명사로 which로 바꾸어 쓸 수 있다. ❸ goldfish: 금붕어 ❹ that은 금붕어가 실제로는 똑똑하다는 것을 가리킨다. ❺ recognize: 알아보다, 인식하다

 Wrap Up 1

M: Jane, do you usually get news online or from the newspaper?

W: Well, I usually watch TV news.

M: TV news? Is there any special reason?

W: I think ❶TV is the most useful way to get news.

M: Why do you say so?

W: I have to ❷spend too much time reading all the news online or in the newspaper. So, I just watch the main news on TV.

M: ❸I see your point.

❶ 접속사 that이 생략되어 있다. ❷ spend time ～ing: ～하는 데 시간을 보내다 ❸ I see your point.: 무슨 말인지 알겠다.

● 다음 우리말과 일치하도록 빈칸에 알맞은 말을 쓰시오.

Listen & Talk 1 A-1

W: I think I _____ _____ _____ because I didn't dress _____ yesterday.

M: Well, I've read an _____ saying that you don't catch a cold because your _____ _____ is low.

W: Really? Can you tell me _____ _____ _____?

M: The article said that people catch colds _____ _____.

Listen & Talk 1 A-2

W: I usually drink _____ _____ _____ _____ _____ _____ before I go to bed, but it doesn't help me _____ _____.

M: I saw a show on TV, and a doctor said that a glass of warm milk doesn't actually _____ you _____ asleep.

W: Oh, it doesn't? Can you _____ _____ _____ _____ _____?

M: Milk has special _____ that make people sleepy. But the _____ in a glass is _____ small _____ have any _____.

Listen & Talk 2 A-1

W: _____ _____ _____ _____, John?

M: I'm reading a book of _____.

W: Riddles? Aren't they _____ children?

M: _____, no. Books of riddles are really _____ _____ _____.

W: Really? Why do you _____ _____?

M: They help us think more _____. We need to _____ _____ _____ _____ to find the answers.

Listen & Talk 2 A-2

M: Are these all _____ _____?

W: Yeah. These are all poems _____ by children.

M: By children?

W: Yeah. I think children _____ _____ poems than adults.

M: Why do you _____ _____?

W: They're really _____ about their _____ and much _____ _____ than adults.

해석

W: 어제 옷을 따뜻하게 입지 않아서 감기에 걸린 것 같아.
M: 글쎄, 체온이 낮다고 해서 감기에 걸리지는 않는다고 쓰여 있는 기사를 읽었어.
W: 정말? 그것에 대해 더 말해 줄 수 있니?
M: 기사에서는 사람들이 바이러스 때문에 감기에 걸린다고 했어.

W: 나는 보통 잠자리에 들기 전에 따뜻한 우유 한 잔을 마시는데, 그것이 잠드는 데 도움이 되지 않아.
M: 내가 텔레비전 프로그램에서 봤는데, 어떤 의사가 따뜻한 우유 한 잔이 실제로 잠드는 데 도움을 주는 건 아니라고 말했어.
W: 오, 그래? 그것에 대해 더 말해 줄 수 있니?
M: 우유에는 사람들을 졸리게 만드는 특별한 성분이 있어. 하지만 한 잔에 있는 양이 너무 적어서 효과가 없어.

W: 무엇을 읽고 있니, John?
M: 나는 수수께끼 책을 읽고 있어.
W: 수수께끼? 그거 아이들용 아니니?
M: 사실, 그렇지 않아. 수수께끼 책은 어른들에게 굉장히 유용해.
W: 정말? 왜 그렇게 생각해?
M: 그 책들은 우리가 더 창의적으로 생각하도록 도와. 우리는 답을 찾기 위해 고정관념에서 벗어나야 하거든.

M: 이거 전부 시집이니?
W: 응. 이것들은 모두 아이들이 쓴 시야.
M: 아이들이?
W: 응. 내 생각에 아이들이 어른들보다 더 좋은 시를 쓰는 것 같아.
M: 왜 그렇게 생각해?
W: 아이들은 그들의 감정에 아주 솔직하고 어른들보다 훨씬 더 창의적이거든.

Listen & Talk 2 B

M: Hey, Sandy. Do you think _____ _____ _____ _____? It is said that it can help me _____ _____.

W: Let me read the _____ more _____. Hmm, it looks a bit _____ to me, David.

M: Why do _____ _____ _____?

W: There isn't _____ _____ about _____ in the _____.

M: Oh, you're _____.

W: Also, it doesn't tell you _____ _____ _____ _____ _____ _____ to lose weight.

Communication

W: There are so many pieces of _____ we call "_____" that are _____ _____.

M: Why do you say so?

W: I read a book, and there were a lot of _____ of these _____ _____ _____ _____.

M: Like _____?

W: Well, most people think _____ are not smart. But, _____ are actually smart.

M: Really? Can you tell me more about that?

W: They can _____ _____ _____.

M: Oh, I didn't _____ _____.

Wrap Up 2

W: I read an _____ _____ about the Black Sea. Do you know _____ _____ _____ _____?

M: Yes. It's _____ Eastern Europe _____ Western Asia, right?

W: Right. _____ _____ do you think it is?

M: Well, black, I _____.

M: No, it isn't. It's blue.

M: Really? Then why is it _____ the Black Sea? Can you tell me more about it?

W: People call it the Black Sea because it is very _____.

해석

M: 안녕, Sandy. 너는 내가 이 음료를 사야 한다고 생각해? 내가 살을 빼는 것을 도와줄 수 있다고 적혀 있어.

W: 라벨을 더 자세히 읽어 볼게. 음, 내가 보기에 좀 이상해, David.

M: 왜 그렇게 생각해?

W: 음료 안에 무엇이 들었는지에 대한 충분한 정보가 없어.

M: 오, 네 말이 맞아.

W: 게다가, 체중을 감량하려면 얼마나 마셔야 하는지도 나와 있지 않아.

W: 우리가 '사실'이라고 말하는 정보 중에 완전히 틀린 것들이 너무 많아.

M: 왜 그렇게 생각해?

W: 내가 책을 읽었는데, 거기에는 이러한 틀린 '사실'의 예시가 많이 있었어.

M: 예를 들면 어떤 것?

W: 음, 대부분의 사람들은 금붕어가 똑똑하지 않다고 생각해. 하지만 금붕어는 사실 똑똑해.

M: 정말? 그것에 대해 더 말해 줄 수 있니?

W: 그들은 그들의 주인을 알아 볼 수 있어.

M: 오, 그건 몰랐어.

W: 나는 흑해에 관한 흥미로운 기사를 읽었어. 너 그게 어디에 있는지 아니?

M: 응. 그것은 동유럽과 서아시아 사이에 있어, 그렇지?

W: 맞아. 그게 무슨 색일 거라고 생각해?

M: 글쎄, 검은색일 것 같아.

W: 아니야, 그렇지 않아. 그것은 파란색이야.

M: 정말? 그럼 왜 흑해라고 불리는 거야? 그것에 대해 더 말해 줄 수 있니?

W: 사람들이 흑해라고 부르는 이유는 그곳이 매우 위험하기 때문이야.

[01~02] 다음 대화를 읽고 물음에 답하시오.

> **Suji:** I usually drink a glass of warm milk ⓐbefore I go to bed, but it doesn't help me fall asleep.
>
> **Minsu:** I saw a show on TV, and a doctor said ⓑthat a glass of warm milk doesn't actually help you fall asleep.
>
> **Suji:** Oh, it doesn't? Can you tell me ⓒmore about it?
>
> **Minsu:** Milk has special chemicals that ⓓmakes people sleepy. But the amount in a glass is too ⓔsmall to have any effect.

01 위 대화의 밑줄 친 ⓐ~ⓔ 중 어법상 틀린 것을 찾아 바르게 고치시오.

➡ _____

02 다음 대화의 내용과 일치하지 않는 것은?

① 수지는 자기 전에 따뜻한 우유 한 잔을 마신다.
② 자기 전에 따뜻한 우유 한 잔은 수지가 잠드는 데 도움이 되지 않았다.
③ 민수는 TV에서 어떤 의사가 따뜻한 우유 한 잔이 실제로 잠드는 데 도움을 주는 건 아니라고 말하는 것을 들었다.
④ 우유에는 사람들을 졸리게 만드는 특별한 성분이 있다.
⑤ 우유 한 잔에 있는 특별한 성분의 양으로 숙면을 취할 수 있다.

[03~04] 다음 대화를 읽고 물음에 답하시오.

> **W:** I think I caught a cold because I didn't dress ⓐwarmly yesterday.
>
> **M:** Well, I've read an article ⓑsaying that you don't catch a cold because your body temperature is low.
>
> **W:** Really? Can you tell me more ⓒabout it?
>
> **M:** The article said that people catch colds ⓓbecause viruses.

03 위 대화에서 밑줄 친 ⓐ~ⓓ 중 어법상 틀린 것을 찾아 바르게 고치시오

➡ _____

04 위 대화의 내용과 일치하도록 빈칸을 완성하시오.

> According to the article, people catch colds not because of
> (A)_____ but because of (B)_____.

[01~02] 다음 대화를 읽고 물음에 답하시오.

Jane: I read an article ⓐsaying that Napoleon was actually fairly tall.

Tom: Oh, really? Can you tell me more about it?

Jane: According to the article, a French doctor ⓑwrote down Napoleon's height according to the French measuring system, not the English ⓒone.

Tom: What was the difference?

Jane: At that time, an inch in France was ⓓlonger than an inch in England. So, Napoleon was actually about 168 cm tall, ⓔthat was not that short in those times.

 서답형

01 위 대화의 밑줄 친 ⓐ~ⓔ 중 어법상 **틀린** 것을 찾아 바르게 고치시오.

➡ _____

02 위 대화의 내용과 일치하지 **않는** 것은?

① Jane은 나폴레옹이 실제로 꽤 키가 컸다는 기사를 읽었다.

② 기사에 따르면 프랑스 의사는 나폴레옹의 키를 프랑스 측정 체계에 따라 기록했다.

③ 나폴레옹 시대에 프랑스의 1인치는 영국의 1인치보다 더 길었다.

④ 나폴레옹은 실제로 약 168 cm로 그 당시에는 작은 편이 아니었다.

⑤ 프랑스 측정 체계와 영국의 측정 체계는 다르지 않았다.

[03~05] 다음 대화를 읽고 물음에 답하시오.

Suji: I usually drink a glass of warm milk before I go to bed, but it doesn't help me fall asleep.

Minsu: I saw a show on TV, and a doctor said that a glass of warm milk doesn't actually help you fall asleep.

Suji: Oh, it doesn't? Can you tell me more about it?

Minsu: Milk has special chemicals that make people sleepy. But the amount in a glass is too small to have any effect.

서답형

03 What does Suji do before going to bed?

➡ _____

서답형

04 What is the effect of special chemicals in milk?

➡ _____

서답형

05 Why are the chemicals in a glass of warm milk not helpful for falling asleep?

➡ _____
_____

서답형

06 다음 대화가 자연스럽게 이어지도록 순서대로 배열하시오.

M: Are these all poetry books?

(A) By children?

(B) Why do you say so?

(C) Yeah. These are all poems written by children.

(D) Yeah. I think children write better poems than adults.

(E) They're really honest about their feelings and much more creative than adults.

➡ _____

Conversation **17**

다음 짝지어진 대화가 어색한 것은?

① A: Did you know that bats aren't blind?

B: No. Can you tell me more about it?

② A: Books of riddles are really useful for adults.

B: Why do you say so?

③ A: Actually, frozen fruits are as good as fresh ones.

B: Really? Can you give me more information about it?

④ A: You know what? I'm planning to visit Canada this summer vacation.

B: I'm wondering if you could tell me more about your vacation plan.

⑤ A: Did you know that Bill's birthday is on May 4th?

B: I see your point.

[08~09] 다음 대화를 읽고 물음에 답하시오.

Susan: What are you reading, John?

John: I'm reading a book of riddles.

Susan: Riddles? Aren't they for children?

John: Actually, no. Books of riddles are really useful for adults.

Susan: Really? (A)_____

John: They help us think more creatively. (B)_____

08 위 대화의 빈칸 (A)에 들어갈 말로 나머지와 의도가 <u>다른</u> 것은?

① Why do you say so?

② What makes you say so?

③ What makes you think so?

④ Can you tell me the reason why?

⑤ What do you think about it?

09 위 대화의 빈칸 (B)에 들어갈 말을 보기에 주어진 단어들을 모두 배열하여 완성하시오.

┌─ 보기 ┐

need / we / to / find / to / the answers / outside / think / the box

➡ _____

_____

[10~12] 다음 대화를 읽고 물음에 답하시오.

Mike: Are these all poetry books?

Sue: Yeah. These are all poems (A)_____ (write) by children.

Mike: By children?

Sue: Yeah. I think children write better poems than adults.

Mike: (B)Why do you say so?

Sue: (C)They're really honest about their feelings and much more creative than adults.

10 위 대화의 빈칸 (A)에 주어진 단어를 알맞은 형태로 쓰시오.

➡ _____

11 위 대화의 밑줄 친 (B)와 바꾸어 쓰기에 <u>어색한</u> 것은?

① Why do you think so?

② What makes you say so?

③ What makes you think so?

④ Can you tell me why?

⑤ How do you feel about that?

12 위 대화의 밑줄 친 (C)가 가리키는 것을 찾아 쓰시오.

➡ _____

[01~02] 다음 대화를 읽고 물음에 답하시오.

W: I think I caught a cold because I didn't dress warmly yesterday.
M: Well, I've read an article saying that you don't catch a cold because your body temperature is low.
W: Really? (A)_____?
M: The article said that people catch colds because of viruses.

01 위 대화의 빈칸 (A)에 들어갈 말을 〈보기〉에 주어진 단어들을 배열하여 완성하시오.

┌─ 보기 ├─
you / more / it / can / about / tell / me

➡ _____?

2 Why does the woman think she caught a cold?

➡ _____
_____

03 다음 대화의 내용과 일치하도록 기사를 완성하시오.

Jane: I read an article saying that Napoleon was actually fairly tall.
Tom: Oh, really? Can you tell me more about it?
Jane: According to the article, a French doctor wrote down Napoleon's height according to the French measuring system, not the English one.
Tom: What was the difference?
Jane: At that time, an inch in France was longer than an inch in England. So, Napoleon was actually about 168 cm tall, which was not that short in those times.

↓
Daily News, May 7th 2020
Was (A)_____ Really Short?
We have been wrong about Napoleon's (B)_____. The misunderstanding came from the difference between (C)_____ _____ and (D)_____ _____. He was actually about 168 cm tall!

[04~06] 다음 대화를 읽고 물음에 답하시오.

Mike: Are these all poetry books?
Sue: Yeah. These are all poems written by children.
Mike: By children?
Sue: Yeah. I think children write better poems than adults.
Mike: (A)왜 그렇게 생각해? (say)
Sue: They're really honest about their feelings and much more creative than adults.

04 위 대화의 밑줄 친 (A)의 우리말을 주어진 단어를 사용하여 5 단어로 영작하시오.

➡ _____

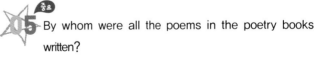**5** By whom were all the poems in the poetry books written?

➡ _____

06 Why does Sue think that children write better poems than adults?

➡ _____
_____

Grammar

1 분사구문

> • Let's look into some articles **thinking about the hidden motives.** 숨겨진 동기를 생각하면서 몇 가지 뉴스 기사를 살펴보자.

■ 분사가 이끄는 구를 분사구문이라고 하며, 이유, 조건, 시간, 동시동작, 양보 등의 뜻을 나타낸다. 분사구문은 '접속사+주어+동사'로 이루어진 부사절의 주어가 주절의 주어와 일치할 때 접속사와 주어를 생략하고 동사를 분사(동사원형+-ing)로 만든 구문이다. 이때 생략되는 접속사에 따라 뜻이 달라진다.

　• When I arrived at the party, it began to rain. → **Arriving at the party**, it began to rain. (시간) (파티에 도착했을 때 비가 내리기 시작했다.)

■ 부사절과 주절의 주어가 다를 때는 부사절의 주어를 생략하지 않고 사용하며 이것을 독립분사구문이라고 한다. 일반인이 주어일 경우에는 생략한다.(비인칭 독립분사구문)

　• As it was raining, we couldn't go out. → **It being raining**, we couldn't go out. (우리는 비가 오고 있었기 때문에 나갈 수가 없었다.)

■ 분사구문의 부정은 분사 앞에 'not'이나 'never'를 쓴다.

　• As he didn't feel well, he took the last Wednesday off. → **Not feeling well**, he took the last Wednesday off. (그는 지난 수요일 몸이 불편하여 쉬었다.)

■ 분사구문의 뜻을 명확히 하기 위해 접속사를 생략하지 않기도 한다. 이 경우는 부사절에서 '주어+be동사'를 생략한 것과 같은 형태가 된다.

　• I mailed a letter **while taking a walk**. (나는 산책을 하면서 편지를 부쳤다.)

■ 부사절의 시제가 주절보다 앞선 경우에는 완료분사구문(having+과거분사)으로 쓴다.

　• As he had done it before, he was going to do it.
　　= **Having done it before**, he was going to do it.

■ 과거분사로 시작되는 분사구문은 being이 생략된 것으로 수동의 의미를 갖는다.

　• **Written in English**, the book is not easy to read. (영어로 쓰여졌기 때문에, 그 책은 읽기에 쉽지 않다.)

핵심 Check

1. 다음 괄호 안에서 알맞은 말을 고르시오.

　(1) (Live / Living) next door, I often see Billy.

　(2) (Listening / Listened) to the music, she stayed up late.

② so that ~ can ...

• They made up this fake article **so that** they **could** draw the readers' attention.
그들은 독자들의 주의를 끌기 위해 이 가짜 기사를 지어냈다.

■ so that은 '~하기 위해', '~하고자', '~하도록'의 의미로 '목적'이나 '의도'를 나타낸다. 일반적으로 '주절+so that+주어+can/will+동사원형 ~'의 형태로 쓰인다.
 • He tried to make friends with him **so that** he **could** get help from the wolf. (그는 늑대로부터 도움을 받을 수 있도록 그와 친구가 되려고 하였다.)
 • She worked hard **so that** everything **would** be ready in time. (그녀는 모든 것이 제 시간에 준비될 수 있도록 열심히 일을 했다.)

■ 'so that ~ can …'은 'in order that ~ can …'으로 바꿔 쓸 수 있으며, 주절과 종속절의 주어가 같은 경우 '(in order[so as]) to부정사'로 바꿔 쓸 수 있다.
 • I borrowed a book **so that** I **could** read during weekends. (나는 주말 동안 읽으려고 책을 한 권 빌렸다.)
  = I borrowed a book **in order that** I **could** read during weekends.
  = I borrowed a book **to read** during weekends. 〈to부정사의 부사적 용법 – 목적〉
  = I borrowed a book **in order to read** during weekends.
  = I borrowed a book **so as to read** during weekends.

■ so that을 기준으로 앞과 뒤의 동사의 시제를 일치시킨다.
 • He takes a taxi **so that** he **won't** be late. (그는 지각하지 않기 위해 택시를 탄다.)
 • He took a taxi **so that** he **wouldn't** be late. (그는 지각하지 않기 위해 택시를 탔다.)

■ 'so that'은 '결과'의 부사절을 이끌어 '그래서, 그러므로'의 의미를 갖는 접속사로 쓰이기도 하는데, 대개 앞에 쉼표(,)가 온다.
 • He always breaks his promises, **so that** he has no friends. (그는 항상 약속을 어긴다. 그래서 그는 친구가 없다.)

■ so와 that 사이에 수식어가 오면, '너무 ~해서 결국 …하다'라는 뜻이 되며, 'so+형용사[부사]+that+주어+can …(매우 ~해서 …할 수 있는)'은 '형용사+enough to …(…할 정도로 충분히 ~한)'로 바꿔 쓸 수 있으며, 'so+형용사[부사]+that+주어+can't …(너무 ~해서 …할 수 없는)'은 'too+형용사[부사]+to부정사(…하기에 너무 ~한)'로 바꿔 쓸 수 있다.
 • I got **so** excited **that** I was at a loss for words. (나는 너무 흥분한 나머지 말문이 막혔다.)
 • He was **so** happy **that** he could dance. (그는 뛸 듯이 기뻐했다.)
  = He was happy **enough to** dance.

핵심 Check

2. 다음 괄호 안에서 알맞은 말을 고르시오.
 (1) She hurried up so (that / which) she could get there on time.
 (2) Use a hand signal (in that / so that) drivers can see you.

01 다음 우리말에 맞게 빈칸에 알맞은 것은?

> 당신이 그 곳에 제 시간에 도착할 수 있게 빨리 몰겠습니다.
> = I'll drive fast so _____ you can get there in time.

① this   ② that   ③ what
④ which   ⑤ it

02 다음 괄호 안에서 알맞은 말을 고르시오.

(1) (Have / Having) no money, I couldn't buy a new bike.

(2) (Knowing not / Not knowing) what to do, I was at my wits' end.

(3) I went to the zoo (though / so that) my sister could see wild animals.

(4) I was very excited, (because / so that) I couldn't get to sleep.

03 다음 빈칸에 들어갈 말로 알맞은 것은?

> _____ me, the man ran off.

① Seeing   ② Seen   ③ Sees
④ Saw   ⑤ See

04 다음 우리말에 맞게 주어진 어휘를 바르게 배열하시오.

(1) 성적표를 보면서, 엄마의 얼굴이 어두워졌다.

(mom's face, the report card, looking, darkened, at)

➡ _____

(2) 우리는 책을 빌릴 수 있도록 도서관에 갈 것이다.

(we, we, can, are, borrow, going, so, books, the library, that, to)

➡ _____

01 다음 중 어법상 어색한 것은?

① Feeling happy, she sang a song.

② Working in the hospital, my aunt helped many people.

③ Aaron danced on the stage listened to the music.

④ He uses his cellphone while walking on the street.

⑤ Turning left, you can find the bus stop.

02 다음 중 어법상 바르지 않은 것은?

① Speak clearly so that we can understand you.

② I had to save much money to buy a new car.

③ The bird practiced flying hard so to fly up high.

④ I took a taxi in order that I could be there on time.

⑤ She arrived early in order to get a good seat.

03 다음 빈칸에 알맞은 말이 바르게 짝지어진 것은?

• He is eating his favorite egg sandwich _____ a newspaper.

• Put on a helmet _____ that you can protect your head.

---

① reading – so

② reading – for

③ reads – so

④ reads – for

⑤ read – in

04 다음 괄호 안에서 알맞은 말을 고르시오.

(1) Save electricity so (that / as) we can save polar bears.

(2) He noted every detail so (as / that) to fix the scene in his mind.

(3) Come early in (order / condition) that you can see him.

(4) (Neglected / Neglecting) his duty, he was fired.

(5) When (process / processing) your request, an error occurred.

(6) (Knowing not / Not knowing) what to do, I asked for my mom's advice.

05 주어진 두 문장을 한 문장으로 바꿀 때 옳지 않은 것은?

• I arrived home late at night.

• I saw some fruits and ate them.

---

① When I arrived home late at night, I saw some fruits and ate them.

② As I arrived home late at night, I saw some fruits and ate them.

③ Arriving home late at night, I saw some fruits and ate them.

④ When arriving home late at night, I saw some fruits and ate them.

⑤ When arrived home late at night, I saw some fruits and ate them.

06 빈칸 (A)와 (B)에 알맞은 것으로 바르게 짝지어진 것은?

- Get up early ___(A)___ as to be in time for the first train.
- He is ___(B)___ rich that he can buy the sports car.

	(A)	(B)
①	too	so
②	too	too
③	so	so
④	so	too
⑤	enough	as

07 다음 문장의 밑줄 친 부분 중 어법상 어색한 것은?

David, ⓐthought ⓑthat ⓒit ⓓwould soon pass, ⓔignored his headache.

① ⓐ   ② ⓑ   ③ ⓒ
④ ⓓ   ⑤ ⓔ

08 다음 밑줄 친 부분과 바꿔 쓸 수 있는 것은?

Jim sold his watch <u>so that</u> he could buy the coat.

① in that   ② so as to   ③ to
④ in order   ⑤ in order that

서답형

09 다음 두 문장을 한 문장으로 바꿔 쓸 때 빈칸에 들어갈 한 단어를 쓰시오.

- You cross the street.
- You should be careful.
= _____ the street, you should be careful.

10 다음 우리말을 바르게 영작한 것을 고르시오.

네가 건강해질 수 있도록 채소를 더 많이 먹어야 한다.

① You should eat more vegetables so what you can be healthy.
② You should eat more vegetables so that you can be healthy.
③ You should eat more vegetables in that you can be healthy.
④ You should eat more vegetables so as you can be healthy.
⑤ You should eat more vegetables so to you can be healthy.

11 분사구문의 의미가 밑줄 친 부분과 같은 것은?

<u>Being</u> small, the kitchen is well designed.

① <u>Having</u> nothing to do, I went for a walk to the park.
② The sun <u>being</u> shining, it wasn't very warm.
③ We need luck when <u>taking</u> tests.
④ He told me a shocking story while <u>having</u> lunch together.
⑤ Not <u>paying</u> the rent, you'll be thrown out.

서답형

12 다음 문장에서 생략할 수 있는 것을 찾아 쓰시오.

(1) Though he was young, he had much gray hair.
➡ _____

(2) She had her picture taken when she was in Italy.
➡ _____

13 다음 문장과 뜻이 같은 것을 고르시오.

> The girl is too shy to speak in front of others.

① The girl is shy so that she can't speak in front of others.
② The girl is so that shy she can't speak in front of others.
③ The girl is so shy that can't speak in front of others.
④ The girl is so shy that she can't speak in front of others.
⑤ The girl is too shy to she can't speak in front of others.

서답형

14 다음 문장에서 어법상 어색한 것을 바르게 고쳐 다시 쓰시오.

(1) Don't throw trash in the sea in order for animals can live safely.

➡ _____

(2) Look for hidden ideas so as that you can see what the writer really means.

➡ _____

(3) Swum in the pond, she wore her swimming cap.

➡ _____

(4) Being fine, we went for a walk to the beach.

➡ _____

(5) Seeing from high above, the cars looked tiny.

➡ _____

15 다음 우리말을 바르게 영작한 것을 고르시오.

> Kathryn은 그들의 이름을 들었지만, 그들을 구별하지 못했다.

① Although she hearing their names, Kathryn couldn't recognize them.
② She having heard their names, Kathryn couldn't recognize them.
③ Having heard their names, Kathryn not recognizing them.
④ Kathryn having heard their names, she couldn't recognize them.
⑤ Having heard their names, Kathryn couldn't recognize them.

중요

16 다음 중 어법상 어색한 것을 모두 고르시오. (2개)

① She became too weak to move her own body easily.
② I was enough stupid to believe him.
③ Come early so as that you can have plenty of time.
④ Do not use smartphones so that others can study in a quiet place.
⑤ They made up this fake article so that they could draw the readers' attention.

서답형

17 다음 두 문장을 'so that'을 이용하여 한 문장으로 바꿔 쓰시오.

> • They confessed that they made it up.
> • They could draw the readers' attention to the unsafe conditions at the zoo.

➡ _____

_____

01 다음 문장을 분사구문으로 바꿔 쓰시오.

(1) Because my mom caught a bad cold, she couldn't get to work.

➡ _____

_____

(2) After I finished breakfast, I took a taxi to school.

➡ _____

(3) If you mix blue and yellow, you get green.

➡ _____

(4) Although she was nervous, she said it was a good experience.

➡ _____

_____

(5) Because I didn't know what happened, I called my friend, Sam.

➡ _____

_____

(6) If it is fine tomorrow, I will go hiking.

➡ _____

02 'so that'을 이용하여 다음 두 문장을 한 문장으로 바꿔 쓰시오.

(1) • Read the book carefully.

• You can find hidden ideas.

➡ _____

_____

(2) • Sally bought a camera.

• She could take great pictures.

➡ _____

_____

03 다음 우리말에 맞게 주어진 단어를 바르게 배열하시오.

(1) 그 뉴스가 거짓이라는 것을 알지 못했기 때문에 많은 사람이 겁에 질려 어쩔 줄 몰랐다. (people, the news, was, knowing, panicked, many, not, false)

➡ _____

_____

(2) 일찍 떠났지만, 그는 회의에 늦었다. (he, the meeting, was, leaving, early, late, for)

➡ _____

(3) 그는 매우 열심히 공부해서 마침내 변호사가 되었다. (he, he, a lawyer, that, worked, became, hard, finally, so)

➡ _____

_____

(4) 그는 일찍 일어나서 첫 버스를 탈 수 있었다. (he, he, bus, catch, could, got, that, the, early, first, so, up)

➡ _____

_____

04 다음 문장에서 어법상 어색한 부분을 바르게 고치시오.

(1) Exhausting from the work, he lay down on the sofa.

➡ _____

(2) Failing twice, Jaden didn't want to try again.

➡ _____

05 그림을 보고 주어진 어휘를 이용하여 빈칸을 알맞게 채우시오.

(1) Mina reads newspapers every day
_____ keep up with
current affairs. (can, as)

(2) Mina reads newspapers every day
_____ keep up with
current affairs. (to, in)

(3) Mina reads newspapers every day
_____ keep up with
current affairs. (to, so)

06 중요 그림을 보고 접속사 없이 주어진 어휘를 이용하여 빈칸을 알맞게 채우시오.

(1) _____ rainy, they cannot go for a
walk. (be)

(2) _____ the rain, they are talking
about whether to go shopping. (watch)

07 중요 다음 우리말을 괄호 안의 지시대로 영작하시오.

(1) 왼쪽으로 돌면, 그 집을 찾을 겁니다.

➡ _____

(분사구문을 써서)

➡ _____

(접속사를 써서)

(2) 그녀는 아파서 학교에 결석했다.

➡ _____

(분사구문을 써서)

➡ _____

(접속사를 써서)

(3) Lisa는 그녀의 엄마가 오렌지 주스를 만들 수
있도록 오렌지를 좀 샀다.

➡ _____

_____

(that을 써서)

08 다음 문장에서 <u>잘못된</u> 것을 알맞게 고쳐 다시 쓰시오.

(1) Judy practices playing the piano in
order to that she can win the top prize.

➡ _____

_____

(2) I got up early so as to I could go
jogging.

➡ _____

_____

(3) Arrived late at the station, I saw the
train leaving.

➡ _____

_____

Can You Spot Fake News?

Every day we watch, hear, or read interesting news. However, have you ever seriously considered whether an article is really true?
└─ 현재완료(경험) ─┘   '~인지 아닌지'라는 뜻의 접속사

Everyone likes an interesting news story but what if it is completely
~이라면 어떻게 될까?

made up?

Fake news can be very harmful in that it can make people less
~이므로, ~라는 점에서

informed or even misled. Nevertheless, there have been various fake
목적격보어로 수동의 의미를 지닌 과거분사를 사용   그럼에도 불구하고,   현재완료(계속)

news reports throughout history. Why have some people written such

false information? Let's look into some articles thinking about the
동시동작을 나타내는 분사구문

hidden motives behind them.

AWFUL DISASTER

Last night, an angry group of rhinoceroses broke down the walls
a group of: '~의 무리',   break down: ~을 부수다, 무너뜨리다

of the cage at the zoo and escaped. They also broke down the walls

of the other wild animals' cages. These animals ran down the streets

and injured hundreds of people. Twelve of the animals are still on the
수백의

loose. Citizens should stay indoors until further notice.
잡히지 않은, 탈주 중인   farther(×)

* Not a single act or incident described above has taken place.
과거분사로, 앞에 나온 명사 act와 incident를 수식   현재완료

| spot 발견하다, 찾아내다 |
| fake 가짜의, 거짓의 |
| seriously 진지하게, 심각하게 |
| harmful 해로운, 유해한 |
| mislead 잘못 이끌다, 오해하게 하다 |
| nevertheless 그럼에도 불구하고 |
| motive 동기, 이유 |
| make up 지어내다, 만들어 내다 |
| awful 끔찍한, 지독한 |
| disaster 참사, 재난 |
| escape 달아나다, 탈출하다, 벗어나다 |
| injure 부상을 입히다 |
| citizen 시민 |
| incident 사건 |
| describe 기술하다 |
| rhinoceros 코뿔소 |
| break down ~을 부수다, ~을 무너뜨리다 |
| on the loose 잡히지 않은, 탈주 중인 |
| single 단 하나의 |
| act 행동 |

• 다음 문장이 본문의 내용과 일치하면 T, 일치하지 않으면 F를 쓰시오.

1 Each day we watch, hear, or read interesting news. ☐

2 Fake news can make people well-informed. ☐

3 There have been various fake news reports throughout history. ☐

4 All the acts or incidents described in the article above actually took place. ☐

At that time, those who read the article carefully laughed out loud.
= the people   크게 웃었다

Those who didn't read it to the end got really worried. Not knowing
주격 관계대명사절 who didn't read it to the end가 선행사 Those를 수식   이유를 나타내는 분사구문의 부정

the news was false, many people panicked. Some tried to escape the
Because they didn't know the news was false.

city while others went into the parks with guns to hunt the animals.
= other people

So why did *The Herald* make up such news? Later, they confessed
(남을 속이거나 즐겁게 하기 위해 이야기 등을) 지어내다, 만들어 내다   = The Herald

that they made it up so that they could draw the readers' attention to
= such news   (in order) to draw

the unsafe conditions at the zoo.

SLAV SHOOTS A FRIEND IN ARGUMENT

Mejk Swenekafew, a Slav worker at the Columbia Coal Mine, was
Mejk Swenekafew와 a Slav worker at the Columbia Coal Mine은 동격

shot and seriously wounded by John Pecitello near the mining camp

Thursday evening.

The two men had an argument during a meeting. The argument led
언쟁을 벌였다, 말다툼을 했다   during+기간을 나타내는 명사

to a fight, and Pecitello shot Swenekafew twice, in the chest and leg.

He is now at the hospital in critical condition. Pecitello ran away after
be in critical condition: 위독한 상태에 있다

the shooting. The police are searching for him now and are warning
복수 취급   search for: ~을 찾다   are searching and are warning: 접속사 and에 의해 병렬 구조로 연결되어 있음.

citizens that he is extremely dangerous.

panic 겁에 질려 어쩔 줄 모르다	
confess 고백하다, 인정하다	
unsafe 안전하지 않은	
condition 상태	
Slav 슬라브인	
shoot (총 등을) 쏘다	
argument 논쟁, 언쟁	
mine 광산, 채굴하다	
lead to ~을 이끌다	
twice 두 번	
wound 상처를 입히다	
chest 가슴, 흉부	
critical 위험한, 위독한	
extremely 극도로, 극히	
run away 도망치다	

확인문제

● 다음 문장이 본문의 내용과 일치하면 T, 일치하지 <u>않으면</u> F를 쓰시오.

1 At that time, those who read the article carefully laughed out loud. ☐

2 Those who read the article to the end got really worried. ☐

3 As they didn't know the news was false, many people panicked. ☐

4 John Pecitello was shot and seriously wounded by Mejk Swenekafew Thursday evening. ☐

5 Swenekafew is now at the hospital in critical condition. ☐

6 The police are warning citizens that Swenekafew is extremely dangerous. ☐

Is there anything strange about the article? Read the Slav's name backwards; it spells, "we-fake-news." Who wrote this and why?

the Slav's name. 즉 'Swenekafew'를 가리킨다. fake: '위조하다, 조작하다'

The Daily Telegram published this fake article so that they could
= in order to prove

prove if *The Daily News*, their competitor, was stealing their articles.
if(= whether): '~인지 아닌지'라는 의미의 명사절을 이끄는 접속사.

The Daily News published the same article about "Swenekafew" the next day and thus got caught stealing. The people at *The Daily News*
잡혔다, 포착되었다

had to admit their act and were harshly criticized by the public.
그동안 몰래 데일리 텔레그램 사의 기사를 훔쳤던 행위
The people at The Daily News를 주어로 하는 수동태 문장. 'The public harshly criticized the people at The Daily News .'(능동태)

The two articles were special cases, but there are many "fake" news
there+be동사: '~이 있다'는 의미. 주어는 many "fake" news articles

articles published every day. As readers, we need to read critically
과거분사로 앞에 나온 명사 articles를 수식

and judge whether the news is real or fake.
'~인지 아닌지'라는 의미의 접속사 = if

How to spot fake news!
how+to부정사: ~하는 방법

Consider the Source
기사의 출처인 원본 자료나 뉴스의 정보원 혹은 소식통을 의미

Is it from a reliable source?
Can we trust the writer?

Check the Date
Is it a new or an old story?
Is it related to current events?
be related to: ~와 관련이 있다

Read Beyond the Headlines
단순히 기사 제목만 읽고 뉴스의 내용을 짐작하여 판단하지 말고, 그 기사의 내용까지 모두 읽으라는 의미

Does the headline match the content?

Find Supporting Sources
Do other related stories provide similar content?

spell 철자를 말하다(쓰다)
publish 발행하다, 출판하다, 게재하다
competitor 경쟁자, 경쟁 상대
admit 인정하다, 자백하다
criticize 비난하다
public 대중, 일반 사람들
critically 비판적으로
judge 판단하다
source 출처, 자료
reliable 믿을 만한, 신뢰할 만한
current 현재의, 지금의
support 뒷받침하다

확인문제

- 다음 문장이 본문의 내용과 일치하면 T, 일치하지 <u>않으면</u> F를 쓰시오.

1 *The Daily Telegram* published this fake article so that they could prove that *The Daily News* was stealing their articles. ☐

2 *The Daily News* published a little bit different article about "Swenekafew" the next day. ☐

3 The people at *The Daily News* were harshly criticized by the public. ☐

4 To spot fake news, we need not check many sources. ☐

5 To spot fake news, it is necessary to check the date. ☐

6 To spot fake news, we shouldn't read beyond the headlines. ☐

● 우리말을 참고하여 빈칸에 알맞은 말을 쓰시오.

1 Can You _____ _____ _____?

2 Every day we watch, hear, or read _____ _____.

3 However, have you ever seriously considered _____ an article is really true?

4 Everyone likes an interesting news story but _____ _____ it is completely _____ _____?

5 Fake news can be very harmful _____ _____ it can make people _____ _____ or even _____.

6 _____, there have been various fake news reports _____ _____.

7 Why have some people written _____ _____ _____?

8 Let's look into some articles _____ about _____ _____ _____ behind them.

9 _____ DISASTER

10 Last night, an angry group of rhinoceroses _____ _____ the walls of the cage at the zoo and escaped.

11 They also broke down the walls of _____ _____ wild animals' cages.

12 These animals ran down the streets and injured _____ _____ people.

13 Twelve of the animals are still _____ _____ _____ _____.

14 Citizens should stay indoors _____ _____ _____ _____.

15 Not a single act or incident _____ _____ has taken place.

16 At that time, those who read the article carefully _____ _____ _____.

---

1 당신은 가짜 뉴스임을 알아챌 수 있는가?

2 매일 우리는 흥미로운 뉴스를 보고, 듣고, 읽는다.

3 그러나 당신은 뉴스 기사가 정말로 진실인지 심각하게 고려해 본 적이 있는가?

4 모든 사람이 흥미로운 뉴스 기사를 좋아하지만, 만약 그것이 완전히 지어낸 것이라면 어떻게 할 것인가?

5 가짜 뉴스는 사람들에게 정보를 부족하게 제공하거나 사람들을 잘못 이끌 수 있다는 점에서 매우 해로울 수 있다.

6 그럼에도 불구하고, 역사를 통틀어 다양한 가짜 뉴스 보도들이 존재해 왔다.

7 왜 어떤 사람들은 그러한 거짓 정보를 써 왔던 것일까?

8 그 뒤에 숨겨진 동기를 생각하면서 몇 가지 뉴스 기사를 살펴보자.

9 끔찍한 참사

10 어젯밤, 화가 난 코뿔소 떼가 동물원 우리의 벽을 부수고 도망쳤다.

11 그들은 또한 다른 야생 동물 우리의 벽도 부수었다.

12 이 동물들은 거리를 뛰어다니며 수백 명의 사람들에게 부상을 입혔다.

13 그중 열두 마리의 동물들이 아직 잡히지 않았다.

14 시민들은 추후 안내가 있을 때까지 집 안에 머물러야 한다.

15 위에 기술된 어떤 행동이나 사건도 일어나지 않았다.

16 그 당시 이 기사를 주의 깊게 읽었던 사람들은 크게 웃었다.

17 Those who didn't read it to the end _____ _____ _____ .

18 _____ _____ the news was false, many people _____ .

19 _____ tried to escape the city while _____ went into the parks with guns to hunt the animals.

20 So why did *The Herald* _____ _____ _____ _____ ?

21 Later, they confessed that they _____ _____ _____ _____ _____ they _____ draw the readers' attention to the unsafe conditions at the zoo.

22 SLAV SHOOTS A FRIEND _____ _____

23 Mejk Swenekafew, a Slav worker at the Columbia Coal Mine, _____ _____ and seriously _____ by John Pecitello near the mining camp Thursday evening.

24 The two men _____ _____ _____ during a meeting.

25 The argument _____ _____ a fight, and Pecitello shot Swenekafew twice, _____ _____ _____ and leg.

26 He is now at the hospital _____ _____ _____ .

27 Pecitello ran away _____ _____ _____ .

28 The police _____ _____ _____ him now and _____ _____ citizens that he is extremely dangerous.

29 Is there _____ _____ about the article?

30 Read the Slav's name _____ ; it spells, "we-fake-news."

31 Who wrote this and _____ ?

17 그것을 끝까지 읽지 않은 사람들은 정말로 걱정하였다.

18 그 기사가 거짓이라는 것을 알지 못했기 때문에 많은 사람이 겁에 질려 어쩔 줄 몰랐다.

19 어떤 사람들은 도시를 빠져나가려고 했고 다른 사람들은 그 동물들을 사냥하기 위해 총을 들고 공원으로 나갔다.

20 그렇다면 왜 헤럴드 사는 이러한 뉴스를 만들어 냈을까?

21 나중에 그들은 동물원의 안전하지 않은 상태에 대해 독자들의 주의를 끌기 위해 그 기사를 지어냈다고 고백했다.

22 슬라브인이 언쟁 중에 친구에게 총을 쏘다

23 목요일 저녁 채굴 야영지 근처에서, 컬럼비아 광산 소속의 슬라브인 노동자 Mejk Swenekafew가 John Pecitello에 의해 총상을 입어 심각하게 다쳤다.

24 그 두 사람은 회의 중에 언쟁을 벌였다.

25 언쟁이 싸움으로 번졌고, Pecitello가 Swenekafew의 가슴과 다리에 두 번 총을 쏘았다.

26 현재 그는 위독한 상태로 입원 중이다.

27 Pecitello는 총격 이후 도주했다.

28 경찰이 지금 그를 찾고 있으며, 그가 극히 위험하다고 시민들에게 경고하고 있다.

29 이 기사에 뭔가 이상한 점이 있는가?

30 그 슬라브인의 이름을 거꾸로 읽어 보아라. 그것의 철자는 "우리는 뉴스를 조작한다."가 된다.

31 누가 이것을 썼고 왜 그랬을까?

32 *The Daily Telegram* published this fake article _____ _____ they _____ prove _____ *The Daily News*, their competitor, was stealing their articles.

33 *The Daily News* published the same article about "Swenekafew" the next day and thus _____ _____ _____.

34 The people at *The Daily News* had to _____ their act and _____ _____ _____ by the public.

35 The two articles were special cases, but there are many "fake" news articles _____ every day.

36 _____ readers, we need to read critically and judge _____ the news is real _____ fake.

37 _____ _____ _____ fake news!

38 Consider the _____

39 Is it from a _____ source?

40 Can we _____ the writer?

41 _____ the Date

42 Is it a _____ or an _____ story?

43 _____ it _____ _____ _____ events?

44 Read _____ _____ _____

45 Does the headline _____ _____ _____?

46 Find _____ Sources

47 Do other _____ stories provide _____ content?

32 데일리 텔레그램 사는 그들의 경쟁자인 데일리 뉴스 사가 그들의 기사를 훔치는지를 증명하기 위해서 이 거짓 기사를 발행했다.

33 데일리 뉴스 사는 그 다음 날 'Swenekafew'에 대한 동일한 기사를 발행했고 그래서 훔친 것이 발각되었다.

34 데일리 뉴스 사의 사람들은 그들의 행동을 인정해야만 했고 대중들로부터 혹독한 비난을 받았다.

35 이 두 기사는 특별한 경우였지만, 매일 발행되는 '가짜' 뉴스 기사는 많이 있다.

36 독자로서, 우리는 비판적으로 읽고 그 뉴스가 진짜인지 가짜인지 판단할 필요가 있다.

37 가짜 뉴스 판별 방법!

38 출처를 고려하라

39 그것은 믿을 만한 출처에서 온 것인가?

40 우리는 그 필자를 신뢰할 수 있는가?

41 날짜를 확인하라

42 그것은 새로운 이야기인가 혹은 오래된 이야기인가?

43 그것은 현재의 사건들과 관련된 것인가?

44 기사 제목 그 이상을 읽어라

45 기사 제목이 기사 내용과 일치하는가?

46 뒷받침하는 자료를 찾아라

47 다른 관련된 이야기도 비슷한 내용을 제공하는가?

● 우리말을 참고하여 본문을 영작하시오.

1 ▶ 당신은 가짜 뉴스임을 알아챌 수 있는가?

➡ _____

2 ▶ 매일 우리는 흥미로운 뉴스를 보고, 듣고, 읽는다.

➡ _____

3 ▶ 그러나 당신은 뉴스 기사가 정말로 진실인지 심각하게 고려해 본 적이 있는가?

➡ _____

4 ▶ 모든 사람이 흥미로운 뉴스 기사를 좋아하지만, 만약 그것이 완전히 지어낸 것이라면 어떻게 할 것인가?

➡ _____

5 ▶ 가짜 뉴스는 사람들에게 정보를 부족하게 제공하거나 사람들을 잘못 이끌 수 있다는 점에서 매우 해로울 수 있다.

➡ _____

6 ▶ 그럼에도 불구하고, 역사를 통틀어 다양한 가짜 뉴스 보도들이 존재해 왔다.

➡ _____

7 ▶ 왜 어떤 사람들은 그러한 거짓 정보를 써 왔던 것일까?

➡ _____

8 ▶ 그 뒤에 숨겨진 동기를 생각하면서 몇 가지 뉴스 기사를 살펴보자.

➡ _____

9 ▶ 끔찍한 참사

➡ _____

10 ▶ 어젯밤, 화가 난 코뿔소 떼가 동물원 우리의 벽을 부수고 도망쳤다.

➡ _____

11 ▶ 그들은 또한 다른 야생 동물 우리의 벽도 부수었다.

➡ _____

12 ▶ 이 동물들은 거리를 뛰어다니며 수백 명의 사람들에게 부상을 입혔다.

➡ _____

13 ▶ 그중 열두 마리의 동물들이 아직 잡히지 않았다.

➡ _____

14 ▶ 시민들은 추후 안내가 있을 때까지 집 안에 머물러야 한다.

➡ _____

15 ▶ 위에 기술된 어떤 행동이나 사건도 일어나지 않았다.

➡ _____

16 ▶ 그 당시 이 기사를 주의 깊게 읽었던 사람들은 크게 웃었다.

➡ _____

17 그것을 끝까지 읽지 않은 사람들은 정말로 걱정하였다.

➡ _____

18 그 기사가 거짓이라는 것을 알지 못했기 때문에 많은 사람이 겁에 질려 어쩔 줄 몰랐다.

➡ _____

19 어떤 사람들은 도시를 빠져나가려고 했고 다른 사람들은 그 동물들을 사냥하기 위해 총을 들고 공원으로 나갔다.

➡ _____

20 그렇다면 왜 헤럴드 사는 이러한 뉴스를 만들어 냈을까?

➡ _____

21 나중에 그들은 동물원의 안전하지 않은 상태에 대해 독자들의 주의를 끌기 위해 그 기사를 지어냈다고 고백했다.

➡ _____

_____

22 슬라브인이 언쟁 중에 친구에게 총을 쏘다

➡ _____

23 목요일 저녁 채굴 야영지 근처에서, 컬럼비아 광산 소속의 슬라브인 노동자 Mejk Swenekafew가 John Pecitello에 의해 총상을 입어 심각하게 다쳤다.

➡ _____

_____

24 그 두 사람은 회의 중에 언쟁을 벌였다.

➡ _____

25 언쟁이 싸움으로 번졌고, Pecitello가 Swenekafew의 가슴과 다리에 두 번 총을 쏘았다.

➡ _____

26 현재 그는 위독한 상태로 입원 중이다.

➡ _____

27 Pecitello는 총격 이후 도주했다.

➡ _____

28 경찰이 지금 그를 찾고 있으며, 그가 극히 위험하다고 시민들에게 경고하고 있다.

➡ _____

29 이 기사에 뭔가 이상한 점이 있는가?

➡ _____

30 그 슬라브인의 이름을 거꾸로 읽어 보아라. 그것의 철자는 "우리는 뉴스를 조작한다."가 된다.

➡ _____

31 누가 이것을 썼고 왜 그랬을까?

➡ _____

32 데일리 텔레그램 사는 그들의 경쟁자인 데일리 뉴스 사가 그들의 기사를 훔치는지를 증명하기 위해서 이 거짓 기사를 발행했다.

➡ _____

33 데일리 뉴스 사는 그 다음 날 'Swenekafew'에 대한 동일한 기사를 발행했고 그래서 훔친 것이 발각되었다.

➡ _____

34 데일리 뉴스 사의 사람들은 그들의 행동을 인정해야만 했고 대중들로부터 혹독한 비난을 받았다.

➡ _____

34 이 두 기사는 특별한 경우였지만, 매일 발행되는 '가짜' 뉴스 기사는 많이 있다.

➡ _____

36 독자로서, 우리는 비판적으로 읽고 그 뉴스가 진짜인지 가짜인지 판단할 필요가 있다.

➡ _____

37 가짜 뉴스 판별 방법!

➡ _____

38 출처를 고려하라

➡ _____

39 그것은 믿을 만한 출처에서 온 것인가?

➡ _____

40 우리는 그 필자를 신뢰할 수 있는가?

➡ _____

41 날짜를 확인하라

➡ _____

42 그것은 새로운 이야기인가 혹은 오래된 이야기인가?

➡ _____

43 그것은 현재의 사건들과 관련된 것인가?

➡ _____

44 기사 제목 그 이상을 읽어라

➡ _____

45 기사 제목이 기사 내용과 일치하는가?

➡ _____

46 뒷받침하는 자료를 찾아라

➡ _____

47 다른 관련된 이야기도 비슷한 내용을 제공하는가?

➡ _____

[01~04] 다음 글을 읽고 물음에 답하시오.

Every day we watch, hear, or read interesting news. ___ⓐ___, have you ever seriously considered whether an article is really true? (①) Everyone likes an interesting news story but what if it is completely made up? (②)
ⓑFake news can be very harmful in that they can make people less informed or even misled. (③) Why have some people written such false information? (④) Let's look into some articles thinking about the hidden motives behind them. (⑤)

01 위 글의 빈칸 ⓐ에 들어갈 알맞은 말을 고르시오.

① In addition   ② In other words
③ Therefore   ④ However
⑤ For example

02 위 글의 흐름으로 보아, 주어진 문장이 들어가기에 가장 적절한 곳은?

> Nevertheless, there have been various fake news reports throughout history.

①   ②   ③   ④   ⑤

03 According to the passage, which is NOT true?

① Day after day we watch, hear, or read interesting news.
② There is no one that doesn't like an interesting news story.
③ Fake news can be very damaging.
④ People may be well-informed because of fake news.
⑤ Fake news can mislead people.

04 위 글의 밑줄 친 ⓑ에서 어법상 틀린 부분을 찾아 고치시오.

➡ _____

[05~07] 다음 글을 읽고 물음에 답하시오.

AWFUL DISASTER
  Last night, an angry group of rhinoceroses broke down the walls of the cage at the zoo and escaped. They also broke down the walls of the other wild animals' cages. These animals ran down the streets and injured hundreds of people. Twelve of the animals are still ___ⓐ___ the loose. Citizens should stay indoors ___ⓑ___ further notice.
  *Not ⓒa single act or incident described above has ⓓtaken place.

05 위 글의 빈칸 ⓐ와 ⓑ에 들어갈 전치사가 바르게 짝지어진 것은?

　　　ⓐ　ⓑ　　　　　　　ⓐ　ⓑ
① at – by   ② on – until
③ in – until   ④ at – for
⑤ on – with

06 다음 중 위 글의 밑줄 친 ⓒ에 해당하지 않는 것을 고르시오.

① 어젯밤, 화가 난 코뿔소 떼가 동물원 우리의 벽을 부수고 도망쳤다.
② 코뿔소 떼가 다른 야생 동물 우리의 벽도 부수었다.
③ 이 동물들이 거리를 뛰어다녔다.
④ 수백 명의 사람들이 부상을 입었다.
⑤ 그 중 열두 마리의 동물들이 잡혔다.

07 위 글의 밑줄 친 ⓓtaken place와 바꿔 쓸 수 있는 말을 모두 고르시오.

① been held
② happened
③ occurred
④ been hosted
⑤ arisen

[08~10] 다음 글을 읽고 물음에 답하시오.

At that time, those who read the article carefully laughed out loud. Those who didn't read it to the end got really worried. ⓐNot knowing the news was false, many people panicked. Some tried to escape the city while others went into the parks with guns to hunt the animals.

So why did *The Herald* ⓑmake up such news? Later, they confessed that they made it up so that they could draw the readers' attention to the unsafe conditions at the zoo.

08 아래 〈보기〉에서 위 글의 밑줄 친 ⓐ와 분사구문의 용법이 다른 것의 개수를 고르시오.

┌─ 보기 ┐
① Not having much money, he acted like a rich man.
② Having nothing to do, I went to bed earlier than usual.
③ Finding my son in the mall, please let me know.
④ Not failing the test, she still looked miserable.
⑤ Being sick, she decided not to go to school.
└─────────┘

① 1개   ② 2개   ③ 3개   ④ 4개   ⑤ 5개

09 위 글의 밑줄 친 ⓑmake up과 같은 의미로 쓰인 것을 고르시오.

① He likes to make up fun songs.
② Can I leave early this afternoon and make up the time tomorrow?
③ They fight and make up quite often.
④ Eleven players make up a team.
⑤ I make up my face to look like a clown.

10 위 글의 주제로 알맞은 것을 고르시오.

① the laughter of the readers who read the article carefully
② the worry of the readers who didn't read the article to the end
③ the reason why many people panicked
④ the false news to draw the readers' attention
⑤ the unsafe conditions at the zoo

[11~13] 다음 글을 읽고 물음에 답하시오.

SLAV SHOOTS A FRIEND IN ARGUMENT
Mejk Swenekafew, a Slav worker at the Columbia Coal Mine, was (A)[shot / shut] and seriously wounded by John Pecitello near the mining camp Thursday evening.

The two men had an argument during a meeting. The argument led to a fight, and Pecitello shot Swenekafew twice, in the chest and leg. ⓐHe is now at the hospital in critical condition. Pecitello ran away after the shooting. The police (B)[is / are] searching for him now and (C)[is / are] warning citizens that he is extremely dangerous.

서답형

11 위 글의 괄호 (A)~(C)에서 문맥이나 어법상 알맞은 낱말을 골라 쓰시오.

➡ (A)_____ (B)_____ (C)_____

서답형

12 위 글의 밑줄 친 ⓐHe가 가리키는 것을 본문에서 찾아 쓰시오.

➡ _____

중요

13 위 글을 읽고 Mejk Swenekafew에 대해 알 수 없는 것을 고르시오.

① Where did he work?

② Why did he have an argument with John Pecitello?

③ When was he shot?

④ How many times was he shot?

⑤ Where is he now?

[14~16] 다음 글을 읽고 물음에 답하시오.

Every day we watch, hear, or read interesting news. However, ⓐhave you ever seriously considered whether an article is really true? Everyone likes an interesting news story but what if it is completely made up?

Fake news can be very harmful (A)[in that / in which] it can make people less informed or even (B)[misleading / misled]. Nevertheless, there have been various fake news reports throughout history. Why have some people written (C)[so / such] false information? Let's look into some articles thinking about the hidden motives behind them.

서답형

14 위 글의 괄호 (A)~(C)에서 어법상 알맞은 낱말을 골라 쓰시오.

➡ (A)_____ (B)_____ (C)_____

15 위 글의 밑줄 친 문장 ⓐ의 현재완료 have considered와 용법이 같은 것을 모두 고르시오.

① How many times have you done it?

② He has gone to New York.

③ He has been ill for two weeks.

④ She has seen my brother before.

⑤ I have just finished my homework.

중요

16 Which question CANNOT be answered after reading the passage?

① How many interesting news do we watch, hear, or read each day?

② What kind of news story does everyone like?

③ Can fake news make people less informed?

④ Can fake news mislead people?

⑤ Have there been various fake news reports throughout history?

[17~19] 다음 글을 읽고 물음에 답하시오.

The two articles were special cases, but there are many "fake" news articles _ⓐ_ every day. As readers, we need to read critically and judge whether the news is real or fake.

How to spot fake news!

Consider the Source

Is it from a reliable source?

Can we trust the writer?

Check the Date

Is it a new or an old story?

Is it related to ⓑcurrent events?

Read Beyond the Headlines

Does the headline match the content?

Find Supporting Sources

Do other related stories provide similar content?

17 위 글의 빈칸 ⓐ에 publish를 알맞은 형태로 쓰시오.

➡ _____

18 위 글의 밑줄 친 ⓑcurrent와 같은 의미로 쓰인 것을 고르시오.

① These words are no longer current.

② He swam to the shore against a strong current.

③ The direct current flows in one direction.

④ Do you know the budget for the current year?

⑤ He doesn't want to swim against the current.

19 위 글을 읽고 가짜 뉴스 판별 방법에 해당하지 않는 것을 고르시오.

① to consider the source

② to guess the content by the headlines

③ to check the date

④ to read beyond the headlines

⑤ to find supporting sources

[20~23] 다음 글을 읽고 물음에 답하시오.

> Is there anything strange about the article? ⓐ Read the Slav's name forward; it spells, "we-fake-news." Who wrote this and why?
>
> *The Daily Telegram* published this fake article so that they could prove ⓑif *The Daily News*, their competitor, was stealing their articles. *The Daily News* published the same article about "Swenekafew" the next day and thus got caught stealing. The people at *The Daily News* had to admit their act and were harshly criticized by the public.

20 위 글의 밑줄 친 ⓐ에서 흐름상 어색한 부분을 찾아 고치시오.

➡ _____

21 위 글의 밑줄 친 ⓑif와 문법적 쓰임이 같은 것을 모두 고르시오.

① I can come at once if necessary.

② You can stay for the weekend if you like.

③ Do you know if he's married?

④ She will forgive you if you apologize to her.

⑤ I wonder if I should wear a coat.

22 According to the passage, which is NOT true?

① *The Daily Telegram* published this fake article.

② *The Daily News* was the competitor of *The Daily Telegram*.

③ *The Daily Telegram* published the same article about "Swenekafew" the next day.

④ *The Daily News* got caught stealing.

⑤ *The Daily News* were harshly criticized by the public.

23 다음 주어진 영영풀이에 해당하는 단어를 본문에서 찾아 쓰시오.

not genuine or real

➡ _____

[24~26] 다음 글을 읽고 물음에 답하시오.

Every day we watch, hear, or read interesting news. However, have you ever seriously considered whether an article is really true? Everyone likes an interesting news story but what if it is completely made up?

Fake news can be very harmful in that it can make people less informed or even misled. ⓐ Nevertheless, there have been various fake news reports throughout history. Why have some people written such false information? Let's look into some articles thinking about the hidden motives behind ⓑthem.

24 위 글의 밑줄 친 ⓐNevertheless와 바꿔 쓸 수 있는 말을 모두 고르시오.

① Despite ② Therefore
③ Still ④ Otherwise
⑤ Nonetheless

25 위 글의 밑줄 친 ⓑthem이 가리키는 것을 본문에서 찾아 쓰시오.

➡ _____

26 위 글의 제목으로 알맞은 것을 고르시오.

① Do You Want to Spot Fake News?
② Have You Considered If the News Is True?
③ Who Doesn't Like an Interesting News Story?
④ Harmful but Continuous Fake News Reports
⑤ Let's Write Faithful News Reports from Now on.

[27~29] 다음 글을 읽고 물음에 답하시오.

At that time, those who read the article carefully laughed out loud. (A)그것을 끝까지 읽지 않은 사람들은 정말로 걱정하였다. Not knowing the news was false, many people panicked. ⓐ tried to escape the city while ⓑ went into the parks with guns to hunt the animals.

So why did The Herald make up such news? (B)Later, they confessed that they made up it so that they could draw the readers' attention to the unsafe conditions at the zoo.

27 위 글의 빈칸 ⓐ와 ⓑ에 들어갈 알맞은 말을 고르시오.

① One – the other
② Some – the others
③ Another – the other
④ The first – the second
⑤ Some – others

28 위 글의 밑줄 친 (A)의 우리말에 맞게 주어진 어휘를 알맞게 배열하시오.

worried / end / who / to / didn't / got / it / those / really / the / read

➡ _____

29 위 글의 밑줄 친 (B)에서 어법상 틀린 부분을 찾아 고치시오.

➡ _____

[01~03] 다음 글을 읽고 물음에 답하시오.

Every day we watch, hear, or read interesting news. However, have you ever seriously considered whether an article is really true? Everyone likes an interesting news story but what (A)[if / whether] it is completely made up?

Fake news can be very (B)[harmful / harmless] in that it can make people less (C)[informing / informed] or even misled. Nevertheless, there have been various fake news reports throughout history. ⓐ왜 어떤 사람들은 그러한 거짓 정보를 써 왔던 것일까? Let's look into some articles ⓑthinking about the hidden motives behind them.

01 위 글의 괄호 (A)~(C)에서 문맥이나 어법상 알맞은 낱말을 골라 쓰시오.

➡ (A) _____ (B) _____ (C) _____

02 위 글의 밑줄 친 ⓐ의 우리말에 맞게 주어진 어휘를 알맞게 배열하시오.

> people / false / written / some / information / why / such / have / ?

➡ _____

_____

03 위 글의 밑줄 친 ⓑ를 부사절로 고치시오.

➡ _____

_____

[04~06] 다음 글을 읽고 물음에 답하시오.

AWFUL DISASTER

Last night, an angry group of rhinoceroses broke down the walls of the cage at the zoo and escaped. They also broke down the walls of the other wild animals' cages. These animals ran down the streets and injured hundreds of people. Twelve of the animals are still ⓐ_____ _____ _____. Citizens should stay indoors until further notice.

*ⓑNot a single act or incident described above has been taken place.

04 주어진 영영풀이를 참고하여 빈칸 ⓐ에 철자 o로 시작하는 어구를 쓰시오.

> having escaped; not under control

➡ _____

05 위 글의 밑줄 친 ⓑ에서 어법상 틀린 부분을 찾아 고치시오.

➡ _____

06 Actually how many people were injured by the escaped animals from the zoo last night? Fill in the blanks (A) and (B) with suitable words.

> (A)_____ one was injured by the escaped animals from the zoo because the animals didn't (B)_____ from the zoo last night in reality.

[07~08] 다음 글을 읽고 물음에 답하시오.

At that time, those who read the article carefully laughed out loud. Those who didn't read it to the end got really worried. Not knowing the news was false, many people panicked. Some tried to escape the city while ⓐothers went into the parks with guns to hunt the animals.

So why did *The Herald* make up such news? Later, they confessed that they made ⓑit up so that they could draw the readers' attention to the unsafe conditions at the zoo.

07 위 글의 밑줄 친 ⓐ를 다음과 같이 바꿔 쓸 때 빈칸에 들어갈 알맞은 말을 쓰시오.

➡ others went into the parks with guns

_____ they _____

hunt the animals

08 위 글의 밑줄 친 ⓑit이 가리키는 것을 본문에서 찾아 쓰시오.

➡ _____

[09~10] 다음 글을 읽고 물음에 답하시오.

SLAV SHOOTS A FRIEND IN ARGUMENT

Mejk Swenekafew, a Slav worker at the Columbia Coal Mine, was shot and seriously wounded ①by John Pecitello ②near from the mining camp Thursday evening.

The two men had an argument during a meeting. The argument led to a fight, and Pecitello shot Swenekafew twice, ③in the chest and leg. He is now at the hospital ④ in critical condition. Pecitello ran away after the shooting. The police are searching ⑤for him now and are warning citizens that he is extremely dangerous.

09 위 글의 밑줄 친 ①~⑤에서 어법상 어색한 것을 찾아 알맞게 고치시오.

➡ _____

10 본문의 내용과 일치하도록 다음 빈칸 (A)와 (B)에 알맞은 단어를 쓰시오.

> Mejk Swenekafew (A)_____ _____ _____ with John Pecitello during a meeting and Pecitello shot him. Swenekafew is now at the hospital and his condition is (B)_____.

[11~12] 다음 글을 읽고 물음에 답하시오.

Is there anything strange about the article? Read the Slav's name backwards; it spells, "we-fake-news." Who wrote this and why?

The Daily Telegram published this fake article so that they could prove ⓐif *The Daily News*, their competitor, was stealing their articles. *The Daily News* published the same article about "Swenekafew" the next day and thus got caught stealing. The people at *The Daily News* had to admit ⓑtheir act and were harshly criticized by the public.

11 위 글의 밑줄 친 ⓐif와 바꿔 쓸 수 있는 말을 쓰시오.

➡ _____

12 위 글의 밑줄 친 ⓑtheir act가 가리키는 것을 본문에서 찾아 쓰시오.

➡ _____

_____

Wrap Up 3

A: Wow! The news title says "Longer Vacation for Students." Hey, we're going

to have a longer vacation!

B: Wait! We should check first if it is true.
　　　　　　　　　　　　　　　　= whether

A: Why do you say so?

B: Some news uses a shocking title but its content may tell a different story.
　　　　　　　단수 동사　　　　　　　　　　　　　추측의 조동사

A: Oh, I see. I should read beyond the news title.

구문해설 • shocking: 충격적인 • content: 내용

해석

A: 와! 뉴스 제목이 "학생들을 위한 더 긴 방학"이야. 이봐, 우리 더 긴 방학을 갖나봐!

B: 기다려! 우리는 먼저 이게 사실인지를 확인해야 해.

A: 왜 그렇게 생각해?

B: 어떤 뉴스는 충격적인 제목을 사용하지만 그 내용은 다른 이야기를 할지도 몰라.

A: 오, 알았다. 뉴스 제목 너머를 읽어야 하는구나.

Read & Think After You Read B

Reporter: Why did *The Herald* write the "Awful Disaster" story, Mr. Right?

Mr. Right: They just wanted to draw the readers' attention to the unsafe
　　　　　　　　　　　　　　draw one's attention to ~: ~에 …의 주의를 끌다
　　　　conditions at the zoo.

Reporter: Actually, readers were very upset to find that it was false. How
　　　= In fact/As a matter of fact: 사실.　　　　　　　　to부정사의 부사적 용법(원인)
　　　　about "Slav Shoots a Friend in Argument?" What was the motive?
　　　= What about ~?: ~은 어떤가?

Mr. Right: *The Daily Telegram* wanted to prove that *The Daily News* was
　　　　　　　　　　　　　　　　　명사절(목적어)을 이끄는 접속사(생략 가능)
　　　　stealing their articles.
　　　　　　　= The Daily Telegram's

구문해설 • awful: 끔찍한 • disaster: 참사, 재난 • unsafe: 안전하지 않은 • upset: 속상한, 마음이 상한
• motive: 동기 • article: 기사

기자: 왜 헤럴드 사는 〈끔찍한 참사〉 이야기를 썼을까요, Right 씨?

Mr. Right: 그들은 단지 동물원의 안전하지 않은 상태에 대해 독자들의 주의를 끌고 싶었답니다.

기자: 사실, 독자들은 그것이 거짓이라는 것을 알고 매우 화가 났어요. 〈슬라브인이 언쟁 중에 친구에게 총을 쏘다〉는 어떤가요? 동기가 무엇이었나요?

Mr. Right: 데일리 텔레그램 사는 데일리 뉴스 사가 그들의 기사를 훔치고 있다는 것을 증명하기를 원했어요.

Read & Think After You Read C

A: Among the four tips, which do you think is the most important, and why?
간접의문문(= Do you think? + Which is the most important?)이며 think 동사가 있어서 의문사 which가 문두로 이동 뒤에 do you think it is
　　　　　　　　　　　　　　　　　　　　　　　　　　the most important 생략

B: I think finding supporting sources is the most important because I can
　　　　　동명사 주어　현재분사로 sources 수식　동명사 주어는 단수 취급　　간접의문문으로 명사절을 이끄는 접속사(~인지 아닌지)
　　check if the information is correct.

구문해설 • tip: 조언 • support: (진술 따위를) 입증하다, 뒷받침하다 • source: 자료

A: 네 가지 조언 중에서 너는 어떤 것이 가장 중요하다고 생각하며, 그 이유는 무엇이니?

B: 나는 뒷받침하는 자료들을 찾는 것이 가장 중요하다고 생각하는데, 그 정보가 올바른지 확인할 수 있기 때문이야.

01 다음 짝지어진 단어의 관계가 같도록 빈칸에 알맞은 말을 쓰시오.

> lead : mislead = understand : _____

02 다음 중 밑줄 친 부분의 뜻풀이가 바르지 <u>않은</u> 것은?

① People <u>panicked</u> and screamed when the hotel caught on fire. (겁에 질렸다)
② <u>Nevertheless</u>, many people came to the festival. (더욱이, 게다가)
③ These exercises help keep your <u>muscles</u> strong. (근육)
④ The <u>motive</u> for the fight between them was unknown. (동기)
⑤ News often <u>misleads</u> us with wrong information. (잘못 이끌다)

03 다음 문장의 빈칸에 들어갈 말을 <보기>에서 골라 쓰시오.

> ┤ 보기 ├
> riddle / seriously / reliable / source / shoot

(1) We are looking for someone who is honest and _____.
(2) Solve this _____, or you can't open the door.
(3) He can't talk now because he is _____ hurt.
(4) They will _____ arrows at bottles.
(5) He couldn't find the _____ of the story.

04 다음 영영풀이가 가리키는 것을 고르시오.

> to suddenly feel so worried that you cannot be reasonable

① panic
② reliable
③ current
④ critical
⑤ private

05 다음 주어진 문장의 밑줄 친 current와 <u>다른</u> 의미로 쓰인 것은?

> Did you have any idea about the <u>current</u> issue?

① I'll interview the <u>current</u> Olympic title-holder soon.
② Corona 19 seems so serious that the <u>current</u> situation will continue.
③ We got together here to find the solution to the <u>current</u> crisis.
④ You can check the <u>current</u> price by visiting our website.
⑤ Mike swam to the shore against a strong <u>current</u>.

06 다음 우리말에 맞게 빈칸에 알맞은 말을 쓰시오.

(1) 소방관들은 집으로 들어가기 위해 문을 부숴야 했다.
➡ The firefighters had to _____ _____ the door to get into the house.
(2) 계획에 따르면, 그들은 목요일까지 그것을 끝내야 한다.
➡ _____ _____ the plan, they should finish it by Thursday.
(3) 그녀는 잠잘 때 보는 무서운 동화를 만들어 냈다.
➡ She _____ _____ a scary bedtime story.

07 다음 우리말을 주어진 단어를 이용하여 영작하시오.

(1) 그녀는 지난밤에 있었던 일을 기술했다.
(happened) (6 words)

➡ _____

(2) 이것은 최악의 자연 재난 중의 하나이다.
(worst) (8 words)

➡ _____

(3) 사자가 한 시간 전에 동물원에서 탈출했다.
(ago, a lion) (9 words)

➡ _____

Conversation

08 다음 대화가 자연스럽게 이어지도록 순서대로 배열하시오.

Chris: Jane, do you usually get news online or from the newspaper?
Jane: Well, I usually watch TV news.
(A) I see your point.
(B) Why do you say so?
(C) TV news? Is there any special reason?
(D) I think TV is the most useful way to get news.
(E) I have to spend too much time reading all the news online or in the newspaper. So, I just watch the main news on TV.

➡ _____

[09~10] 다음 대화를 읽고 물음에 답하시오.

David: Hey, Sandy. Do you think I should buy this drink? It is said that it can help me lose weight.
Sandy: Let me read the label more closely. Hmm, it looks a bit strange to me, David.
David: Why do you say so?
Sandy: There isn't enough information about what's in the drink.

David: Oh, you're right.
Sandy: Also, it doesn't tell you how much you have to drink to lose weight.

09 위 대화에서 나타난 Sandy의 성격으로 적절한 것은?

① careful ② diligent
③ creative ④ adventurous
⑤ hardworking

10 위 대화의 내용과 일치하지 <u>않는</u> 것은?

① David is wondering if he should buy the drink.
② It is said that the drink can be helpful to lose weight.
③ Sandy finds out something strange about the drink.
④ There isn't enough information about how much David should drink to lose weight.
⑤ There's some information about what the drink is made of.

[11~12] 다음 대화를 읽고 물음에 답하시오.

Susan: What are you reading, John?
John: I'm reading a book of riddles.
Susan: Riddles? Aren't they for children?
John: Actually, no. Books of riddles are really useful for adults.
Susan: Really? Why do you say so?
John: They help us think more creatively. We need to think outside the box to find the answers.

11 Why does John think books of riddles are useful for adults?

➡ _____

12 What do we need to do to find the answers to riddles?

➡ _____

[13~14] 다음 대화를 읽고 물음에 답하시오.

> W: I think I caught a cold because I didn't dress warmly yesterday.
> M: Well, I've read an article saying that you don't catch a cold because your body temperature is low.
> W: Really? _____
> M: The article said that people catch colds because of viruses.

13 위 대화의 빈칸에 들어갈 말로 나머지와 의도가 <u>다른</u> 것은?

① Can you tell me more about it?
② Could you give me more information?
③ Can you explain more in detail?
④ Could you be more specific?
⑤ Can you give me your hand?

14 위 대화의 내용과 일치하지 <u>않는</u> 것은?

① The woman was not feeling well.
② The man read the article related to catching a cold.
③ The woman didn't dress warmly yesterday.
④ The article explained that people catch colds due to viruses.
⑤ The woman caught a cold because her body temperature was low.

Grammar

15 다음 두 문장을 괄호 안의 단어를 이용하여 한 문장으로 바꾸시오.

(1) • Linda was stupid.
 • She made a big mistake. (enough)

 ➡ _____

(2) • Bill is very poor.
 • So he can't buy the house. (too)

 ➡ _____

16 다음 밑줄 친 부분과 바꿔 쓸 수 있는 것은?

> Slow down <u>so that</u> children can cross the street safely.

① in order that
② in order to
③ so as to
④ such that
⑤ so which

17 다음 문장 중에서 어법상 어색한 문장을 고르시오.

① Not knowing the language, we had to use sign language.
② Working in a hospital, John is always busy.
③ Things getting more difficult, we should draw on our wisdom.
④ Arriving at the store, I found it closed.
⑤ Not handing out the report, she is responsible for the result.

18 다음 문장을 바꿔 썼을 때 빈칸에 알맞은 말을 쓰시오.

(1) The two articles having been special cases, there are many "fake" news articles published every day.

 ➡ _____,
 there are many "fake" news articles published every day.

(2) In the morning Harold greeted her smiling brightly.

 ➡ In the morning Harold greeted her
 _____.

(3) Being tired from the work, I fell asleep.

 ➡ _____,
 I fell asleep.

19 다음 문장의 공통으로 빈칸에 알맞은 것은?

> • He sat smiling, _____ his legs crossed.
> • Don't speak _____ your mouth full.

① in   ② with
③ of   ④ from
⑤ along

Reading

[20~23] 다음 글을 읽고 물음에 답하시오.

①Every day we watch, hear, or read interesting news. However, have you ever seriously considered ②whether an article is really true? Everyone likes an interesting news story but ③what if it is completely made up?

Fake news can be very harmful ④in that it can make people less informed or even misled. ⓐ , there have been various fake news reports throughout history. Why have some people written such false information? Let's look ⓑ some articles thinking about the hidden ⑤motives behind them.

20 위 글의 빈칸 ⓐ에 알맞은 것을 고르시오.

① Furthermore   ② Nevertheless
③ Likewise   ④ That is
⑤ Thus

21 다음 중 위 글의 밑줄 친 ①~⑤와 바꿔 쓸 수 있는 말로 옳지 않은 것을 고르시오.

① Each day
② if
③ what would happen if
④ in the sense that
⑤ themes

22 위 글의 빈칸 ⓑ에 알맞은 것을 고르시오.

① for   ② at
③ on   ④ with
⑤ into

23 위 글의 뒤에 올 내용으로 가장 알맞은 것을 고르시오.

① the way we can spot fake news
② various kinds of interesting news we watch, hear, or read every day
③ some fake news articles through which we can think about the hidden motives behind them
④ people who are less informed or even misled by fake news
⑤ the harmful effects of fake news

[24~26] 다음 글을 읽고 물음에 답하시오.

AWFUL DISASTER

Last night, an angry group of rhinoceroses ⓐ broke down the walls of the cage at the zoo and escaped. They also broke down the walls of (A)[another / the other] wild animals' cages. These animals ran down the streets and injured hundreds of people. ⓑ그중 열두 마리의 동물들이 아직 잡히지 않았다. Citizens should stay indoors until (B)[farther / further] notice.
*Not a single act or incident (C)[describing / described] above has taken place.

24 위 글의 밑줄 친 ⓐbroke down과 같은 의미로 쓰인 것을 고르시오.

① The peace talks between them broke down.
② Our car broke down on the freeway.
③ His health broke down under the pressure of work.
④ In the stomach, acids broke down food into bits.
⑤ The telephone system broke down.

25 위 글의 괄호 (A)~(C)에서 문맥이나 어법상 알맞은 낱말을 골라 쓰시오.

➡ (A)＿＿＿＿ (B)＿＿＿＿ (C)＿＿＿＿

26 위 글의 밑줄 친 ⓑ의 우리말에 맞게 주어진 어휘를 이용하여 9 단어로 영작하시오.

loose, of

➡ ＿＿＿＿＿＿＿＿＿＿＿＿

[27~28] 다음 글을 읽고 물음에 답하시오.

SLAV SHOOTS A FRIEND IN ARGUMENT
Mejk Swenekafew, a Slav worker at the Columbia Coal Mine, was shot and seriously wounded by John Pecitello near the mining camp Thursday evening. (①)
The two men had an argument during a meeting. (②) He is now at the hospital in critical condition. (③) Pecitello ran away after the shooting. (④) The police are searching for him now and are warning citizens that ⓐhe is extremely dangerous. (⑤)

27 위 글의 밑줄 친 ⓐhe가 가리키는 것을 본문에서 찾아 쓰시오.

➡ ＿＿＿＿＿＿＿＿＿＿＿＿

28 위 글의 흐름으로 보아, 주어진 문장이 들어가기에 가장 적절한 곳은?

The argument led to a fight, and Pecitello shot Swenekafew twice, in the chest and leg.

①　　②　　③　　④　　⑤

[29~30] 다음 글을 읽고 물음에 답하시오.

Reporter: Why did *The Herald* write ⓐthe "Awful Disaster" story, Mr. Right?
Mr. Right: They just wanted to draw the readers' attention to the unsafe conditions at the zoo.
Reporter: Actually, readers were very upset to find that it was false. How about "ⓑSlav Shoots a Friend in Argument?" What was the motive?
Mr. Right: *The Daily Telegram* wanted to prove that *The Daily News* was stealing their articles.

29 위 글의 종류로 알맞은 것을 고르시오.

① article
② essay
③ review
④ interview
⑤ summary

30 위 글을 읽고 The Herald가 가짜 기사인 ⓐthe "Awful Disaster" story를 지어낸 동기와, The Daily Telegram이 가짜 기사인 ⓑSlav Shoots a Friend in Argument를 지어낸 동기를 각각 본문에서 찾아, to부정사로 시작하여 쓰시오.

➡ ⓐ ＿＿＿＿＿＿＿＿＿＿＿＿
＿＿＿＿＿＿＿＿＿＿＿＿
ⓑ ＿＿＿＿＿＿＿＿＿＿＿＿
＿＿＿＿＿＿＿＿＿＿＿＿

01 다음 영영풀이가 가리키는 것을 고르시오.

> to form words with the letters in the correct order

① shoot　　　　② spot
③ support　　　④ strengthen
⑤ spell

[02~03] 다음 대화를 읽고 물음에 답하시오.

Suji: I usually drink a glass of warm milk before I go to bed, but it doesn't help me fall asleep.

Minsu: I saw a show on TV, and a doctor said that a glass of warm milk doesn't actually help you fall asleep.

Suji: Oh, it doesn't? (A)Can you tell me more about it? (information)

Minsu: Milk has special chemicals that make people sleepy. But the amount in a glass is too small to have any effect.

02 위 대화의 밑줄 친 (A)와 의도가 같도록 주어진 어휘를 사용하여 다시 쓰시오.

➡ _____

03 위 대화를 읽고 대답할 수 없는 것은?

① What's the matter with Suji?
② What does Suji do before going to bed?
③ What is the effect of special chemicals in milk?
④ Why are the chemicals in a glass of warm milk not helpful for falling asleep?
⑤ How many glasses of milk should Suji drink to sleep better?

[04~05] 다음 대화를 읽고 물음에 답하시오.

Jane: I read an article saying that Napoleon was actually fairly tall. (A)

Tom: Oh, really? (B)

Jane: According to the article, a French doctor wrote down Napoleon's height according to the French measuring system, not the English one. (C)

Tom: What was the difference? (D)

Jane: At that time, an inch in France was longer than an inch in England. So, Napoleon was actually about 168 cm tall, which was not that short in those times. (E)

04 위 대화의 (A)~(E) 중 주어진 문장이 들어가기에 적절한 곳은?

> Can you tell me more about it?

① (A)　② (B)　③ (C)　④ (D)　⑤ (E)

05 위 대화를 읽고 대답할 수 없는 것은?

① What is the article about?
② Who wrote down Napoleon's height?
③ In what way was Napoleon's height written down?
④ Why was an inch in France different from an inch in England?
⑤ What was the difference between French and English measuring systems?

[06~07] 다음 대화를 읽고 물음에 답하시오.

Susan: What are you reading, John?

John: I'm reading a book of riddles.

Susan: Riddles? Aren't they for children?

John: Actually, no. Books of riddles are really useful for adults.

Susan: Really? Why do you say so?

John: They help us think more creatively. We need to think outside the box to find the answers.

06 위 대화에서 다음 영영풀이가 가리키는 말을 찾아 쓰시오.

> a question that is difficult to understand, and that has a surprising answer, that you ask somebody as a game

➡ _____

07 위 대화의 내용과 일치하지 <u>않는</u> 것은?

① John은 수수께끼 책을 읽고 있다.

② 수수께끼 책은 어른들에게 유용하다.

③ 수수께끼 책은 좀 더 창의적으로 생각하도록 돕는다.

④ 수수께끼 답을 찾기 위해 고정관념에서 벗어날 필요가 있다.

⑤ 수수께끼 답을 찾기 위해 상자를 밖으로 꺼내야 한다.

[08~09] 다음 대화를 읽고 물음에 답하시오.

W: I read an interesting article about the Black Sea. Do you know ⓐwhere is it?

M: Yes. It's ⓑbetween Eastern Europe and Western Asia, right?

W: Right. ⓒWhat color do you think it is?

M: Well, black, I guess.

W: No, it isn't. It's blue.

M: Really? Then why is it ⓓcalled the Black Sea? Can you tell me more about it?

W: People call it the Black Sea ⓔbecause it is very dangerous.

08 위 대화의 밑줄 친 ⓐ~ⓔ 중 어법상 <u>틀린</u> 것을 찾아 바르게 고치시오.

➡ _____

09 위 대화의 내용과 일치하지 <u>않는</u> 것은?

① 여자는 흑해에 관한 흥미로운 기사를 읽었다.

② 흑해는 동유럽과 서아시아 사이에 있다.

③ 흑해는 검은색이 아니라 파란색이다.

④ 사람들이 흑해라고 부르는 이유는 그곳이 매우 위험하기 때문이다.

⑤ 남자는 사람들이 흑해하고 부르는 이유에 대해 알고 있었다.

10 다음 중 어법상 <u>어색한</u> 문장을 고르시오.

① He didn't want to be late, so that he took a taxi.

② Put it down gently so that it doesn't break.

③ She was so tired to think straight.

④ Is she healthy enough to travel?

⑤ I studied Italian so that I would be able to read Dante in the original.

출제율 95%

11 다음 분사구문을 접속사를 이용한 문장으로 바꿔 쓰시오.

(1) Driving my car, I couldn't reply to your text message.

➡ _____

_____

(2) Walking down the street, I met my friend.

➡ _____

_____

(3) There being no work to do, he remained at his office until late.

➡ _____

_____

출제율 90%

12 다음 그림을 보고 주어진 어휘를 이용하여 빈칸을 알맞게 채우시오.

Mary was sitting on the sofa, _____

_____. (play, the guitar)

출제율 100%

13 다음 중 의미가 다른 문장을 고르시오.

① Don't waste water so that we can prevent water shortages.

② Don't waste water in order that we can prevent water shortages.

③ Don't waste water so as to prevent water shortages.

④ Don't waste water in order can prevent water shortages.

⑤ Don't waste water to prevent water shortages.

[14~16] 다음 글을 읽고 물음에 답하시오.

Every day we watch, hear, or read interesting news. However, have you ever seriously considered whether an ⓐarticle is really true? Everyone likes an interesting news story but what if it is completely made up?

Fake news can be very harmful in that it can make people less informed or even misled. Nevertheless, there have been various fake news reports throughout history. Why have some people written such false information? Let's look into some articles ⓑthinking about the hidden motives behind them.

출제율 90%

14 위 글의 밑줄 친 ⓐarticle과 같은 의미로 쓰인 것을 모두 고르시오.

① Bread is an article of food.

② He contributed an article to a journal.

③ That word has to have a definite article before it.

④ I read every last article in the newspaper.

⑤ I'm looking for an article of clothing.

출제율 95%

15 위 글의 밑줄 친 ⓑthinking과 문법적 쓰임이 같은 것을 모두 고르시오.

① My hobby is reading books.

② Who is the girl playing the piano?

③ I saw the boy eating an apple.

④ Taking a walk every day is very good for you.

⑤ He is collecting stamps.

출제율 100%

16 위 글의 주제로 알맞은 것을 고르시오.

① We are living in a flood of information.

② Everyone likes an interesting news story.

③ It is difficult to spot fake news.

④ There are many ways to write news reports faithfully.

⑤ Despite their harmful effects, there have been various fake news reports.

[17~19] 다음 글을 읽고 물음에 답하시오.

At that time, those who read the article carefully laughed out loud. Those who didn't read it to the end got really worried. (A)<u>Not knowing the news was false</u>, many people ⓐ_____ . Some tried to escape the city while others went into the parks with guns to hunt the animals.

So why did *The Herald* make up such news? Later, they confessed that they made it up so that they could draw the readers' attention to the unsafe conditions at the zoo.

17 위 글의 빈칸 ⓐ에 panic을 알맞은 형태로 쓰시오. (one word)

➡ _____

18 위 글의 밑줄 친 (A)를 부사절로 고치시오.

➡ _____

19 According to the passage, which is NOT true?

① The readers who read the article carefully laughed out loud.

② Some of the readers who didn't read the article to the end tried to escape the city.

③ Some of the readers who didn't read the article to the end went into the parks with guns to hunt the animals.

④ *The Herald* made up such false news to scare people.

⑤ The conditions of the zoo were unsafe.

[20~22] 다음 글을 읽고 물음에 답하시오.

Is there anything strange about the article? Read the Slav's name backwards; it spells, "we-fake-news." Who wrote this and why?

The Daily Telegram published this fake article so that they could prove if *The Daily News*, their competitor, was stealing (A)<u>their</u> articles. *The Daily News* published the same article about "Swenekafew" the next day and ⓐ_____ got caught stealing. The people at *The Daily News* had to admit (B)<u>their</u> act and (C) <u>were harshly criticized by the public.</u>

20 위 글의 빈칸 ⓐ에 들어갈 알맞은 말을 고르시오.

① additionally　　② alternatively

③ on the other hand　④ moreover

⑤ thus

21 위 글의 밑줄 친 (A)their와 (B)their가 가리키는 것을 각각 본문에서 찾아 쓰시오.

➡ (A) _____
(B) _____

22 위 글의 밑줄 친 (C)를 능동태로 고치시오.

➡ _____
_____

[01~03] 다음 대화를 읽고 물음에 답하시오.

Jane: I read an article saying that Napoleon was actually fairly tall.

Tom: Oh, really? Can you tell me more about it?

Jane: According to the article, a French doctor wrote down Napoleon's height according to the French measuring system, not the English one.

Tom: What was the difference?

Jane: At that time, an inch in France was longer than an inch in England. So, Napoleon was actually about 168 cm tall, which was not that short in those times.

01 What does the article say about Napoleon's height?

➡ _____

02 Who wrote down Napoleon's height and in what way was it written down?

➡ _____

_____

03 What was the difference between French and English measuring systems?

➡ _____

04 분사구문은 부사절로, 부사절은 분사구문으로 바꿔 쓰시오.

(1) Winning the first prize, Jenny was so happy.

➡ _____

_____

(2) Walking with Wing Walker, you burn more calories and get slimmer.

➡ _____

_____

(3) Because they use the hidden board technology, they strengthen leg muscles.

➡ _____

_____

(4) She studied very hard and passed the exam.

➡ _____

05 다음 문장을 같은 뜻을 갖는 문장으로 바꿔 쓰려고 한다. 빈칸을 알맞게 채우시오.

(1) I want to have Harry Potter's magic cloak so that I could become invisible.

= I want to have Harry Potter's magic cloak _____ _____ _____ I could become invisible.

(2) Take a rest every hour so that you can keep warm.

= Take a rest every hour _____ _____ _____ keep warm.

(3) Be so humble that you can learn from your mistakes.

= Be humble _____ _____ learn from your mistakes.

(4) It was so hot that we couldn't go out.

= It was _____ _____ for us _____ go out.

Every day we watch, hear, or read interesting news. ⓐHowever, have you ever seriously considered that an article is really true? Everyone likes an interesting news story but ⓑ만약 그것이 완전히 지어낸 것이라면 어떻게 할 것인가?

Fake news can be very harmful in that it can make people less informed or even misled. Nevertheless, there have been various fake news reports throughout history. Why have some people written such false information? Let's look into some articles thinking about the hidden motives behind them.

06 위 글의 밑줄 친 ⓐ에서 어법상 틀린 부분을 찾아 고치시오.

➡ _____

07 위 글의 밑줄 친 ⓑ의 우리말에 맞게 주어진 어휘를 이용하여 7 단어로 영작하시오.

what, made, completely

➡ _____

08 본문의 내용과 일치하도록 다음 빈칸 (A)와 (B)에 공통으로 들어갈 알맞은 단어를 쓰시오.

Though people can be less informed or even misled because of (A)_____ _____, there have been various (B)_____ _____ reports throughout history.

At that time, those who read the article carefully laughed out loud. Those who didn't read ⓐit to the end got really worried. Not knowing the news was false, many people panicked. Some tried to escape the city while others went into the parks with guns to hunt the animals.

So why did *The Herald* make up such news? Later, they confessed that they made it up ⓑso that they could draw the readers' attention to the unsafe conditions at the zoo.

09 위 글의 밑줄 친 ⓐit이 가리키는 것을 본문에서 찾아 쓰시오.

➡ _____

10 위 글의 밑줄 친 ⓑ를 to부정사를 사용하여 고치시오.

➡ _____

_____

11 How did the readers who didn't know the news was false react? Fill in the blanks (A) and (B) with suitable words.

Some tried to (A)_____ _____ _____ while others (B)_____ _____ _____ _____ with guns to hunt the animals.

01 다음 대화를 읽고 Suji의 일기를 완성하시오.

> Suji: I usually drink a glass of warm milk before I go to bed, but it doesn't help me fall asleep.
>
> Minsu: I saw a show on TV, and a doctor said that a glass of warm milk doesn't actually help you fall asleep.
>
> Suji: Oh, it doesn't? Can you tell me more about it?
>
> Minsu: Milk has special chemicals that make people sleepy. But the amount in a glass is too small to have any effect.

> Recently, I couldn't sleep well, so (A)_____ before I went to bed. However, it didn't work at all. I talked about it to Minsu. He explained that (B)_____ _____. According to the doctor, there are special chemicals in milk that (C)_____, but the (D)_____ in a glass is too small. I think I should find another way to get a sound sleep.

02 다음 내용을 바탕으로 제품의 광고 내용에 대해 문의하는 게시 글을 쓰시오.

> Q1 What product are they advertising?
>
> A1 They are advertising the walking shoes, Wing Walker.
>
> Q2 What are the strong points of the product?
>
> A2 Walking with Wing Walker, people burn more calories and get slimmer. They also strengthen leg muscles because they use the hidden board technology.
>
> Q3 What information is not shown in the ad?
>
> A3 First, is it scientifically proven that walking with Wing Walker, people burn more calories? Second, what materials are used for the hidden board?

> I saw the ad about (A)_____. It says that walking with Wing Walker, people (B)_____. They also strengthen leg muscles because they use (C)_____. But here are some questions. First, is it (D)_____ that walking with Wing Walker, people burn more calories? Second, (E)_____ are used for the hidden board? It would be great if you could answer my questions.

단원별 모의고사

01 다음 대화가 자연스럽게 이어지도록 순서대로 배열하시오.

> (A) Really? Can you tell me more about it?
>
> (B) The article said that people catch colds because of viruses.
>
> (C) Well, I've read an article saying that you don't catch a cold because your body temperature is low.
>
> (D) I think I caught a cold because I didn't dress warmly yesterday.

➡ _____

02 다음 우리말에 맞게 빈칸에 알맞은 말을 쓰시오.

(1) 저 치즈의 냄새는 지독하다.
➡ The smell of that cheese is _____.

(2) 너는 이 화학 물질을 다룰 때 장갑을 껴야만 한다.
➡ You must wear gloves when you handle these _____.

(3) 그는 가슴 위로 팔짱을 꼈다.
➡ He crossed his arms over his _____.

(4) 그는 한국인 여인과 결혼해서 한국 시민이 되었다.
➡ He married a Korean woman and became a Korean _____.

03 다음 문장의 빈칸에 들어갈 말을 〈보기〉에서 골라 알맞은 형태로 쓰시오.

> ┌─ 보기 ─┐
> public / recognize / publish / prove / poems

(1) He enjoys writing _____ in his free time.

(2) She should _____ they are wrong.

(3) The museum will be open to the _____ next month.

(4) He has _____ several novels, and I have read them all.

(5) I was able to _____ my old friend by her voice.

04 다음 문장에 공통으로 들어갈 말을 고르시오.

> • My grandfather used to work in the gold _____.
> • The _____ was closed because of the safety problem.
> • People _____ for coal in this area.
> • Half of the money was _____.

① panic   ② condition
③ mine   ④ strengthen
⑤ support

[05~06] 다음 대화를 읽고 물음에 답하시오.

Suji: There are so many pieces of information we call "facts" that are completely wrong.

Jack: (A) Why do you say so?

Suji: (B) I read a book, and there were a lot of examples of these facts that are wrong.

Jack: (C) Like what?

Suji: (D) But goldfish are actually smart.

Jack: (E) Really? Can you tell me more about that?

Suji: They can recognize their owners.

Jack: Oh, I didn't know that.

05 위 대화의 (A)~(E) 중 주어진 문장이 들어가기에 적절한 곳은?

> Well, most people think goldfish are not smart.

① (A)   ② (B)   ③ (C)   ④ (D)   ⑤ (E)

06 위 대화를 읽고 대답할 수 <u>없는</u> 것은?

① What did Suji read about?

② What do most people think about goldfish?

③ What can goldfish actually do?

④ Why does Suji think that goldfish are smart?

⑤ How can goldfish recognize their owners?

[07~09] 다음 대화를 읽고 물음에 답하시오.

David: Hey, Sandy. Do you think I should buy this drink? It is said that it can help me lose weight.

Sandy: Let me read the label more closely. Hmm, it looks a bit strange to me, David.

David: Why do you say so?

Sandy: There isn't enough information about what's in the drink.

David: Oh, you're right.

Sandy: Also, it doesn't tell you how much you have to drink to lose weight.

07 What does Sandy read closely?

➡ _____

08 Why does Sandy think that David shouldn't buy the drink?

➡ _____

_____

09 What are the two things that are not shown on the label?

➡ _____

_____

[10~11] 다음 대화를 읽고 물음에 답하시오.

Susan: What are you reading, John?

John: I'm reading a book of riddles.

Susan: Riddles? Aren't they for children?

John: Actually, no. Books of riddles are really (A)[useful / useless] for adults.

Susan: Really? Why do you say so?

John: They help us think more (B)[ordinarily / creatively]. We need to think (C)[inside / outside] the box to find the answers.

10 위 대화의 (A)~(C)에 들어갈 말로 바르게 짝지어진 것은?

	(A)	(B)	(C)
①	useful	ordinarily	inside
②	useful	creatively	outside
③	useful	creatively	inside
④	useless	creatively	outside
⑤	useless	ordinarily	inside

11 위 대화를 읽고 대답할 수 <u>없는</u> 것은?

① What is John reading now?

② Are the books of riddles for children?

③ Why are the books of riddles useful for adults?

④ What should people do to find the answers to the riddles?

⑤ What is there outside John's box?

12 다음 우리말을 주어진 단어를 이용하여 영작하시오.

(1) 비판적으로 생각하고 그들이 너에게 말하는 모든 것을 믿지는 마라. (critically)

　➡ _____

_____

(2) 너의 학급 친구들을 비난하거나 놀리지 마라. (of, fun)

　➡ _____

(3) 이것이 너의 현재 주소니? (current)

　➡ _____

(4) 그것이 맞는지 아닌지는 판단하기가 어렵다. (whether, difficult, judge)

　➡ _____

13 다음 문장에서 어법상 어색한 것을 바르게 고쳐 다시 쓰시오.

(1) Sam saved some money so as to he could buy a new backpack.

　➡ _____

_____

(2) You must follow the rules in order to everyone enjoy the experience.

　➡ _____

_____

_____

(3) She saw Thomas entered the classroom.

　➡ _____

(4) Very embarrassing, she didn't tell us that news.

　➡ _____

_____

14 다음 우리말을 주어진 어휘를 이용하여 영작하시오.

(1) 할 일이 없을 때, 그는 낚시하러 간다. (have, work, do, 8 단어)

　➡ _____

(2) Susan은 다른 사람들이 그녀의 목소리를 들을 수 없도록 조용히 얘기했다. (other people, voice, that, speak, hear, quietly, 11 단어)

　➡ _____

_____

15 Which is grammatically wrong?

① Getting up late, I brought some bread to school for breakfast.

② Never use your phone in order to always look in front of you.

③ Wear a swimming cap in order to the pool be kept clean.

④ Wear bright-colored clothes in order that people can see you at night.

⑤ Let's plant many trees so that they can help provide fresh air.

16 다음 중 어법상 옳은 문장을 모두 고르시오.

① Starting a class, my teacher plays a pop song.

② Pass the exam, I felt really happy.

③ After taking a walk in the park, I went to bed.

④ He plays computer games with his friends having some snacks.

⑤ Feeling not hungry, I concentrated on reading.

⑥ Meeting her several times, he noticed her immediately.

17 다음 두 문장을 해석하고 그 차이를 설명하시오.

(1) Jinho studied English hard so that he could talk with foreigners in English.

➡ 해석 _____

_____

차이 _____

_____

(2) Jinho studied English so hard that he could talk with foreigners in English.

➡ 해석 _____

_____

차이 _____

_____

[18~19] 다음 글을 읽고 물음에 답하시오.

Every day we watch, hear, or read interesting news. However, have you ever seriously considered whether an article is really true? Everyone likes an interesting news story but what if ⓐit is completely made up?

Fake news can be very harmful in that it can make people less informed or even misled. Nevertheless, there ⓑhave been various fake news reports throughout history. Why have some people written such false information? Let's look into some articles thinking about the hidden motives behind them.

18 아래 〈보기〉에서 위 글의 밑줄 친 ⓑhave been과 현재완료의 용법이 같은 것의 개수를 고르시오.

┌─── 보기 ├───
① I have lost my cellphone.
② Have you finished reading the book yet?
③ I have studied English since the third grade of elementary school.
④ He has now completed the project.
⑤ She has been to Japan twice.
└────────────┘

① 1개 ② 2개 ③ 3개 ④ 4개 ⑤ 5개

19 위 글의 밑줄 친 ⓐit이 가리키는 것을 본문에서 찾아 쓰시오.

➡ _____

[20~22] 다음 글을 읽고 물음에 답하시오.

At that time, those who read the article carefully laughed out loud. (①) Those who didn't read it ⓐ_____ the end got really worried. (②) Not knowing the news was false, many people panicked. (③) Some tried to escape the city (A)while others went into the parks with guns to hunt the animals.

(④) Later, they confessed that they made it up so that they could draw the readers' attention ⓑ_____ the unsafe conditions at the zoo. (⑤)

20 위 글의 빈칸 ⓐ와 ⓑ에 공통으로 들어갈 알맞은 전치사를 고르시오.

① of   ② from
③ to   ④ at
⑤ for

21 위 글의 밑줄 친 (A)while과 의미와 문법적 쓰임이 같지 않은 것을 고르시오.

① I've read fifty pages, while he's read only twenty.
② Some are rich, while others are poor.
③ They chatted for a while.
④ Tom's very good at science, while his brother is absolutely hopeless.
⑤ The walls are green, while the ceiling is white.

22 위 글의 흐름으로 보아, 주어진 문장이 들어가기에 가장 적절한 곳은?

> So why did *The Herald* make up such news?

①   ②   ③   ④   ⑤

[23~26] 다음 글을 읽고 물음에 답하시오.

ⓐ _____

  Mejk Swenekafew, a Slav worker at the Columbia Coal Mine, was shot and seriously wounded by John Pecitello near the mining camp Thursday evening.
ⓑ그 두 사람은 회의 중에 언쟁을 벌였다. The argument led to a fight, and Pecitello shot Swenekafew twice, in the chest and leg. He is now at the hospital in critical condition. Pecitello ran ___ⓒ___ after the shooting. The police are searching for him now and are warning citizens that he is extremely dangerous.

23 위 글의 빈칸 ⓐ에 들어갈 제목으로 알맞은 것을 고르시오.

① A Slav Worker at the Columbia Coal Mine
② Argument Near the Mining Camp
③ Swenekafew Is in Critical Condition
④ Extremely Dangerous Criminal
⑤ Slav Shoots a Friend in Argument

24 위 글의 밑줄 친 ⓑ의 우리말에 맞게 주어진 어휘를 알맞게 배열하시오.

> during / men / a / argument / two / had / an / meeting / the

➡ _____
_____

25 위 글의 빈칸 ⓒ에 알맞은 것은?

① in   ② to
③ away   ④ from
⑤ along

26 According to the passage, which is NOT true?

① Mejk Swenekafew was a Slav worker at the Columbia Coal Mine.
② Mejk Swenekafew was seriously wounded by John Pecitello.
③ Swenekafew was shot in the chest and leg.
④ The police are searching for Swenekafew.
⑤ The police are warning citizens that Pecitello is extremely dangerous.

MEMO

Lesson

6

Words of Wisdom

 의사소통 기능

- 상대방을 안심시키기

  A: I keep making mistakes. I'm so worried.

  B: **Don't worry about** making mistakes.

- 상상한 내용 묻기

  A: **What would you do if** you had a magic carpet?

  B: I would fly to wherever I want.

 언어 형식

- 'It ~ that ...' 강조 구문

  It was this wisdom **that** our father tried to explain.

- have+목적어+과거분사

  I **had** my bed **designed** by experts.

Words & Expressions

교과서

Key Words

- □ **captain** [kǽptin] 몡 선장
- □ **carpet** [kɑ́:rpit] 몡 카펫, 양탄자
- □ **castle** [kǽsl] 몡 성
- □ **character** [kǽriktər] 몡 등장인물
- □ **chat** [ʧæt] 툉 한가롭게 이야기하다, 담소하다
- □ **chef** [ʃef] 몡 요리사
- □ **comfortably** [kʌ́mfərtəbli] 閉 편안하게
- □ **confusing** [kənfjú:ziŋ] 혱 혼란스러운, 헷갈리는
- □ **continue** [kʌntínju:] 툉 계속하다
- □ **deadline** [dédlain] 몡 기한, 마감 일자
- □ **death** [deθ] 몡 죽음
- □ **design** [dizáin] 툉 설계하다
- □ **dragon** [drǽgən] 몡 용
- □ **dwarf** [dwɔ:rf] 몡 난장이
- □ **exhibit** [igzíbit] 툉 전시하다
- □ **expensive** [ikspénsiv] 혱 비싼, 돈이 많이 드는
- □ **expert** [ékspə:rt] 몡 전문가
- □ **explain** [ikspléin] 툉 설명하다
- □ **express** [iksprés] 툉 표현하다
- □ **failure** [féiljər] 몡 실패
- □ **far-away** [fɑ́rəwei] 혱 멀리 떨어진

- □ **foolish** [fú:liʃ] 혱 어리석은, 바보 같은
- □ **forest** [fɔ́:rist] 몡 숲, 삼림, 산림
- □ **forever** [fərévər] 閉 영원히
- □ **freedom** [frí:dəm] 몡 자유
- □ **hire** [haiər] 툉 고용하다
- □ **lastly** [lǽstli] 閉 마지막으로, 끝으로
- □ **luxurious** [lʌgʒúəriəs] 혱 사치스러운, 호화로운
- □ **magical** [mǽdʒikəl] 혱 마술의, 마력이 있는
- □ **matter** [mǽtər] 툉 중요하다
- □ **motto** [mátou] 몡 좌우명
- □ **past** [pæst] 몡 과거
- □ **pot** [pɑt] 몡 항아리, 단지, 독
- □ **priceless** [práislis] 혱 대단히 귀중한, 값을 매길 수 없는
- □ **puzzled** [pʌ́zld] 혱 당혹스러운, 어리둥절한
- □ **reward** [riwɔ́:rd] 몡 보상
- □ **situation** [sìtʃuéiʃən] 몡 상황, 환경
- □ **stardom** [stɑ́:rdəm] 몡 스타덤, 스타의 반열
- □ **suppose** [səpóuz] 툉 추측하다, 추정하다
- □ **twin** [twin] 혱 쌍둥이의
- □ **wisdom** [wízdəm] 몡 지혜, 현명함

Key Expressions

- □ **after a hard day's work** 하루 종일 열심히 일하고 나서
- □ **be stuck on** ~에 갇히다
- □ **bring back** 돌려주다
- □ **come true** 이루어지다, 실현되다
- □ **deserted island** 무인도
- □ **explain oneself** 심중을 털어놓다
- □ **fill up** 채우다
- □ **from head to toe** 머리에서 발끝까지
- □ **get lost** 길을 잃다
- □ **go wrong** 잘못하다, 실수를 하다

- □ **live by** (신조, 원칙 등)에 따라 살다
- □ **lock up** 투옥시키다
- □ **look after** ~을 살피다, ~을 돌보다
- □ **make friends** 친구를 사귀다
- □ **pass away** 세상을 떠나다, 돌아가시다
- □ **run out of** ~이 없어지다, ~이 다 떨어지다
- □ **settle in** ~에 자리 잡다, ~에 정착하다
- □ **take one's share** 자기 몫을 차지하다[취하다]
- □ **throughout one's life** 일생을 통해
- □ **with open arms** 두 팔을 벌리고

Word Power

※ 서로 비슷한 뜻을 가진 어휘

- □ **bring back** 돌려주다 – **return** 돌려주다, 반납하다
- □ **expensive** 비싼 – **costly** 값비싼
- □ **far-away** 멀리 떨어진 – **distant** 먼, 떨어져 있는
- □ **hire** 고용하다 – **employ** 고용하다
- □ **puzzled** 당혹스러운, 어리둥절한 – **confused** 혼란스러운
- □ **priceless** 대단히 귀중한, 값을 매길 수 없는 – **invaluable** 값을 헤아릴 수 없는

- □ **exhibit** 전시하다 – **show** 보여주다
- □ **explain** 설명하다 – **describe** 묘사하다
- □ **forever** 영원히 – **perpetually** 영원히
- □ **look after** 돌보다 – **take care of** 돌보다
- □ **return** 돌려주다 – **bring back** 돌려주다

※ 서로 반대의 뜻을 가진 어휘

- □ **comfortably** 편안하게 ↔ **uncomfortably** 불편하게
- □ **continue** 계속하다 ↔ **stop** 멈추다, 그만두다
- □ **expensive** 비싼, 돈이 많이 드는 ↔ **inexpensive** 비싸지 않은
- □ **hire** 고용하다 ↔ **fire** 해고하다
- □ **priceless** 대단히 귀중한, 값을 매길 수 없는 ↔ **worthless** 가치 없는, 보잘 것 없는

- □ **confusing** 혼란스러운 ↔ **clear** 명료한
- □ **death** 죽음 ↔ **life** 삶, 인생, 생명
- □ **failure** 실패 ↔ **success** 성공
- □ **lastly** 마지막으로, 끝으로 ↔ **firstly** 첫째로

※ 접두사 ex- (밖으로)

- □ **ex-** + **ceed** → **exceed** 능가하다, 초과하다
- □ **ex-** + **clude** → **exclude** 배제하다, 제외하다
- □ **ex-** + **plain** → **explain** 설명하다
- □ **ex-** + **press** → **express** 표현하다

- □ **ex-** + **change** → **exchange** 교환하다
- □ **ex-** + **hibit** → **exhibit** 전시하다
- □ **ex-** + **port** → **export** 수출하다
- □ **ex-** + **tend** → **extend** 확장시키다

※ 접미사 –dom (영역, 상태)

- □ **bore** + **-dom** → **boredom** 지루함, 따분함
- □ **free** + **-dom** → **freedom** 자유
- □ **star** + **-dom** → **stardom** 스타덤

- □ **fan** + **-dom** → **fandom** 팬덤, 팬층
- □ **king** + **-dom** → **kingdom** 왕국
- □ **wis** + **-dom** → **wisdom** 지혜

English Dictionary

- □ **character** 등장인물
  → a person represented in a film, play, or story
  영화나 연극 혹은 이야기 속에 나오는 사람

- □ **expert** 전문가
  → a person with a high level of knowledge or skill relating to a particular subject or activity
  특정한 주제나 활동에 관련된 높은 수준의 지식이나 기술을 가진 사람

- □ **explain** 설명하다
  → to make something clear or easy to understand by describing or giving information about it
  어떤 것에 대한 정보를 묘사하거나 제공함으로써 분명하거나 이해하기 쉽게 만들다

- □ **express** 표현하다
  → to show what you think or feel
  당신이 생각하거나 느끼는 것을 보여주다

- □ **failure** 실패
  → a lack of success in doing or achieving something, especially in relation to a particular activity
  특히 특정 활동과 관련해서 어떤 일을 하거나 성취하는 데 있어서 성공의 결여

- □ **hire** 고용하다
  → to employ a person or pay him to do a particular job for you
  당신을 위해 특정한 일을 하도록 어떤 사람에게 일을 주거나 그에게 돈을 지불하다

- □ **luxurious** 사치스러운, 호화로운
  → very comfortable and expensive
  매우 편안하고 비용이 많이 드는

- □ **priceless** 대단히 귀중한, 값을 매길 수 없는
  → worth a large amount of money
  많은 양의 돈의 가치가 있는

- □ **reward** 보상
  → something given in exchange for good behavior or good work, etc.
  좋은 행동이나 업적 등의 대가로 주어지는 어떤 것

- □ **wisdom** 지혜, 현명함
  → the ability to use your knowledge and experience to make good decisions and judgments
  좋은 결정이나 판단을 할 수 있는 지식과 경험을 사용하는 능력

01 접미사 -dom을 붙여 명사로 만들 수 <u>없는</u> 것을 고르시오.

① wise ② free ③ bore
④ novel ⑤ fan

02 다음 밑줄 친 부분과 의미가 가장 가까운 것을 고르시오.

He is a person with a <u>priceless</u> ability to make people feel comfortable around him.

① valueless ② worthless
③ precious ④ economic
⑤ expensive

03 다음 빈칸 (A)와 (B)에 들어갈 말이 바르게 짝지어진 것을 고르시오.

• After he had traveled for years, he settled (A)_____ New York.
• If you get stuck (B)_____ a difficult word, just ask for help.

① for – in ② in – on
③ for – on ④ in – to
⑤ for - to

서답형
04 다음 괄호 안의 단어를 문맥에 맞게 변형하여 빈칸을 채우시오.

His new film was a complete _____. (fail)

05 다음 밑줄 친 부분의 의미로 알맞지 <u>않은</u> 것은?

① He is the funniest <u>character</u> in this film. (등장인물)
② I would like to <u>express</u> my thanks to my friend, Jina. (설명하다)
③ They gave him a <u>reward</u> for his hard work. (보상)
④ It's a difficult <u>situation</u> and I don't know what to do. (상황)
⑤ My grandmother lived on a <u>far-away</u> mountain. (멀리 떨어진)

06 다음 영영풀이가 나타내는 단어를 고르시오.

to employ someone or pay him to do a particular job for you

① hire ② afford
③ demand ④ require
⑤ encourage

07 다음 빈칸에 공통으로 들어갈 말을 고르시오.

• I _____ many friends at the summer camp.
• As they watched the shooting star, they _____ a wish.

① found ② went ③ put
④ took ⑤ made

01 다음 짝지어진 단어의 관계가 같도록 빈칸에 알맞은 말을 쓰시오.

> hire : employ = return : b_____

02 다음 우리말에 맞게 주어진 단어를 이용하여 빈칸을 채우시오.

(1) 하루 종일 열심히 일하고 나서, 나는 매우 피곤했다. (after)

➡ _____, I was very tired.

(2) 나는 그 사건에 대해서 내 심중을 털어놓고 싶지 않았다. (explain)

➡ I didn't want to _____ about the incident.

03 다음 밑줄 친 부분과 바꿔 쓸 수 있는 말을 주어진 철자로 시작하여 쓰시오.

> Who's going to <u>look after</u> the children while you're away?

➡ t_____ (3 단어)

04 다음 빈칸에 공통으로 들어갈 단어를 쓰시오.

> • I didn't finish the test – I _____ out of time.
> • I _____ to school as fast as possible.

05 다음 우리말에 맞게 주어진 단어를 바르게 배열하시오.

(1) 너는 일생을 통해 배울 것이 매우 많다.
(your, to, so, you, throughout, have, learn, much, life)

➡ _____

(2) 가격은 이번 주에 내려갈 것으로 추측된다.
(this, to, is, the, go, week, price, supposed, down)

➡ _____

(3) 모든 학생들은 그 질문에 어리둥절했다.
(question, were, all, by, the, puzzled, students, the)

➡ _____

(4) 이 상황이 아주 중요하다.
(situation, a, matters, lot, this)

➡ _____

(5) 그건 내가 삶에서 신조로 삼을 만한 철학이다.
(that's, I, live, could, philosophy, a, by)

➡ _____

06 다음 그림에 맞게 빈칸에 알맞은 말을 쓰시오.

➡ My aunt welcomed me _____ _____ _____.

Conversation

1 상대방을 안심시키기

A: I'm so worried about going to high school. 고등학교 올라가는 게 너무 걱정돼.

B: Don't worry about it. It'll be a great chance to get to know new people.
걱정하지 마. 새로운 사람들을 알게 되는 좋은 기회가 될 거야.

■ 상대방을 안심시키는 표현으로는 'Don't worry about ~.'이라는 말을 쓸 수 있다. 이와 같은 표현으로는 'Don't let ~ bother you.(~에 대해 너무 신경 쓰지 마.)', 'Don't sweat over ~.(~에 대해 너무 걱정하지 마.)' 등이 있다.

■ 'Don't worry about ~.'은 뭔가에 대하여 걱정을 하는 상대방을 안심시킬 때 사용하고, 이와 유사한 표현으로 'Never mind.'를 사용하기도 한다. 'Never mind.'는 '걱정하지 마.'의 의미 이외에도 '괜찮아.' 혹은 '신경 쓰지 마.' 등 다양한 의미로도 쓰인다.

상대방을 안심시키기

- Don't worry about ~.
- Don't let ~ bother you.
- Don't think twice about ~.
- Don't sweat it.

 핵심 Check

1. 다음 대화의 빈칸에 들어갈 말로 적절하지 <u>않은</u> 것은?

> A: I don't have anything to wear to the party. I can't afford to it.
> B: _____, Cinderella. The fairy Godmother will make a dress for you.

① Don't forget about it

② Don't let it bother you

③ Don't think twice about it

④ Don't sweat it

⑤ Don't worry about it

② 상상한 내용 묻기

A: What would you do if you could time travel? 만약 네가 시간 여행을 할 수 있다면 무엇을 하겠니?

B: I would travel to the 1940s and prevent World War Ⅱ. How about you? 나는 1940년대로 가서 제2차 세계 대전을 막고 싶어. 너는 어때?

A: I would go to the Joseon Dynasty and meet King Sejong. 나는 조선 시대로 가서 세종 대왕을 만나고 싶어.

■ 상상한 내용을 묻는 표현으로는 'What would you do if ~?(~라면 무엇을 할 거니?)'가 있다. 이와 같은 표현으로는 'Imagine that ~. What would you do?', 'If you were ~, what would you do?', 'Let's say that you ~. What would you do?' 등이 있다.

■ 가정법 과거 – if +주어+동사의 과거형, 주어+조동사의 과거형+동사원형 ~.(~라면 …할 텐데) 현재 사실과 반대되는 상황이나 일에 대해 가정하거나 현재 사실에 대한 후회나 아쉬움을 강조할 때, 가정법 과거를 쓴다. 즉, 현재 사실과 반대이므로, 과거 시제를 쓴다. 조건절은 'if+주어+동사의 과거형'으로, 주절은 '주어+would/should/could/might+동사원형 ~'을 쓴다. 이때 해석은 '~라면 …할 텐데.'라고 해석한다.

■ 'What would you do if ~?'는 거의 일어날 가능성이 없는 상황에서 무엇을 할 것인가에 대한 질문인 반면, 'What will you do if ~?'는 미래의 계획이나 가능성을 묻는 질문이다.

상상한 내용 묻기

• What would you do if you ~?
• Imagine that ~. What would you do?
• If you were ~, what would you do?
• Let's say that you ~. What would you do?

핵심 Check

2. 다음 대화의 빈칸에 들어갈 말이 바르게 짝지어진 것은?

> A: What would you do if you __(A)__ a million dollars?
> B: I __(B)__ buy a car. How about you?
> A: I __(C)__ donate the half of it for the poor.

	(A)		(B)		(C)			(A)		(B)		(C)
①	have	–	would	–	could		②	have	–	will	–	can
③	had	–	would	–	can		④	had	–	will	–	can
⑤	had	–	would	–	would							

Listen & Talk 1 A-1

W: James, why are you still ❶up? It's 11 o'clock!

M: I can't sleep ❷because ❸I'm worried about the Bookworm Competition tomorrow.

W: You've read all of the books on the list. What do you ❹have to worry about?

M: Some of the writers' names are ❺confusing, so ❻I'm worried that I might not remember them.

W: ❼Don't worry about something ❽that hasn't happened yet. You'll do fine.

M: Thanks. I'll try ❾not to worry so much.

W: James, 왜 아직 깨어 있니? 11시야!

M: 내일 있을 책벌레 경연 대회가 걱정되어서 저는 잠을 잘 수가 없어요.

W: 너는 목록에 있는 책들을 다 읽었잖아. 뭐가 걱정이니?

M: 몇몇 작가들의 이름이 헷갈려서 그들을 기억하지 못할까봐 걱정이 돼요.

W: 아직 일어나지 않은 일을 걱정하지 마. 너는 잘할 거야.

M: 고마워요. 너무 걱정하지 않도록 해 볼게요.

❶ up은 부사로 '기상하여, 잠이 깨어'의 의미로 사용되었다.
❷ 자지 못하는 이유를 설명하기 위해 접속사 because를 사용하였다. because 대신에 접속사 since, as를 사용할 수도 있다.
❸ 'I'm worried about ~.'은 '나는 ~에 대해 걱정한다.'의 의미로 걱정을 나타낼 때 사용하는 표현이다. 같은 의미의 표현으로 'I'm anxious about ~.', 'I'm concerned about ~.' 등이 있다.
❹ have to 동사원형: ~해야 한다
❺ confusing: 혼란스러운
❻ 'I'm worried (that)+주어+동사.'는 '나는 (주어)가 ~인 것이 걱정돼.'라는 의미로 that절 이하에 걱정하는 내용이 온다.
❼ 상대방을 안심시키는 표현으로는 'Don't worry about ~.'이라는 말을 쓸 수 있다. 이와 같은 표현으론 'Don't let ~ bother you.(~에 대해 너무 신경 쓰지 마.)', 'Don't sweat over ~.(~에 대해 너무 걱정하지 마.)' 등이 있다.
❽ that은 something을 수식하는 주격 관계대명사이다.
❾ to worry는 try의 목적어이다. to부정사를 부정하기 위해서 앞에 not을 썼다. 'try to 동사원형'은 '~하도록 노력하다'라는 의미이므로, 'try not to 동사원형'은 '~하지 않도록 노력하다'로 해석할 수 있다.

Check(√) True or False

(1) James read all of the books on the list for the Bookworm Competition.　　T ☐ F ☐

(2) James needs to worry about something that hasn't happened yet.　　T ☐ F ☐

Listen & Talk 2 C

A: What would you do ❶if you had a magic carpet?

B: ❷I would never walk, and always fly to ❸wherever I want.

A: 마법 양탄자를 갖는다면 무엇을 하겠니?

B: 나는 절대 걷지 않고 항상 내가 원하는 어디든지 날아다닐 거야.

❶ 실제로는 일어나기 어려운 상황을 가정하거나 상상하여 물을 때 가정법 과거를 사용하여 'If you+동사의 과거형 ~, what would you+동사원형 ~?'으로 묻는다.
❷ 'If you+동사의 과거형 ~, what would you+동사원형 ~?'에 답을 할 때는 'I would+동사원형 ~.'을 쓴다.
❸ whenever는 '~할 때는 언제든지'의 의미를 가지며 부사절을 이끈다.

Check(√) True or False

(3) B had a magic carpet.　　T ☐ F ☐

(4) B would never walk if she or he had a magic carpet.　　T ☐ F ☐

Listen and Speak 2 A-2

W: Jason, what are you reading?

M: I'm reading a book ❶called *Three Wishes*.

W: Oh, ❷I've heard about it. A genie ❸makes a boy's wishes ❹ come true, right?

M: Yeah. ❺What would you do if you could make one wish?

W: I ❻would make the genie stay with me forever. Then, I could make all my wishes come true.

M: That's smart!

W: Jason, 무엇을 읽고 있니?

M: 나는 〈세 가지 소원〉이라는 책을 읽고 있어.

W: 오, 그것에 대해 들어 본 적 있어. 요정이 어떤 남자아이의 소원을 들어주는 거지, 그렇지?

M: 맞아. 만약 소원 하나를 빌 수 있다면 너는 무엇을 할 거니?

W: 나는 요정을 영원히 내 옆에 있도록 만들 거야. 그러면, 나는 나의 모든 소원들을 이룰 수 있어.

M: 그거 똑똑한데!

❶ called는 과거분사로 '~라는 이름의, ~라고 불려지는'의 의미로 앞에 있는 명사 a book을 수식하고 있다.

❷ have heard는 현재완료의 '경험' 용법으로 '들어본 적이 있다'로 해석한다.

❸ make는 '…에게 ~하게 하다'라는 의미를 가지는 사역동사로, 목적격보어로 동사원형을 쓴다. 여기서 목적어는 a boy's wishes이며 목적격보어는 come true이다.

❹ come true: 이루어지다, 실현되다

❺ 실제로는 일어나기 어려운 상황을 가정하거나 상상하여 물을 때 'If you+동사의 과거형 ~, what would you+동사원형 ~?'의 형태인 가정법 과거를 사용하여 현재 사실과 반대되는 것을 말할 수 있다.

❻ 'If you+동사의 과거형 ~, what would you+동사원형 ~?'에 대한 응답은 'I would ~.'가 주로 사용되는데 would는 조동사이므로 뒤에 동사원형이 와야 한다.

Check(√) True or False

(5) W never heard about the book, *Three Wishes*.　　　　T ☐ F ☐

(6) In the book, a genie makes a boy's wishes come true.　　　　T ☐ F ☐

Wrap Up 1

M: ❶I've heard that you're going to be in the writing contest next week.

W: Yeah, it's already next week.

M: You ❷look worried. What's wrong?

W: ❸I'm worried that the topic would be too difficult for me.

M: Don't worry about something ❹you can't change. Just ❺ believe in yourself.

W: Thanks. I'll try.

M: 네가 다음 주에 글쓰기 대회에 나간다고 들었어.

W: 맞아, 그게 벌써 다음 주야.

M: 너 걱정스러워 보인다. 무슨 일이니?

W: 주제가 나에게 너무 어려울까봐 걱정이야.

M: 네가 바꿀 수 없는 것에 대해 걱정하지 마. 그저 자신을 믿어봐.

W: 고마워. 그렇게 해 볼게.

❶ 'I've heard (that) 주어+동사 ~.'는 '나는 ~하다는 것을 들었어.'라는 뜻으로 알고 있음을 표현하는 말이다.

❷ look+형용사: ~하게 보이다

❸ 'be worried (that) 주어+동사'는 '(주어)가 ~인 것이 걱정이다.'라는 의미로 걱정을 표현할 때 사용하는 표현이다.

❹ something과 you can't change 사이에 목적격 관계대명사 that이 생략되어 있다.

❺ believe in 사람: ~을[~의 능력을] 믿다

Check(√) True or False

(7) W will participate in the writing contest next week.　　　　T ☐ F ☐

(8) W is concerned about the writing contest.　　　　T ☐ F ☐

Listen & Talk 1 A-2

M: Sujin, what are you doing this weekend?

W: Nothing special, why?

M: I ❶have to go to Busan for a family trip tomorrow but I can't find anyone ❷to feed my dog, Lucy.

W: Don't worry about Lucy. I'll take care of her.

M: Oh, thank you so much. I was so worried.

W: I'll ❸take her for a walk in the park, too. The weather's ❹supposed to be nice tomorrow.

❶ have to 동사원형: ~해야 한다
❷ to feed 이하는 앞의 명사 anyone을 수식하는 형용사적 용법이다.
❸ take ~ for a walk: ~를 산책하러 데리고 가다
❹ suppose: 추측하다, 추정하다

Listen & Talk 1 B

M: Jane, you look worried. What's the matter?

W: I got a big part in the school musical.

M: I heard you singing. You sound great!

W: It's just that I ❶keep ❷making mistakes. I'm so worried.

M: Oh, you just need a little more practice. Don't ❸worry about making mistakes. You can actually learn from them.

W: Thanks, Dad. ❹I hope I do a good job.

M: You'll do great.

❶ keep은 동명사를 목적어로 받는다. ❷ make a mistake: 실수하다
❸ worry about (동)명사: ~에 대해 걱정하다
❹ 'I hope (that) 주어+동사 ~.'나 'I hope to 동사원형'을 사용해 희망이나 바람을 나타낼 수 있다.

Listen & Talk 2 A-1

M: Caroline, have you read the book, *Tuck Everlasting*?

W: Yeah, it is about a family that drank magical water and lived forever, right?

M: Right. ❶What would you do if you could live forever?

W: Well, ❷I would live in different cities all around the world.

M: Really? I would collect interesting items and make a museum.

W: Cool.

❶ '만약 ~라면 어떻게 하겠니?'라고 실제가 아닌 상황이나 사실을 가정하여 물어볼 때는 가정법 과거를 이용하여 'What would you do if you+과거시제 ~?'로 표현한다.
❷ 'What would you do if you+과거시제 ~?'에 대한 대답으로 '나는 ~할 거야.'라는 의미로 'I would 동사원형 ~.' 형태의 가정법 과거를 사용하여 대답한다.

Listen & Talk 2 B

W: What are you doing, Jinho?

M: I'm writing a review of the movie, *The Time Traveler's Wife*.

W: I saw that movie, too. It's ❶one of my favorite romantic movies.

M: I loved it, too. Emily, ❷what would you do if you could time travel?

W: I would travel to the 1940s and prevent World War II. How about you?

M: I would go to the Joseon Dynasty and meet King Sejong. I'm a big fan of him.

❶ one of 복수명사: ~중의 하나
❷ 현재 사실과 반대되는 상황이나 일에 대해 가정하거나 현재 사실에 대한 후회나 아쉬움을 강조할 때, 가정법 과거를 쓴다.

Communication Step A

M: How's your online story going, Amy?

W: Not well. The deadline is this weekend but I ❶ran out of ideas.

M: Don't worry about it. I can help you.

W: That would be great. My main character has special powers. What would you do if you were able to read people's minds?

M: Well, I would find out ❷if the girl I like likes me.

W: That's a good idea. Thanks.

❶ run out of: ~이 없어지다, 다 떨어지다
❷ 여기서 if의 의미는 '~인지 아닌지'로 whether로 바꿔 쓸 수 있다.

● 다음 우리말과 일치하도록 빈칸에 알맞은 말을 쓰시오.

Listen & Talk 1 A

1. **W:** James, why are _____ _____ _____? It's 11 o'clock!

   M: I can't sleep _____ _____ _____ _____ the Bookworm Competition tomorrow.

   W: _____ _____ all of the books on the list. What do you _____ _____ _____ _____?

   M: Some of the writers' names are _____, so I'm _____ _____ I might not remember them.

   W: Don't worry about something _____ _____ _____ yet. You'll do fine.

   M: Thanks. I'll _____ _____ _____ _____ so much.

2. **M:** Sujin, what are you doing this weekend?

   W: _____ _____, why?

   M: I _____ _____ _____ _____ Busan for a family trip tomorrow but I _____ _____ _____ to feed my dog, Lucy.

   W: Don't _____ _____ Lucy. I'll take care of her.

   M: Oh, thank you so much. I was so _____.

   W: I'll take her for a walk in the park, too. The weather's _____ _____ _____ nice tomorrow.

Listen & Talk 1 B

M: Jane, you look _____. What's the matter?

W: I _____ _____ _____ _____ _____ the school musical.

M: I heard you singing. You sound great!

W: It's just that I _____ _____ _____. I'm so worried.

M: Oh, you just need a little more _____. Don't worry about _____ _____. You can actually learn from them.

W: Thanks, Dad. I hope I do a good job.

M: You'll do great.

해석

1. W: James, 왜 아직 깨어 있니? 11시 야!

   M: 내일 있을 책벌레 경연 대회가 걱 정되어서 저는 잠을 잘 수가 없어 요.

   W: 너는 목록에 있는 책들을 다 읽었 잖아. 뭐가 걱정이니?

   M: 몇몇 작가들의 이름이 헷갈려서 그들을 기억하지 못할까봐 걱정이 돼요.

   W: 아직 일어나지 않은 일을 걱정하 지 마. 너는 잘할 거야.

   M: 고마워요. 너무 걱정하지 않도록 해 볼게요.

2. M: 수진아, 이번 주말에 뭐 할 거야?

   W: 특별한 일은 없어, 왜?

   M: 내일 부산으로 가족 여행을 가야 하는데 내 개 Lucy에게 먹이를 줄 사람을 아무도 찾을 수가 없어.

   W: Lucy에 대해서는 걱정하지 마. 내 가 그 개를 돌봐 줄게.

   M: 오, 정말 고마워. 나 너무 걱정했 거든.

   W: 내가 그 개를 데리고 공원에서 산 책도 시켜 줄게. 내일 날씨가 좋을 거래.

M: Jane, 너 걱정스러워 보이는구나. 무 슨 일 있니?

W: 제가 학교 뮤지컬에서 큰 역할을 맡 았어요.

M: 네가 노래하는 것을 들었어. 잘하던 데!

W: 그냥 제가 자꾸만 실수하는 거예요. 저는 너무 걱정돼요.

M: 오, 너는 그저 조금만 더 연습하면 돼. 실수하는 것에 대해서는 걱정하지 마. 사실 실수로부터 배울 수 있어.

W: 고마워요, 아빠. 제가 잘하면 좋겠어 요.

M: 너는 아주 잘해 낼 거야.

Listen & Talk 2 A

1. M: Caroline, have you read the book, *Tuck Everlasting*?

   W: Yeah, it is about a family that drank magical water and _____ _____, right?

   M: Right. _____ _____ _____ _____ _____ you could live forever?

   W: Well, I _____ live in different cities all around the world.

   M: Really? I would collect _____ items and make a museum.

   W: Cool.

2. W: Jason, what are you reading?

   M: I'm reading a book _____ *Three Wishes*.

   W: Oh, I've _____ about it. A genie makes a boy's wishes _____ _____, right?

   M: Yeah. What would you do _____ _____ _____ _____ _____?

   W: I _____ _____ the genies _____ with me forever. Then, I could _____ _____ _____ _____ _____ _____.

   M: That's smart!

Listen & Talk 2 B

W: What are you doing, Jinho?

M: I'm writing a review of the movie, *The Time Traveler's Wife*.

W: I saw that movie, too. It's _____ _____ my favorite romantic _____.

M: I loved it, too. Emily, _____ _____ _____ _____ _____ _____ _____ time travel?

W: I would travel to the 1940s and _____ World War II. How about you?

M: I _____ _____ _____ the Joseon Dynasty and _____ King Sejong. I'm a big fan of him.

1. M: Caroline, 너 트리갭의 샘물(Tuck Everlasting)이라는 책을 읽어 봤니?

   W: 응, 그것은 마법의 물을 마시고 영원히 살게 된 한 가족에 대한 이야기잖아, 맞지?

   M: 맞아. 만약 네가 영원히 살게 된다면 너는 뭘 할 거야?

   W: 글쎄, 나는 전 세계의 다양한 도시에서 살고 싶어.

   M: 정말? 나는 흥미로운 물건들을 모아서 박물관을 만들 거야.

   W: 멋지다.

2. W: Jason, 무엇을 읽고 있니?

   M: 나는 〈세 가지 소원〉이라는 책을 읽고 있어.

   W: 오, 그것에 대해 들어 본 적 있어. 요정이 어떤 남자아이의 소원을 들어주는 거지, 그렇지?

   M: 맞아. 만약 소원 하나를 빌 수 있다면 너는 무엇을 할 거니?

   W: 나는 요정을 영원히 내 옆에 있도록 만들 거야. 그러면, 나는 나의 모든 소원들을 이룰 수 있어.

   M: 그거 똑똑한데!

W: 진호야, 무엇을 하고 있니?

M: 나는 〈시간 여행자의 아내〉라는 영화의 후기를 쓰고 있어.

W: 나도 그 영화 봤어. 그건 내가 가장 좋아하는 로맨스 영화 중 하나야.

M: 나도 너무 좋았어. Emily, 만약 네가 시간 여행을 할 수 있다면 무엇을 하겠니?

W: 나는 1940년대로 가서 제2차 세계 대전을 막고 싶어. 너는 어때?

M: 나는 조선 시대로 가서 세종대왕을 만나고 싶어. 나는 그의 엄청난 팬이야.

Communication Step A

M: _____ your online story going, Amy?

W: Not well. The deadline is this weekend but I _____ _____ of ideas.

M: _____ _____ _____ it. I can help you.

W: That would be great. My main _____ has special powers. _____ _____ _____ _____ _____ _____ _____ able to read people's minds?

M: Well, I would _____ _____ _____ the girl I like likes me.

W: That's a good idea. Thanks.

M: 네 온라인 이야기는 어떻게 되어 가고 있니, Amy?

W: 별로야. 마감이 이번 주말인데 아이디어가 다 떨어졌어.

M: 그건 걱정하지 마. 내가 도와줄게.

W: 그럼 정말 좋겠다. 내 주인공은 특별한 능력을 가지고 있어. 만약 네가 사람들의 생각을 읽을 수 있다면 무엇을 하겠니?

M: 음, 나는 내가 좋아하는 여자아이가 나를 좋아하는지 알아보고 싶어.

W: 그거 좋은 생각이다. 고마워.

Wrap Up

1. M: _____ _____ _____ you're going to be in the writing contest next week.

   W: Yeah, it's already next week.

   M: You look _____. What's wrong?

   W: _____ _____ _____ the topic would be _____ _____ for me.

   M: _____ _____ _____ something you can't change. Just _____ _____ _____.

   W: Thanks. I'll try.

1. M: 네가 다음 주에 글쓰기 대회에 나간다고 들었어.

   W: 맞아, 그게 벌써 다음 주야.

   M: 너 걱정스러워 보인다. 무슨 일이니?

   W: 주제가 나에게 너무 어려울까봐 걱정이야.

   M: 네가 바꿀 수 없는 것에 대해 걱정하지 마. 그저 자신을 믿어봐.

   W: 고마워. 그렇게 해 볼게.

2. M: Lisa, have you _____ the movie, *Cast Away*?

   W: No, I haven't. What is it about?

   M: It's about _____ _____ _____ _____ _____ a deserted island for 4 years.

   W: It sounds interesting.

   M: Yeah, the man _____ everything to stay alive. What _____ you do _____ _____ _____ _____?

   W: To stay _____? Well, I would build a tree house and hunt for food.

   M: Yeah, me too. And _____ _____ _____ _____ _____ in the movie.

2. M: Lisa, 영화 〈캐스트 어웨이〉 본 적 있니?

   W: 아니, 없어. 무슨 내용이야?

   M: 4년 동안 외딴섬에 갇힌 어떤 남자에 관한 영화야.

   W: 재미있게 들린다.

   M: 응, 그 남자는 살기 위해 모든 것을 시도해. 만약 네가 그 남자라면 무엇을 하겠니?

   W: 살기 위해서? 글쎄, 나는 나무로 집을 만들고 먹을 것을 사냥할 거야.

   M: 응, 나도. 그리고 그게 그 남자가 영화에서 했던 거야.

[01~02] 다음 대화의 빈칸에 알맞은 것을 고르시오.

01

M: Caroline, have you read the book, *Tuck Everlasting*?

W: Yeah, it is about a family that drank magical water and lived forever, right?

M: Right. What would you do if you could live forever?

W: Well, I would live in different cities all around the world.

M: Really? _____

W: Cool.

① I would like to read many books.

② I want to make all my wishes come true.

③ I will buy every game in the world.

④ I would collect interesting items and make a museum.

⑤ I have become rich.

02

W: James, why are you still up? It's 11 o'clock!

M: I can't sleep because I'm worried about the Bookworm Competition tomorrow.

W: You've read all of the books on the list. What do you have to worry about?

M: Some of the writers' names are confusing, so I'm worried that I might not remember them.

W: _____ You'll do fine.

M: Thanks. I'll try not to worry so much.

① Don't worry about something that hasn't happened yet.

② I'm concerned about the competition, too.

③ You have to remember all of the writers' names.

④ You are supposed to win the competition.

⑤ I've never heard about the tomorrow's competition.

[01~03] 다음 대화를 읽고 물음에 답하시오.

M: How's your online story going, Amy?
W: (①) Not well. The deadline is this weekend (A)_____ I ran out of ideas.
M: (②) I can help you.
W: That would be great. (③) My main character has special powers. What would you do if you (B)_____ able to read people's minds? (④)
M: Well, I would find out if the girl I like likes me. (⑤)
W: That's a good idea. Thanks.

01 위 대화의 ①~⑤ 중 주어진 문장이 들어갈 곳은?

> Don't worry about it.

①　　　②　　　③　　　④　　　⑤

02 빈칸 (A)에 알맞은 말을 고르시오.

① because
② so
③ but
④ therefore
⑤ since

03 빈칸 (B)에 알맞은 말을 고르시오.

① were
② was
③ be
④ will be
⑤ being

04 다음 중 짝지어진 대화가 <u>어색한</u> 것은?

① A: I'm concerned about the final test.
　 B: Don't worry about it. You will do well.
② A: Don't go too far. And you're supposed to be back before dark.
　 B: Don't worry. We'll be back soon.
③ A: What would you do if you were free now?
　 B: I would go to the amusement park with my friends.
④ A: What would you do if you were a fashion model?
　 B: I could be very tall.
⑤ A: What would you do if you were a university student now?
　 B: I would go backpacking all around the world.

[05~06] 다음 대화를 읽고 물음에 답하시오.

M: Caroline, have you read the book, *Tuck Everlasting*?
W: Yeah, it is about a family that drank magical water and lived forever, right?
M: Right. What would you do if (A)_____?
W: Well, I would live in different cities all around the world.
M: Really? I would collect interesting items and make a museum.
W: Cool.

05 빈칸 (A)에 알맞은 말을 고르시오.

① you can time travel
② you could live forever
③ you make all your wishes come true
④ you will have a million dollars
⑤ you may become rich

06 위 대화의 내용과 일치하지 <u>않는</u> 것을 고르시오.

① 영원히 살게 된다면 남자는 흥미로운 물건들을 모아서 박물관을 만들 것이다.

② Caroline은 *Tuck Everlasting*을 읽어본 적이 있다.

③ 영원히 살게 된다면 Caroline은 한 도시에서 오래 살 것이다.

④ *Tuck Everlasting*은 마법의 물을 마시고 영원히 살게 된 한 가족에 대한 이야기이다.

⑤ 남자는 *Tuck Everlasting*을 읽어봤다.

[07~09] 다음 대화를 읽고 물음에 답하시오.

> W: (①) James, why are you still up? It's 11 o'clock!
>
> M: I can't sleep because I'm worried about the Bookworm Competition tomorrow. (②)
>
> W: You've read all of the books on the list. (③)
>
> M: Some of the writers' names are confusing, so (A)_____ (④)
>
> W: Don't worry about something that hasn't happened yet. You'll do fine. (⑤)
>
> M: Thanks. <u>너무 걱정하지 않도록 해 볼게요.</u>(so, to, try, much, I'll, worry, not)

07 위 대화의 ①~⑤ 중 주어진 문장이 들어갈 곳은?

> What do you have to worry about?

①   ②   ③   ④   ⑤

서답형

08 밑줄 친 우리말에 맞게 주어진 단어를 알맞게 배열하시오.

➡ _____

09 빈칸 (A)에 알맞은 말을 고르시오.

① I'm worried about taking care of them.

② I'm so worried about going to high school.

③ I'm worried that I can't find anyone to read them.

④ I'm worried that I might not remember them.

⑤ I'm concerned about knowing new people.

[10~11] 다음 대화를 읽고 물음에 답하시오.

> M: Jane, you look worried. (①) What's the matter?
>
> W: I got a big part in the school musical. (②)
>
> M: I heard you singing. (③) You sound great!
>
> W: It's just that I keep (A)_____. (④) I'm so worried.
>
> M: Oh, you just need a little more practice. Don't worry about making mistakes. (⑤)
>
> W: Thanks, Dad. I hope I do a good job.
>
> M: You'll do great.

10 위 대화의 ①~⑤ 중 주어진 문장이 들어갈 곳은?

> You can actually learn from them.

①   ②   ③   ④   ⑤

11 빈칸 (A)에 알맞은 말을 고르시오.

① avoiding it   ② making mistakes

③ realizing it   ④ wanting to sing

⑤ playing a main character

[01~02] 다음 대화를 읽고 물음에 답하시오.

W: Jason, what are you reading?

M: I'm reading a book _____(call) *Three Wishes*.

W: Oh, I've heard about it. A genie (A)_____ s a boy's wishes come true, right?

M: Yeah. What would you do if you could (B)_____ one wish?

W: I would (C)_____ the genie stay with me forever. Then, I could (D)_____ all my wishes come true.

M: That's smart!

01 괄호 안의 단어를 활용하여 빈칸에 알맞은 말을 쓰시오.

➡ _____

02 빈칸 (A)~(D)에 공통으로 들어갈 말을 쓰시오.

➡ _____

[03~04] 다음 대화를 읽고 물음에 답하시오.

W: James, why are you still up? It's 11 o'clock!

M: I can't sleep because I'm worried (A)_____ the Bookworm Competition tomorrow.

W: You've read all of the books on the list. What do you have to worry about?

M: Some of the writers' names are (B)_____ (confuse), so I'm worried that I might not remember them.

W: Don't worry about something that hasn't happened yet. You'll do fine.

M: Thanks. I'll try not to worry so much.

03 빈칸 (A)에 알맞은 말을 쓰시오.

➡ _____

04 괄호 안의 단어를 활용하여 빈칸 (B)에 알맞은 말을 쓰시오.

➡ _____

[05~06] 다음 대화를 읽고 물음에 답하시오.

M: Caroline, have you read the book, *Tuck Everlasting*?

W: Yeah, it is about a family that drank magical water and lived forever, right?

M: Right. (A)만약 네가 영원히 살게 된다면 너는 뭘 할 거야?

W: Well, I would live in different cities all around the world.

M: Really? (B)I would collect interesting items and made a museum.

W: Cool.

05 밑줄 친 우리말 (A)를 주어진 단어와 대화의 단어를 이용해 영작하시오.

➡ _____

(would, could, if)

06 밑줄 친 문장 (B)에서 흐름상 또는 어법상 어색한 것을 바르게 고치시오.

➡ _____

Grammar

① 'It ~ that ...' 강조 구문

> • **It was** this wisdom **that** our father tried to explain. 우리의 아버지가 설명하려고 하셨던 것은 바로 이 지혜였다.

- 'It+is/was+강조어(구)+that ...'의 형태로 주어나 목적어, 부사(구/절) 등을 강조하기 위해서 쓰이며, 강조하고자 하는 부분을 'it is/was'와 'that' 사이에 쓰고, 나머지 부분을 that 뒤에 그대로 쓴다. 'be'동사는 문장의 시제에 맞춰 'is'나 'was'를 사용하며 이때, 해석은 '~한 것은 바로 …이다'라고 한다.

    • I washed my pet dog from head to toe. 나는 내 애완견을 머리부터 발끝까지 씻겼다.
       → **It was** I **that** washed my pet dog from head to toe. (주어 강조)
       → **It was** my pet dog **that** I washed from head to toe. (목적어 강조)

- 'It ~ that ...' 강조 구문에서 강조하는 대상이 사람일 때는 that 대신에 who[whom], 사물이나 동물일 때는 which로 바꿔 쓸 수 있으며, 시간이나 장소의 부사(구/절)일 경우에는 when(시간) 또는 where(장소)로 바꿔 쓸 수 있다.

    • I bought a book at the bookstore yesterday. 나는 어제 그 서점에서 책을 한 권 샀다.
       → **It was** I **that**[**who**] bought a book at the bookstore yesterday.
       → **It was** a book **that**[**which**] I bought at the bookstore yesterday.
       → **It was** at the bookstore **that**[**where**] I bought a book yesterday.
       → **It was** yesterday **that**[**when**] I bought a book at the bookstore.

- 'It ~ that ...' 강조 구문에서 강조하는 대상이 부사(구/절)일 경우 that 다음에 완전한 절이 나오지만, 그 외의 경우에는 불완전한 절이 나오는 것에 유의한다. 또한 강조되는 부분에 형용사나 동사는 올 수 없다. 동사를 강조할 때는 동사 앞에 조동사 do/does/did를 쓴다.

    • **It was** the meeting **that** changed my life. 내 삶을 바꿔 놓은 것은 바로 그 만남이었다. (that 다음에 불완전한 절)
    • **It was** at this point **that** her acting career really took off. 그녀의 연기가 인기를 얻기 시작한 것은 바로 이 시점이었다. (that 다음에 완전한 절)
    • It was beautiful that she was when young.(✗) (형용사 강조 X)
    • It was cleaned that I my room last night.(✗) (동사 강조 X)

    cf. 강조 구문에서는 'it is/was'와 that을 지우면 완전한 문장이 남지만, 'It(가주어) ~ that(진주어)' 구문에서는 'It is/was'와 that을 지우면 불완전한 문장이 남는다.

핵심 Check

1. 다음 괄호 안에서 알맞은 말을 고르시오.

    (1) (It / That) was in the morning that I drank a cup of coffee.
    (2) It was Nathalie (that / what) came from Russia.

② have+목적어+과거분사

• I **had** my bed **designed** by experts.
나는 내 침대를 전문가들에 의해 설계되게 했다.

■ 'have/has/had+목적어+목적격보어'의 형태로 목적어의 '능동/수동' 여부에 따라 목적격보어 자리에 원형동사 또는 과거분사가 온다. 즉, 목적어가 목적격보어의 동작을 당하는 대상(주로 사물)이면 과거분사를 사용하고, 목적어가 목적격보어의 동작을 하는 주체(주로 사람)면 동사원형을 사용한다. have는 '~하게 시키다, 만들다'라는 의미의 사역동사로 '~이 되도록 누군가를 시키다'라는 의미를 가진다. 해석은 직역보다는 '~가 …되게 했다'라는 뜻으로 의역하면 자연스럽다.

※ have+목적어+동사원형: 목적어가 그 행위를 하는 주체

• I **had** him **wash** my car.

※ have+목적어+과거분사: 목적어는 그 동작을 당하는 대상

• I **had** my car **washed** by him.

■ 'have+목적어+과거분사' 유형은 어떤 일을 간접적으로 행할 때 쓰는 표현이다. 행위의 주체를 밝힐 때에는 'by+사람'의 형태로 쓴다.

• I **had** him **do** the work. 나는 그로 하여금 그 일을 하게 했다. (능동: 동사원형)

• I **had** the work **done** by him. 나는 그 일이 그에 의해 해지도록 했다. (수동: 과거분사)

■ cf. have와 get
get이 'get+목적어+to부정사'나 'get+목적어+과거분사'의 형태로 쓰여 have와 같은 의미를 갖는다.

• She **had** him **fix** the bike. 그녀는 그가 자전거를 고치도록 시켰다.
  = She **got** him **to fix** the bike.
  = She **had**[**got**] the bike **fixed** by him.

• She **had** the letter **written** by him. 그녀는 편지가 그에 의해 쓰여지게 했다.
  = She **got** the letter **written** by him.

■ 'have+목적어+과거분사'에는 '~당하다'라는 피동의 뜻도 있다.

• She **had** her purse **stolen** in the subway. 그녀는 지하철에서 지갑을 도난당했다.

핵심 Check

2. 다음 괄호 안에서 알맞은 말을 고르시오.

(1) She had the students (finish / finishing) their homework.

(2) Jake had his leg (break / broken) in the accident.

(3) The teacher got him (sing / to sing) on the stage.

01 다음 빈칸에 알맞은 것은?

> It was Tom _____ studied math in the library yesterday.

① where   ② when   ③ which
④ that   ⑤ what

02 다음 빈칸에 들어갈 말로 알맞은 것은?

> Sam had the chair _____.

① fixes   ② to fix   ③ fixing
④ fix   ⑤ fixed

03 다음 괄호 안에서 알맞은 말을 고르시오.

(1) I had him (repair / repaired) my watch.

(2) I had my money (steal / stolen) yesterday.

(3) (It / That) was several hours later that he went to the garden.

(4) It was Romeo (which / who) first met Juliet at the party.

04 다음 우리말에 맞게 주어진 어휘를 바르게 배열하시오.

(1) 그 피자를 먹은 사람은 바로 민지였다.

(the pizza, Minji, it, ate, was, that)

➡ _____

(2) 그곳은 윌리엄 왕자가 다녔던 바로 그 학교에요.

(Prince William, it, the school, is, went, that, to)

➡ _____

(3) Della는 Jim의 다리가 부러졌다는 것에 놀랐다.

(Jim, Della, his leg, broken, surprised, had, was, that)

➡ _____

중요
01 다음 중 어법상 <u>어색한</u> 것은?

① It was this wisdom that our father tried to explain.
② It was Lisa who played soccer in the park.
③ It was ended that World War Ⅱ in 1945.
④ It was his advice which prevented me from believing her.
⑤ It was yesterday that I met Jane.

02 다음 중 어법상 <u>어색한</u> 것은?

① I hired people and had the house looked after.
② How did you have him posed for this picture?
③ Lucy had her dog cleaned.
④ She had me help her with her math homework.
⑤ Why don't you have your furniture recycled?

중요
03 다음 빈칸에 알맞은 말이 바르게 짝지어진 것은?

• It was the necklace _____ the princess bought. • My grandfather had his eyes _____.

① that – checked
② what – checked
③ that – checking
④ what – checking
⑤ which – to check

서답형
04 다음 괄호 안에서 알맞은 말을 고르시오.

(1) She had her face (paint / painted) red and blue.
(2) I had him (wash / washed) the dishes after dinner.
(3) Millar got her husband (to bring / bringing) the box.
(4) It was the princess (which / who) killed the dragon.
(5) It was last night (which / when) I sent you the message.
(6) It was at the festival (which / where) Mary went to a face painting booth.

중요
05 주어진 문장의 <u>틀린</u> 부분을 찾아, 올바르게 고친 것을 고르시오.

Do you need to have the computer fixes? Call the Computer Doctor.

① Do you need to have the computer to fix? Call the Computer Doctor.
② Do you need to have the computer fixing? Call the Computer Doctor.
③ Do you need to have the computer to fixing? Call the Computer Doctor.
④ Do you need to have the computer fixed? Call the Computer Doctor.
⑤ Do you need to have the computer fix? Call the Computer Doctor.

06 빈칸 (A)와 (B)에 알맞은 것으로 바르게 짝지어진 것은?

> It is the milk __(A)__ I had __(B)__ every morning.

	(A)	(B)
①	that	deliver
②	that	delivered
③	what	deliver
④	what	delivering
⑤	what	delivered

07 다음 〈보기〉의 밑줄 친 that과 쓰임이 같은 것은?

> **보기**
>
> It was in 1888 that Vincent Gogh painted *Sunflowers*.

① The poison of the cobra is more deadly than that of the rattlesnake.

② Are you sure she's that young?

③ It was the question that aimed at the heart of the matter.

④ We argued it this way and we argued it that way.

⑤ Are you mad that you should do such a thing?

08 다음 문장의 밑줄 친 ⓐ~ⓔ 중 어법상 어색한 것은?

> Your shoes ⓐlook ⓑdirty. Why ⓒdon't you have ⓓthem ⓔclean?

① ⓐ   ② ⓑ   ③ ⓒ

④ ⓓ   ⑤ ⓔ

[09~10] 다음 문장의 빈칸에 알맞은 말을 고르시오.

09

> It was Jean Valjean _____ stole the bread from the bakery.

① that   ② what   ③ when

④ which   ⑤ where

10

> Anna intentionally got the bike _____ by the neighbour.

① to repair   ② repairing

③ had repaired   ④ repaired

⑤ repair

11 다음 우리말을 바르게 영작한 것을 고르시오.

> Gogh가 Arles에서 만난 사람은 바로 Gauguin 이었다.

① It was Gogh that Gauguin met in Arles.

② It was Gauguin whom Gogh met in Arles.

③ It was Gauguin what Gogh met in Arles.

④ It was Gauguin when Gogh met in Arles.

⑤ It was Gauguin which Gogh met in Arles.

서답형

12 다음 문장에서 어법상 어색한 것을 바르게 고쳐 다시 쓰시오.

> Mary had her table make by her brother.

➡ _____

13 다음 중 It ~ that의 쓰임이 나머지와 <u>다른</u> 하나는?

① It is very important that students develop an awareness of how the Internet can be used.

② It was in August that we went hiking together.

③ It was soccer that I played with him yesterday.

④ It was with Jane that I had *gimbap* in the restaurant yesterday.

⑤ It was she that asked me to study math together yesterday.

14 다음 두 문장을 한 문장으로 바꿔 쓰고자 한다. 빈칸에 들어갈 알맞은 말을 쓰시오.

> • Mary asked Simon to buy a used computer.
> • She asked him to repair the computer yesterday.
> = Mary had Simon ＿＿＿＿＿ a used computer and got it ＿＿＿＿＿ by him yesterday.

15 다음 밑줄 친 어휘의 쓰임이 〈보기〉와 <u>다른</u> 것은?

> ┤ 보기 ├
> I had the vegetables and fruit <u>mixed</u> well.

① I had my car <u>washed</u> by my son.

② I had my hair <u>cut</u> yesterday.

③ Her little baby had just <u>woken</u> from a deep sleep.

④ I had what I bought at the store <u>delivered</u> yesterday.

⑤ We had our house <u>decorated</u> with flowers last Christmas.

서답형

16 다음 문장에서 어법상 어색한 것을 바르게 고쳐 다시 쓰시오.

(1) The writer had his book print at his own expense.

➡ ＿＿＿＿＿＿＿＿＿＿＿＿＿＿＿＿＿＿

(2) How can I get him dress better?

➡ ＿＿＿＿＿＿＿＿＿＿＿＿＿＿＿＿＿＿

(3) I found out that it was the price who frightened me.

➡ ＿＿＿＿＿＿＿＿＿＿＿＿＿＿＿＿＿＿

(4) It was when they are heated which metals expand.

➡ ＿＿＿＿＿＿＿＿＿＿＿＿＿＿＿＿＿＿

(5) It was the theater that I met Jack last weekend.

➡ ＿＿＿＿＿＿＿＿＿＿＿＿＿＿＿＿＿＿

중요

17 다음 우리말을 알맞게 영작한 것을 고르시오.

> Jenny가 어제 공원에서 본 것은 바로 별똥별이었다.

① It was a shooting star when Jenny saw at the park yesterday.

② It was at the park that Jenny saw a shooting star yesterday.

③ It was Jenny that saw a shooting star at the park yesterday.

④ It was yesterday that Jenny saw a shooting star at the park.

⑤ It was a shooting star which Jenny saw at the park yesterday.

01 〈보기〉와 같이 두 문장이 비슷한 의미가 되도록 주어진 단어를 활용하여 빈칸을 알맞게 채우시오. (어형 변화 가능.)

> ┤ 보기 ├
>
> Allow the students to play soccer on the playground.
> → Let the students play soccer on the playground. (let)

(1) You'd better ask a catering service to prepare the food.
　➡ Why don't you _____ by a catering service? (have)

(2) The teacher had Harry hand in his report by May 10.
　➡ The teacher _____ _____ by May 10. (get)

(3) She made Nick repair her computer.
　➡ She _____ her computer. (force)

02 다음 우리말에 맞게 주어진 어구를 바르게 배열하시오.

(1) Romeo가 Juliet을 처음 만난 건 바로 파티에서였어. (Romeo, Juliet, the party, that, it, was, first, met, at)
　➡ _____

(2) 내가 빌린 것은 바로 그의 공책이었다. (I, notebook, it, borrowed, was, his, which)
　➡ _____

(3) Jim은 Della가 그녀의 머리카락을 자른 것에 놀랐다. (Jim, Della, hair, surprised, had, was, her, cut, that)
　➡ _____
　_____

(4) 그녀는 차를 세차시킬 필요가 있다. (she, the car, have, needs, washed, to)
　➡ _____

03 다음 문장에서 어법상 어색한 부분을 바르게 고쳐 다시 쓰시오.

(1) Tom made his son have his eyes check.
　➡ _____

(2) He got his brother do his homework for him.
　➡ _____

(3) It was pizza who Jake ate at a cafe.
　➡ _____

(4) It is the restaurant that I'll have dinner with you this evening.
　➡ _____
　_____

(5) It was more carefully that he read the letter again.
　➡ _____

04 그림을 보고, 주어진 어휘를 이용하여 빈칸을 알맞게 채우시오.

(1) The princess _____
her to the castle yesterday. (have, take,
the dragon)

(2) _____ made the
first PC in 1976. (Steve Jobs, who)

05 다음 문장을 have를 이용하여 바꾸어 쓸 때 빈칸에 알맞은
말을 쓰시오.

(1) They asked Zaha Hadid to design
Dongdaemun Design Plaza.

➡ They had Dongdaemun Design Plaza

_____ .

(2) In Korea, some people order groceries
through the Internet and the sellers deliver
them to their homes.

➡ In Korea, some people order groceries
through the Internet and _____
_____ by the sellers.

06 다음 문장을 주어진 단어를 강조하는 문장으로 고쳐 쓰시오.
(that은 사용하지 말 것.)

> Matthew met Jake at the park last weekend.

(1) Matthew

➡ _____

_____

(2) met

➡ _____

(3) Jake

➡ _____

_____

(4) at the park

➡ _____

(5) last weekend

➡ _____

_____

07 다음 문장의 밑줄 친 부분을 강조하는 문장으로 바꿔 쓰시오.

(1) They started a swimming class <u>last
week</u>.

➡ _____

_____

(2) <u>Mary and Mike</u> danced hard to be a
mascot.

➡ _____

_____

(3) Robin broke <u>the vase</u> yesterday.

➡ _____

_____

(4) Did his sister teach <u>him</u> how to play the
guitar?

➡ _____

_____

Reading

교과서

A Father's Wisdom

A rich and wise father had two sons, Puru and Puneet. Before he
two sons와 Puru and Puneet은 동격
passed away, he called his two sons to give them some last words of
to부정사의 부사적 용법 중 목적(~하기 위해서)
advice.

"Listen carefully, my dear sons. Live by these words throughout your
life, and you will be happy," he said.
명령문, ~and ... : ~해라, 그러면 ...

"Build a house in every city. Sleep comfortably. Enjoy your food.
Lastly, spend money like a rich man... ."
전치사(~처럼)

Before he could explain himself, he passed away.
재귀대명사의 재귀적 용법(주어와 목적어가 같을 때 목적어로 재귀대명사 사용)

After his death, the two sons took their share of the father's wealth
and settled in different cities. Five years passed. Puru, who had been
took과 병렬 연결   *과거완료진행형*
following his father's words carefully, had no money left.

But his brother was richer than ever. Puru was puzzled about where
he had gone wrong, so he visited Puneet to find out.
간접의문문(의문사+주어+동사): 전치사 about의 목적어   *부사적 용법(목적)*

Puneet welcomed Puru with open arms. That night, when the brothers
sat down to chat after dinner, Puru asked the question that had been on
주격 관계대명사(선행사: the question)
his mind for days.

"It was our father's advice that I followed, but I am not happy.
It ~ that 강조 구문(I followed our father's advice. but I am not happy.)
I built a house in every city. But because I could not always stay
every+단수명사   *이유를 이끄는 접속사(~이기 때문에)*
there, I hired people and had the house looked after.
사역동사+목적어+p.p.(목적어와 목적격보어의 관계가 수동일 때)

---

wisdom: 지혜, 현명함
comfortably: 편안하게
lastly: 마지막으로
pass away: 세상을 떠나다
live by: (신조, 원칙 등)에 따라 살다
throughout one's life: 일생을 통해
explain oneself: 심중을 털어놓다
death: 죽음
puzzled: 당혹스러운, 어리둥절한
take one's share: 자기 몫을 차지하다
settle in: ~에 자리 잡다
go wrong: 잘못하다, 실수를 하다
with open arms: 두 팔을 벌리고
chat: 한가롭게 이야기하다
hire: 고용하다

📎 **확인문제**

● 다음 문장이 본문의 내용과 일치하면 T, 일치하지 않으면 F를 쓰시오.

1 The father died before he explained his words of advice. ☐

2 Puru, who had been following his father's words carefully, was richer than ever. ☐

3 Puru's houses were looked after by his wife. ☐

4 Puru lived near his brother after his father passed away. ☐

Father said we should sleep comfortably and enjoy our food, so I had my bed designed by experts and my meals prepared by a great chef. He told us to spend like a rich man, so I bought what I wanted without worrying about money. But look at me now! I am empty-handed. Did you not follow our father's wisdom? Tell me, brother, how did you get so rich?"

Puneet smiled and said, "My dear brother, I also followed our father's wisdom. But I understood it a bit differently. When he said 'build a house in every city,' I took it as having a place to stay all around the world. So I made friends in every city and I stayed at their houses when I visited those cities. Also, I slept comfortably each night because I would be tired after a hard day's work, and it did not matter if I was sleeping on a bed or on the hard floor. I ate only when I was hungry, so even a simple meal tasted great."

"Spend money like a rich man?" continued Puneet.

"A rich man knows how to make money grow. So, I tried to spend money on something that would bring me back more money rather than on luxurious things. For me, it was this wisdom that our father tried to explain."

Now Puru realized how foolish he had been. With this wisdom in mind, Puru started a new life.

design: 설계하다; 디자인
expert: 전문가
chef: 요리사
matter: 중요하다
a bit: 조금
make friends: 친구를 사귀다
after a hard day's work: 하루 종일 열심히 일하고 나서
continue: 말을 계속하다
luxurious: 사치스러운, 호화로운
foolish: 어리석은
bring back: 돌려주다

📎 **확인문제**

● 다음 문장이 본문의 내용과 일치하면 T, 일치하지 <u>않으면</u> F를 쓰시오.

1 For Puneet, sleeping on a bed or on the floor didn't matter because he would be tired after a hard day's work. ☐

2 Puneet ate only the delicious food. ☐

3 Puneet tried to spend money on something that would bring him back more money. ☐

4 Puru made his brother realize his foolishness. ☐

5 What Puneet understood about their father's wisdom was different from what Puru understood. ☐

● 우리말을 참고하여 빈칸에 알맞은 말을 쓰시오.

1 A rich and wise father _____ _____ _____, Puru and Puneet.

2 Before he _____ _____, he _____ his two sons _____ _____ _____ some _____ _____ _____ _____ _____.

3 "_____ _____, my dear sons. _____ _____ these words _____ _____ _____, and you will be happy," he said.

4 "_____ a house in _____ _____. Sleep _____. _____ your food. _____, spend money _____ a rich man... ."

5 Before he could _____ _____, he _____ _____.

6 After _____ _____, the two sons took _____ _____ _____ the father's _____ and _____ _____ different cities.

7 Five years passed. Puru, _____ _____ _____ _____ _____ his father's words carefully, had _____ _____ _____.

8 But his brother _____ _____ _____ _____ _____ _____.

9 Puru _____ _____ _____ _____ he _____ _____, so he visited Puneet _____ _____ _____.

10 Puneet _____ Puru _____ _____ _____.

11 That night, when the brothers _____ _____ _____ _____ after dinner, Puru asked the question _____ _____ _____ _____ _____ _____ for days.

12 "_____ _____ our father's advice _____ I followed, but I am not happy. I built a house _____ _____ _____.

13 But because I could not _____ _____ _____, I hired people and _____ the house _____ _____.

14 Father said we should _____ _____ and _____ our food, so I _____ my bed _____ by experts and _____ _____ _____ _____ a great chef.

15 He _____ us _____ _____ _____ a rich man, so I bought _____ _____ _____ without _____ about money.

16 But _____ _____ _____ now! I am _____.

17 Did you _____ _____ our _____ _____?

18 Tell me, brother, _____ _____ you _____ so _____?"

19 Puneet _____ and said, "My dear brother, I _____ _____ our _____ _____.

20 But I understood _____ _____ _____ _____ _____.

21 When he said '_____ a house in every city,' I _____ _____ _____ _____ _____ _____ _____ all around the world.

22 So I _____ _____ in every city and I _____ _____ their houses when I visited _____ _____.

23 Also, I slept _____ each night _____ I would be tired after a hard day's work, and it did not matter _____ _____ _____ _____ on a bed _____ on the hard floor.

24 I ate _____ _____ _____ _____ _____, so even a simple meal _____ _____."

25 "Spend money _____ _____ _____ _____ _____?" _____ Puneet.

26 "A rich man knows _____ _____ _____ _____ _____.

27 So, I tried to spend money _____ something _____ would _____ _____ _____ more money _____ _____ _____ luxurious things.

28 For me, _____ _____ this wisdom _____ our father _____ _____."

29 Now Puru realized _____ _____ _____ _____.

30 _____ this wisdom _____ _____, Puru started a new life.

14 아버지께서 우리는 편하게 자고 음식을 즐겨야 한다고 말씀하셔서 나는 내 침대를 전문가들에 의해 설계되게 했고, 내 식사는 훌륭한 요리사에 의해 준비되도록 했단다.

15 아버지는 우리에게 부자처럼 돈을 쓰라고 하셨으므로, 나는 돈 걱정을 하지 않고 내가 원하는 것을 샀지.

16 그렇지만 지금 나를 봐! 나는 빈 털터리야.

17 너는 우리 아버지의 지혜를 따르지 않았니?

18 나에게 말해 보렴, 동생아. 너는 어떻게 그렇게 부유해졌니?"

19 Puneet은 웃으며 말했다. "친애하는 형님. 저 또한 우리 아버지의 지혜를 따랐습니다.

20 하지만 저는 조금 다르게 이해했지요.

21 아버지가 '모든 도시에 집을 지어라'라고 말하셨을 때, 저는 그것을 전 세계에 머물 수 있는 장소를 가지는 것으로 여겼지요.

22 그래서 저는 모든 도시에서 친구를 사귀었고 그 도시들을 방문했을 때 그들의 집에 머물렀어요.

23 또한, 저는 하루 종일 열심히 일하고 나서 피곤해지곤 했기 때문에 침대에서 자든 딱딱한 바닥에서 자든 상관없이 매일 밤 편안하게 잠을 잤지요.

24 저는 배고플 때만 먹었기 때문에 간단한 식사마저도 훌륭한 맛이 났습니다."

25 "부자처럼 돈을 쓰라고요?" Puneet은 계속했다.

26 "부자는 돈을 불리는 방법을 알고 있어요.

27 그래서 저는 사치스러운 물건에 돈을 쓰는 것보다는 저에게 더 많은 돈을 돌려줄 수 있는 것에 돈을 쓰려고 노력했지요.

28 저에게는 이게 우리의 아버지가 설명하려고 하셨던 바로 그 지혜입니다."

29 이제 Puru는 그가 얼마나 어리석었었는지를 깨달았다.

30 이 지혜를 마음에 새기고, Puru는 새로운 삶을 시작했다.

● 우리말을 참고하여 본문을 영작하시오.

1 ▶ 부유하고 지혜로운 아버지에게 두 아들, Puru와 Puneet이 있었다.

➡ _____

2 ▶ 아버지는 돌아가시기 전에, 마지막 충고의 말을 하기 위해 그의 두 아들을 불렀다.

➡ _____

3 ▶ "주의 깊게 듣거라, 사랑하는 아들들아. 너희의 일생 동안 이 말대로 살면, 행복해질 것이다." 그는 말했다.

➡ _____

4 ▶ "모든 도시에 집을 지어라. 편하게 자거라. 음식을 즐기거라. 마지막으로, 돈을 부자처럼 쓰거라…."

➡ _____

5 ▶ 아버지는 그 말을 설명하기도 전에 돌아가셨다.

➡ _____

6 ▶ 그의 죽음 후에, 두 아들은 아버지의 재산 중 자신들의 몫을 가지고 다른 도시에 정착했다.

➡ _____

7 ▶ 5년이 지났다. 아버지의 말을 신중히 따라온 Puru는 남은 돈이 없었다.

➡ _____

8 ▶ 그러나 그의 동생은 그 어느 때보다 더 부자가 되었다.

➡ _____

9 ▶ Puru는 그가 어디서부터 잘못했는지 어리둥절했고, 그래서 그는 (그것을) 알아내기 위해 Puneet을 방문했다.

➡ _____

10 ▶ Puneet은 Puru를 두 팔 벌려 환영했다.

➡ _____

11 ▶ 그날 밤, 형제가 저녁식사 후 이야기를 하려고 앉았을 때, Puru는 며칠간 자신의 마음에 있었던 그 질문을 했다.

➡ _____

_____

12 ▶ "내가 따른 건 바로 우리 아버지의 조언이었지만, 나는 행복하지 않아. 나는 모든 도시에 집을 지었어.

➡ _____

13 ▶ 그러나 나는 그곳에 항상 머물 수 없었으므로 사람들을 고용하여 집을 돌보게 했지.

➡ _____

14 아버지께서 우리는 편하게 자고 음식을 즐겨야 한다고 말씀하셔서 나는 내 침대를 전문가들에 의해 설계되게 했고, 내 식사는 훌륭한 요리사에 의해 준비되도록 했단다.

➡ _____
_____

15 아버지는 우리에게 부자처럼 돈을 쓰라고 하셨으므로, 나는 돈 걱정을 하지 않고 내가 원하는 것을 샀지.

➡ _____

16 그렇지만 지금 나를 봐! 나는 빈털터리야.

➡ _____

17 너는 우리 아버지의 지혜를 따르지 않았니?

➡ _____

18 나에게 말해 보렴, 동생아, 너는 어떻게 그렇게 부유해졌니?"

➡ _____

19 Puneet은 웃으며 말했다, "친애하는 형님, 저 또한 우리 아버지의 지혜를 따랐습니다.

➡ _____

20 하지만 저는 조금 다르게 이해했지요.

➡ _____

21 아버지가 '모든 도시에 집을 지어라'라고 말하셨을 때, 저는 그것을 전 세계에 머물 수 있는 장소를 가지는 것으로 여겼지요.

➡ _____

22 그래서 저는 모든 도시에서 친구를 사귀었고 그 도시들을 방문했을 때 그들의 집에 머물렀어요.

➡ _____

23 또한, 저는 하루 종일 열심히 일하고 나서 피곤해지곤 했기 때문에 침대에서 자든 딱딱한 바닥에서 자든 상관없이 매일 밤 편안하게 잠을 잤지요.

➡ _____
_____

24 저는 배고플 때만 먹었기 때문에 간단한 식사마저도 훌륭한 맛이 났습니다."

➡ _____

25 "부자처럼 돈을 쓰라고요?" Puneet은 계속했다.

➡ _____

26 "부자는 돈을 불리는 방법을 알고 있어요.

➡ _____

27 그래서 저는 사치스러운 물건에 돈을 쓰는 것보다는 저에게 더 많은 돈을 돌려줄 수 있는 것에 돈을 쓰려고 노력했지요.

➡ _____
_____

28 저에게는 이게 우리의 아버지가 설명하려고 하셨던 바로 그 지혜입니다."

➡ _____

29 이제 Puru는 그가 얼마나 어리석었었는지를 깨달았다.

➡ _____

30 이 지혜를 마음에 새기고, Puru는 새로운 삶을 시작했다.

➡ _____

[01~04] 다음 글을 읽고 물음에 답하시오.

A rich and wise father had two sons, Puru and Puneet. Before he passed away, he called his two sons to give them some last words of advice.

"Listen carefully, my dear sons. Live (A)_____ these words throughout your life, and you will be happy," he said.

"Build a house in every city. Sleep comfortably. Enjoy your food. Lastly, spend money like a rich man... ."

Before he could explain himself, he passed away. After his death, the two sons took their share of the father's wealth and settled in different cities. Five years passed. Puru, who had been following his father's words carefully, had no money left. But his brother was richer than ever. Puru was puzzled about where he had gone wrong, so he visited Puneet to find out.

01 다음 중 빈칸 (A)에 들어갈 말과 같은 말이 들어가는 것은?

① He took part _____ the contest.
② Breakfast consisted _____ bread with butter.
③ As time goes _____, I miss her more and more.
④ We are different _____ each other in many ways.
⑤ Their house is very similar _____ ours, but ours is more beautiful.

02 다음과 같이 풀이되는 말을 위 글에서 찾아 쓰시오.

> the end of life

➡ _____

03 What were the names of the two sons? Answer in English with a full sentence.

➡ _____

04 다음 중 위 글을 읽고 답할 수 있는 것은?

① How rich was the father?
② What made the father rich?
③ How old was the rich man when he died?
④ Where were two sons before their father called them?
⑤ What did the rich man say to his sons when he was dying?

[05~08] 다음 글을 읽고 물음에 답하시오.

Puneet welcomed Puru with open arms. That night, when the brothers sat down ①to chat after dinner, Puru asked the question ② that had been on his mind for days.

"It was our father's advice that I followed, but I am not happy. I built a house in every city. But ③because I could not always stay there, I hired people and had the house ④look after. Father said we should sleep comfortably and enjoy our food, so I had my bed designed by experts and my meals prepared by a great chef. He told us ⑤to spend like a rich man, so I bought what I wanted without worrying about money. But look at me now! I am empty-handed. Did you not follow (A)our father's wisdom? Tell me, brother, how did you get so rich?"

05 What did Puru follow? Answer in English.

➡ _____

06 다음 중 밑줄 친 (A)에 해당하는 것은?

① Be curious about everything.
② Be proud of yourself.
③ Don't spend much money.
④ Take pleasure in eating food.
⑤ Build your house in your hometown.

07 밑줄 친 ①~⑤ 중 어법상 바르지 않은 것은?

①　　②　　③　　④　　⑤

Choose one that is TRUE.

① Puneet didn't like his brother's visit.
② Puru regrets not following his father's advice.
③ Puru had his house designed by experts.
④ Puru was employed by a chef to prepare a meal.
⑤ Puru bought everything he wanted without worrying about money.

[09~12] 다음 글을 읽고 물음에 답하시오.

　Puneet smiled and said, "My dear brother, I also followed our father's wisdom. But I understood it a bit differently. When he said 'build a house in every city,' I took it as having a place to stay all around the world. So I made friends in every city and I stayed at their houses when I visited those cities. (A) Also, I slept comfortably each night because I would be tired after a hard day's work, and it did not matter if I was sleeping on a bed or on the hard floor. I ate only when I was hungry, so even a simple meal tasted great."
"Spend money like a rich man?" continued Puneet.

"A rich man knows how to make money grow. So, I tried to spend money on something that would bring ⓐ_____ rather than on luxurious things. For me, it was this wisdom that our father tried to explain."
Now Puru realized how foolish he had been. With this wisdom in mind, Puru started a new life.

09 위 글의 흐름상 빈칸 ⓐ에 들어갈 말로 가장 적절한 것은?

① you a big fortune
② us happy lives
③ me back more money
④ up my children comfortably
⑤ about a change

10 다음 중 밑줄 친 (A)를 대신하여 쓸 수 있는 것은?

① Therefore　　② For instance
③ In addition　　④ However
⑤ On the other hand

서답형
11 Write the reason why Puneet could be satisfied with only a simple meal. Answer in English with a full sentence.

➡ _____

서답형
12 Where did Puneet stay when he visited cities all around the world? Answer in English.

➡ _____

_____

[13~16] 다음 글을 읽고 물음에 답하시오.

A rich and wise father had two sons, Puru and Puneet. Before he passed away, he called his two sons to give them some last words of advice.

"Listen carefully, my dear sons. Live by these words throughout your life, and you will be happy," he said.

"Build a house in every city. Sleep comfortably. Enjoy your food. Lastly, spend money like a rich man... ." Before he could explain (A)himself, he passed away.

(①) After his death, the two sons took their share of the father's wealth and settled in different cities. (②) Five years passed. (③) Puru, who had been following his father's words carefully, had no money left. (④) Puru was puzzled about where he had gone wrong, so he visited Puneet to find out. (⑤)

13 (①)~(⑤) 중 주어진 문장이 들어가기에 가장 적절한 곳은?

But his brother was richer than ever.

①   ②   ③   ④   ⑤

14 위 글에 이어질 내용으로 가장 적절한 것은?

① Puneet leaving for making more money
② Puneet wanting to help his brother
③ The way Puneet became richer than ever
④ The reason why Puru visited his brother
⑤ Two brothers visiting their father's grave

서답형
15 What happened to Puru five years after his father's death? Answer in English with five words.

➡ _____

16 다음 중 밑줄 친 (A)와 쓰임이 다른 것은?

① They enjoyed themselves a lot.
② He spoke to the principal himself.
③ He cut himself on a knife yesterday.
④ Please help yourself to the salad.
⑤ She couldn't make herself understood.

[17~20] 다음 글을 읽고 물음에 답하시오.

(A)Puneet welcomed Puru with open arms. That night, when the brothers sat down to chat after dinner, Puru asked the question that had been on his mind for days.

"It was our father's advice that I followed, but I am not happy. I built a house in every city. But because I could not always stay there, I hired people and had the house looked after. Father said we should sleep comfortably and enjoy our food, so I had my bed designed by experts and my meals ⓐ_____ by a great chef. He told us to spend like a rich man, so I bought what I wanted without worrying about money. But look at me now! I am empty-handed. Did you not follow our father's wisdom? Tell me, brother, how did you get so rich?"

서답형
17 주어진 단어를 어법에 맞게 빈칸 ⓐ에 쓰시오.

(prepare)

➡ _____

18 밑줄 친 (A)의 의미로 가장 적절한 것은?

① Puru was rejected by Puneet.
② Puru held Puneet by the arm.
③ Puneet welcomed Puru reluctantly.
④ Puneet wanted Puru to go away.
⑤ Puneet gave Puru a warm welcome.

서답형

19 What did Puru do in every city? Answer in English.

➡ _____

중요
20 위 글에 이어질 내용으로 가장 적절한 것은?

① what Puneet did to help his brother
② how Puru became rich again
③ how Puneet became richer
④ what Puru did to follow the advice
⑤ what happened to Puru before he came back

[21~25] 다음 글을 읽고 물음에 답하시오.

Puneet smiled and said, "My dear brother, I also followed our father's wisdom. But I understood it a bit differently. When he said 'build a house in every city,' I took it as having a place to stay all around the world. So I made friends in every city and I stayed at their houses when I visited those cities. ⓐAlso, I slept comfortably each night because I would be tired after a hard day's work, and it did not matter if I was sleeping on a bed or on the hard floor. I ate only when I was hungry, so even a simple meal tasted great."

"Spend money like a rich man?" continued Puneet.

"A rich man knows how to make money grow. So, I tried to spend money on something that would bring me back more money rather than (A)_____ luxurious things. For me, it was this wisdom that our father tried to explain."

Now Puru realized how foolish he had been. With this wisdom in mind, Puru started a new life.

21 빈칸 (A)에 들어갈 말로 적절한 것은?

① at ② on ③ about ④ to ⑤ by

중요
22 According to the underlined ⓐ, what was their father's last word?

① Get a good rest.
② Sleep comfortably.
③ Work like a bee.
④ Make money as I did.
⑤ Always sleep at home.

23 What did Puru do after hearing what his brother said?

① He went home with anger.
② He made his brother start a new life.
③ He went back to his old habit.
④ He made a fresh start.
⑤ He realized his brother's foolishness.

서답형
24 위 글의 내용에 맞게 빈칸에 알맞은 말을 쓰시오.

Both brothers understood their father's wisdom _____.

중요
25 다음 중 위 글의 내용과 일치하지 <u>않는</u> 것은?

① Puru followed his father's advice.
② Their father told them to build a house in every city.
③ Puneet built houses as his father told him to.
④ Puru finally understood what his father tried to say.
⑤ Puneet made his money grow like a rich man does.

[01~05] 다음 글을 읽고 물음에 답하시오.

A rich and wise father had two sons, Puru and Puneet. Before he passed away, he called his two sons to give them some last words of advice.

"Listen carefully, my dear sons. (A)Live by these words throughout your life, and you will be happy," he said.

"Build a house in every city. Sleep comfortably. Enjoy your food. Lastly, spend money like a rich man... ." Before he could explain himself, he passed away.

After his death, the two sons took their share of the father's wealth and settled in different cities. Five years passed. Puru, who had been following his father's words carefully, had no money left. But his brother was richer than ever. Puru was puzzled about where he had gone wrong, so he visited Puneet to find out.

01 Write the reason why the father called his two sons before he passed away. Use the phrase 'It was because.'

➡ _____

_____

02 What had Puru been doing since his father passed away? Answer in English.

➡ _____

03 접속사 if를 사용하여 밑줄 친 (A)와 같은 의미의 문장을 쓰시오.

➡ _____

_____

04 위 글의 내용과 일치하도록 빈칸에 알맞은 말을 쓰시오.

Unlike _____, _____ became richer than ever.

05 What did the two sons do after their father died? Answer in English with a full sentence.

➡ _____

_____

[06~11] 다음 글을 읽고 물음에 답하시오.

Puneet smiled and said, "My dear brother, I also followed our father's wisdom. But I understood it a bit differently. When he said 'build a house in every city,' I took it as having a place to stay all around the world. So I made friends in every city and I stayed at their houses when I visited those cities. Also, I slept comfortably each night because I would be tired after a hard day's work, and it did not matter if I was sleeping on a bed or on the hard floor. I ate only when I was hungry, so even a simple meal tasted great."

"Spend money like a rich man?" continued Puneet.

"A rich man (A)_____. So, I tried to spend money on something that would bring me back more money rather than on luxurious things. For me, it was this wisdom that our father tried to explain."

Now Puru realized how foolish he had been. With this wisdom in mind, Puru started a new life.

06 주어진 단어를 바르게 나열하여 빈칸 (A)에 들어갈 말을 완성하시오.

(grow / knows / make / to / money / how)

➡ _____

07 Why did a simple meal taste great to Puneet? Answer in English and use the word 'because.'

➡ _____

_____

08 What did Puneet do to spend money like a rich man? Answer in English with a full sentence.

➡ _____

_____

_____

09 다음 중 위 글의 내용과 일치하지 않는 곳을 두 군데 찾아 바르게 고쳐 쓰시오.

> Puneet understood what his brother had said differently from Puru. Thanks to his own deep understanding, Puneet became poor and happy.

➡ _____

10 Write the reason why Puneet could sleep anywhere comfortably. Use the phrase 'It was because.'

➡ _____

11 What did Puru realize? Answer in English.

➡ _____

[12~15] 다음 글을 읽고 물음에 답하시오.

Puneet welcomed Puru with open arms. That night, when the brothers sat down to chat after dinner, Puru asked the question that had been on his mind for days.

"It was our father's advice that I followed, but I am not happy. I built a house in every city. But because I could not always stay (A)there, I hired people and (B)집을 돌보게 했지. Father said we should sleep comfortably and enjoy our food, so I had my bed designed by experts and my meals prepared by a great chef. He told us to spend like a rich man, so I bought what I wanted without worrying about money. But look at me now! I am empty-handed. Did you not follow our father's wisdom? Tell me, brother, how did you get so rich?"

12 밑줄 친 (A)there가 의미하는 것을 우리말로 쓰시오.

➡ _____

13 주어진 단어를 활용하여 밑줄 친 우리말 (B)를 5 단어의 영어로 쓰시오.

> (have / look)

➡ _____

14 What did their father tell them to do? Answer in English with a full sentence.

➡ _____

15 위 글의 내용에 맞게 괄호 (A)~(C)에서 적절한 말을 고르시오.

> (A)[Although / Unless] Puru followed his father's advice, he lived an (B)[easy / unhappy] life and became (C)[wealthy / broke].

➡ (A) _____ (B) _____ (C) _____

Language in Use

- Everyone has freedom of speech and expression.
  형용사에 '–dom'을 붙이면 명사가 되어 '영역, 상태'라는 의미가 더해진다.
- Can you explain the rules of the game before we start playing it?
  특정 어근 앞에 'ex–'를 붙이면 '밖으로'라는 의미를 더한다.

구문해설 ・freedom: 자유 ・explain: 설명하다

해석
- 모든 사람들은 언론과 표현의 자유가 있다.
- 우리가 경기를 시작하기 전에 규칙을 설명해 줄래?

Grammar in Real Life B Look and Write

1. Do you need to have the computer fixed? Call the Computer Doctor.
   have+목적어+과거분사: 목적어가 목적격 보어의 동작을 당하는 대상(주로 사물)
2. Why don't you have your hair cut at Susie's Hair Studio?
   ~하는 게 어때?   과거분사(머리카락이 잘리는 것)
3. How about having your pet cleaned from head to toe? Come to Happy Pet.
   ~하는 게 어때?   과거분사(애완동물이 깨끗하게 되는 것)
4. Do you want to have your party room decorated with flowers?
                              과거분사(파티 룸이 장식되는 것)

   Look for Mary's Flowers.

구문해설 ・fix: 수리하다, 고치다 ・toe: 발가락, 발끝 ・decorate: 장식하다

1. 컴퓨터를 고쳐야 하나요? '컴퓨터 닥터'에게 전화하세요.
2. '수지의 헤어 스튜디오'에서 머리카락을 자르는 게 어때요?
3. 당신의 애완동물을 머리부터 발끝까지 깨끗하게 하는 것은 어떨까요? '해피 펫'으로 오세요.
4. 당신의 파티 룸을 꽃으로 장식하고 싶은가요? '메리의 꽃들'을 찾아 주세요.

Think & Write C

Let me introduce my motto.
사역동사+목적어+동사원형
It is "Go for it!"

It means "Go and do things without fear because failure is also a good
                                              이유를 이끄는 접속사
experience." I made it my motto when I was a kicker in the school soccer

team. From the motto, I learned that even the bad kicks made me a better

kicker at the end. It is this motto that changed my life!

구문해설 ・introduce: 소개하다 ・motto: 좌우명 ・failure: 실패

나의 좌우명을 소개하게 해 줘.
그것은 "어서 해!"야.
그것은 "실패 또한 좋은 경험이기 때문에 두려움 없이 무언가를 해'라는 의미야. 나는 학교 축구팀에서 키커였을 때, 그것을 나의 좌우명으로 삼았어. 그 좌우명에서 나는 나쁜 킥들조차 결국엔 나를 더 좋은 키커로 만들어 준다는 것을 배웠지. 나의 삶을 바꾼 것은 바로 이 좌우명이야!

01 다음 밑줄 친 부분의 의미로 알맞지 <u>않은</u> 것은?

① It was really <u>priceless</u> information. (가치 없는)

② My brother is an <u>expert</u> at computer programming. (전문가)

③ She laughed and <u>chatted</u> happily with her family. (담소하다)

④ The princess lived in this old <u>castle</u> for her entire life. (성)

⑤ The <u>chef</u> is famous in Korea for Chinese food. (요리사)

02 다음 괄호 안의 단어를 문맥에 맞게 고쳐 쓰시오.

He has lived on this _____ island alone for 10 years. (desert)

03 다음 빈칸에 알맞은 단어를 고르시오.

We've nearly _____ out of paper. Do you think there's enough for today?

① made   ② taken   ③ run
④ got   ⑤ put

04 다음 밑줄 친 부분과 바꿔 쓸 수 있는 말을 고르시오.

He <u>died</u> at the age of eighty-four.

① passed out   ② passed up
③ got through   ④ passed away
⑤ took back

[05~08] 다음 대화를 읽고 물음에 답하시오.

W: What are you doing, Jinho?
M: (①) I'm writing a (A)_____ of the movie, *The Time Traveler's Wife*. (②)
W: I saw that movie, too. It's one of my favorite romantic movies. (③)
M: (④) Emily, (B)만약 네가 시간 여행을 할 수 있다면 무엇을 하겠니?
W: I would travel to the 1940s and prevent World War II. How about you?
M: I would go to the Joseon Dynasty and meet King Sejong. (⑤) I'm a big fan of him.

05 위 대화의 (①)~(⑤) 중 주어진 문장이 들어갈 곳은?

I loved it, too.

①   ②   ③   ④   ⑤

06 빈칸 (A)에 알맞은 것을 고르시오.

① reward   ② review   ③ wisdom
④ paper   ⑤ motto

07 위 대화를 읽고 답할 수 <u>없는</u> 질문을 고르시오.

① Emily는 시간 여행을 할 수 있다면, 1940년대로 가서 무엇을 하고 싶어 하는가?

② Emily는 <시간 여행자의 아내>라는 영화를 보았는가?

③ 진호는 왜 세종대왕을 만나고 싶어 하는가?

④ 진호는 지금 무엇을 하고 있는가?

⑤ Emily는 어떤 종류의 영화를 좋아하는가?

08 밑줄 친 우리말 (B)를 주어진 단어를 이용하여 영작하시오.

➡ _____

(time travel, will)

[09~11] 다음 대화를 읽고 물음에 답하시오.

M: ⓐ_____'s your online story going, Amy?
W: Not well. The deadline is this weekend but I
ⓑ_____ out of ideas.
M: Don't worry about it. I can help you.
W: That would be great. My main character has special powers. What would you do if you ⓒ_____ able to ⓓ_____ people's minds?
M: Well, I would find out ⓔ_____ the girl I like likes me.
W: That's a good idea. Thanks.

09 빈칸 ⓐ~ⓔ에 들어가지 않는 것을 고르시오. (대·소문자 무시)

① read   ② that   ③ ran
④ how   ⑤ were

10 위 대화에서 다음 영영풀이에 해당하는 단어를 찾아 쓰시오.

a person represented in a film, play, or story

➡ _____

11 위 대화를 읽고 답할 수 없는 질문을 고르시오.

① What power does the main character of her story have?
② What is Amy worried about?
③ Does the man help Amy who worried about the online story?
④ When is the deadline of the online story?
⑤ What would Amy do if she could read people's mind?

12 다음 대화의 빈칸에 들어갈 말을 〈보기〉에서 골라 순서대로 옳게 배열한 것은?

M: _____
W: _____
M: _____
W: _____
M: Really? I would collect interesting items and make a museum.
W: Cool.

┤ 보기 ├

(A) Right. What would you do if you could live forever?
(B) Caroline, have you read the book, *Tuck Everlasting*?
(C) Yeah, it is about a family that drank magical water and lived forever, right?
(D) Well, I would live in different cities all around the world.

① (B) – (A) – (C) – (D)
② (B) – (C) – (A) – (D)
③ (B) – (D) – (A) – (C)
④ (C) – (B) – (A) – (D)
⑤ (C) – (D) – (B) – (A)

Grammar

13 다음 밑줄 친 부분과 바꿔 쓸 수 있는 것은?

It was on the subway that I lost my bag.

① what   ② which   ③ who
④ when   ⑤ where

14 다음 문장 중에서 어법상 <u>어색한</u> 문장을 고르시오.

① David had the TV turned on after dinner.
② I know that my mom had the dishes done by Jake.
③ The government had the markets closed because of the Covid-19.
④ Dad had me returned home as it was very late at night.
⑤ Dad had my elder brother wash the pet dog.

15 다음 주어진 문장과 뜻이 같도록 빈칸을 알맞게 채우시오. (that 사용 금지.)

> The cafe is the place which Jane is reading a comic book at.
>
> ➡ It is ＿＿＿＿＿＿＿＿＿＿ a comic book.

16 다음 ⓐ~ⓖ 중 어법상 옳은 것을 <u>모두</u> 고르시오.

> ⓐ Do you want to have your party room decorated with flowers?
> ⓑ Dad had the tree plant in the yard last Saturday.
> ⓒ Lisa got her daughter come back home by 10 p.m.
> ⓓ It is Mina and Junha that are waiting in line for the roller coaster.
> ⓔ I think it was on the bus when Mina got her wallet steal.
> ⓕ It is in her room which Linda is taking a selfie.
> ⓖ It was the cat that ate the sandwiches on your desk.

➡ ＿＿＿＿＿＿＿＿＿＿

17 다음 우리말을 괄호 안의 조건에 맞게 영작하시오.

> Tom은 Rene에게 자기 대신 공항에서 그의 엄마를 모셔오게 했다.
> (the airport, had, pick up, for 이용, 총 12 단어)

➡ ＿＿＿＿＿＿＿＿＿＿
＿＿＿＿＿＿＿＿＿＿

18 다음 중 어법상 <u>어색한</u> 것을 고르시오. (2개)

① I had my bed design by experts and my meals prepared by a great chef.
② It was the stage that BTS performed their first show.
③ I must have the broken car fixed tomorrow.
④ It was in the morning that the dragon took the princess.
⑤ It was in 1893 that Edvard Munch painted *The Scream*.

19 다음 우리말에 맞게 영작한 것은?

> 아빠가 TV에서 보고 계시던 것은 바로 축구 경기였다.

① It was a soccer game that Dad was watching on TV.
② It was Dad that was watching a soccer game on TV.
③ It was on TV that Dad was watching a soccer game.
④ It was watching on TV that Dad a soccer game.
⑤ Dad watched a soccer game on TV.

20 다음 그림을 보고, 주어진 어휘를 이용하여 빈칸을 알맞게 채우시오.

> They will _____ next week. (the writing contest, have, hold)

Reading

[21~24] 다음 글을 읽고 물음에 답하시오.

Puneet smiled and said, "My dear brother, I also followed our father's wisdom. But I understood it a bit ①differently. When he said 'build a house in every city,' I took it as ② having a place to stay all around the world. So I made friends in every city and I stayed at their houses when I visited ③those cities. Also, I slept comfortably each night because I would be tired after a hard day's work, and it did not matter if I was sleeping on a bed or on the hard floor. I ate only when I was hungry, so even a simple meal tasted ④great."

"Spend money like a rich man?" continued Puneet.

"A rich man knows how to make money ⑤to grow. So, I tried to spend money on something that would bring me back more money rather than on luxurious things. For me, it was this wisdom that our father tried to explain."

Now Puru realized how foolish he had been. With this wisdom ___(A)___ mind, Puru started a new life.

21 ①~⑤ 중 어법상 바르지 않은 것은?

①   ②   ③   ④   ⑤

22 위 글의 빈칸 (A)에 알맞은 것은?

① in   ② to
③ at   ④ with
⑤ from

23 다음과 같이 풀이되는 말을 위 글에서 찾아 쓰시오.

> extremely comfortable or elegant, especially when involving great expense

➡ _____

24 According to what Puneet said, what didn't matter to him after a hard day's work? Answer in English.

➡ _____
_____

[25~26] 다음 글을 읽고 물음에 답하시오.

> Let me introduce my motto
> It is "Go for it!"
> It means "Go and do things without fear because failure is also a good experience." I made it my motto when I was a kicker in the school soccer team. From the motto, I learned that even the bad kicks made me a better kicker at the end. It is this motto that changed my life!

25 Write the reason why the writer tries to go and do things without fear. Use the phrase 'It is because.'

➡ _____

26 Choose one that is TRUE.

① The writer doesn't have her or his own motto yet.
② One of the kickers gave the motto to the writer.
③ The writer thinks she or he can be a better kicker with bad kicks.
④ The writer's life was changed by the school soccer team.
⑤ The writer was not a good kicker.

[27~30] 다음 글을 읽고 물음에 답하시오.

Puneet welcomed Puru with open arms. That night, when the brothers sat down to chat after dinner, Puru asked ⓐthe question that had been on his mind for days.

"(A) He told us to spend like a rich man, so I bought what I wanted without ⓑworrying about money. But look at me now! I am empty-handed. Did you not follow our father's wisdom? Tell me, brother, how did you get so rich?

(B) But because I could not always stay there, I hired people and had the house looked after. Father said we should sleep comfortably and enjoy our food, so I had my bed designed by experts and my meals prepared by a great chef.

(C) It was our father's advice that I followed, but I am not happy. I built a house in every city."

27 자연스러운 글이 되도록 (A)~(C)를 바르게 나열하시오.

➡ _____

28 What does the underlined ⓐ mean?

① how Puru became so wealthy
② how his brother got so rich
③ what made Puru become miserable
④ what made Puneet become unhappy
⑤ why Puru wasn't welcomed by his brother

29 Choose one that is TRUE.

① Puru welcomed his brother heartily.
② Puru hired experts to build houses in every city.
③ Puru took care of all the houses by himself.
④ Puru's houses could be found in every city.
⑤ Puneet didn't offer dinner to his brother, Puru.

30 다음 중 밑줄 친 ⓑ와 쓰임이 다른 하나는?

① Did you enjoy making dinner with her?
② David finished doing his homework already.
③ June was waiting for you at the bus stop.
④ My job is protecting you from dangerous things.
⑤ Tom was fond of listening to music.

01 다음 빈칸에 공통으로 들어갈 접두어를 쓰시오.

> • She _____plained how the machine worked.
> • His paintings have been _____hibited in China.
> • He _____pressed an interest in meeting her.

02 빈칸을 다음 영영풀이에 해당하는 말을 이용하여 채우시오. (주어진 철자로 시작할 것.)

> something given in exchange for good behavior or good work, etc.

> They gave him a _____ for his hard work.

➡ r_____

03 빈칸 (A)와 (B)에 들어갈 말이 바르게 짝지어진 것을 고르시오.

> • It was cold, so I slept with a blanket covering me (A)_____ head to toe.
> • It's hard work to (B)_____ after three children all day.

	(A)	(B)
①	on	look
②	on	take
③	from	look
④	from	take
⑤	from	care

04 밑줄 친 부분과 바꿔 쓸 수 있는 말을 고르시오.

> Lastly, I would like to ask about your future plans.

① In addition
② Therefore
③ Later
④ Finally
⑤ Eventually

[05~06] 다음 대화를 읽고 물음에 답하시오.

> M: Caroline, have you ⓐread the book, *Tuck Everlasting*?
> W: Yeah, it is about a family ⓑthat drank magical water and ⓒlives forever, right?
> M: Right. What (A)_____ you do if you could live forever?
> W: Well, I (B)_____ live in different cities all around the world.
> M: Really? I (C)_____ collect ⓓinteresting items and ⓔmake a museum.
> W: Cool.

05 ⓐ~ⓔ 중 흐름상 또는 어법상 어색한 것을 고르시오.

① ⓐ ② ⓑ ③ ⓒ ④ ⓓ ⑤ ⓔ

06 빈칸 (A)~(C)에 공통으로 들어갈 말을 쓰시오.

➡ _____

[07~09] 다음 대화를 읽고 물음에 답하시오.

> W: What are you doing, Jinho?
> M: I'm writing a review of the movie, *The Time Traveler's Wife*.

W: I saw that movie, too. It's one of my favorite romantic movies.

M: I loved it, too. Emily, (A)_____?

W: I would travel to the 1940s and (B)_____ World War II. How about you?

M: 나는 조선 시대로 가서 세종대왕을 만날 거야. I'm a big fan of him.

07 빈칸 (A)에 알맞은 말을 고르시오.

① what will you do if you can time travel

② what would you do if you have time machine

③ what will you do if you have a magic suit

④ what would you do if you could time travel

⑤ what could you do if you make time machine

08 빈칸 (B)에 알맞은 말을 고르시오.

① prevent　　② express　　③ allow
④ obtain　　⑤ exhibit

09 밑줄 친 우리말과 일치하도록 주어진 단어를 이용해 영작하시오.

➡ I _____
_____. (the Joseon Dynasty, King Sejong)

[10~11] 다음 대화를 읽고 물음에 답하시오.

M: I've heard that you're going to be in the writing contest next week.

W: Yeah, it's already next week.

M: You look worried. What's wrong?

W: I'm worried that the topic would be too difficult for me.

M: 네가 바꿀 수 없는 것에 대해 걱정하지 마. Just believe (A)_____ yourself.

W: Thanks. I'll try.

10 빈칸 (A)에 알맞은 전치사를 쓰시오.

➡ _____

11 밑줄 친 우리말과 일치하도록 주어진 단어를 이용해 영작하시오.

➡ _____
(something, change, about, 7 단어)

12 다음 우리말에 맞게 영작한 것은?

> 나는 그가 내 시계를 수리하게 했다.

① I had my watch repair him.

② I got my watch repaired him.

③ I had him repaired my watch.

④ I had him repair my watch.

⑤ I got him repair my watch.

13 다음 중 어법상 어색한 문장은?

① Ted needs to have the plants watered.

② It was my mom that named my pet dog Lucky.

③ My grandma had me fix her computer last week.

④ It was the amusement park that Minsu rode the roller coaster.

⑤ It was the movie *Parasite* that I watched last Sunday.

14 다음 빈칸에 들어갈 말을 순서대로 바르게 묶은 것은?

> • Mom had the dinner _____ before everyone came.
>
> • It was yesterday _____ I played tennis with Mike.

① prepared – where
② prepared – when
③ prepare – where
④ prepare – what
⑤ prepares – that

15 밑줄 친 부분을 바르게 고쳐 문장을 다시 쓰시오.

(1) My dad has his car to wash once a month.

➡ _____

(2) Mom had a robot vacuum cleaner to clean the floor.

➡ _____
_____

(3) Jane got Richard guessing her age when she first met him.

➡ _____
_____

(4) It was the restaurant which Angelina had dinner with her friends.

➡ _____
_____

(5) It was a knife where I forgot to bring to the cooking class.

➡ _____
_____

16 그림을 보고, 주어진 어휘를 이용하여 빈칸을 알맞게 채우시오. (변형 가능)

It was the princess _____

_____ with flowers. (the table, have, decorate)

[17~20] 다음 글을 읽고 물음에 답하시오.

A rich and wise father had two sons, Puru and Puneet. Before he ①passed away, he called his two sons to give them some last words of advice.

"Listen carefully, my dear sons. ②Live on these words throughout your life, and you will be ③happy," he said.

"Build a house in every city. Sleep comfortably. Enjoy your food. Lastly, spend money like a rich man... ." Before he could ④explain himself, he passed away.

After his death, the two sons took their share of the father's wealth and settled in different cities. Five years passed. Puru, who had been following his father's words carefully, had no money ⑤left. But his brother was richer than ever. Puru was puzzled about where he had gone wrong, so he visited Puneet to find out.

17 ①~⑤ 중 글의 흐름상 어색한 것은?

① 　② 　③ 　④　⑤

18 Who was richer after five years, Puru or Puneet? Answer in English with a full sentence.

➡ _____

19 Choose one that is TRUE.

① The father passed away without saying a word.
② Two sons couldn't watch their father pass away.
③ The father left nothing for his two sons.
④ Two sons settled in the same city where they grew up together.
⑤ Puru stuck to what his father had said.

20 How did Puru feel about his brother's news? Answer in English with three words.

➡ _____

[21~24] 다음 글을 읽고 물음에 답하시오.

  Puneet smiled and said, "My dear brother, I also followed our father's wisdom. (①) But I understood (A)it a bit differently. (②) When he said 'build a house in every city,' I took it as having a place (B)to stay all around the world. (③) Also, I slept comfortably each night because I would be tired after a hard day's work, and it did not matter if I was sleeping on a bed or on the hard floor. I ate only when I was hungry, so even a simple meal tasted great." (④)
  "Spend money like a rich man?" continued Puneet. (⑤)
  "A rich man knows how to make money grow. So, I tried to spend money on something that would bring me back more money rather than on luxurious things. For me, it was this

wisdom that our father tried to explain."
  Now Puru realized how foolish he had been. (C)With this wisdom in mind, Puru started a new life.

21 (①)~(⑤) 중 주어진 문장이 들어가기에 가장 적절한 곳은?

So I made friends in every city and I stayed at their houses when I visited those cities.

①   ②   ③   ④   ⑤

22 밑줄 친 (A)it이 가리키는 것을 위 글에서 찾아 쓰시오.

➡ _____

23 다음 중 밑줄 친 (B)와 쓰임이 같은 것은?

① He went out to find some food.
② Did they want you to do it?
③ It was interesting to see the movie.
④ That is the simple way to do it.
⑤ She was very sad to hear the news.

24 What does underlined (C) mean?

① He didn't bother to remember the wisdom.
② He tried to bear the wisdom in mind.
③ He didn't understand what his brother said.
④ He often forgot keeping the wisdom in mind.
⑤ He wondered how his brother made money.

01 대화의 흐름상 빈칸에 들어갈 말을 주어진 〈조건〉에 맞춰 쓰시오.

> M: Lisa, have you watched the movie, *Cast Away*?
> W: No, I haven't. What is it about?
> M: It's about a man who was stuck on a deserted island for 4 years.
> W: It sounds interesting.
> M: Yeah, the man tries everything to stay alive. _____
> W: To stay alive? Well, I would build a tree house and hunt for food.
> M: Yeah, me too. And that's what the man did in the movie.

┌─ 조건 ─
│ • 상상한 내용을 묻기
│ • will, be, do, him을 이용할 것 (형태 변화 가능)
│ • 총 8 단어

➡ _____

02 다음 대화에서 흐름상 어색한 것을 찾아 바르게 고치시오.

> M: ①I've heard that you're going to be in the writing contest next week.
> W: Yeah, it's already next week.
> M: ②You look worried. What's wrong?
> W: ③I'm worried that the topic would be too easy for me.
> M: ④Don't worry about something you can't change. ⑤Just believe in yourself.
> W: Thanks. I'll try.

➡ _____

03 다음 대화의 밑줄 친 부분과 같은 뜻이 되도록 빈칸에 알맞은 말을 쓰시오.

> M: Sujin, what are you doing this weekend?
> W: Nothing special, why?
> M: I have to go to Busan for a family trip tomorrow but I can't find anyone to feed my dog, Lucy.
> W: Don't worry about Lucy. <u>I'll take care of her.</u>

➡ I'll _____ after her.

04 다음 문장에서 틀린 것을 고쳐 다시 쓰시오.

(1) Why don't you have the groceries to deliver to your home?

➡ _____
_____

(2) The students got their classroom paint.

➡ _____

(3) It was Matt which had coffee at the office this morning.

➡ _____
_____

[05~08] 다음 글을 읽고 물음에 답하시오.

Puneet welcomed Puru with open arms. That night, when the brothers sat down to chat after dinner, Puru asked the question that had been on his mind for days.

"It was our father's advice that I followed, but I am not happy. I built a house in every city. But because I could not always stay there, I hired people and had the house looked after. Father said we should sleep comfortably and enjoy our food, so I had my bed designed by experts and my meals prepared by a great chef. (A)그는 우리에게 부자처럼 돈을 쓰라고 했어, so I bought what I wanted without worrying about money. But look at me now! I am empty-handed. Did you not follow our father's wisdom? Tell me, brother, how did you get so rich?"

Puneet smiled and said, "My dear brother, I also followed our father's wisdom. But I understood it a bit differently. When he said 'build a house in every city,' I took it as having a place to stay all around the world. So I made friends in every city and I stayed at their houses when I visited those cities. Also, I slept comfortably each night because I would be tired after a hard day's work, and it did not matter if I was sleeping on a bed or on the hard floor. I ate only when I was hungry, so even a simple meal tasted great."

05 What did they do after dinner? Answer in English with a full sentence.

➡ _____

06 How did Puneet take his father's advice of building a house in every city? Answer in English with eleven words including 'making', 'living', 'different.'

➡ _____

_____

07 빈칸에 알맞은 말을 넣어, 아버지의 유언을 형제가 어떻게 해석했는지 정리하시오.

(1) Build a house in every city.

Puru: I _____ _____ _____ in every city.

Puneet: I _____ _____ in every city.

(2) Sleep comfortably.

Puru: I had _____ _____

_____ _____ experts.

Puneet: I slept comfortably because I would be _____ after

_____ _____ _____

_____.

(3) Enjoy your food.

Puru: I had _____ _____ _____ by a great chef.

Puneet: I ate only when _____

_____ _____.

08 주어진 단어를 활용하여 밑줄 친 우리말 (A)를 영어로 쓰시오.

(tell / like / man)

➡ _____

[09~10] 다음 글을 읽고 물음에 답하시오.

Let me (A)_____ my motto.
It is "Go for it!"
It means "Go and do things without fear because failure is also a good experience." I made it my motto when I was a kicker in the school soccer team. From the motto, I learned that even the bad kicks made me a better kicker at the end. It is this motto that changed my life!

09 빈칸 (A)에 introduce를 알맞게 쓰시오.

➡ _____

10 What does "Go for it" mean? Answer in English with a full sentence.

➡ _____

_____

01 다음 질문에 자유롭게 대답하시오.

> Q: What would you do if you were invisible for a day?

> A: _____
> _____

02 다음 문장을 'have+목적어+목적격보어' 유형을 사용하여 비슷한 뜻으로 바꾸어 쓰시오.

> (1) She checked her ears.
> ➡ _____
>
> (2) They asked Jørn Utzon to design the Opera House in Sydney.
> ➡ _____
> ➡ _____
>
> (3) Mom allowed me to play a computer game after dinner.
> ➡ _____
> ➡ _____

03 다음 내용을 바탕으로 제품의 광고 내용에 대해 문의하는 게시 글을 쓰시오.

> Q: What is your motto?
> A: It's "No Pain, No Gain."
> Q: What does it mean?
> A: It means "Without hard work, you can get nothing as a reward."
> Q: When did you make it your motto?
> A: I made it my motto when I was a kicker in the school soccer team.
> Q: What did the motto help you learn?
> A: I learned that even the bad kicks made me a better kicker at the end.

> Let me introduce my motto.
> It is "_____"
> It means "_____" I made it my motto when
> _____. From the motto, I learned that _____
> _____. It is this motto that changed my life!

단원별 모의고사

01 다음 짝지어진 단어의 관계가 <u>다른</u> 하나를 고르시오.

① puzzled – confused
② hire – fire
③ priceless – worthless
④ death – life
⑤ lastly – firstly

02 다음 빈칸에 가장 알맞은 말을 고르시오.

> A: I will have a soccer game tomorrow.
>   I'm so nervous.
> B: _____ yourself. You're a good
>   soccer player.

① Live by
② Explain
③ Look after
④ Believe in
⑤ Worry about

03 다음 빈칸에 공통으로 들어갈 말을 쓰시오.

> • I'm going to _____ the dog for a walk.
> • He's old enough to _____ care of himself.
> • He only wanted to _____ his share.

04 다음 영영풀이에 해당하는 말을 주어진 철자로 시작하여 쓰시오.

> very comfortable and expensive

➡ l_____

[05~06] 다음 대화를 읽고 물음에 답하시오.

> M: Jane, you look ⓐ_____. What's the matter?
> W: I ⓑ_____ a big part in the school musical.
> M: I heard you ⓒ_____. You sound great!
> W: It's just that I keep ⓓ_____ mistakes. I'm so worried.
> M: Oh, you just need a little more practice. <u>실수하는 것에 대해서는 걱정하지 마.</u> You can actually ⓔ_____ from them.
> W: Thanks, Dad. I hope I do a good job.
> M: You'll do great.

05 빈칸 ⓐ~ⓔ에 들어가지 <u>않는</u> 말을 고르시오.

① singing
② worried
③ learn
④ got
⑤ to make

06 밑줄 친 우리말과 일치하도록 주어진 단어를 이용하여 영작하시오.

➡ _____

(about, mistakes, 5 단어)

07 다음 대화의 흐름상 빈칸에 들어갈 말을 주어진 단어를 이용해 문장을 완성하시오.

> A: _____
>   (have, will, if, a magic carpet, 형태변형 가능)
> B: I would never walk, and always fly to wherever I want.

[08~09] 다음 대화를 읽고 물음에 답하시오.

A: I'm worried (A)[that / what / about] I can't finish my online story by the deadline.
B: 그건 걱정하지 마. I can help you.
A: That would be great. My main (B)[character / director / letter] has special powers. What would you do (C)[when / whether / if] you could change (D)[you / yours / yourself] into anyone every day?
B: Well, I would change myself into famous people and live different lives.

08 위 대화의 괄호 (A)~(D)에서 적절한 것을 골라 쓰시오.

➡ (A) _____ (B) _____
　 (C) _____ (D) _____

09 밑줄 친 우리말과 일치하도록 주어진 단어를 이용해 영작하시오.

➡ (1) _____ (it, worry)
　 (2) _____ (it, bother)

[10~13] 다음 대화를 읽고 물음에 답하시오.

M: Sujin, what are you doing this weekend?
W: (①) Nothing special, why?
M: (②) I have to go to Busan for a family trip tomorrow (A)_____ I can't find anyone to feed my dog, Lucy.
W: (③) I'll (B)_____ of her.
M: Oh, thank you so much. (④) I was so worried. (⑤)
W: I'll take her for a walk in the park, too. The weather's (C)_____ to be nice tomorrow.

10 ①~⑤ 중 주어진 문장이 들어갈 곳은?

Don't worry about Lucy.

① 　　② 　　③ 　　④ 　　⑤

11 빈칸 (A)에 들어갈 말을 고르시오.

① but 　　② since 　　③ if
④ because 　　⑤ when

12 위 대화의 흐름상 빈칸 (B)에 들어갈 말을 쓰시오. (2 단어)

➡ _____

13 빈칸 (C)에 들어갈 말을 고르시오.

① worried 　　② explained
③ expressed 　　④ taken
⑤ supposed

14 다음 중 어법상 옳은 문장을 모두 고르시오.

① Why don't we have it brought to our hotel room?
② How about having your pet to clean from head to toe?
③ Why don't you go to see a dentist and have the tooth pulled out?
④ It was a book that Jack bought for his sister.
⑤ It was in the street which I saw Jane this morning.
⑥ It was our father's advice that I followed.
⑦ It was a cat what went to save the princess.

15 다음 문장에서 어법상 <u>어색한</u> 것을 바르게 고쳐 다시 쓰시오.

(1) It was many bugs where were in the bottle.

➡ _____

(2) It was at the concert I saw her.

➡ _____

(3) This morning I had my watch that I had bought last month repair.

➡ _____

_____

(4) I'll help you so that you can have your homework finish before the movie starts.

➡ _____

_____

16 괄호 안의 단어를 이용하여 다음 대화의 빈칸을 완성하시오.

> A: I have to return the book I borrowed from the library but I feel sick.
> B: Don't worry. I'll _____ for sure. (return, have)

17 Which is grammatically WRONG?

① It was not until then that I learned Hangeul.

② The princess had her dress designed by a famous designer.

③ It was at the park which I met Tim last Sunday.

④ It was pasta that I made for Lucy the other day.

⑤ It wouldn't be a good idea to have your dream job fixed now.

[18~21] 다음 글을 읽고 물음에 답하시오.

Puneet welcomed Puru with open arms. That night, when the brothers sat down to chat after dinner, Puru asked the question that had been on his mind for days.

"It was our father's advice that I followed, but I am ①<u>not happy</u>. I built a house in every city. But because I could not always stay there, I hired people and had the house ②<u>looked after</u>. Father said we should ③<u>sleep comfortably</u> and enjoy our food, so I had my bed designed by experts and my meals prepared by a great chef. He told us to spend like a rich man, so I bought (A)_____ I wanted ④<u>with</u> worrying about money. But look at me now! I am ⑤ <u>empty-handed</u>. Did you not follow our father's wisdom? Tell me, brother, how did you get so rich?"

18 다음 중 빈칸 (A)에 들어갈 말과 같은 말이 들어가는 것은?

① I don't believe _____ he made a mistake.

② There is one problem _____ you need to be aware of.

③ The news _____ he was alive made people shocked.

④ Kevin said _____ we had to accept his apology.

⑤ So, did you give him _____ he wanted from you?

19 ①~⑤ 중 글의 흐름상 <u>어색한</u> 것은?

①　　　②　　　③　　　④　　　⑤

20 Write the reason why Puru had his meals prepared by a great chef. Use the phrase 'in order to.'

➡ _____

_____

21 다음 중 위 글을 읽고 답할 수 있는 것은?

① How many people did Puru hire to look after his houses?

② How big were the houses that Puru built?

③ Why did Puru employ experts?

④ When did Puru visit his brother Puneet?

⑤ How did Puneet become so rich?

[22~26] 다음 글을 읽고 물음에 답하시오.

A rich and wise father had two sons, Puru and Puneet. Before ①he passed away, he called his two sons to give them some last words of advice.

"Listen carefully, my dear sons. Live by these words throughout your life, and you will be happy," ②he said.

"Build a house in every city. Sleep comfortably. Enjoy your food. Lastly, spend money like a rich man... ." Before (A)he could explain himself, ③he passed away. After ④ his death, the two sons took their share of the father's wealth and settled in different cities. Five years passed. Puru, who had been following his father's words carefully, had no money left. But his brother was richer than ever. Puru was puzzled about where ⑤he had gone wrong, so he visited Puneet to find out.

22 What does the underlined (A) mean?

① wanting to hear some explanation

② telling what he meant by those words

③ putting his sons in a difficult situation

④ letting the sons explain what the words meant

⑤ making the situation worse than before

23 위 글의 내용에 맞게 빈칸에 알맞은 말을 바르게 짝지은 것은?

A wise and rich man gave his two sons some last words of advice, which would be ⓐ_____ for them to live happy life. However, two sons lived a ⓑ_____ life.

① harmful – similar

② helpful – similar

③ harmful – contrasting

④ helpful – contrasting

⑤ beneficial – various

24 Write the reason why Puru visited Puneet. Use the word 'because.'

➡ _____

_____

25 What did the two brothers do after their father's death? Answer in English.

➡ _____

_____

26 위 글의 밑줄 친 ①~⑤에서 가리키는 대상이 다른 하나는?

①   ②   ③   ④   ⑤

Spend Wisely

🎙 의사소통 기능

- 어떤 것에 만족하거나 불만이 있는지 묻기

  A: How do you like this dress?

  B: The design is cool and interesting.

- 후회하는 일 말하기

  A: What's wrong with your laptop?

  B: It makes too much noise and gets overheated.
  I should have read more reviews.

🎙 언어 형식

- 접속사 as

  As more and more people get on the bandwagon, others are more likely to get on it.

- 수의 일치

  Half of the boys on his soccer team **wear** those shoes.

Words & Expressions

교과서

Key Words

- **aboard**[əbɔ́ːrd] 부 ~에 탑승하고, ~에 타서
- **above**[əbʌ́v] 전 ~ 위에
- **affect**[əfékt] 동 ~에 영향을 주다
- **allowance**[əláuəns] 명 용돈
- **although**[ɔ:lðóu] 접 비록 ~이지만
- **anchor**[ǽŋkər] 명 닻 동 닻을 내리다
- **behavior**[bihéivjər] 명 행동, 행위
- **billion**[bíljən] 명 10억
- **combine**[kəmbáin] 동 결합하다
- **compare**[kəmpέər] 동 비교하다
- **compete**[kəmpíːt] 동 경쟁하다
- **complete**[kəmplíːt] 동 완성하다
- **concept**[kánsept] 명 개념
- **consume**[kənsúːm] 동 소비하다, 소모하다
- **convenient**[kənvíːnjənt] 형 편리한, 간편한
- **deal**[diːl] 명 거래
- **difference**[dífərəns] 명 차이, 차이점
- **disappear**[dìsəpíər] 동 사라지다
- **discount**[dískaunt] 명 할인 동 할인하다
- **effect**[ifékt] 명 효과
- **encourage**[inkə́ːridʒ] 동 부추기다, 조장하다
- **endanger**[indéindʒər] 동 위험에 빠뜨리다
- **even though** 비록 ~이지만
- **fix**[fiks] 동 고정하다
- **furniture**[fə́ːrnitʃər] 명 가구

- **immediately**[imíːdiətli] 부 즉시, 바로
- **influence**[ínfluəns] 동 ~에 영향을 주다
- **lack**[læk] 명 부족, 결핍
- **laptop**[lǽptɑp] 명 휴대용 노트북 컴퓨터
- **last**[læst] 동 오래가다, (기능이) 지속되다
- **match**[mætʃ] 동 어울리다
- **mention**[ménʃən] 동 언급하다, 말하다
- **miss**[mis] 동 놓치다
- **overheated**[ouvərhítid] 형 지나치게 뜨거운, 과열된
- **parade**[pəréid] 명 행렬, 퍼레이드
- **purchase**[pə́ːrtʃəs] 동 구매하다, 구입하다
- **quality**[kwáləti] 명 질, 품질, 특성, 자질
- **quarter**[kwɔ́ːrtər] 명 4분의 1
- **raise**[reiz] 동 기르다, 키우다
- **refund**[rifʌ́nd] 명 환불
- **release**[rilíːs] 동 출시하다, 발매하다
- **replace**[ripléis] 동 바꾸다, 교체하다
- **spending**[spéndiŋ] 명 지출
- **striped**[straipt] 형 줄무늬가 있는
- **suit**[suːt] 동 어울리다
- **tight**[tait] 형 꽉 조이는, 딱 붙는
- **unplanned**[ənplǽnd] 형 미리 계획하지 않은
- **wagon**[wǽgən] 명 사륜 마차, 짐마차
- **waste**[weist] 동 낭비하다, 소모하다

Key Expressions

- **as such** 그러한 결과로
- **at a glance** 한눈에, 즉시
- **a pair of** ~ 한 짝의 ~
- **be likely to** ~할 가능성이 있다, ~하기 쉽다
- **end up –ing** 결국 ~하게 되다
- **for a moment** 잠깐
- **go well with** ~와 잘 어울리다
- **go window shopping** 진열된 상품을 구경하고 다니다
- **in comparison** 비교해 보면
- **in this way** 이런 방식으로

- **just because** 단지 ~라는 이유로
- **keep track of** ~을 기록하다
- **lead to** ~로 이어지다
- **more and more** 점점 더 많은
- **more than half** 반 이상의
- **on display** 진열된, 전시된
- **soon after** 직후
- **spend A on 동사ing** A를 ~하는 데 쓰다
- **the next time 주어+동사** 다음번에 ~할 때에
- **when it comes to** ~에 관해서, ~에 대해 말하자면

Word Power

※ 서로 비슷한 뜻을 가진 어휘

□ **affect** ~에 영향을 주다 – **influence** ~에 영향을 주다

□ **effect** 결과, 효과 – **result** 결과, 성과

□ **lack** 부족, 결핍 – **shortage** 결핍, 부족

□ **purchase** 구매하다, 구입하다 – **buy** 사다

□ **replace** 바꾸다, 교체하다 – **substitute** 대신하다

□ **complete** 완성하다 – **perfect** 완벽하게 하다

□ **immediately** 즉시, 바로 – **at once** 즉시

□ **mention** 언급하다, 말하다 – **refer to** 언급하다

□ **quality** 질, 품질 – **characteristic** 특질, 특징

□ **suit** 어울리다 – **match** 어울리다

※ 서로 반대의 뜻을 가진 어휘

□ **above** ~ 위에 ↔ **under** ~ 아래에

□ **difference** 차이(점) ↔ **similarity** 유사(성)

□ **encourage** 부추기다, 조장하다 ↔ **discourage** 낙담시키다

□ **purchase** 구매하다, 구입하다 ↔ **sell** 팔다

□ **unplanned** 미리 계획하지 않은 ↔ **planned** 미리 계획된

□ **convenient** 편리한, 간편한 ↔ **inconvenient** 불편한, 곤란한

□ **disappear** 사라지다 ↔ **appear** 나타나다

□ **endanger** 위험에 빠뜨리다 ↔ **save** 구하다

□ **tight** 꽉 조이는, 딱 붙는 ↔ **loose** 헐거운, 느슨한

□ **waste** 낭비하다, 소모하다 ↔ **save** 절약하다

※ 접두사 en-: en-+특정 어근: 동사로 만들어 '~하게 하다', '어떤 상태가 되게 하다', '안에'라는 의미를 더함.

□ **en-** + **able** → **enable** 가능케 하다

□ **en-** + **courage** → **encourage** 조장하다, 권유하다

□ **en-** + **hance** → **enhance** 향상시키다, 높이다

□ **en-** + **rich** → **enrich** 풍부하게 하다

□ **en-** + **close** → **enclose** 에워싸다, 둘러싸다

□ **en-** + **force** → **enforce** 집행하다, 강요하다

□ **en-** + **large** → **enlarge** 확대하다, 확장하다

□ **en-** + **danger** → **endanger** 위험에 빠뜨리다

※ 접두사 com-: com-+특정 어근: '함께'라는 의미를 더함.

□ **com-** + **bine** → **combine** 결합하다

□ **com-** + **pare** → **compare** 비교하다

□ **com-** + **pile** → **compile** 편찬하다

□ **com-** + **pound** → **compound** 합성의

□ **com-** + **pany** → **company** 회사, 동료

□ **com-** + **pete** → **compete** 경쟁하다

□ **com-** + **pose** → **compose** 구성하다

□ **com-** + **promise** → **compromise** 타협하다

English Dictionary

□ **affect** ~에 영향을 주다
→ to have an influence on someone or something, or to cause a change in someone or something
어떤 사람이나 사물에 영향을 미치다, 혹은 어떤 사람이나 사물에 변화를 야기하다

□ **combine** 결합하다
→ to join together to make a single thing or group
하나의 물건 혹은 하나의 집단으로 만들기 위해 합치다

□ **concept** 개념
→ a principle or idea
어떤 원리나 생각

□ **consume** 소비하다, 소모하다
→ to use fuel, energy, or time, especially in large amounts or to eat or drink, especially a lot of something
연료, 에너지, 혹은 시간을 특히 많은 양으로 쓰다, 또는 특히 어떤 것을 많이 먹고 마시다

□ **convenient** 편리한, 간편한
→ suitable for your purposes and needs and causing the least difficulty
목적이나 필요에 맞고 어려움을 최소한으로 야기하는

□ **encourage** 부추기다, 조장하다
→ to support an activity or make it more likely
어떤 활동을 지원하거나 더 쉽게 만들다

□ **endanger** 위험에 빠뜨리다
→ to put someone or something at risk or in danger of being harmed, damaged, or destroyed
어떤 사람이나 사물을 해를 입고 망가지고 파괴되는 위험에 처하게 하다

□ **lack** 부족, 결핍
→ a condition of not having any or enough of something, especially something necessary or wanted
특히 필요하거나 원하는 어떤 것이 조금도 없거나 충분하지 않은 상태

□ **suit** 어울리다
→ to be right for a particular person, situation, or occasion
어떤 특정한 사람이나 상황, 또는 경우에 알맞다

□ **tight** 꽉 조이는, 딱 붙는
→ rather small and fit closely to your body
다소 작거나 몸에 밀착되게 맞는

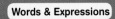
01 접두사 en-을 붙여 동사를 만들 때, en이 '~하게 하다'의 의미를 가지지 <u>않는</u> 단어를 고르시오.

① enlarge   ② enclose   ③ enable
④ enforce   ⑤ enrich

02 다음 밑줄 친 부분과 의미가 가장 가까운 것을 고르시오.

We have to <u>change</u> this carpet soon.

① replace   ② repair   ③ remove
④ impact   ⑤ preserve

03 [서답형] 다음 주어진 단어를 이용하여 우리말에 맞도록 빈칸에 알맞은 말을 쓰시오.

축구에 관해서라면, Mark가 최고의 선수이다.
➡ _____ soccer, Mark is the best player. (when, come)

04 다음 영영풀이에 해당하는 단어로 알맞은 것은?

to use fuel, energy, or time, especially in large amounts or to eat or drink, especially a lot of something

① contain   ② require
③ maintain   ④ assume
⑤ consume

05 다음 짝지어진 단어의 관계가 〈보기〉와 같은 것끼리 짝지어진 것을 고르시오.

┌─── 보기 ├───
│ quality – characteristic │

ⓐ tight – loose
ⓑ endanger – save
ⓒ effect – result
ⓓ replace – substitute
ⓔ encourage – discourage

① ⓐ, ⓑ   ② ⓐ, ⓔ   ③ ⓑ, ⓒ
④ ⓒ, ⓓ   ⑤ ⓓ, ⓔ

06 다음 밑줄 친 부분의 의미로 알맞지 <u>않은</u> 것은?

① His words had a soothing <u>effect</u>. (효과)
② It is difficult to define the <u>concept</u> of beauty. (개념)
③ Your opinion will <u>affect</u> many people. (영향을 주다)
④ I receive an <u>allowance</u> from my parents. (허락)
⑤ The bus was nearly empty as she stepped <u>aboard</u>. (~에 타서)

07 다음 빈칸에 알맞은 단어를 고르시오.

The shirt is beautiful. _____, it is cheap.

① Thus   ② Although
③ Furthermore   ④ Therefore
⑤ Likewise

01 다음 빈칸에 공통으로 들어갈 접두사를 쓰시오.

> • I made the two plans for _____parison.
> • We finally reached a _____promise.
> • Three judges _____pose the committee.

02 다음 주어진 우리말에 맞게 빈칸을 채우시오.

(1) 그 학생들 중 3분의 1이 그들의 지출을 기록한다.
➡ One third of the students record their _____. (one word)

(2) 다음번에 우리가 만날 때, 나는 더 건강해질 것이다.
➡ The _____ we meet, I will be healthier. (two words)

(3) 날씨가 좋지 않았음에도 불구하고 우리는 하이킹을 갔다.
➡ We went hiking _____ the weather was not good. (two words)

(4) 너는 보통 진열된 상품을 구경하고 다니는 것을 좋아하니?
➡ Do you usually like to _____ _____? (three words)

03 다음 빈칸에 공통으로 들어갈 말을 쓰시오.

> • The painting is currently _____ display in New York.
> • Tickets are _____ sale from the booking office.

04 다음 빈칸에 들어갈 전치사를 〈보기〉에서 골라 쓰시오.

> ┤ 보기 ├
> at   for   in   with   as

(1) I think this blouse goes well _____ the skirt you are wearing.
(2) _____ comparison to her problems, mine seems small.
(3) You should hold your breath _____ a moment.
(4) I noticed what had happened _____ a glace.
(5) _____ such, he was a man with persistence.

05 다음 빈칸에 알맞은 말을 〈보기〉에서 골라 쓰시오. (한 단어는 한 번만 사용할 것, 형태 변화 가능.)

> ┤ 보기 ├
> combine   compare   endanger   mention

(1) Did I _____ that I will move to Canada next month?
(2) You should _____ prices before you buy things.
(3) He wants to _____ his job with pleasure.
(4) The fire _____ animals in the forest.

교과서
Conversation

1 어떤 것에 만족하거나 불만이 있는지 묻기

> **A:** Can I try on that cap with stars over there? 저기 별들이 그려진 모자를 써 볼 수 있나요?
>
> **B:** Sure. How do you like it? 그럼요. 어떠세요?
>
> **A:** The design is nice, but I don't think the color suits me. Do you have it in black? 디자인은 좋은데, 색이 제게 안 어울리는 것 같아요. 이거 검은색으로 있나요?

■ 어떤 것에 만족하거나 불만이 있는지 물어보는 표현으로 'How do you like it?(마음에 드니?)'을 쓸 수 있다. 이외에도 'Are you satisfied with ~?(~에 만족하십니까?)', 'How is ~?(~는 어떠십니까?)', 'Are you enjoying ~?(~이 마음에 드십니까?)' 등이 있다.

어떤 것에 만족하거나 불만이 있는지 묻기

- How do you like ~?
- Are you satisfied[happy] with ~?
- How is ~?
- Are you enjoying ~?
- Do you like ~?

■ 'How do you like ~?'는 상대방의 의견 혹은 만족 여부를 물을 때 사용한다. 이미 지난 일에 대한 만족 여부를 물을 때는 'How did you like ~?'를 쓸 수 있다. 'Do you like ~?'는 상대방의 구체적인 의견보다는 단순히 만족 여부에 초점을 둘 때 사용한다.

■ 'How do you like ~?'는 상대방의 만족이나 불만족을 묻는 표현이고, 'What do you like?'은 '무엇을 좋아하니?'라는 의미로 상대방이 좋아하는 것을 묻는 표현이다.

핵심 Check

1. 다음 대화의 빈칸에 들어갈 말로 가장 적절한 것은?

> **A:** Hi, I'm looking for a backpack for hiking.
>
> **B:** These two are popular among hikers. _____
>
> **A:** The green one is lighter than the blue one. I'll take the lighter one.

① How were the backpacks?
② How do you like them?
③ Did you enjoy the backpacks?
④ What do you like?
⑤ What is your favorite?

2 후회하는 일 말하기

A: What's wrong with your laptop? 노트북에 무슨 문제가 있어?

B: It makes too much noises and gets overheated. I should have read more reviews. 소음이 너무 심하고 과열이 돼. 난 후기를 더 많이 읽어 봤어야 했어.

- 'I should have p.p. ~.'는 어떤 일을 했어야 했다고, 또는 하지 말았어야 했다고 후회할 때 사용한다. 예를 들어, 공부를 열심히 하지 않은 것을 후회하며 더 열심히 공부했어야 했다고 말할 때는 'I should have studied harder!'라고 말할 수 있다.

- 과거 사실에 대해 후회나 유감을 나타낼 때 '~했어야 했다'는 의미로 'should have p.p. ~'를 쓴다. 이 때 조동사 should 뒤에는 과거의 일을 의미하므로 동사원형 대신 'have+p.p.'를 써야 한다. 이외에도 'I regret -ing ~.', 'I wish I had p.p. ~.', 'If I could, I would+동사원형 ~.' 등으로 쓸 수 있다.

- 'should have p.p.'는 '~했어야 했는데 (못했다)'라는 후회의 의미이고, 'could have p.p.'는 '~할 뻔 했다'라는 가능성의 의미이고, 'must have p.p.'는 '~이었음이 틀림없다'라는 추측의 의미를 갖는다.

후회하는 일 말하기

- I should have checked the size before buying it.
  = I regret not checking the size before buying it.
  = I wish I had checked the size before buying it.
  = If I could, I would check the size before buying it.

핵심 Check

2. 괄호 안에 주어진 단어를 이용하여 밑줄 친 우리말을 영작하시오.

> **A:** Are you okay? You look tired today.
> **B:** Yeah, I missed the school bus again. <u>내가 더 일찍 일어났어야 했는데.</u> (get up earlier)

➡ _____

Listen & Talk 1 A-2

M: Good morning. Welcome to Kelly's Sporting Goods Store.

W: Hi, I'm ❶looking for a backpack for hiking.

M: These two are ❷popular among hikers. ❸How do you like them?

W: The green one is ❹lighter than the blue one. I'll take the lighter one.

M: Great choice.

M: 안녕하세요. Kelly의 스포츠 용품 가게에 오신 것을 환영합니다.

W: 안녕하세요. 저는 하이킹할 때 쓸 배낭을 찾고 있어요.

M: 이 두 개가 하이킹하시는 분들 사이에서 인기가 있어요. 어떠세요?

W: 초록색 배낭이 파란색 배낭보다 더 가볍네요. 더 가벼운 걸로 할게요.

M: 탁월한 선택입니다.

❶ look for: ~을 찾다
❷ popular: 인기 있는 among: ~ 중에, ~ 사이에
❸ 'How do you like ~?'는 어떤 사물이나 사건 등에 관해 상대방의 만족이나 불만족을 묻고자 할 때 사용한다.
❹ lighter는 light(가벼운)의 비교급이다.

Check(√) True or False

(1) The woman will buy the green backpack.   T ☐ F ☐

(2) The woman wants to buy a backpack for books.   T ☐ F ☐

Listen & Talk 2 A-1

M: Oh, this coat is ❶too uncomfortable.

W: Why? ❷What's wrong with it?

M: It's too ❸tight.

W: Didn't you ❹try it on before buying it?

M: No. It was my size, so I just bought it. I ❺should have tried it on.

M: 오, 이 코트는 너무 불편해.
W: 왜? 무슨 문제가 있니?
M: 너무 꽉 껴.
W: 사기 전에 입어 보지 않았어?
M: 아니. 내 사이즈여서 그냥 사 버렸어. 난 그것을 입어 봤어야 했어.

❶ too: 너무 uncomfortable: 불편한
❷ 'What's wrong with you?'는 '무슨 문제가 있니?'라는 의미로 불만족의 원인이나 걱정을 물을 때 사용하는 표현이다.
❸ tight: 꽉 조이는, 딱 붙는
❹ try on: (옷 등을 시험 삼아) 입어 보다
❺ 'I should have p.p. ~.'는 어떤 일을 했어야 했다고, 했다고 후회할 때 사용한다.

Check(√) True or False

(3) The man tried on the coat before he bought it.   T ☐ F ☐

(4) The coat is comfortable but tight.   T ☐ F ☐

Listen & Talk 2 A-2

W: Hey, Eric. Camilla and I ❶are going to watch a movie. Do you want to join us?

M: I'd love to, but I can't. ❷I've spent all of my ❸allowance for this week.

W: Didn't you just get ❹it a few days ago? How did you spend it all?

M: I'm not sure. I ❺should have kept track of my ❻spending.

W: 안녕, Eric. Camilla랑 나는 영화를 보러 갈 거야. 우리랑 같이 갈래?

M: 그러고 싶지만, 안 돼. 이번 주 용돈을 전부 써 버렸거든.

W: 너 고작 며칠 전에 받지 않았어? 어떻게 다 써 버렸어?

M: 잘 모르겠어. 내 지출을 기록했어야 했어.

❶ be going to 동사원형: ~할 것이다
❷ have spent는 현재완료형으로 여기에서는 '완료' 용법으로 사용하였다.
❸ allowance: 용돈
❹ it은 allowance를 가리킨다.
❺ 과거 사실에 대해 후회나 유감을 나타낼 때 '~했어야 했다'는 의미로 'should have p.p. ~'를 쓴다. '주어 should have p.p. ~'와 같은 의미로 '주어+regret not+동명사 ~.', '주어+wish+주어+had p.p. ~.', 'If+주어+could, 주어+would+동사원형 ~.' 등이 있다. keep track of: ~을 기록하다
❻ spending: 지출

Check(√) True or False

(5) Eric received an allowance a few days ago. T ☐ F ☐

(6) Camilla and Eric are going to watch a movie. T ☐ F ☐

Wrap Up 1

M: Good morning. May I help you?

W: ❶I'd like to buy a T-shirt for my sister. She's eleven years old.

M: ❷How do you like this red one? This character is ❸quite popular among children.

W: Well, she doesn't like animation characters that much. Can I see the blue one?

M: You mean this blue striped T-shirt? Its design is simple and cool.

W: Yes, ❹I think my sister will like it. I'll take it.

M: 안녕하세요. 도와 드릴까요?

W: 저는 여동생에게 티셔츠를 사 주고 싶어요. 그 애는 11살이에요.

M: 이 빨간색 티셔츠는 어떠세요? 이 캐릭터는 아이들 사이에서 꽤 인기가 있어요.

W: 글쎄요, 그 애는 만화 캐릭터를 그다지 좋아하지 않아요. 파란색 티셔츠 좀 볼 수 있을까요?

M: 파란색 줄무늬 티셔츠 말씀이시죠? 그건 디자인이 단순하고 멋있어요.

W: 네, 제 여동생이 좋아할 것 같아요. 그걸로 할게요.

❶ would like to 동사원형: ~하고 싶다(= want to 동사원형)
❷ 'How do you like ~?'는 '~는 어떠니?'라는 뜻으로 어떤 것에 대한 의견을 물을 때 쓰인다. 비슷한 표현인 'Are you satisfied[happy] with ~?'는 직접적으로 만족이나 불만족 여부를 물을 때 쓸 수 있다.
❸ quite는 부사로 '꽤, 상당히'의 의미이다.
❹ think의 목적어는 that my sister will like it이다. 접속사 that은 생략했다

Check(√) True or False

(7) The woman wants to buy a T-shirt with animation characters for her sister. T ☐ F ☐

(8) What the woman will choose is the blue striped T-shirt. T ☐ F ☐

Listen & Talk 1 A-1

M: Hi, can I help you with anything?

W: Yes, can I ❶try on that cap with stars ❷ over there?

M: Sure. ❸How do you like it?

W: The design is nice, but I don't think the color ❹suits me. Do you have it in black?

M: Yes. I'll get one from the back. *(pause)* Here it is.

W: Great. I'll take it.

❶ try on: (옷 등을 시험 삼아) 입어 보다

❷ over there: 저기에, 저쪽에

❸ 'How do you like ～?'는 '～는 어때?'라는 의미로 상대방에게 어떤 것에 대한 만족 또는 불만족을 묻는 표현이다.

❹ suit: 어울리다

Listen & Talk 1 B

W: Hi, Luke. Is that a new speaker?

M: Yes, I ❶bought it a few weeks ago.

W: It looks cool. ❷How do you like it?

M: It's ❸convenient. I can take it anywhere and listen to music. The sound ❹quality is good, too.

W: Great. How long does the battery ❺last?

M: About 2 hours. The battery doesn't last long.

W: That's too bad.

M: Yeah, but I'm ❻pretty happy with it, anyway.

❶ bought는 buy(사다)의 과거형이다.

❷ 'How do you like ～?'는 '너는 ～이 어떠니?'라는 뜻으로 어떤 것에 대한 만족이나 불만족을 묻는 표현이다. 바꿔 쓸 수 있는 표현으로 'Are you satisfied [happy] with ～?', 'How is ～?', 'Are you enjoying ～?', 'Do you like ～?' 등이 있다.

❸ convenient: 편리한, 간편한 ❹ quality: 질, 품질

❺ last: 오래가다, (기능이) 지속되다 ❻ pretty: 아주, 매우

Listen & Talk 2 B

M: Did you get a new phone, Jamie? It's just like mine.

W: Yeah, I got it last weekend ❶on sale.

M: It was on sale? But it ❷has just been ❸ released, hasn't it?

W: Right, but the store on Green Street is

having ❹a year-end sale.

M: Oh, I bought mine ❺at full price!

W: Really? That's too bad. They're selling them at a 40 percent discount.

M: I ❻should have checked the sales before buying mine.

❶ on sale: 할인 중인

❷ 현재완료형인 have+p.p.와 부사 just를 사용하면 '방금 ～하다'로 해석된다. (완료 용법)

❸ release: 출시하다, 발매하다 ❹ a year-end sale: 연말 세일

❺ at full price: 정가에, 제값에

❻ 'should have p.p. ～'는 '～했어야 했는데 (사실은 하지 않았다)'의 뜻으로 과거 사실에 대한 유감을 나타내는 표현이다. '주어+regret not+동명사 ～.', '주어+wish+주어+had p.p ～.', 'If+주어+could, 주어+would+동사원형 ～.' 등으로 바꿔 쓸 수 있다.

Communication Step A

M: Hi, Riley. ❶I heard that you bought a laptop online. ❷How do you like it?

W: Oh, ❸I'm not happy with it.

M: Why? What's wrong?

W: It makes too much noise and ❹gets overheated. ❺I should have read more reviews.

M: Oh, then you should ❻ask for your money back.

W: The online store won't ❼give me back my money because I've used it for a week.

M: ❽How about calling the online shop and explaining your problem?

W: Yeah, I think I should ❾do that.

❶ 어떤 내용을 들어서 알고 있음을 표현할 때 'I heard that+주어+동사'의 형태로 말할 수 있다.

❷ 'How do you like ～?'는 어떤 물건이나 사건 등에 관해 상대방의 만족이나 불만족을 묻고자 할 때 사용한다.

❸ 어떤 것에 대해 만족이나 불평을 표현할 때 '나는 ～이 만족스럽다/그다지 만족스럽지 않다'라는 의미의 'I'm (not) really[so] happy[satisfied] with ～.'로 말할 수 있다. 만족스럽지 않은 경우에 'I want to complain about ～.'으로도 바꿔 말할 수 있다.

❹ makes와 gets는 문장의 동사로, 접속사 and로 연결되어 있다. get 다음에 형용사가 오면, '(～의 상태가) 되다, (～하기에) 이르다'의 의미이다.

❺ 'I should have p.p. ～.'는 어떤 일을 했어야 했다고 후회할 때 사용한다.

❻ ask for: 요청하다 ❼ give back: 돌려주다

❽ 'How about ～?'은 '～하는 게 어때?'라는 뜻으로 상대방에게 권유할 때 사용하는 표현이고, about은 전치사이기 때문에 뒤에 명사나 동명사가 올 수 있다. explaining은 calling과 접속사 and로 연결되어 있다.

❾ do that은 'call the online shop and explain my problem'을 의미한다.

● 다음 우리말과 일치하도록 빈칸에 알맞은 말을 쓰시오.

Listen & Talk 1 A

1. M: Hi, can I _____ you with anything?

   W: Yes, can I _____ _____ that cap with stars over there?

   M: Sure. _____ _____ _____ _____ it?

   W: The design is nice, _____ I don't think the color _____ me. Do you _____ it in black?

   M: Yes. I'll get _____ from the back. *(pause)* Here it is.

   W: Great. I'll take it.

2. M: Good morning. Welcome _____ Kelly's Sporting Goods Store.

   W: Hi, _____ _____ _____ a backpack for hiking.

   M: These two are _____ _____ hikers. _____ _____ _____ _____ them?

   W: The _____ _____ _____ _____ _____ the blue _____. I'll take the lighter one.

   M: Great choice.

Listen & Talk 1 B

W: Hi, Luke. Is that a new speaker?

M: Yes, I _____ it a few weeks _____.

W: It _____ cool. _____ _____ _____ _____ it?

M: It's _____. I can take it _____ and listen to music. The sound _____ is good, too.

W: Great. _____ _____ does the battery _____?

M: About 2 hours. The battery _____ _____ long.

W: That's _____ _____.

M: Yeah, but I'm _____ _____ with it, anyway.

해석

1. M: 안녕하세요, 무엇을 도와 드릴까요?
   W: 네, 저기 별들이 그려진 모자를 써 볼 수 있나요?
   M: 그럼요. 어떠세요?
   W: 디자인은 좋은데, 색이 제게 안 어울리는 것 같아요. 이거 검은색으로 있나요?
   M: 네. 제가 안쪽에서 가져다 드릴게요. (잠시 후) 여기 있어요.
   W: 좋아요. 그걸로 할게요.

2. M: 안녕하세요. Kelly의 스포츠 용품 가게에 오신 것을 환영합니다.
   W: 안녕하세요, 저는 하이킹할 때 쓸 배낭을 찾고 있어요.
   M: 이 두 개가 하이킹하시는 분들 사이에서 인기가 있어요, 어떠세요?
   W: 초록색 배낭이 파란색 배낭보다 더 가볍네요. 더 가벼운 걸로 할게요.
   M: 탁월한 선택입니다.

W: 안녕, Luke. 그거 새 스피커니?
M: 응, 몇 주 전에 샀어.
W: 멋져 보인다. 그거 어때?
M: 편리해. 나는 그것을 어디든지 가져가서 음악을 들을 수 있어. 음질도 좋아.
W: 좋다. 배터리가 얼마나 오래가니?
M: 2시간 정도야. 배터리가 그렇게 오래 가지 않아.
W: 그거 안타깝구나.
M: 응, 하지만 어쨌든 나는 꽤 만족해.

Listen & Talk 2 A

1. **M:** Oh, this coat is _____ _____.

   W: Why? _____ _____ _____ _____?

   M: It's too _____.

   W: Didn't _____ _____ _____ _____ _____ _____
   it?

   M: No. It was my size, _____ I just bought it. I _____ _____
   _____ it _____.

2. **W:** Hey, Eric. Camilla and I _____ _____ _____ _____ a
   movie. Do you want to join us?

   M: I'd love to, but I can't. _____ _____ all of my _____ for
   this week.

   W: Didn't you just _____ _____ a few days ago? How did you
   spend it all?

   M: I'm not sure. I _____ _____ _____ _____ _____
   _____ _____.

1. **M:** 오, 이 코트는 너무 불편해.
   W: 왜? 무슨 문제가 있니?
   M: 너무 꽉 껴.
   W: 사기 전에 입어 보지 않았어?
   M: 아니. 내 사이즈여서 그냥 사 버렸어. 난 그것을 입어 봤어야 했어.

2. **W:** 안녕, Eric. Camilla랑 나는 영화를 보러 갈 거야. 우리랑 같이 갈래?
   M: 그러고 싶지만, 안 돼. 이번 주 용돈을 전부 써 버렸거든.
   W: 너 고작 며칠 전에 받지 않았어? 어떻게 다 써 버렸어?
   M: 잘 모르겠어. 내 지출을 기록했어야 했어.

Listen & Talk 2 B

M: Did you get a new phone, Jamie? It's just like mine.

W: Yeah, I got it last weekend _____ _____.

M: It was _____ _____? But it _____ _____ _____
_____, hasn't it?

W: Right, but the store on Green Street _____ _____ a year-end
sale.

M: Oh, I bought mine _____ _____ _____!

W: Really? That's too bad. They're selling them _____ a 40 percent
_____.

M: I _____ _____ _____ _____ _____ _____ buying
mine.

M: 새 전화기를 샀니, Jamie? 내 것과 똑같다.
W: 응, 나는 이것을 지난주 할인할 때 샀어.
M: 그거 할인 중이었어? 하지만 그것은 막 출시되었잖아, 그렇지 않아?
W: 맞아, 하지만 Green가에 있는 가게에서 연말 할인 판매를 하더라.
M: 오, 나는 내 것을 정가를 주고 샀는데!
W: 정말? 그것 참 안됐다. 40퍼센트 할인하여 팔고 있어.
M: 내 것을 사기 전에 할인 판매를 확인했어야 했어.

Communication Step A

M: Hi, Riley. I _____ _____ _____ _____ a laptop online. How do you like it?

W: Oh, I'm _____ _____ with _____.

M: _____? _____ wrong?

W: It makes too much noise and _____ _____. I should _____ _____ more reviews.

M: Oh, then you should ask _____ your money back.

W: The online store _____ _____ _____ _____ my money because _____ _____ it for a week.

M: How about _____ the online shop and _____ your problem?

W: Yeah, I think I should _____ that.

Wrap Up

1. M: Good morning. May I help you?

   W: _____ _____ _____ buy a T-shirt for my sister. She's eleven years old.

   M: _____ _____ _____ _____ _____ _____ _____? This character is quite popular among children.

   W: Well, she doesn't like animation characters _____ much. Can I see the blue _____?

   M: You mean this blue _____ T-shirt? _____ design is simple and cool.

   W: Yes, I think my sister will like it. I'll _____ it.

2. W: Jake, here's a package for you.

   M: It's my helmet. I bought it at an _____ _____ _____ a few days ago.

   W: Oh, open it and _____ _____ _____ it.

   M: Okay. *(pause)* Oh, this outer part _____ _____ _____ _____. The seller _____ _____ it's perfectly fine though.

   W: Didn't you check the pictures of the helmet _____ you bought it?

   M: No, _____ _____ _____ the seller. I _____ _____ _____ _____ _____.

   W: You _____ _____ the seller and _____ _____ _____ _____.

해석

M: 안녕, Riley. 네가 온라인으로 노트북을 샀다고 들었어. 그거 어때?
W: 아, 나는 별로 마음에 들지 않아.
M: 왜? 무슨 문제가 있어?
W: 소음이 너무 심하고 과열이 돼. 난 후기를 더 많이 읽어 봤어야 했어.
M: 오, 그럼 환불을 요청해 봐.
W: 내가 그것을 일주일 동안 사용했기 때문에 온라인 가게는 환불을 해 주지 않을 거야.
M: 온라인 가게에 전화해서 문제를 설명하는 건 어때?
W: 응, 그렇게 해야 할 것 같아.

1. M: 안녕하세요. 도와 드릴까요?
   W: 저는 여동생에게 티셔츠를 사 주고 싶어요. 그 애는 11살이에요.
   M: 이 빨간색 티셔츠는 어떠세요? 이 캐릭터는 아이들 사이에서 꽤 인기가 있어요.
   W: 글쎄요, 그 애는 만화 캐릭터를 그다지 좋아하지 않아요. 파란색 티셔츠 좀 볼 수 있을까요?
   M: 파란색 줄무늬 티셔츠 말씀이시죠? 그건 디자인이 단순하고 멋있어요.
   W: 네, 제 여동생이 좋아할 것 같아요. 그걸로 할게요.

2. W: Jake, 여기 네 소포가 있어.
   M: 그거 내 헬멧이야. 며칠 전에 온라인 중고 가게에서 샀어.
   W: 오, 열어서 보여 줘.
   M: 그래. (잠시 후) 아, 이 바깥 부분이 조금 깨졌어. 하지만 판매자는 이것이 완벽하게 괜찮다고 말했어.
   W: 사기 전에 헬멧 사진을 확인해 보지 않았니?
   M: 아니, 나는 그냥 판매자를 믿었어. 조금 더 확인을 했어야 했어.
   W: 너는 판매자에게 전화해서 환불을 요청해야 해.

01 다음 대화의 빈칸에 알맞은 것을 고르시오.

> M: Hi, can I help you with anything?
> W: Yes, can I try on that cap with stars over there?
> M: Sure. _____
> W: The design is nice, but I don't think the color suits me. Do you have it in black?
> M: Yes. I'll get one from the back. *(pause)* Here it is.
> W: Great. I'll take it.

① What do you think of this black hat?

② How do you like it?

③ What do you like?

④ Which cap do you like better, the one with stars or black one?

⑤ Please tell me where to buy it.

[02~03] 다음 대화를 읽고 물음에 답하시오.

> M: _____
> W: _____
> M: _____
> W: _____
> M: No. It was my size, so I just bought it. I ⓐ _____.

02 위 대화의 빈칸에 들어갈 말을 〈보기〉에서 골라 순서대로 바르게 배열한 것은?

┤ 보기 ├

(A) Didn't you try it on before buying it?
(B) It's too tight.
(C) Oh, this coat is too uncomfortable.
(D) Why? What's wrong with it?

① (B) – (A) – (C) – (D) ② (B) – (C) – (A) – (D)

③ (C) – (A) – (B) – (D) ④ (C) – (B) – (A) – (D)

⑤ (C) – (D) – (B) – (A)

03 위 대화의 빈칸 ⓐ에 알맞은 것을 고르시오.

① should have tried it on ② should not have tried it on

③ cannot have tried it on ④ must have tried it on

⑤ may have tried it on

중요
01 다음 대화의 빈칸에 들어갈 알맞은 것을 <u>모두</u> 고르면?

A: _____
B: I love them. They are very comfortable.

① What do you like in your new pants?
② How do you like your new pants?
③ Are you concerned about your new pants?
④ Are you enjoying your new pants?
⑤ Are you satisfied with your new pants?

[02~03] 다음 대화를 읽고 물음에 답하시오.

M: Oh, this coat is too uncomfortable.
W: Why? (A)_____
M: It's too tight.
W: (B)_____
M: No. It was my size, so I just bought it. 난 그것을 입어 봤어야 했어.

서답형
02 위 대화의 빈칸 (A)와 (B)에 들어갈 말을 〈보기〉에서 골라 기호를 쓰시오.

┌─── 보기 ───┐
ⓐ What do you think of this coat?
ⓑ Didn't you try it on before buying it?
ⓒ How about trying it on?
ⓓ Can I help you with anything?
ⓔ What's wrong with it?
ⓕ Can I see the loose one?
└────────┘

➡ (A) _____ (B) _____

서답형
03 밑줄 친 우리말에 맞게 주어진 단어를 알맞게 배열하시오.

➡ _____ (it, have, on, should, tried, I)

04 다음 빈칸에 가장 알맞은 말을 고르시오.

A: I heard that you bought some iced tea online. How do you like it?
B: Oh, I'm not happy with it.
A: Why? What's wrong?
B: There is too much sugar in it.
_____

① I should not have read more reviews.
② I should bring more food with less sugar.
③ I should have checked the nutrition facts first.
④ I should buy it at online used store a few days ago.
⑤ I should have kept track of my spending.

중요
05 다음 중 짝지어진 대화가 <u>어색한</u> 것은?

① A: I bought a new cell phone last week.
   B: How do you like it?
   A: I like it a lot. It's very light.
② A: Are you happy with your new books?
   B: Yes, I am. They are interesting.
③ A: How did you like it?
   B: I liked it a lot. It was delicious.
④ A: How do you like the weather there?
   B: I love it. It's sunny and warm.
⑤ A: I watched a new movie last Sunday.
   B: It looks really interesting. How did you like it?
   A: No, I'm not. It's boring.

[06~07] 다음 대화를 읽고 물음에 답하시오.

M: Did you get a new phone, Jamie? It's just like mine. (①)

W: Yeah, I got it last weekend on sale.

M: It was on sale? (②) But it (A)_____, hasn't it?

W: Right, but the store on Green Street is having a year-end sale. (③)

M: Oh, I bought mine at full price!

W: Really? (④) They're selling them at a 40 percent discount.

M: I (B)_____ the sales before buying mine. (⑤)

06 위 대화의 ①~⑤ 중 주어진 문장이 들어갈 곳은?

| That's too bad. |

①   ②   ③   ④   ⑤

07 다음 빈칸 (A)와 (B)에 들어갈 말로 알맞게 짝지어진 것은?

        (A)   (B)

① has just released – should check

② has just released – should not have checked

③ has just been released – should check

④ has just been released – should have checked

⑤ has just been released – should not have checked

[08~09] 다음 대화를 읽고 물음에 답하시오.

W: Hi, Luke. Is that a new speaker?

M: Yes, I bought it a few weeks ago.

W: It looks cool. (A)_____

M: It's convenient. I can take it anywhere and listen to music. The sound quality is good, too.

W: Great. How long does the battery last?

M: About 2 hours. The battery doesn't last long.

W: That's too bad.

M: Yeah, but I'm pretty happy with it, anyway.

08 위 대화의 빈칸 (A)에 알맞은 말을 고르시오.

① When did you buy it?

② How long can you use it?

③ How do you like it?

④ What's wrong with it?

⑤ How do you get it?

 위 대화를 읽고 답할 수 <u>없는</u> 질문을 고르시오.

① How is the sound quality of the new speaker?

② What will Luke use the new speaker for?

③ When did Luke buy the new speaker?

④ Are Luke satisfied with the new speaker?

⑤ How long does the battery last?

01 그림을 보고, should have와 주어진 단어를 이용해 빈칸을 채우시오.

Alison

A: What's the problem?

B: Alison _____.
(warm, wear, jacket)

[02~04] 다음 대화를 읽고 물음에 답하시오.

M: Hi, Riley. I heard that you bought a laptop online. (A)_____

W: Oh, I'm not happy with it.

M: Why? What's wrong?

W: It makes too much noise and gets overheated. (a)난 후기를 더 많이 읽어 봤어야 했어.

M: Oh, then you should ask for your money back.

W: The online store won't give me back my money because I've used it for a week.

M: How about calling the online shop and (B)_____(explain) your problem?

W: Yeah, I think I should do that.

02 대화의 흐름상 빈칸 (A)에 들어갈 말을 주어진 단어를 이용해 문장을 완성하시오.

➡ _____ (like, it)

03 빈칸 (B)에 괄호 안의 단어를 문맥에 맞게 고쳐 채우시오.

➡ _____

04 밑줄 친 우리말 (a)를 주어진 단어를 이용해 영작하시오.

➡ _____
(reviews, read, more)

[05~06] 다음 대화를 읽고 물음에 답하시오.

M: Did you get a new phone, Jamie? It's just like mine.

W: Yeah, I got it last weekend (A)_____ sale.

M: It was (A)_____ sale? But it has just been released, hasn't it?

W: Right, but the store on Green Street is having a year-end sale.

M: Oh, I bought mine (B)_____ full price!

W: Really? That's too bad. They're selling them at a 40 percent discount.

M: (C)_____ (buying, sales, checked, mine, before, should, I, have, the)

05 빈칸 (A)와 (B)에 알맞은 전치사를 쓰시오.

➡ (A) _____ (B) _____

06 빈칸 (C)를 괄호 안에 주어진 단어를 알맞게 배열하여 채우시오.

➡ _____
_____

Grammar

1 접속사 as

> • **As** more and more people get on the bandwagon, others are more likely to get on it. 더 많은 사람들이 밴드왜건에 올라탈수록 다른 사람들이 더욱 그것에 올라타려고 한다.

- 접속사 as는 보통 'as+주어+동사 ~, 주어+동사 ….'의 형태로 사용하며, 종속절을 문장의 주절에 연결하는 종속접속사로서 부사절을 이끈다.
  - **As** I entered the room, they applauded. 내가 방안에 들어서자 그들은 박수를 쳤다.
- 접속사 **as**의 역할
  (1) 비례, 추이: ~함에 따라서, ~에 비례하여
  - **As** it grew darker, it became colder. 어두워짐에 따라 더욱 추워졌다.
  (2) 시간: ~할 때, ~하는 동안, ~하면서
  - He came up **as** she was speaking. 그녀가 이야기하고 있을 때 그가 왔다.
  (3) 이유: ~해서, ~이므로, ~ 때문에
  - **As** I am ill, I will not go. 몸이 아파서 나는 안 가겠다.
  (4) 방식(양태): ~하듯이, ~하는 것처럼, ~ 같이, ~하는 대로, ~와 마찬가지로
  - **As** food nourishes our body, so books nourish our mind. 음식이 몸의 영양이 되는 것처럼 책은 마음의 영양이 된다.
  (5) 비교: ~와 같이, ~와 같은 정도로, ~만큼
  - She can walk as quickly **as** I can. 그녀는 나만큼 빨리 걸을 수 있다.
  (6) 양보: 비록 ~할지라도, ~이지만, ~이긴 하나
  - Rich **as** she is, she is not happy. 그녀는 부자이긴 하지만 행복하지는 않다.
- 전치사 **as**: ~ 같이, ~로서(자격)
  전치사 as 뒤에는 명사나 명사구가 오지만 접속사 as 뒤에는 '주어+동사'가 오는 것에 유의한다.
  - It can be used **as** a knife. (전치사) 그건 나이프 대용으로 쓸 수가 있다.
  - We didn't go, **as** it rained hard. (접속사) 비가 몹시 쏟아져서 우리는 가지 않았다.

핵심 Check

1. 다음 빈칸에 공통으로 들어갈 알맞은 단어를 고르시오. (대 · 소문자 구분 안 함)

> • _____ she grew older, she became weaker.
> • Do _____ I tell you.

① that   ② what   ③ since   ④ as   ⑤ for

② 수의 일치

> • **Half of the boys** on his soccer team **wear** those shoes. 그의 축구팀에 있는 소년들의 반이 그 축구화를 신는다.

■ '부분을 나타내는 명사+of' 다음에 명사가 올 때 동사의 수를 명사의 수에 일치시킨다.
 ※ 부분을 나타내는 말+단수 명사: 단수 동사
  부분을 나타내는 말+복수 명사: 복수 동사
 • **Some of the music was** weird. 그 음악의 일부는 기묘했다.
 • **Some of the studies show** positive results. 그 연구들 중 일부는 긍정적인 결과를 보여준다.

■ 부분을 나타내는 명사에는 most, all, some, half, percent, rest, part, 분수(one-third, two-thirds) 등이 있다.
 • **Most of the rooms face** the sea. 그 방들의 대부분은 바다를 향하고 있다.

 cf. 1. many of/(a) few of/a number of+복수 명사+복수 동사
   much of/(a) little of/+단수 명사, the number of+단수(복수) 명사+단수 동사

 • **Many of the pictures show** violence. 많은 장면들이 폭력을 보여줍니다.
 • **Much of the region is** lowland. 그 지역은 많은 부분이 저지대이다.

 cf. 2. one of+복수 명사+단수 동사

 • **One** of the screws **is** loose. 그 나사들 중 하나가 헐겁다.

 cf. 3. none of+단수 명사+단수 동사
   none of+복수 명사+단수 동사[복수 동사]

 • **None** of these computers **works[work]**. 이 컴퓨터들이 하나도 작동이 안 된다.

 cf. 4. every, each, -thing, -one, -body, 시간, 거리, 금액, 무게, 학문 이름+단수 명사+단수 동사

 • **Every** move **was** painful. 몸을 움직일 때마다 아팠다.

 ※ 시제의 일치
  주어와 종속절의 시제를 일치시켜야 한다.
  주절의 동사가 현재시제인 경우 종속절에는 모든 시제를 쓸 수 있지만, 주절의 동사가 과거시제인 경우 종속절의 시제는 과거나 과거완료가 온다.
  주절의 시제가 과거일지라도 종속절이 불변의 진리, 격언, 현재의 습관, 과학적 사실 등을 나타내면 현재시제를 쓴다.
 • She **said** that knowledge **is** power.(진리) 그녀는 지식은 힘이라고 말했다.

핵심 Check

2. 괄호 안에 주어진 어휘를 빈칸에 현재형으로 알맞게 쓰시오.
   (1) The rest of the paper _____ on the table. (be)
   (2) Quite a few of the members _____ present. (be)
   (3) More than one third of wage earners _____ concerned about reduced wages. (be)

01 다음 각 문장의 빈칸에 as를 넣을 때 어색한 것은?

① Leave the papers _____ they are.
② My mother was crying _____ I waved her goodbye.
③ _____ he aged, his memory got worse.
④ The trouble is _____ we are short of money.
⑤ Her voice lowered _____ she spoke.

02 다음 빈칸에 알맞은 것을 고르시오.

Half of the money _____ mine.

① being   ② to be   ③ was
④ were   ⑤ are

03 다음 문장의 빈칸에 가장 알맞은 말은?

_____ he grows older, Ted gets more popular.

① As   ② Because   ③ What
④ Whether   ⑤ That

04 다음 빈칸에 들어갈 수 있는 말이 다른 하나는?

① The orchestra was tuning up _____ we entered the hall.
② _____ she gave no sign, I was sure she had seen me.
③ The new rules could mean the end of football _____ we know it.
④ _____ we get older, our bodies become less efficient at burning up calories.
⑤ I like him _____ he is honest.

05 다음 우리말을 괄호 안에 주어진 어휘를 이용하여 영작하시오.

시간이 지날수록 나는 너를 사랑한다. (as, go by, 7 단어)

➡ _____

01 다음 밑줄 친 as 중 나머지 넷과 쓰임이 다른 하나는?

① As the prices of the tickets increase, people are less likely to go to concerts.
② As I was tired, I fell asleep early.
③ You don't need to be unconfident, as you are perfect the way you are.
④ We are, as you know, a leading company in the industry of benchmarking.
⑤ He is widely acknowledged as the best player in the world.

02 다음 밑줄 친 as 중 나머지 넷과 그 뜻이 다른 하나는?

① As you grow older, you will become wiser.
② The game was called off as it rained cats and dogs.
③ As she practiced the piano, she enjoyed it more and more.
④ As the movie progresses, the tension builds.
⑤ As she got older, offers of modelling work began to dry up.

03 다음 두 문장을 한 문장으로 바꾸어 쓸 때 알맞게 표현한 것을 고르시오.

> • The graph shows.
> • People are spending more and more money on food.

① Although the graph shows, people are spending more and more money on food.
② If the graph shows, people are spending more and more money on food.
③ As the graph shows, people are spending more and more money on food.
④ Since the graph shows, people are spending more and more money on food.
⑤ After the graph shows, people are spending more and more money on food.

04 다음 빈칸에 공통으로 들어갈 알맞은 말을 고르시오.

> (1) All of my songs _____ written by myself.
> (2) A quarter of all the people surveyed _____ don't-knows.
> (3) Only half of the rooms _____ occupied at that time.

① to be　　② being　　③ be
④ was　　⑤ were

05 다음 중 어법상 어색한 것은?

① Most of the students listen to music while studying.
② Some of the pie is missing.
③ Thirty percent of the country is plains.
④ About one third of all the students in our school wears glasses.
⑤ One of the most important things in a partner is a sense of humor.

06 [서답형] 다음 문장에서 어법상 어색한 단어 한 개를 찾아서 고치시오.

> One fourth of the students likes to go on a picnic, but the others don't.

➡ _____

07 [중요] 다음 빈칸에 공통으로 들어갈 알맞은 말을 고르시오. (대·소문자 무시)

> (1) _____ you spend more time giving thanks, you will be happier.
> (2) More people want to buy them _____ the price of apples falls.
> (3) They were all dressed _____ clowns.

① because ② as ③ while
④ when ⑤ what

[08~09] 다음 우리말을 어법상 알맞게 영작한 것을 고르시오.

08

> 햄버거를 더 많이 먹음에 따라, 우리는 더 많은 소를 키워야 한다.

① As we eat more hamburgers, we need to raise more cows.
② Because we eat more hamburgers, we need to raise more cows.
③ Even though we eat more hamburgers, we need to raise more cows.
④ Since we eat more hamburgers, we need to raise more cows.
⑤ If we eat more hamburgers, we need to raise many cows.

09

> 그 문제를 축소하기 위해 많은 조치가 취해졌다.

① The number of measures was taken to reduce the problem.
② The number of measures were taken to reduce the problem.
③ A number of measures was taken to reduce the problem.
④ A number of measures were taken to reduce the problem.
⑤ A great deal of measures were taken to reduce the problem.

10 [중요] 다음 밑줄 친 as가 어법상 문장 속에서 바르게 쓰인 것을 고르시오.

① <u>As</u> every product sells well, being tested before being sold.
② Do you think <u>as</u> these latest changes will do any good?
③ Ann got a lot of experience <u>as</u> she traveled a lot.
④ Now she's caught up in a love triangle and doesn't know <u>as</u> to do.
⑤ In addition, <u>as</u> they were unable to mobilize the resources they needed.

11 다음 빈칸에 들어갈 말이 나머지와 <u>다른</u> 하나는?

① Half of the money _____ mine.
② Seventy percent of the participants _____ Asian.
③ Some of the teachers _____ criticized for poor performance.
④ The old part of the cities _____ destroyed during the war.
⑤ Most of the houses _____ built of stone.

12 다음 주어진 문장의 밑줄 친 as와 가장 가까운 뜻의 as가 쓰인 것을 고르시오.

> As more and more people get on the bandwagon, others are more likely to get on or follow it.

① Famous as she is, she is still quite modest.

② As it was raining heavily, we couldn't go out.

③ As she was advised, she practiced speaking constantly.

④ The audience fell silent as the curtain rose.

⑤ Picasso became more and more famous as he painted with more freedom.

13 다음 두 문장을 한 문장으로 연결할 때 가장 적절한 것은?

> • Nick tried many Korean dishes while he was in Seoul.
> • Nick tried *samgyupsal*.

① Nick tried many Korean dishes while he was in Seoul *samgyupsal* was one of the dishes.

② Nick tried *samgyupsal* that he tried Korean dishes while he was in Seoul.

③ Nick tried many Korean dishes while he was in Seoul that *samgyupsal* was.

④ One of the Korean dishes Nick tried in Seoul was *samgyupsal*.

⑤ One of the dishes which Nick tried were *samgyupsal*.

14 다음 중 밑줄 친 as의 쓰임이 적절하지 않은 것을 고르시오.

① As you exercise harder, your heart rate will increase.

② A monkey is a monkey as he wears a gold ring.

③ As time went by, we became more confident and happy to meet them.

④ You'll experience more things as you grow up.

⑤ As you read more, you will be able to read faster.

 15 다음 우리말을 바르게 영작한 것을 고르시오.

> 그녀는 그녀의 남편이 매일 아침 커피 한 잔을 마신다고 말했다.

① She said that her husband drinks a cup of coffee every morning.

② She says that her husband drinks a cup of coffee every morning.

③ She said that her husband has drunk a cup of coffee every morning.

④ She said that her husband had drunk a cup of coffee every morning.

⑤ She says that her husband drank a cup of coffee every morning.

서답형
16 우리말과 일치하도록 괄호 안에 주어진 어휘를 바르게 배열하시오.

> 비록 이상해 보일지 모르지만, 그것들은 실제 사람들이 일상생활에서 마주하고 있는 공포다.
> → (it, as, seem, strange, may), they are actually real fears that people confront every day.

➡ _____

01 다음 우리말과 일치하도록 괄호 안에 주어진 어구를 바르게 배열하여 영작하시오.

(1) 로마에 가면 로마인 방식대로 해라. (Rome, the Romans, you, are, do, do, as, when, in)

➡ _____

(2) 그 노래가 더 유명해질수록, 그는 더 많은 사람들에게 알려졌다. (he, people, the song, known, was, became, popular, more, more, as, to)

➡ _____
_____

(3) 그 물의 절반 가량이 미국에서 동물을 키우기 위해 사용된다. (half, animals, the water, about, is, raise, used, the U.S., to, in, of)

➡ _____
_____

(4) 전체 인구의 약 14퍼센트는 교육의 부족으로 읽는 법을 알지 못한다. (all people, 14 percent, education, lack, know, don't, read, due, how, about, to, to, of, of)

➡ _____
_____

(3) Each blind student were paired with a sighted student.

➡ _____
_____

(4) Jeff buys soccer shoes because more than half of the boys on his team wears them.

➡ _____
_____

(5) Most of the allowance are spent on clothes and one fourth of the allowance are spent on snacks.

➡ _____
_____

02 다음 문장에서 어법상 <u>어색한</u> 것을 바르게 고쳐 다시 쓰시오.

(1) I caught him just though he was leaving the building.

➡ _____

(2) As brave he was, he could not help weeping at the sight.

➡ _____
_____

03 다음 문장을 as를 이용하여 같은 뜻의 문장으로 바꿔 쓰시오.

(1) The more love you give, the more love you will receive.

➡ _____
_____

(2) The harder you exercise, the healthier you become.

➡ _____
_____

04 그림을 보고, 주어진 어휘를 이용하여 빈칸을 알맞게 채우시오.

Only one of them at the party _____ on the sofa. (sit)

05 그림을 보고, 주어진 어휘를 이용하여 빈칸을 알맞게 채우시오.

_____ at night, you will get fatter. (eat more)

06 괄호 안에 주어진 동사를 어법에 맞게 빈칸에 쓰시오.

(1) Most of the boys _____ to eat hamburgers. (like)

(2) All of the stars seen in the sky _____ part of our Milky Way Galaxy. (be)

(3) None of the audience really _____ me. (know)

(4) The teacher told us that the Moon _____ around the earth once in 30 days. (go)

(5) The number of students _____ day by day. (decrease)

(6) I knew that World War II _____ in 1945. (end)

07 주어진 두 문장을 〈보기〉처럼 하나의 문장으로 쓰시오.

┤ 보기 ├

• Julie gave Edan some money.
• Edan bought a new backpack with only half of the money.
→ Only half of the money that Julie gave to Edan was used to buy a new backpack by him.

(1) • Sophie wrote many books.
   • Steve read about two thirds of them.
   ➡ _____
   _____

(2) • Mom made the food.
   • Mike threw away some of the food.
   ➡ _____
   _____

(3) • Dominic has a few hobbies.
   • Basketball is his hobby.
   ➡ _____

Why We Buy What We Buy

Have you ever wondered why you've bought things that you don't
간접의문문(의문사+주어+동사)　　　목적격 관계대명사
even want or need? Let's consider what affects us when it comes to
간접의문문(의문사(주어)+동사+목적어)
buying things.
동명사(to의 목적어)

Why do I want to buy what my friends bought?

Jeff goes to the shopping center and sees a pair of soccer shoes on
display. He recognizes the shoes at a glance because more than half of
이유를 이끄는 접속사(~ 때문에)
the boys on his soccer team wear them. Although he already has many
half of+명사: 명사에 수의 일치 (the boys에 수의 일치를 하여 복수동사 wear)　양보의 부사절을 이끄는 접속사
pairs of soccer shoes, he ends up buying another new pair.

We can use the "bandwagon effect" to explain Jeff's behavior. A
to부정사의 부사적 용법 중 목적(~하기 위해서)
bandwagon is a wagon in a parade that encourages people to jump
encourage+목적어+to부정사
aboard and enjoy the music. As more and more people get on the
접속사(~함에 따라)
bandwagon, others are more likely to get on or follow it. In this way,
people tend to buy something just because other people have bought it.
단지 ~이기 때문에

Why do I buy a pair of pants and a bag after I have bought a new coat?

Lisa buys a coat that she really loves. Immediately, she realizes that
목적격 관계대명사(+불완전한 절)　　　　　　명사절 접속사(+완전한 절)
her pants do not match her new coat. So, she buys new pants that go
perfectly with her new coat. But she sees that none of her bags match
none of+명사: 명사에 수의 일치
her new clothes. So, she buys a new bag. Most of her money is spent
Most of+명사: 명사에 수의 일치(단수동사 is)
on buying the new items to complete her new look.
= in order to complete

---

affect: ~에 영향을 주다
when it comes to: ~에 관해서, ~에 대해 말하자면
effect: 효과
behavior: 행동, 행위
wagon: 사륜마차, 짐마차
parade: 행렬, 퍼레이드
encourage: 부추기다
aboard: 탑승하고
on display: 진열된, 전시된
at a glance: 한눈에, 즉시
be likely to: ~하기 쉽다
immediately: 즉시
match: 어울리다

 확인문제

● 다음 문장이 본문의 내용과 일치하면 T, 일치하지 않으면 F를 쓰시오.

1 Jeff sees a pair of soccer shoes on display in the shopping center. ☐

2 As more and more people get on the bandwagon, others are more likely to avoid it. ☐

What made Lisa search for new items immediately after buying
_{사역동사+목적어+동사원형}
a new coat? The "Diderot effect" may explain it. Denis Diderot, a
French writer, received a new gown as a gift. Soon after receiving
_{Denis Diderot와 동격}   _{= After he received the gift.}
the gift, he noticed that all of his furniture did not go well with his
new gown. So, he ended up replacing most of it. The Diderot effect,
_{end up Ving: 결국 V하게 되다}
therefore, is the concept that purchasing a new item often leads to
_{the concept를 설명하는 동격의 명사절을 이끎}
more unplanned purchases.

Why do I buy things just because they are on sale?

Nathan goes window shopping and sees a pair of headphones. He
checks the price and finds out that they are $200. He thinks that the
_{checks와 병렬 연결   finds out의 목적어를 이끄는 명사절 접속사}
headphones are too expensive. The sales person approaches him and
says, "You can get a 20 percent discount on those headphones." Even
though the discounted price is still not very low, Nathan decides to
_{양보절 접속사(비록 ~일지라도)}
buy the headphones.

The situation described above is an example of the "anchoring
_{(which is) described}
effect."

The price mentioned first affects our opinion of prices mentioned
_{The price를 수식하는 과거분사}
afterwards. For example, if we start with $200, then $160 will seem
cheap in comparison. Furthermore, as the difference of the two prices
_{접속사(~함에 따라, ~할수록)}
becomes bigger, the effect will be more powerful. As such, the price
mentioned first acts as an "anchor" that fixes our thoughts about the
price of an item.

Just like Jeff and his friends, we tend to buy things without seriously
considering why we are buying them. As these effects have shown,
_{간접의문문(의문사+주어+동사)   접속사(~하듯이)}
many things influence our purchases. The next time you decide to buy
_{접속사구(다음번에 ~할 때에)}
something, think for a moment about why you are buying it.
_{간접의문문(의문사+주어+동사)}

furniture: 가구	
replace: 바꾸다	
concept: 개념	
purchase: 구입, 구매	
go well with: ~와 잘 어울리다	
lead to: ~로 이어지다	
discount: 할인; 할인하다	
mention: 언급하다, 말하다	
furthermore: 더욱이	
anchor: 닻; 닻을 내리다	
fix: 고정하다	
go window shopping: 진열된 상품을 구경하며 다니다	
in comparison: 비교해 보면	
influence: ~에 영향을 주다	
for a moment: 잠깐	

확인문제

● 다음 문장이 본문의 내용과 일치하면 T, 일치하지 <u>않으면</u> F를 쓰시오.

1 Most of Lisa's money is spent on repairing the new items. ☐

2 A French writer, Denis Diderot, received a new gown as a gift. ☐

3 Nathan decides to buy the headphones because the discounted price is low. ☐

● 우리말을 참고하여 빈칸에 알맞은 말을 쓰시오.

1 Have you ever wondered _____ _____ _____ _____ you don't even want or need?

2 Let's consider _____ _____ _____ when it comes to _____ things.

3 Why do I want to buy _____ _____ _____?

4 Jeff _____ to the shopping center and _____ _____ _____ _____ soccer shoes _____ _____.

5 He _____ the shoes at a glance _____ more than _____ _____ _____ _____ on his soccer team _____ them.

6 _____ he already has _____ _____ _____ soccer shoes, he _____ _____ _____ another new pair.

7 We can use the "_____ _____" _____ _____ Jeff's behavior.

8 A bandwagon is a wagon in a parade _____ _____ people _____ _____ _____ and enjoy the music.

9 As _____ _____ _____ _____ get on the bandwagon, _____ _____ more _____ _____ _____ _____ or follow it.

10 In this way, people tend _____ something _____ _____ other people _____ _____.

11 Why do I _____ _____ _____ _____ pants and a bag _____ I _____ _____ a new coat?

12 Lisa buys a coat _____ she really loves. Immediately, she _____ _____ her pants do not _____ her new coat.

13 So, she buys new pants _____ _____ perfectly _____ her new coat.

14 But she sees _____ _____ _____ _____ her new clothes.

15 So, she _____ a new bag. _____ _____ _____ _____ _____ spent _____ buying the new items _____ _____ her new look.

16 What _____ Lisa _____ _____ new items immediately _____ _____ a new coat?

1 여러분은 원하거나 필요로 하지도 않는 것들을 자신이 왜 구입했는지 궁금해 한 적이 있는가?

2 물건들을 구입하는 것에 관하여 무엇이 우리에게 영향을 주는지 생각해 보자.

3 나는 왜 친구들이 산 것을 사고 싶은 걸까?

4 Jeff는 쇼핑센터에 가서 진열되어 있는 축구화 한 켤레를 보게 된다.

5 그의 축구팀에 있는 소년들의 반 이상이 그 축구화를 신기 때문에 그는 그 신발을 한눈에 알아챈다.

6 이미 그에게는 축구화가 많이 있지만 결국 그는 또 다른 새 축구화를 사 버리고 만다.

7 우리는 Jeff의 행동을 설명하기 위해 '밴드왜건 효과'를 이용할 수 있다.

8 밴드왜건(악대차)은 사람들이 올라타서 음악을 즐기게끔 부추기는 퍼레이드에 있는 사륜마차이다.

9 더 많은 사람들이 밴드왜건에 올라탈수록 다른 사람들이 더욱 그것에 올라타거나 그것을 따라가려 한다.

10 이런 식으로, 사람들은 단지 다른 사람들이 어떤 것을 샀다는 이유로 그것을 구매하는 경향이 있다.

11 나는 왜 새 코트를 구입한 후에 바지와 가방을 사는 걸까?

12 Lisa는 정말 마음에 드는 코트를 산다. 그녀는 그녀의 바지가 새 코트와 어울리지 않는다는 것을 즉시 알아차린다.

13 그래서 그녀는 새 코트와 완벽하게 어울리는 새 바지를 구입한다.

14 하지만 그녀는 자신의 가방 중 어느 것도 새로운 옷들과 어울리지 않는다는 것을 알게 된다.

15 그래서 그녀는 새 가방을 산다. 그녀의 돈 대부분이 그녀의 새로운 모습을 완성하기 위하여 새로운 물품을 사는 데 쓰인다.

16 무엇이 Lisa로 하여금 새 코트를 산 후 즉시 새로운 물품을 찾게 했을까?

17 The "Diderot effect" may _____ _____. Denis Diderot, a French writer, _____ a new gown _____ a gift.

18 Soon _____ _____ the gift, he _____ _____ all of his _____ did not _____ _____ with his new gown. So, he ended up _____ _____ _____ _____ .

19 The Diderot effect, _____, is the concept _____ _____ _____ _____ _____ often _____ _____ more _____ purchases.

20 Why do I buy things just because _____ _____ _____ ?

21 Nathan _____ _____ _____ _____ and _____ a pair of headphones.

22 He _____ the price and _____ _____ _____ they are $200. He thinks _____ the headphones are _____ _____ .

23 The sales person _____ _____ and says, "You can get a 20 percent _____ _____ those headphones."

24 _____ _____ the discounted price _____ _____ not very _____, Nathan decides _____ _____ the headphones.

25 The situation _____ _____ is an example of the " _____ _____ ."

26 The price _____ first _____ our _____ _____ _____ mentioned afterwards.

27 _____ _____ , if we start with $200, then $160 will _____ _____ _____ _____ .

28 _____ , as the difference of the two prices _____ _____ , the effect will _____ _____ _____ .

29 _____ _____ , the price _____ _____ acts as an " _____ " that _____ _____ _____ _____ about the price of an item.

30 _____ _____ Jeff and his friends, we tend _____ _____ things without seriously _____ _____ _____ them.

31 _____ these effects _____ _____ , many things _____ our purchases.

32 _____ _____ _____ you decide to buy something, _____ for a moment _____ _____ _____ _____ it.

17 '디드로 효과'가 그것을 설명해 줄지도 모른다. 프랑스 작가인 Denis Diderot는 선물로 새 가운을 받았다.

18 그 선물을 받은 후에 곧 그는 그의 모든 가구가 새로운 가운과 어울리지 않는다는 것을 알아챘다. 그래서 그는 결국 대부분의 가구를 바꾸고 말았다.

19 그러므로 디드로 효과는 새로운 물품을 구입하는 것이 흔히 계획에 없던 더 많은 구매로 이어진다는 개념이다.

20 나는 왜 단지 할인 중이라는 이유로 물건을 구입하는 걸까?

21 Nathan은 진열된 상품을 구경하러 가서 헤드폰을 하나 본다.

22 그는 가격을 확인하고 그것이 200달러임을 알게 된다. 그는 그 헤드폰이 너무 비싸다고 생각한다.

23 점원이 그에게 다가와 "이 헤드폰에 20퍼센트 할인을 받을 수 있어요."라고 말한다.

24 비록 할인된 가격이 여전히 별로 저렴하지는 않지만 Nathan은 그 헤드폰을 사기로 결심한다.

25 위에 기술된 상황은 '앵커링 효과'의 한 예이다.

26 처음에 언급된 가격이 이후에 언급되는 가격에 대한 우리의 의견에 영향을 미친다.

27 예를 들어, 만약 우리가 200달러로 시작한다면, 비교해 볼 때 160달러는 저렴해 보일 것이다.

28 그뿐만 아니라, 두 가격의 차이가 커질수록 그 효과는 더욱 강력해질 것이다.

29 이와 같이 처음에 언급된 가격이 물건의 가격에 대한 우리의 생각을 고정하는 '닻'으로서 작동한다.

30 Jeff와 그의 친구들처럼, 우리는 우리가 왜 물건들을 사는지 진지하게 고려하지 않고 그것들을 구입하는 경향이 있다.

31 이러한 효과들이 보여 주듯이, 많은 것들이 우리의 구매에 영향을 미친다.

32 다음번에 여러분이 어떤 것을 구매하려고 결정할 때에는, 자신이 그것을 왜 사려는지 잠시 동안 생각해 보아라.

● 우리말을 참고하여 본문을 영작하시오.

1 여러분은 원하거나 필요로 하지도 않는 것들을 자신이 왜 구입했는지 궁금해 한 적이 있는가?
➡ _____

2 물건들을 구입하는 것에 관하여 무엇이 우리에게 영향을 주는지 생각해 보자.
➡ _____

3 나는 왜 친구들이 산 것을 사고 싶은 걸까?
➡ _____

4 Jeff는 쇼핑센터에 가서 진열되어 있는 축구화 한 켤레를 보게 된다.
➡ _____

5 그의 축구팀에 있는 소년들의 반 이상이 그 축구화를 신기 때문에 그는 그 신발을 한눈에 알아챈다.
➡ _____

6 이미 그에게는 축구화가 많이 있지만 결국 그는 또 다른 새 축구화를 사 버리고 만다.
➡ _____

7 우리는 Jeff의 행동을 설명하기 위해 '밴드왜건 효과'를 이용할 수 있다.
➡ _____

8 밴드왜건(악대차)은 사람들이 올라타서 음악을 즐기게끔 부추기는 퍼레이드에 있는 사륜마차이다.
➡ _____

9 더 많은 사람들이 밴드왜건에 올라탈수록 다른 사람들이 더욱 그것에 올라타거나 그것을 따라가려 한다.
➡ _____

10 이런 식으로, 사람들은 단지 다른 사람들이 어떤 것을 샀다는 이유로 그것을 구매하는 경향이 있다.
➡ _____

11 나는 왜 새 코트를 구입한 후에 바지와 가방을 사는 걸까?
➡ _____

12 Lisa는 정말 마음에 드는 코트를 산다. 그녀는 그녀의 바지가 새 코트와 어울리지 않는다는 것을 즉시 알아차린다.
➡ _____

13 그래서 그녀는 새 코트와 완벽하게 어울리는 새 바지를 구입한다.
➡ _____

14 하지만 그녀는 자신의 가방 중 어느 것도 새로운 옷들과 어울리지 않는다는 것을 알게 된다.
➡ _____

15 그래서 그녀는 새 가방을 산다. 그녀의 돈 대부분이 그녀의 새로운 모습을 완성하기 위하여 새로운 물품을 사는 데 쓰인다.
➡ _____

16 무엇이 Lisa로 하여금 새 코트를 산 후 즉시 새로운 물품을 찾게 했을까?
➡ _____

17 '디드로 효과'가 그것을 설명해 줄지도 모른다. 프랑스 작가인 Denis Diderot는 선물로 새 가운을 받았다.
➡ _____

18 그 선물을 받은 후에 곧 그는 그의 모든 가구가 새로운 가운과 어울리지 않는다는 것을 알아챘다. 그래서 그는 결국 대부분의 가구를 바꾸고 말았다.
➡ _____

19 그러므로 디드로 효과는 새로운 물품을 구입하는 것이 흔히 계획에 없던 더 많은 구매로 이어진다는 개념이다.
➡ _____
_____

20 나는 왜 단지 할인 중이라는 이유로 물건을 구입하는 걸까?
➡ _____

21 Nathan은 진열된 상품을 구경하러 가서 헤드폰을 하나 본다.
➡ _____

22 그는 가격을 확인하고 그것이 200달러임을 알게 된다. 그는 그 헤드폰이 너무 비싸다고 생각한다.
➡ _____

23 점원이 그에게 다가와 "이 헤드폰에 20퍼센트 할인을 받을 수 있어요."라고 말한다.
➡ _____

24 비록 할인된 가격이 여전히 별로 저렴하지는 않지만 Nathan은 그 헤드폰을 사기로 결심한다.
➡ _____

25 위에 기술된 상황은 '앵커링 효과'의 한 예이다.
➡ _____

26 처음에 언급된 가격이 이후에 언급되는 가격에 대한 우리의 의견에 영향을 미친다.
➡ _____

27 예를 들어, 만약 우리가 200달러로 시작한다면, 비교해 볼 때 160달러는 저렴해 보일 것이다.
➡ _____

28 그뿐만 아니라, 두 가격의 차이가 커질수록 그 효과는 더욱 강력해질 것이다.
➡ _____

29 이와 같이 처음에 언급된 가격이 물건의 가격에 대한 우리의 생각을 고정하는 '닻'으로서 작동한다.
➡ _____
_____

30 Jeff와 그의 친구들처럼, 우리는 우리가 왜 물건들을 사는지 진지하게 고려하지 않고 그것들을 구입하는 경향이 있다.
➡ _____

31 이러한 효과들이 보여 주듯이, 많은 것들이 우리의 구매에 영향을 미친다.
➡ _____

32 다음번에 여러분이 어떤 것을 구매하려고 결정할 때에는, 자신이 그것을 왜 사려는지 잠시 동안 생각해 보아라.
➡ _____

[01~04] 다음 글을 읽고 물음에 답하시오.

Have you ever wondered why you've bought things that you don't even want or need? Let's consider what affects us when it comes to buying things.

Why do I want to buy (A)_____?

Jeff goes to the shopping center and sees a pair of soccer shoes on display. He recognizes the shoes at a glance because more than half of the boys on his soccer team wear them. Although he already has many pairs of soccer shoes, he ends up buying another new pair.

We can use the "bandwagon effect" to explain Jeff's behavior. A bandwagon is a wagon in a parade that encourages people to jump aboard and enjoy the music. As more and more people get on the bandwagon, others are more likely to get on or follow it. In this way, people tend to buy something just because other people have bought it.

01 다음 중 빈칸 (A)에 들어갈 말로 가장 적절한 것은?

① luxurious things
② what my friends bought
③ what my friends want me to buy
④ things that is not good for me
⑤ what I need most

서답형

02 Where does Jeff go? Answer in English with a full sentence.

➡ _____

서답형

03 다음과 같이 풀이되는 말을 위 글에서 찾아 쓰시오.

the things that a person or an animal does

➡ _____

04 다음 중 위 글을 읽고 답할 수 있는 것은?

① What did Jeff want to buy at the shopping center?
② How many pairs of soccer shoes does Jeff have?
③ When Jeff sees the shoes on display, what does he do?
④ How many members are there on Jeff's soccer team?
⑤ When did people start to use a bandwagon?

[05~08] 다음 글을 읽고 물음에 답하시오.

Why do I buy a pair of pants and a bag after I have bought a new coat?

Lisa buys a coat that she really loves. Immediately, she realizes that her pants do not match her new coat. So, she buys new pants that go perfectly with her new coat. (①) But she sees that none of her bags match her new clothes. (②) So, she buys a new bag. Most of her money is spent on buying the new items to complete her new look. (③)

What made Lisa search for new items immediately after buying a new coat? (④) Denis Diderot, a French writer, received a new gown as a gift. Soon after receiving the gift, he noticed that all of his furniture did not go well with his new gown. (⑤) So, he ended up replacing most of it. The Diderot effect, therefore, is the concept that purchasing a new item often leads to more unplanned purchases.

05 (①)~(⑤) 중 주어진 문장이 들어가기에 적절한 곳은?

The "Diderot effect" may explain it.

①   ②   ③   ④   ⑤

06 Choose two things that Lisa didn't buy.

① a hat   ② a coat   ③ pants

④ shoes   ⑤ a bag

07 다음 중 글의 내용과 일치하는 것은?

① Lisa bought two pairs of pants.

② Denis Didreot is one of Lisa's friends.

③ Denis gave someone a new gown as a gift.

④ Lisa spent money on what she planned to buy.

⑤ What Lisa wanted was to complete her new look.

서답형

08 What did Lisa do after buying her new clothes? Answer in English.

➡ _____

[09~13] 다음 글을 읽고 물음에 답하시오.

Why do I buy things just because they are ①on sale?

Nathan goes window shopping and sees a pair of headphones. He checks the price and finds out that they are $200. He thinks that the headphones are ②too expensive. The sales person approaches him and says, "You can get a 20 percent discount on those headphones." Even though the discounted price is still not very ③low, Nathan decides to buy the headphones.

The situation described above is an example of the "anchoring effect." The price mentioned first affects our opinion of prices mentioned ④before. (A)_____, if we start with $200, then $160 will seem cheap in comparison. Furthermore, as the difference of the two prices

becomes ⑤bigger, the effect will be more powerful. As such, the price mentioned first acts as an "anchor" that fixes our thoughts about the price of an item.

09 밑줄 친 ①~⑤ 중 글의 흐름상 어색한 것은?

①   ②   ③   ④   ⑤

10 빈칸 (A)에 들어갈 말로 가장 적절한 것은?

① Nevertheless   ② Therefore

③ For example   ④ However

⑤ On the other hand

11 What is the passage mainly talking about?

① What makes people buy things they don't need?

② The reason we buy something only because it is on sale.

③ The reason some products are constantly on sale while others are not.

④ Who determines a price of a product on sale?

⑤ What kind of products attract people most?

서답형

12 According to the passage, what is the price of the headphones which fixes Nathan's thought about the price of them? Answer in English.

➡ _____

서답형

13 What does the sales person say when he approaches Nathan? Answer in English.

➡ _____

_____

[14~18] 다음 글을 읽고 물음에 답하시오.

Have you ever wondered why you've bought things ①that you don't even want or need? Let's consider what affects us when it comes to ②buy things.

Why do I want to buy ③what my friends bought?

(A) Although he already has many pairs of soccer shoes, he ends up buying another new pair.

(B) As more and more people get on the bandwagon, others are more likely to get on or follow it. In this way, people tend to buy something just because ④other people have bought it.

(C) Jeff goes to the shopping center and sees a pair of soccer shoes on display. He recognizes the shoes at a glance because more than half of the boys on his soccer team wear them.

(D) We can use the "bandwagon effect" ⑤ to explain Jeff's behavior. A bandwagon is a wagon in a parade that encourages people to jump aboard and enjoy the music.

14 자연스러운 글이 되도록 (A)~(D)를 바르게 나열한 것은?

① (B)–(A)–(C)–(D) ② (B)–(D)–(A)–(C)
③ (C)–(A)–(D)–(B) ④ (C)–(B)–(A)–(D)
⑤ (D)–(A)–(B)–(C)

15 밑줄 친 ①~⑤ 중 어법상 바르지 <u>않은</u> 것은?

①   ②   ③   ④   ⑤

16 What does Jeff see at the shopping center? Answer in English.

➡ _____

17 위 글의 제목으로 가장 적절한 것은?

① What Makes You Survive?
② What Makes You Feel Happy?
③ Things That Money Can't Buy
④ What Makes Us Spend Money?
⑤ Ways To Be a Good Consumer: Follow Your Friends

18 What can we use to explain Jeff's behavior?

➡ _____

[19~22] 다음 글을 읽고 물음에 답하시오.

Why do I buy a pair of pants and a bag (A)_____?

Lisa buys a coat that she really loves. Immediately, she realizes that her pants do not match her new coat. So, she buys new pants that go perfectly with her new coat. But she sees that none of her bags match her new clothes. So, she buys a new bag. Most of her money is spent (B)_____ buying the new items to complete her new look.

What made Lisa search for new items immediately after buying a new coat? The "Diderot effect" may explain it. Denis Diderot, a French writer, received a new gown as a gift. Soon after receiving the gift, he noticed that all of his furniture did not go well with his new gown. So, he ended up replacing most of (C)it. The Diderot effect, therefore, is the concept (D)that purchasing a new item often leads to more unplanned purchases.

19 주어진 단어를 활용하여 빈칸 (A)에 들어갈 말을 완성하시오.

(after / have bought)

➡ _____

20 빈칸 (B)에 들어갈 말과 같은 말이 들어가는 것은?

① The refrigerator broke _____.
② What does the T.C. stand _____?
③ Jina was brought _____ by her sister.
④ Don't put _____ what you have to do today.
⑤ What does the insect mainly live _____?

서답형
21 밑줄 친 (C)가 가리키는 것을 위 글에서 찾아 쓰시오.

➡ _____

22 밑줄 친 (D)와 쓰임이 다른 것은?

① The fact that she betrayed us is true.
② They thought that you lied to them.
③ The name that he mentioned is yours.
④ It is true that the earth is round.
⑤ The news that he won first prize is true.

[23~25] 다음 글을 읽고 물음에 답하시오.

Why do I buy things just ①because they are on sale?

Nathan goes window shopping and sees a pair of headphones. He checks the price and finds out ②that they are $200. He thinks that the headphones are too expensive. The sales person ③approaches to him and says, "You can get a 20 percent discount on those headphones." Even though the discounted price is still not very low, Nathan decides ④to buy the headphones.

The situation described above is an example of the "anchoring effect." The price mentioned first affects our opinion of prices mentioned afterwards. For example, if we start with $200, then $160 will seem cheap in comparison. Furthermore, as the difference of the two prices ⑤becomes bigger, the effect will be more powerful. As such, the price mentioned first acts as an "anchor" that fixes our thoughts about the price of an item.

Just like Jeff and his friends, we tend to buy things without seriously considering why we are buying them. As (a)these effects have shown, many things influence our purchases. The next time you decide to buy something, think for a moment about (A)_____.

23 밑줄 친 ①~⑤ 중 어법상 바르지 않은 것은?

①   ②   ③   ④   ⑤

24 빈칸 (A)에 들어갈 말로 가장 적절한 것은?

① who made you spend money
② why you are buying it
③ when you started to think
④ what influences your life style
⑤ how you spend money wisely

서답형
25 What have the underlined (a)these effects shown?

➡ _____
_____

[01~05] 다음 글을 읽고 물음에 답하시오.

Have you ever wondered why you've bought things that you don't even want or need? Let's consider (A)물건을 구매하는 것에 관하여 무엇이 우리에게 영향을 주는지.

Why do I want to buy what my friends bought?

Jeff goes to the shopping center and sees a pair of soccer shoes on display. He recognizes the shoes at a glance because more than half of the boys on his soccer team ⓐwear them. Although he already has many pairs of soccer shoes, he ends up buying another new pair.

We can use the "bandwagon effect" to explain Jeff's behavior. A bandwagon is a wagon in a parade that encourages people to jump aboard and enjoy the music. As more and more people get on the bandwagon, others are more likely to get on or follow ⓑit. In this way, people tend to buy something just because other people have bought it.

 01 주어진 단어를 활용하여 밑줄 친 우리말 (A)를 영어로 쓰시오.

> (affect / when / come)

➡ _____

02 밑줄 친 ⓐ를 어법에 맞게 쓰시오.

➡ _____

03 밑줄 친 ⓑ가 가리키는 것을 위 글에서 찾아 쓰시오.

➡ _____

04 What is likely to happen when more and more people get on the bandwagon? Answer in English.

➡ _____

_____

05 According to the "bandwagon effect," why do people tend to buy something?

➡ _____

[06~09] 다음 글을 읽고 물음에 답하시오.

Why do I buy a pair of pants and a bag after I have bought a new coat?

Lisa buys a coat that she really loves. Immediately, she realizes that her pants do not match her new coat. So, she buys new pants that go perfectly with her new coat. But she sees that none of her bags match her new clothes. So, she buys a new bag. Most of her money is spent on buying the new items to complete her new look.

What made Lisa search for new items immediately after buying a new coat? The "Diderot effect" may explain it. Denis Diderot, a French writer, received a new gown as a gift. Soon after receiving the gift, he noticed that all of his furniture did not go well with his new gown. So, he ended up replacing most of it. The Diderot effect, therefore, is the concept that purchasing a new item often leads to more unplanned purchases.

06 What does Lisa buy at first?

➡ _____

07 What does Lisa realize after buying a new coat? Answer in English.

➡ _____

_____

08 Write the reason why Diderot replaced most of his furniture after receiving a new gown as a gift. Use the phrase 'It was because.'

➡ _____

_____

09 다음 중 위 글의 내용과 일치하지 <u>않는</u> 곳을 한 군데 찾아 바르게 고쳐 쓰시오.

> Lisa buys a series of new items because, according to the "Diderot effect," one new item leads to a series of planned purchases.

➡ _____

[10~13] 다음 글을 읽고 물음에 답하시오.

Why do I buy things just because they are on sale?

Nathan goes window shopping and sees a pair of headphones. He checks the price and finds out that they are $200. He thinks that the headphones are too expensive. The sales person approaches him and says, "You can get a 20 percent discount on those headphones." Even though the discounted price is still not very low, Nathan decides to buy the headphones.

The situation described above is an example of the "anchoring effect." The price mentioned first affects our opinion of prices mentioned afterwards. For example, if we start with $200, then $160 will seem cheap in comparison.

Furthermore, as the difference of the two prices becomes bigger, the effect will be more powerful. As such, the price mentioned first acts as an "anchor" that fixes our thoughts about the price of an item.

Just like Jeff and his friends, we tend to buy things without seriously considering why we are buying them. As these effects have shown, many things influence our purchases. The next time you decide to buy something, think for a moment about why you are buying it.

10 What does Nathan see when he goes window shopping? Answer in English.

➡ _____

11 What does Nathan find out when he checks the price of the headphone?

➡ _____

12 다음과 같이 풀이되는 말을 위 글에서 찾아 쓰시오.

> a heavy object that is dropped into the water to prevent a boat from moving

➡ _____

13 What does the writer suggest we should do the next time we decide to buy something? Answer in English.

➡ _____

_____

Reading **153**

구석구석

Language in Use

- It is difficult to compare the results in detail.
  특정 어근 앞에 com-을 붙이면 '함께'라는 의미를 더한다. com-+pare(가지런히 놓다) → compare(비교하다)
- We encourage children to think for themselves.

구문해설 · in detail: 상세히 · for oneself: 스스로

- 결과를 상세히 비교하는 것은 어렵다.
- 우리는 아이들이 스스로 생각하도록 장려한다.

Grammar in Real Life B Look and Write

1. About half of the water is used to raise animals in the U.S.
   부분을 나타내는 말은 뒤에 오는 명사의 수에 따라 그 수가 결정된다.(the water/is)
2. One third of the world's food is wasted —1.3 billion tons every year.
   the world's food에 맞춰 is
3. In Somalia, only ten percent of the children go to school.
   the children에 맞춰 go
4. About fourteen percent of all people don't know how to read due to lack of
   약   all people에 맞춰 don't know   의문사+to부정사(= how they should read)
   education.

구문해설 · raise: 키우다 · waste: 낭비하다 · billion: 10억 · due to: ~ 때문에 · lack: 부족, 결핍
· education: 교육

1. 물의 절반 가량이 미국에서 동물을 키우기 위해 사용된다.
2. 세계 식량의 삼분의 일, 즉 매년 13억 톤이 낭비된다.
3. 소말리아에서는 단지 10퍼센트의 아이들이 학교에 다닌다.
4. 전체 인구의 약 14퍼센트는 교육의 부족으로 읽는 법을 알지 못한다.

Think & Write C

I did a survey about allowance. First, I asked 10 students how often they get
                                                      간접의문문(의문사+주어+동사) ask의 직접목적어
an allowance. Twenty percent of the students get an allowance every week and
                              the students에 수의 일치
seventy percent of the students get an allowance every month. Second, I asked
them what they spend most of their allowance on. Most of the allowance is
      asked와 on의 목적어 역할을 함.   the allowance에 수의 일치
spent on clothes and one fourth of the allowance is spent on snacks.
                      4분의 1(분자는 기수, 분모는 서수)
Lastly, I asked them whether they think that they should get a higher
                     ask의 직접목적어(명사절 접속사: ~인지 아닌지)
allowance. Ninety percent of the students think that they should get a higher
allowance.

구문해설 · survey: 설문 조사 · allowance: 용돈 · spend+시간/돈+on ~: ~에 시간이나 돈을 쓰다
· whether: ~인지 아닌지

저는 용돈에 관하여 설문 조사를 했습니다. 우선, 저는 10명의 학생들에게 그들이 얼마나 자주 용돈을 받는지 물었습니다. 20퍼센트의 학생들은 매주 용돈을 받고, 70퍼센트의 학생들은 매달 용돈을 받습니다. 두 번째로, 저는 학생들에게 어디에 용돈의 대부분을 쓰는지 물었습니다. 대부분의 용돈은 옷에 쓰이고, 용돈의 4분의 1은 간식에 쓰입니다. 마지막으로, 저는 학생들에게 그들이 더 많은 용돈을 받아야 한다고 생각하는지 물었습니다. 학생들의 90퍼센트는 그들이 더 많은 용돈을 받아야 한다고 생각합니다.

영역별 핵심문제

01 다음 밑줄 친 부분과 의미가 가장 가까운 것을 고르시오.

> Young people tend to be greatly <u>affected</u> by their peer group.

① invented   ② controlled

③ improved   ④ generated

⑤ influenced

02 다음 빈칸에 들어갈 알맞은 말을 고르시오.

> That jacket _____ your skirt perfectly.

① matches   ② consumes   ③ lasts

④ replaces   ⑤ adapts

03 다음 괄호 안의 단어를 문맥에 맞게 고쳐 문장을 완성하시오.

> The new teacher _____ students to think creatively. (courage)

04 다음 빈칸에 공통으로 들어갈 말을 쓰시오.

> • _____ and more people are using the Internet.
> • The roads were closed for _____ than half an hour.

[05~06] 다음 대화를 읽고 물음에 답하시오.

W: Hey, Eric. Camilla and I are going to watch a movie. (①) Do you want to join us?

M: I'd love to, but I can't. (②) I've spent all of my allowance for this week. (③)

W: Didn't you just get it a few days ago? (④)

M: I'm not sure. (⑤) (A)내 지출을 기록했어야 했어. (keep, spending, track)

05 ①~⑤ 중 주어진 문장이 들어갈 곳은?

> How did you spend it all?

①   ②   ③   ④   ⑤

06 밑줄 친 (A)의 우리말과 일치하도록 주어진 단어를 이용하여 영작하시오.

➡ _____

[07~08] 다음 대화를 읽고 물음에 답하시오.

A: I heard (A)_____ you bought some iced tea online. (a)How do you like it?

B: Oh, I'm (B)_____ with it.

A: Why? What's wrong?

B: There is too much sugar in it. I (C)_____ the nutrition facts first.

07 다음 빈칸 (A)~(C)에 들어갈 말이 알맞게 짝지어진 것은?

① what – not happy – should check

② what – satisfied – should have checked

③ that – satisfied – should check

④ that – satisfied – should have checked

⑤ that – not happy – should have checked

08 밑줄 친 (a)와 바꿔 쓸 수 <u>없는</u> 것을 고르시오.

① Are you satisfied with it?

② Are you enjoying it?

③ Do you like it?

④ Why do you like it?

⑤ Are you happy with it?

[09~10] 다음 대화를 읽고 물음에 답하시오.

M: Good morning. May I help you?

W: I'd like to buy a T-shirt for my sister. She's eleven years old. (①)

M: How do you (A)_____ this red one? (②) This character is quite popular among children. (③)

W: Well, she doesn't (B)_____ animation characters that much. (④)

M: You mean this blue striped T-shirt? Its design is simple and cool. (⑤)

W: Yes, I think my sister will like it. I'll take it.

09 ①~⑤ 중 주어진 문장이 들어갈 곳은?

> Can I see the blue one?

①   ②   ③   ④   ⑤

10 빈칸 (A)와 (B)에 공통으로 들어갈 말을 쓰시오.

➡ _____

[11~12] 다음 대화를 읽고 물음에 답하시오.

M: Good morning. Welcome to Kelly's Sporting Goods Store.

W: Hi, I'm looking for a backpack for hiking.

M: These two are popular among hikers. _____

W: The green one is lighter than the blue one. I'll take the lighter one.

M: Great choice.

11 대화의 흐름상 빈칸에 들어갈 말을 주어진 단어를 이용해 문장을 완성하시오.

➡ (1) _____ (how, like)

(2) _____ (satisfied)

12 〈보기〉의 ⓐ~ⓓ 중 대화를 읽고 답할 수 있는 것을 <u>모두</u> 고른 것은?

┤ 보기 ├

ⓐ Which backpack does the woman take, the green one or the blue one?

ⓑ Which backpack is lighter, the green one or the blue one?

ⓒ What will the woman use a backpack for?

ⓓ Which backpack is more popular, the green one or the blue one?

① ⓐ, ⓑ   ② ⓐ, ⓑ, ⓒ

③ ⓐ, ⓑ, ⓒ, ⓓ   ④ ⓑ, ⓒ

⑤ ⓑ, ⓒ, ⓓ

Grammar

13 다음 중 어법상 옳지 <u>않은</u> 것은?

① As you learn more, you can achieve more.

② As the price goes up, the demand goes down.

③ As you were reborn as an animal, which animal would you be?

④ You have to show your ticket as you go in.

⑤ I couldn't borrow the book from him as James was not at home.

14 다음 중 어법상 옳은 문장을 모두 고르시오.

① One of the highlights were seeing the Taj Mahal.

② 10 percent of the students work to earn money.

③ The number of employees were reduced from 40 to 25.

④ The rest of the money are used to run other government programs.

⑤ Two hours is enough for me to take a walk.

15 다음 밑줄 친 부분이 어법상 옳지 <u>않은</u> 것을 고르시오.

① <u>As she entered the room</u>, she turned the TV on.

② Furthermore, <u>as the difference of the two prices becomes bigger</u>, the effect will be more powerful.

③ <u>As the study shows</u>, those who drink diet sodas tend to get fatter.

④ She earns her living <u>as a freelance journalist</u>.

⑤ Jane met him <u>so as he was leaving the building</u>.

16 다음 문장의 빈칸에 들어갈 말로 알맞은 말은?

> Last weekend, a few of his friends _____ at the party.

① is   ② are   ③ was
④ were   ⑤ has been

17 다음 문장의 밑줄 친 as와 의미상 쓰임이 같은 것을 고르시오.

> <u>As</u> you make more money, you'll want to spend more.

① <u>As</u> the weather gets hotter, more people go to the beach.

② <u>As</u> she was sick, he cared for his wife day and night.

③ <u>As</u> I would not be a slave, so I would not be a master.

④ I wish I could speak English as easily <u>as</u> Korean.

⑤ She was liked by many people <u>as</u> she was honest.

18 다음 문장에서 어법상 어색한 것을 바르게 고쳐 다시 쓰시오.

(1) One third of the students is here.

➡ _____

(2) Much of the house were ruined by the heavy rain.

➡ _____

(3) Ten percent of the girls wants to learn Spanish.

➡ _____

(4) None of the furniture in our house are made of wood.

➡ _____

(5) Last night she said that she took a shower every day.

➡ _____

19 다음 문장에서 잘못된 것을 내용에 맞게 한 단어만 고치시오.

(1) She never took a taxi, as she could afford to.

➡ _____

(2) I usually sleep with the window open as it's really cold.

➡ _____

(3) Korea is regarded like the Mecca of cosmetic surgery.

➡ _____

20 다음 문장에서 어법상 틀린 부분을 찾아 바르게 고쳐 쓰시오.

Only 20 percent of students in my school enjoys outdoor activities.

➡ _____

Reading

[21~24] 다음 글을 읽고 물음에 답하시오.

Have you ever wondered why you've bought things that you don't even want or need? Let's consider ①what affects us when it comes to buying things.

Why do I want to buy what my friends bought?

Jeff goes to the shopping center and ② sees a pair of soccer shoes ③on display. He recognizes the shoes at a glance because more than half of the boys on his soccer team wear them. Although he already has many pairs of soccer shoes, he ends up (A)_____.

We can use the "bandwagon effect" to explain Jeff's behavior. A bandwagon is a wagon in a parade that encourages people to jump aboard and ④enjoys the music. As more and more people get on the bandwagon, others are more likely to get on or follow it. In this way, people tend to buy something just because other people have bought ⑤it.

21 글의 흐름상 빈칸 (A)에 들어갈 말로 가장 적절한 것은?

① throwing them away
② passing by them in the end
③ buying his friends new soccer shoes
④ focusing on playing games
⑤ buying another new pair

22 ①~⑤ 중 어법상 바르지 않은 것을 찾아 바르게 고쳐 쓰시오.

➡ _____

23 다음 중 글의 내용과 일치하지 않는 곳을 한 군데 찾아 바르게 고쳐 쓰시오.

As people jump on the bandwagon in a parade, people tend to buy things just because no other people have bought them.

➡ _____

24 다음 중 위 글을 읽고 답할 수 있는 것은?

① How often does Jeff go to the shopping center?
② What does Jeff recognize as soon as he sees the shoes?
③ What makes Jeff go to the shopping center?
④ Who invented the term "bandwagon effect" first?
⑤ Who made a bandwagon first in the world?

[25~28] 다음 글을 읽고 물음에 답하시오.

Why do I buy a pair of pants and a bag after I have bought a new coat?

Lisa buys a coat that she really loves. Immediately, she realizes that her pants do not match her new coat. So, she buys new pants that go perfectly with her new coat. But she sees that none of her bags match her new clothes. So, she buys a new bag. Most of her money is spent on buying the new items to complete her new look.

What made Lisa search for new items immediately after buying a new coat? The "Diderot effect" may explain it. Denis Diderot, a French writer, received a new gown as a gift. Soon after receiving the gift, he noticed that all of his furniture did not go well with his new gown. So, he ended up replacing most of it. The Diderot effect, (A)_____, is the concept that purchasing a new item often leads to more unplanned purchases.

25 빈칸 (A)에 들어갈 말로 가장 적절한 것은?

① on the other hand   ② however

③ therefore   ④ for instance

⑤ furthermore

26 What does Lisa buy after buying a new coat?

➡ _____

27 What did Diderot do when he noticed all of his furniture didn't go well with his new gown? Answer in English.

➡ _____

28 Choose one that is TRUE.

① Lisa receives a coat as a gift.

② Lisa keeps buying new items because she needs them.

③ Lisa already had a pair of pants perfectly matching her new coat.

④ What Lisa planned to buy was just a coat.

⑤ Diderot was not satisfied with the new gown, so he replaced it with a new one.

[29~30] 다음 글을 읽고 물음에 답하시오.

I did a survey about allowance. First, I asked 10 students (A)_____. Twenty percent of the students get an allowance every week and seventy percent of the students get an allowance every month. Second, I asked them what they spend most of their allowance on. Most of the allowance is spent on clothes and one fourth of the allowance is spent on snacks. Lastly, I asked them whether they think that they should get a higher allowance. Ninety percent of the students think that they should get a higher allowance.

29 빈칸 (A)에 들어갈 말로 가장 적절한 것은?

① how they usually spend their allowance

② how much allowance they save

③ how often they buy things with their allowance

④ how much allowance they get

⑤ how often they get an allowance

30 On what is most of the allowance spent? Answer in English.

➡ _____

01 출제율 90%

다음 짝지어진 단어의 관계가 같도록 빈칸에 알맞은 단어를 주어진 철자로 시작하여 쓰시오.

(1) immediately : at once = buy : p_____

(2) waste : save = loose : t_____

02 출제율 95%

다음 괄호 안의 단어를 문맥에 맞게 고쳐 빈칸에 쓰시오.

What's the _____ between these two computers? (differ)

03 출제율 100%

빈칸 (A)~(C)에 들어갈 말이 바르게 짝지어진 것을 고르시오.

- We're spending a lot more (A)____ food than we used to.
- We need a system to (B)____ track of all our expenses.
- There is no doubt that stress can (C)____ to physical illness.

	(A)	(B)	(C)
①	on	have	result
②	on	make	lead
③	on	keep	lead
④	in	keep	lead
⑤	in	make	result

04 출제율 90%

다음 영영풀이 해당하는 단어를 주어진 철자로 시작하여 빈칸에 쓰고, 알맞은 것을 골라 문장을 완성하시오.

- a_____ : to have an influence on someone or something, or to cause a change in someone or something
- c_____ : to join together to make a single thing or group
- c_____ : a principle or idea

(1) We need to come up with a new _____ now.

(2) Every choice you make _____ your life.

(3) He wants to _____ his job with pleasure.

05 출제율 95%

다음 대화의 빈칸에 들어갈 말을 <보기>에서 골라 순서대로 배열하시오.

W: Hi, Luke. Is that a new speaker?
M: _____
W: _____
M: _____
W: _____
M: About 2 hours. The battery doesn't last long.
W: That's too bad.
M: Yeah, but I'm pretty happy with it, anyway.

(A) Great. How long does the battery last?
(B) It looks cool. How do you like it?
(C) It's convenient. I can take it anywhere and listen to music. The sound quality is good, too.
(D) Yes, I bought it a few weeks ago.

➡ _____

[06~07] 다음 대화를 읽고 물음에 답하시오.

M: Hi. (A)_____

W: Yes, can I try on that cap with stars over there?

M: Sure. (B)_____

W: The design is nice, but I don't think the color suits me. (C)_____

M: Yes. I'll get one from the back. *(pause)* Here it is.

W: Great. I'll take it.

출제율 95%

06 위 대화의 빈칸 (A)~(C)에 들어갈 말을 <보기>에서 골라 기호를 쓰시오.

┌─ 보기 ─────────────────────────┐
ⓐ Are you enjoying your new cap?
ⓑ How do you like it?
ⓒ What's wrong?
ⓓ Can I help you with anything?
ⓔ Do you have it in black?
ⓕ Didn't you check the picture of it?
ⓖ How about trying on that cap?
└─────────────────────────────────┘

➡ (A) _____ (B) _____ (C) _____

출제율 90%

07 위 대화에서 다음 영영풀이에 해당하는 단어를 찾아 쓰시오.

┌─────────────────────────────────┐
to be right for a particular person, situation, or occasion
└─────────────────────────────────┘

➡ _____

[08~11] 다음 대화를 읽고 물음에 답하시오.

M: Hi, Riley. (①) I heard that you bought a laptop online. How do you like it?

W: Oh, I'm not happy with it.

M: Why? What's wrong?

W: (②) I should have read more reviews.

M: (③) Oh, then you should ask (A)_____ your money back.

W: (④) The online store won't give me back my money (B)_____ I've used it for a week.

M: (⑤) How about calling the online shop and explaining your problem?

W: Yeah, I think I should (a)do that.

출제율 100%

08 ①~⑤ 중 주어진 문장이 들어갈 곳은?

┌─────────────────────────────────┐
It makes too much noise and gets overheated.
└─────────────────────────────────┘

①   ②   ③   ④   ⑤

출제율 90%

09 빈칸 (A)에 알맞은 전치사를 쓰시오.

➡ _____

출제율 95%

10 빈칸 (B)에 알맞은 말을 고르시오.

① therefore　　② because
③ but　　④ before
⑤ until

출제율 90%

11 밑줄 친 (a)do that이 가리키는 것을 쓰시오.

➡ _____

12 다음 빈칸에 알맞은 말을 고르시오.

> A: Clara, are you okay?
> B: Yeah, I missed the school bus again.
> _____

① I should have gotten up earlier.
② I should have stayed home in bed.
③ I should not have the alarm.
④ I must have told it earlier.
⑤ I must have taken the subway.

13 다음 밑줄 친 as의 쓰임이 다른 하나를 고르시오.

① As he grew up, he got more interested in history.
② As we need more land to raise cows on, we cut more trees to make land.
③ We soon went back as it was getting darker.
④ As a joke to please her, Jake told a story that he made up.
⑤ As he ran faster and faster, his heart pounded loudly.

14 다음 문장에서 어법상 틀린 부분을 찾아 바르게 고쳐 쓰시오.

> The greater part of the expenses was collected from the members.

➡ _____

15 다음 두 문장을 접속사 as를 이용하여 한 문장으로 고치시오.

> • People eat more junk food.
> • They may gain more weight.

➡ _____
_____

16 다음 빈칸에 들어갈 말이 나머지와 다른 하나는?

① Most of the kids _____ wearing caps.
② Some of the pie _____ missing.
③ There _____ several reasons why I can't come.
④ None of the books _____ worth reading.
⑤ A number of new homes _____ being built in this area.

17 다음 문장을 접속사 as를 이용하여 바꿔 쓰시오.

> The more you run, the stronger you become.

➡ _____

[18~21] 다음 글을 읽고 물음에 답하시오.

> **Why do I buy things just because they are (A) [for sale / on sale]?**
> Nathan goes window shopping and sees a pair of headphones. He checks the price and finds out that they are $200. He thinks that the headphones are too expensive. The sales person approaches him and says, "You can get a 20 percent discount on those headphones." (B)[Even though / Because] the discounted price is still not very low, Nathan decides to buy the headphones.
> The situation described above is an example of the "anchoring effect." The price mentioned first affects our opinion of prices mentioned afterwards. For example, if we start with $200, then $160 will seem cheap in comparison. Furthermore, as the difference of the two prices becomes bigger, the effect will be ⓐ_____. As such, the price mentioned first acts as an "anchor" that (C)[fixes / releases] our thoughts about the price of an item.

Just like Jeff and his friends, we tend to buy things without seriously considering why we are buying them. As these effects have shown, many things influence our purchases. The next time you decide to buy something, think for a moment about why you are buying it.

📝 출제율 100%

18 (A)~(C)에서 글의 흐름상 옳은 것끼리 바르게 짝지어진 것은?

① for sale – Even though – fixes
② for sale – Even though – releases
③ on sale – Even though – fixes
④ on sale – Because – releases
⑤ on sale – Because - fixes

📝 출제율 95%

19 위 글의 내용에 맞게 빈칸에 알맞은 말을 쓰시오.

> The price mentioned first works like an _____. If the price mentioned later is _____ than the first, you will think that the item is cheap.

📝 출제율 100%

20 Choose one that is TRUE.

① Our purchases are influenced by only one thing.
② Nathan finds out on his own that the headphone is on sale.
③ Nathan thinks the price of the headphones is reasonable.
④ The headphone is on Nathan's shopping list.
⑤ Nathan buys the headphone because he is affected by the anchoring effect.

📝 출제율 95%

21 According to the "anchoring effect," what affects our opinion of prices mentioned afterwards? Answer in English.

➡ _____
_____

[22~24] 다음 글을 읽고 물음에 답하시오.

I did a survey about allowance. First, I asked 10 students how often they get an allowance. Twenty percent of the students ①get an allowance every week and seventy percent of the students get an allowance every month. Second, I asked them ②what they spend most of their allowance on. Most of the allowance ③is spent on clothes and one fourth of the allowance is spent ④on snacks. Lastly, I asked them ⑤ that they think that they should get a higher allowance. Ninety percent of the students think that they should get a higher allowance.

📝 출제율 95%

22 밑줄 친 ①~⑤ 중 어법상 바르지 않은 것은?

①　　②　　③　　④　　⑤

📝 출제율 90%

23 What do nine students think about their allowance? Answer in English.

➡ _____

📝 출제율 100%

24 위 글을 읽고 답할 수 있는 것은?

① When was the survey conducted?
② How many students were asked for the survey?
③ How often do they buy clothes?
④ How much allowance do they want to get?
⑤ How long does it take them to spend all of their allowance?

01 그림을 보고 괄호 안에 주어진 어휘를 이용하여 과거 사실에 대해 유감을 나타내는 말로 빈칸을 채우시오.

A: What's the problem?

B: Sam and Ted _____
_____. (an umbrella, bring, should)

02 밑줄 친 문장과 비슷한 뜻을 가진 문장을 주어진 단어를 이용하여 쓰시오.

A: <u>How do you like this dress?</u>

B: The design is cool and interesting.

➡ (1) (enjoy) _____
(2) (satisfied) _____
(3) (happy) _____

03 대화의 흐름상 빈칸에 들어갈 말을 주어진 〈조건〉에 맞춰 쓰시오.

┤ 조건 ├
• 6 단어로 후회하는 일 말하기
• 대화에 나와 있는 어휘 이용하기

M: Oh, this coat is too uncomfortable.

W: Why? What's wrong with it?

M: It's too tight.

W: Didn't you try it on before buying it?

M: No. It was my size, so I just bought it.

_____

➡ _____

04 〈보기〉에 주어진 단어를 활용하여 빈칸을 알맞게 채우시오.

┤ 보기 ├
be   die   have   spend

(1) Half of the money _____ for children in need last month.

(2) Economics _____ not the subject which I'm good at.

(3) I knew that Frida Kahlo _____ in 1954.

(4) The number of homeless people _____ increased dramatically.

05 다음 우리말에 맞도록 괄호 안에 주어진 어휘를 알맞게 배열하시오.

(1) 내가 말하고 있을 때, Jason이 내게 다가왔다. (Jason, I, me, speaking, came, was, to, as, up)

➡ _____

(2) 그는 젊지만 아주 현명했다. (he, he, young, wise, was, was, very, as)

➡ _____

(3) 이러한 효과들이 보여 주듯이, 많은 것들이 우리의 구매에 영향을 미친다. (effects, things, influence, purchases, these, many, shown, our, have, as)

➡ _____
_____

(4) 세계 식량의 삼분의 일이 낭비된다. (one, third, of, the world's food, is, wasted)

➡ _____

Have you ever wondered why you've bought things that you don't even want or need? Let's consider what affects us when it comes to buying things.

Why do I want to buy what my friends bought?

Jeff goes to the shopping center and sees a pair of soccer shoes on display. He recognizes the shoes at a glance because more than half of the boys on his soccer team wear them. Although he already has many pairs of soccer shoes, he ends up buying another new pair.

We can use the "bandwagon effect" to explain Jeff's behavior. A bandwagon is a wagon in a parade that encourages people to jump aboard and enjoy the music. As more and more people get on the bandwagon, others are more likely to get on or follow it. In this way, people tend to buy something just because other people have bought it.

06 According to the passage, why does Jeff buy a pair of soccer shoes on display? Answer in English with a full sentence.

➡ _____

_____

07 What kind of wagon is a bandwagon? Answer in English with a full sentence.

➡ _____

_____

Why do I buy a pair of pants and a bag after I have bought a new coat?

Lisa buys a coat that she really loves. Immediately, she realizes that her pants do not match her new coat. So, she buys new pants that go perfectly with her new coat. But she sees that none of her bags match her new clothes. So, she buys a new bag. Most of her money is spent on buying the new items to complete her new look.

What made Lisa search for new items immediately after buying a new coat? The "Diderot effect" may explain it. Denis Diderot, a French writer, received a new gown as a gift. Soon after receiving the gift, he noticed that all of his furniture did not go well with his new gown. So, he ended up replacing most of it. The Diderot effect, therefore, is the concept that purchasing a new item often leads to more unplanned purchases.

08 Why does Lisa spend most of her money on buying new items? Answer in English with a full sentence.

➡ _____

09 What may explain Lisa's spending? Answer in English.

➡ _____

10 What concept is the "Diderot effect?" Answer in English.

➡ _____

_____

01 다음 문장의 빈칸에 알맞은 말을 〈조건〉에 맞춰 쓰시오.

조건
- 후회하는 일 말하기
- should 이용하기

I went to school yesterday, even though I felt sick. Today I feel even worse. I _____ _____ .

02 〈보기〉와 같이, 주어진 문장의 빈칸을 채워 본인만의 문장을 쓰시오.

보기

As the night becomes darker, the stars become brighter.

(1) As I understood her better, _____ .
(2) As I didn't eat anything, _____ .
(3) As I spend more money, _____ .
(4) As the boy grows older, _____ .

03 10명의 학생을 대상으로 한 설문 조사의 응답을 읽고 그 결과를 설명하는 글을 완성하시오.

Q: How often do you get an allowance?
  □ every week (2명) □ every month (7명)
Q: What do you spend most of your allowance on?
  □ clothes (용돈의 대부분) □ snacks (용돈의 4분의 1)
Q: Do you think you should get a higher allowance?
  □ Yes (9명)   □ No (1명)

I did a survey about allowance. First, I asked 10 students _____ . _____ percent of the students get an allowance _____ and _____ _____ . Second, I asked them what they spend most of their allowance on. Most of the allowance is _____ and _____ is spent on snacks. Lastly, I asked them _____ _____ . _____ _____ .

단원별 모의고사

01 다음 빈칸에 공통으로 들어갈 말을 쓰시오.

> • Which shoes _____ best with this dress?
> • I will _____ window shopping with my friend next weekend.

02 다음 우리말에 맞도록 빈칸에 알맞은 말을 쓰시오. (주어진 단어를 이용하고, 철자가 주어진 경우 주어진 철자로 시작할 것.)

(1) 나는 다음 해에 티켓이 더 비싸질 가능성이 있다고 생각한다. (likely)
➡ I think tickets _____ more expensive next year.

(2) 나는 이 딱 붙는 바지가 편하지 않다.
➡ I am not _____ in these tight pants.

(3) 나는 내가 한 말을 곧 후회했다.
➡ I regretted my words s_____ a_____.

(4) 나는 무슨 일이 일어났었는지 한눈에 알아챘다.
➡ I noticed what had happened _____ _____. (at)

03 다음 빈칸에 알맞은 단어를 〈보기〉에서 골라 쓰시오

> ┤ 보기 ├
> although   because   when

(1) _____ it comes to cooking, he is better than me.

(2) Just _____ I don't complain, people think I'm satisfied.

(3) _____ the sun was shining, it wasn't very warm.

04 다음 괄호 안의 단어를 문맥에 맞게 고쳐 빈칸에 쓰시오.

> In _____ there are those living in wealth and luxury. (compare)

[05~06] 다음 대화를 읽고 물음에 답하시오.

M: Good morning. ⓐMay I help you?
W: ⓑI'd like to buy a T-shirt for my sister. She's eleven years old.
M: (A)이 빨간색 티셔츠는 어떠세요? This character is quite popular among children.
W: Well, ⓒshe likes animation characters that much. Can I see the blue one?
M: You mean this blue striped T-shirt? ⓓIts design is simple and cool.
W: ⓔYes, I think my sister will like it. I'll take it.

05 밑줄 친 ⓐ~ⓔ 중 흐름상 또는 어법상 어색한 것을 고르시오.

① ⓐ   ② ⓑ   ③ ⓒ   ④ ⓓ   ⑤ ⓔ

06 밑줄 친 (A)의 우리말과 일치하도록 주어진 단어를 이용하여 영작하시오. (like, how)

➡ _____

[07~08] 다음 대화를 읽고 물음에 답하시오.

M: Did you get a new phone, Jamie? It's just like mine.
W: Yeah, I got it last weekend on sale.
M: It was on sale? But it has just been released, hasn't it?

W: Right, but the store on Green Street is having a year-end sale.

M: Oh, I bought mine at full price!

W: Really? That's too bad. They're selling them at a 40 percent discount.

M: (A)I should have checked the sales before buying mine.

07 밑줄 친 (A)의 문장과 바꿔 쓸 수 있는 문장을 주어진 단어를 이용하여 쓰시오.

➡ _____
_____ (regret)

➡ _____
_____ (wish)

08 위 대화의 내용과 일치하지 않는 것을 고르시오.

① 남자는 정가에 전화기를 샀다.
② 여자는 지난 주말에 새 전화기를 샀다.
③ 남자는 할인 판매를 확인했었다.
④ 여자는 남자와 같은 전화기를 샀다.
⑤ 전화기는 출시된 지 얼마 되지 않았다.

[09~10] 다음 대화를 읽고 물음에 답하시오.

M: Hi, Riley. I heard that you bought a laptop online. How do you like it?

W: Oh, I'm not happy with it.

M: Why? What's wrong?

W: It makes too much noise and gets overheated. I (A)_____ have read more reviews.

M: Oh, then you (B)_____ ask for your money back.

W: The online store (C)_____ give me back my money because I've used it for a week.

M: How about calling the online shop and explaining your problem?

W: Yeah, I think I (D)_____ do that.

09 빈칸 (A)~(D)에 들어갈 말을 〈보기〉에서 골라 쓰시오. (중복 사용가능)

┌─ 보기 ┤
should   shouldn't   will   won't
└─────────

➡ (A) _____   (B) _____
(C) _____   (D) _____

10 위 대화의 내용과 일치하지 않는 것을 고르시오.

① Riley가 산 노트북은 소음이 심하고 과열이 된다.
② Riley는 새로 산 노트북이 문제가 있어 마음에 들어 하지 않는다.
③ 남자는 전화해서 문제를 설명하라고 Riley에게 조언해 주었다.
④ Riley는 온라인으로 노트북을 샀다.
⑤ Riley는 환불을 받을 수 있을 것이다.

[11~12] 다음 대화를 읽고 물음에 답하시오.

W: ⓐJake, here's a package for you.

M: It's my helmet. I bought it at an online (A)_____ (use) store a few days ago.

W: Oh, open it and let me (B)_____ (see) it.

M: Okay. (pause) Oh, this outer part is a little (C)_____ (break). ⓑThe seller said that it's perfectly fine though.

W: ⓒDidn't you check the pictures of the helmet before you bought it?

M: No, I just trusted the seller. ⓓI must have checked a bit more.

W: ⓔYou should call the seller and ask for a refund.

11 빈칸 (A)~(C)에 괄호 안의 단어를 문맥에 맞게 고쳐 빈칸을 채우시오.

➡ (A) _____ (B) _____ (C) _____

12 밑줄 친 ⓐ~ⓔ 중 흐름상 또는 어법상 어색한 것을 고르시오.

① ⓐ ② ⓑ ③ ⓒ ④ ⓓ ⑤ ⓔ

13 다음 문장에 공통으로 들어갈 알맞은 말을 고르시오. (대·소문자 구분 안 함.)

• _____ you go up a mountain, it gets cooler.
• Treat me _____ a friend.
• Leave the documents _____ they are.

① when ② since ③ as
④ that ⑤ if

[14~15] 다음 우리말에 맞게 주어진 어휘를 활용하여 영작하시오.

14

우리가 땅을 만들기 위해서 더 많은 나무를 베어냄에 따라, 더 많은 숲들이 지구에서 사라진다.
(forests, trees, land, make, disappear, cut, on Earth, to)

➡ _____

_____

15

여러분의 몸이 소비하는 힘의 3분의 1은 여러분이 먹는 음식으로부터 나옵니다. (the power, food, consume, come, from, eat)

➡ _____

_____

[16~19] 다음 글을 읽고 물음에 답하시오.

Why do I buy things just because they are on sale?

Nathan goes window shopping and sees a pair of headphones. He checks the price and finds out that they are $200. He thinks that the headphones are too (A)_____. The sales person approaches him and says, "You can get a 20 percent discount on those headphones." Even though the discounted price is still not very low, Nathan decides to buy the headphones.

The situation described above is an example of the "anchoring effect." The price mentioned first affects our opinion of prices mentioned afterwards. For example, if we start with $200, then $160 will seem cheap in comparison. Furthermore, as the difference of the two prices becomes bigger, the effect will be more powerful. As such, the price mentioned first acts as an "anchor" that fixes our thoughts about the price of an item.

16 빈칸 (A)에 들어갈 말로 적절한 것을 모두 고르시오.

① costly ② pricy ③ low
④ bargain ⑤ expensive

17 How much is the discounted price of the headphones?

➡ _____

18 What acts as an anchor that fixes our thoughts about the price of an item?

➡ _____

19 위 글의 내용을 바르게 이해한 사람은?

① Ann: Like Nathan, I buy things just because they are famous among friends.

② Kirl: Nathan will buy the headphones whether or not they are on sale.

③ Lisa: The price acting as an anchor here is the discounted price.

④ Paul: The price mentioned later makes the price mentioned first seem more expensive.

⑤ Jake: The effect will be more influential if Nathan gets a 10 percent discount on the headphones.

[20~21] 다음 글을 읽고 물음에 답하시오.

Why do I want to buy what my friends bought?

Jeff goes to the shopping center and sees a pair of soccer shoes on display. He recognizes the shoes at a glance because more than half of the boys on his soccer team wear them. Although he already has many pairs of soccer shoes, he ends up buying another new pair.

We can use the "bandwagon effect" to explain Jeff's behavior. A bandwagon is a wagon in a parade that encourages people to jump aboard and enjoy the music. As more and more people get on the bandwagon, others are more likely to (A)_____ . In this way, people tend to buy something just because other people have bought it.

20 위 글의 흐름상 빈칸 (A)에 들어갈 말로 가장 적절한 것은?

① get off or take off from it

② jump on or fight off each other

③ get on or follow it

④ move on and find other wagons

⑤ come along and get ahead of it

21 다음 중 밴드왜건 효과의 영향을 받은 사람은?

① Andrea: I bought another new sweater to complete my new look.

② Paul: I bought a yellow shirt to look fancier than other friends.

③ Chris: I bought a bike because it was on sale.

④ Dave: I bought several notes because I needed them.

⑤ Ethan: I bought a laptop computer because most of my friends have one.

[22~23] 다음 글을 읽고 물음에 답하시오.

What made Lisa search for new items immediately after buying a new coat?

(A) Soon after receiving the gift, he noticed that all of his furniture did not go well with his new gown.

(B) The "Diderot effect" may explain it. Denis Diderot, a French writer, received a new gown as a gift.

(C) So, he ended up replacing most of it. The Diderot effect, therefore, is the concept that purchasing a new item often leads to more unplanned purchases.

22 자연스러운 글이 되도록 (A)~(C)를 바르게 나열하시오.

➡ _____

23 위 글의 내용에 맞게 빈칸에 들어갈 말이 바르게 짝지어진 것은?

The "Diderot effect"explains that there can be _____ because of _____ .

① planned purchases – their expectancy

② unexpected expenditures – one new item

③ unplanned purchases – their greed

④ careful expenditures – their carefulness

⑤ unplanned explorations – one new item

INSIGHT
on the textbook

교과서 파헤치기

※ 다음 영어를 우리말로 쓰시오.

01 seriously

02 admit

03 critically

04 awful

05 extremely

06 fake

07 confess

08 critical

09 harmful

10 citizen

11 mislead

12 height

13 strengthen

14 adult

15 argument

16 publish

17 recognize

18 incident

19 criticize

20 prove

21 current

22 disaster

23 escape

24 judge

25 describe

26 nevertheless

27 reliable

28 wound

29 muscle

30 support

31 mine

32 measure

33 source

34 chest

35 be related to

36 look into

37 make up

38 break down

39 according to

40 draw one's attention to

41 think outside the box

42 be useful for

43 on the loose

※ 다음 우리말을 영어로 쓰시오.

01 인정하다, 자백하다

02 근육

03 그럼에도 불구하고

04 경쟁자, 경쟁 상대

05 진지하게, 심각하게

06 성인, 어른

07 잘못 이끌다,
　 오해하게 하다

08 광산; 채굴하다

09 비난하다

10 입증하다, 증명하다

11 비판적으로

12 참사, 재난

13 달아나다, 탈출하다

14 대중, 일반 사람들

15 강하게 하다,
　 더 튼튼하게 하다

16 가짜의, 거짓의

17 고백하다, 인정하다

18 극도로, 극히

19 해로운, 유해한

20 사건

21 논쟁, 언쟁

22 믿을 만한, 신뢰할 만한

23 끔찍한, 지독한

24 시민

25 판단하다

26 측정하다, 재다

27 현재의, 지금의

28 발행하다, 출판하다

29 위험한, 위독한

30 알아보다

31 출처, 자료

32 기술하다

33 (사실임을) 입증하다,
　 뒷받침하다

34 상처를 입히다

35 조사하다, 들여다보다

36 ~을 찾다

37 ~와 연관되다

38 ~의 관심을 ...로 끌다

39 잠들다

40 ~을 부수다, ~을 무너뜨리다

41 ~에 따르면

42 ~에게 유용하다

43 지어내다, 만들어 내다

※ 다음 영영풀이에 알맞은 단어를 <보기>에서 골라 쓴 후, 우리말 뜻을 쓰시오.

1 _____ : to fire a weapon: _____

2 _____ : not genuine; appearing to be something it is not: _____

3 _____ : a person who lives in a particular city: _____

4 _____ : an event causing great harm, damage, or suffering: _____

5 _____ : to say or write what someone or something is like: _____

6 _____ : to suddenly feel so worried that you cannot be reasonable:

       _____

7 _____ : the upper front part of the body of humans: _____

8 _____ : to form words with the letters in the correct order: _____

9 _____ : to express disapproval of someone or something: _____

10 _____ : a place, person, or thing from which something comes: _____

11 _____ : to injure someone or something by cutting or breaking the skin:

       _____

12 _____ : an unexpected and usually unpleasant thing that happens: _____

13 _____ : to prepare and produce a book, magazine, etc. for sale: _____

14 _____ : to believe that someone is honest or will not do anything bad or wrong:

       _____

15 _____ : to show the existence, truth, or correctness of something by using

       evidence, logic, etc.: _____

16 _____ : a conversation or discussion in which two or more people disagree, often

       angrily: _____

보기			
trust	publish	fake	citizen
incident	criticize	source	panic
prove	wound	spell	disaster
shoot	argument	chest	describe

※ 다음 우리말과 일치하도록 빈칸에 알맞은 말을 쓰시오.

Listen & Talk 1 A-1

W: I think I _____ _____ _____ _____ I didn't _____ _____ yesterday.

M: Well, I've read an _____ saying that you don't catch a _____ because your _____ _____ is _____.

W: Really? Can you tell me _____ _____ _____?

M: The article said that people catch colds _____ _____.

Listen & Talk 1 A-2

W: I usually drink _____ _____ _____ _____ _____ before I go to bed, but it doesn't help me _____ _____.

M: I saw a show on TV, and a doctor said that a glass of warm milk doesn't actually _____ you _____ _____.

W: Oh, it doesn't? Can you _____ _____ _____ _____ _____?

M: Milk has special _____ that _____ people _____. But the _____ in a glass is _____ small _____ have any _____.

Listen & Talk 2 A-1

W: _____ _____ _____ _____, John?

M: I'm reading a book of _____.

W: Riddles? Aren't they _____ children?

M: _____, no. Books of riddles are really _____ _____ _____.

W: Really? Why do you _____ _____?

M: They _____ us _____ more _____. We need to _____ _____ _____ _____ _____ _____ the answers.

Listen & Talk 2 A-2

M: Are these all _____ _____?

W: Yeah. These are all poems _____ _____ children.

M: By children?

W: Yeah. I think children _____ _____ _____ than adults.

M: Why do you _____ _____?

W: They're really _____ about their _____ and much _____ _____ _____.

W: 어제 옷을 따뜻하게 입지 않아서 감기에 걸린 것 같아.

M: 글쎄, 체온이 낮다고 해서 감기에 걸리지는 않는다고 쓰여 있는 기사를 읽었어.

W: 정말? 그것에 대해 더 말해 줄 수 있니?

M: 기사에서는 사람들이 바이러스 때문에 감기에 걸린다고 했어.

W: 나는 보통 잠자리에 들기 전에 따뜻한 우유 한 잔을 마시는데, 그것이 잠드는 데 도움이 되지 않아.

M: 내가 텔레비전 프로그램에서 봤는데, 어떤 의사가 따뜻한 우유 한 잔이 실제로 잠드는 데 도움을 주는 건 아니라고 말했어.

W: 오, 그래? 그것에 대해 더 말해 줄 수 있니?

M: 우유에는 사람들을 졸리게 만드는 특별한 성분이 있어. 하지만 한 잔에 있는 양이 너무 적어서 효과가 없어.

W: 무엇을 읽고 있니, John?

M: 나는 수수께끼 책을 읽고 있어.

W: 수수께끼? 그거 아이들용 아니니?

M: 사실은, 그렇지 않아. 수수께끼 책은 어른들에게 굉장히 유용해.

W: 정말? 왜 그렇게 생각해?

M: 그 책들은 우리가 더 창의적으로 생각하도록 도와. 우리는 답을 찾기 위해 고정관념에서 벗어나야 하거든.

M: 이거 전부 시집이니?

W: 응. 이것들은 모두 아이들이 쓴 시야.

M: 아이들이?

W: 응. 내 생각에 아이들이 어른들보다 더 좋은 시를 쓰는 것 같아.

M: 왜 그렇게 생각해?

W: 아이들은 그들의 감정에 아주 솔직하고 어른들보다 훨씬 더 창의적이거든.

Listen & Talk 2 B

M: Hey, Sandy. Do you think _____ _____ _____ _____ _____? It is said that it can _____ me _____ _____.

W: _____ _____ _____ the _____ more _____. Hmm, it looks a bit _____ to me, David.

M: Why do _____ _____ _____?

W: There isn't _____ _____ about _____ in the _____.

M: Oh, you're _____.

W: Also, it doesn't tell you _____ _____ _____ _____ _____ _____ _____ _____.

M: 안녕, Sandy. 너는 내가 이 음료를 사야 한다고 생각해? 내가 살을 빼는 것을 도와줄 수 있다고 적혀 있어.

W: 라벨을 더 자세히 읽어 볼게. 음, 내가 보기에 좀 이상해, David.

M: 왜 그렇게 생각해?

W: 음료 안에 무엇이 들었는지에 대한 충분한 정보가 없어.

M: 오, 네 말이 맞아.

W: 게다가, 체중을 감량하려면 얼마나 마셔야 하는지도 나와 있지 않아.

Communication

W: There are so many _____ _____ _____ we call " _____ " that are _____ _____.

M: Why do you say so?

W: I read a book, and _____ _____ a lot of _____ of these _____ _____ _____ _____.

M: Like _____?

W: Well, most people think _____ are not smart. But, _____ are _____ _____.

M: Really? Can you _____ me _____ about that?

W: They can _____ _____ _____.

M: Oh, I didn't _____ _____.

W: 우리가 '사실'이라고 말하는 정보 중에 완전히 틀린 것들이 너무 많아.

M: 왜 그렇게 생각해?

W: 내가 책을 읽었는데, 거기에는 이러한 틀린 '사실'의 예시가 많이 있었어.

M: 예를 들면 어떤 것?

W: 음, 대부분의 사람들은 금붕어가 똑똑하지 않다고 생각해. 하지만 금붕어는 사실 똑똑해.

M: 정말? 그것에 대해 더 말해 줄 수 있니?

W: 그들은 그들의 주인을 알아 볼 수 있어.

M: 오, 그건 몰랐어.

Wrap Up 2

W: I read an _____ _____ about the Black Sea. Do you know _____ _____ _____ _____?

M: Yes. It's _____ Eastern Europe _____ Western Asia, _____?

W: Right. _____ _____ do you think _____ _____?

M: Well, black, I _____.

M: No, it isn't. It's blue.

M: Really? Then why is it _____ the Black Sea? Can you _____ _____ _____ about it?

W: People call it the Black Sea _____ it is very _____.

W: 나는 흑해에 관한 흥미로운 기사를 읽었어. 너 그게 어디에 있는지 아니?

M: 응. 그것은 동유럽과 서아시아 사이에 있어, 그렇지?

W: 맞아. 그게 무슨 색일 거라고 생각해?

M: 글쎄, 검은색일 것 같아.

W: 아니야, 그렇지 않아. 그것은 파란색이야.

M: 정말? 그럼 왜 흑해라고 불리는 거야? 그것에 대해 더 말해 줄 수 있니?

W: 사람들이 흑해라고 부르는 이유는 그곳이 매우 위험하기 때문이야.

※ 다음 우리말에 맞도록 대화를 영어로 쓰시오.

Listen & Talk 1 A-1

W: _____

M: _____

_____

W: _____

M: _____

W: 어제 옷을 따뜻하게 입지 않아서 감기에 걸린 것 같아.
M: 글쎄, 체온이 낮다고 해서 감기에 걸리지는 않는다고 쓰여 있는 기사를 읽었어.
W: 정말? 그것에 대해 더 말해 줄 수 있니?
M: 기사에서는 사람들이 바이러스 때문에 감기에 걸린다고 했어.

Listen & Talk 1 A-2

W: _____

_____

M: _____

_____

W: _____

M: _____

W: 나는 보통 잠자리에 들기 전에 따뜻한 우유 한 잔을 마시는데, 그것이 잠드는 데 도움이 되지 않아.
M: 내가 텔레비전 프로그램에서 봤는데, 어떤 의사가 따뜻한 우유 한 잔이 실제로 잠드는 데 도움을 주는 건 아니라고 말했어.
W: 오, 그래? 그것에 대해 더 말해 줄 수 있니?
M: 우유에는 사람들을 졸리게 만드는 특별한 성분이 있어. 하지만 한 잔에 있는 양이 너무 적어서 효과가 없어.

Listen & Talk 2 A-1

W: _____

M: _____

W: _____

M: _____

W: _____

M: _____

W: 무엇을 읽고 있니, John?
M: 나는 수수께끼 책을 읽고 있어.
W: 수수께끼? 그거 아이들용 아니니?
M: 사실은, 그렇지 않아. 수수께끼 책은 어른들에게 굉장히 유용해.
W: 정말? 왜 그렇게 생각해?
M: 그 책들은 우리가 더 창의적으로 생각하도록 도와. 우리는 답을 찾기 위해 고정관념에서 벗어나야 하거든.

Listen & Talk 2 A-2

M: _____

W: _____

M: _____

W: _____

M: _____

W: _____

M: 이거 전부 시집이니?
W: 응. 이것들은 모두 아이들이 쓴 시야.
M: 아이들이?
W: 응. 내 생각에 아이들이 어른들보다 더 좋은 시를 쓰는 것 같아.
M: 왜 그렇게 생각해?
W: 아이들은 그들의 감정에 아주 솔직하고 어른들보다 훨씬 더 창의적이거든.

Listen & Talk 2 B

M: _____
_____

W: _____

M: _____

W: _____

M: _____

W: _____

Communication

W: _____
_____

M: _____

W: _____

M: _____

W: _____

M: _____

W: _____

M: _____

Wrap Up 2

W: _____

M: _____

W: _____

M: _____

W: _____

M: _____

W: _____

M: 안녕, Sandy. 너는 내가 이 음료를 사야 한다고 생각해? 내가 살을 빼는 것을 도와줄 수 있다고 적혀 있어.
W: 라벨을 더 자세히 읽어 볼게. 음, 내가 보기에 좀 이상해, David.
M: 왜 그렇게 생각해?
W: 음료 안에 무엇이 들었는지에 대한 충분한 정보가 없어.
M: 오, 네 말이 맞아.
W: 게다가, 체중을 감량하려면 얼마나 마셔야 하는지도 나와 있지 않아.

W: 우리가 '사실'이라고 말하는 정보 중에 완전히 틀린 것들이 너무 많아.
M: 왜 그렇게 생각해?
W: 내가 책을 읽었는데, 거기에는 이러한 틀린 '사실'의 예시가 많이 있었어.
M: 예를 들면 어떤 것?
W: 음, 대부분의 사람들은 금붕어가 똑똑하지 않다고 생각해. 하지만 금붕어는 사실 똑똑해.
M: 정말? 그것에 대해 더 말해 줄 수 있니?
W: 그들은 그들의 주인을 알아 볼 수 있어.
M: 오, 그건 몰랐어.

W: 나는 흑해에 관한 흥미로운 기사를 읽었어. 너 그게 어디에 있는지 아니?
M: 응. 그것은 동유럽과 서아시아 사이에 있어, 그렇지?
W: 맞아. 그게 무슨 색일 거라고 생각해?
M: 글쎄, 검은색일 것 같아.
W: 아니야, 그렇지 않아. 그것은 파란색이야.
M: 정말? 그럼 왜 흑해라고 불리는 거야? 그것에 대해 더 말해 줄 수 있니?
W: 사람들이 흑해라고 부르는 이유는 그곳이 매우 위험하기 때문이야.

※ 다음 우리말과 일치하도록 빈칸에 알맞은 것을 골라 쓰시오.

1 Can You _____ _____ _____?
  A. News　　　　　　B. Spot　　　　　　C. Fake

2 Every day we _____, _____, or read _____ _____.
  A. news　　　　　B. hear　　　　C. watch　　　　D. interesting

3 However, have you ever _____ _____ _____ an _____ is really true?
  A. article　　　B. considered　　　C. seriously　　　D. whether

4 Everyone likes an interesting news story but _____ _____ it is completely _____ _____?
  A. if　　　　　　B. up　　　　　C. what　　　　D. made

5 Fake news can be very _____ in that it can make people _____ _____ or even _____.
  A. misled　　　B. less　　　C. harmful　　　D. informed

6 _____, there have been _____ fake news reports _____ _____.
  A. various　　B. throughout　　C. nevertheless　　D. history

7 Why have some people _____ _____ _____ _____?
  A. written　　　B. false　　　C. such　　　D. information

8 Let's look into some articles _____ about the _____ _____ _____ them.
  A. hidden　　　B. thinking　　　C. behind　　　D. motives

9 _____ _____
  A. DISATER　　　B. AWFUL

10 Last night, an angry group of rhinoceroses _____ the walls of the _____ at the zoo and _____.
  A. down　　　B. escaped　　　C. broke　　　D. cage

11 They also _____ _____ the walls of the _____ wild animals' _____.
  A. other　　　B. broke　　　C. cages　　　D. down

12 These animals _____ _____ the streets and _____ _____ of people.
  A. hundreds　　　B. ran　　　C. injured　　　D. down

13 Twelve of the animals are _____ _____ _____ _____.
  A. the　　　　B. on　　　C. still　　　D. loose

14 Citizens should _____ indoors _____ _____ _____.
  A. further　　　B. stay　　　C. notice　　　D. until

15 Not a single act or _____ _____ above has _____ _____.
  A. described　　　B. place　　　C. incident　　　D. taken

16 At that time, those who read the _____ carefully _____ _____.
  A. out　　　B. article　　　C. loud　　　D. laughed

1 당신은 가짜 뉴스임을 알아챌 수 있는가?

2 매일 우리는 흥미로운 뉴스를 보고, 듣고, 읽는다.

3 그러나 당신은 뉴스 기사가 정말로 진실인지 심각하게 고려해 본 적이 있는가?

4 모든 사람이 흥미로운 뉴스 기사를 좋아하지만, 만약 그것이 완전히 지어낸 것이라면 어떻게 할 것인가?

5 가짜 뉴스는 사람들에게 정보를 부족하게 제공하거나 사람들을 잘못 이끌 수 있다는 점에서 매우 해로울 수 있다.

6 그럼에도 불구하고, 역사를 통틀어 다양한 가짜 뉴스 보도들이 존재해 왔다.

7 왜 어떤 사람들은 그러한 거짓 정보를 써 왔던 것일까?

8 그 뒤에 숨겨진 동기를 생각하면서 몇 가지 뉴스 기사를 살펴보자.

9 끔찍한 참사

10 어젯밤, 화가 난 코뿔소 떼가 동물원 우리의 벽을 부수고 도망쳤다.

11 그들은 또한 다른 야생 동물 우리의 벽도 부수었다.

12 이 동물들은 거리를 뛰어다니며 수백 명의 사람들에게 부상을 입혔다.

13 그중 열두 마리의 동물들이 아직 잡히지 않았다.

14 시민들은 추후 안내가 있을 때까지 집 안에 머물러야 한다.

15 위에 기술된 어떤 행동이나 사건도 일어나지 않았다.

16 그 당시 이 기사를 주의 깊게 읽었던 사람들은 크게 웃었다.

17 _____ who didn't read it to the end _____ _____ _____.

A. worried   B. those   C. got   D. really

18 _____ _____ the news was _____, many people _____.

A. false   B. knowing   C. panicked   D. not

19 _____ tried to _____ the city while _____ went into the parks with guns to _____ the animals.

A. others   B. hunt   C. escape   D. some

20 So why did *The Herald* _____ _____ _____ _____?

A. such   B. make   C. news   D. up

21 Later, they _____ that they made it _____ so that they could draw the readers' _____ to the _____ conditions at the zoo.

A. attention   B. confessed   C. unsafe   D. up

22 _____ _____ A FRIEND _____ _____

A. IN   B. SLAV   C. ARGUMENT   D. SHOOTS

23 Mejk Swenekafew, a Slav worker at the Columbia Coal Mine, was _____ and seriously _____ by John Pecitello _____ the _____ camp Thursday evening.

A. shot   B. near   C. wounded   D. mining

24 The two men _____ an _____ _____ a meeting.

A. argument   B. had   C. during

25 The argument _____ to a fight, and Pecitello _____ Swenekafew _____, in the _____ and leg.

A. twice   B. led   C. chest   D. shot

26 He is now at the hospital _____ _____ _____.

A. critical   B. in   C. condition

27 Pecitello _____ _____ _____ the _____.

A. away   B. shooting   C. after   D. ran

28 The police are _____ for him now and are _____ _____ that he is extremely _____.

A. warning   B. searching   C. dangerous   D. citizens

29 Is _____ _____ _____ about the _____?

A. article   B. strange   C. anything   D. there

30 _____ the Slav's name _____; it _____, "we-fake-news."

A. backwards   B. read   C. spells

31 _____ _____ this and _____?

A. wrote   B. why   C. who

17 그것을 끝까지 읽지 않은 사람들은 정말로 걱정하였다.

18 그 기사가 거짓이라는 것을 알지 못했기 때문에 많은 사람이 겁에 질려 어쩔 줄 몰랐다.

19 어떤 사람들은 도시를 빠져나가려고 했고 다른 사람들은 그 동물들을 사냥하기 위해 총을 들고 공원으로 나갔다.

20 그렇다면 왜 헤럴드 사는 이러한 뉴스를 만들어 냈을까?

21 나중에 그들은 동물원의 안전하지 않은 상태에 대해 독자들의 주의를 끌기 위해 그 기사를 지어냈다고 고백했다.

22 슬라브인이 언쟁 중에 친구에게 총을 쏘다

23 목요일 저녁 채굴 야영지 근처에서, 컬럼비아 광산 소속의 슬라브인 노동자 Mejk Swenekafew가 John Pecitello에 의해 총상을 입어 심각하게 다쳤다.

24 그 두 사람은 회의 중에 언쟁을 벌였다.

25 언쟁이 싸움으로 번졌고, Pecitello가 Swenekafew의 가슴과 다리에 두 번 총을 쏘았다.

26 현재 그는 위독한 상태로 입원 중이다.

27 Pecitello는 총격 이후 도주했다.

28 경찰이 지금 그를 찾고 있으며, 그가 극히 위험하다고 시민들에게 경고하고 있다.

29 이 기사에 뭔가 이상한 점이 있는가?

30 그 슬라브인의 이름을 거꾸로 읽어 보아라. 그것의 철자는 "우리는 뉴스를 조작한다."가 된다.

31 누가 이것을 썼고 왜 그랬을까?

32 *The Daily Telegram* published this fake article _____ they could prove if *The Daily News*, their _____, was _____ their articles.

A. stealing B. that C. competitor D. so

33 *The Daily News* _____ the same _____ about "Swenekafew" the next day and thus got _____ _____.

A. caught B. published C. stealing D. article

34 The people at *The Daily News* had to _____ their act and were _____ _____ by the _____.

A. criticized B. admit C. harshly D. public

35 The two articles were _____ _____, but there are many "fake" news _____ _____ every day.

A. cases B. published C. articles D. special

36 As readers, we need to read _____ and _____ the news is real or _____.

A. whether B. fake C. critically D. judge

37 _____ _____ _____ fake news!

A. to B. how C. spot

38 _____ the _____

A. Source B. Consider

39 Is it _____ a _____ _____?

A. sources B. from C. reliable

40 _____ we _____ the _____?

A. trust B. can C. writer

41 _____ the _____

A. Date B. Check

42 Is it a _____ or an _____ _____?

A. old B. new C. story

43 _____ it _____ _____ events?

A. to B. is C. current D. related

44 Read _____ _____ _____

A. Headlines B. the C. Beyong

45 Does the _____ _____ the _____?

A. content B. match C. headline

46 Find _____ _____

A. Sources B. Supporting

47 Do other _____ stories _____ _____ _____?

A. content B. related C. similar D. provide

32 데일리 텔레그램 사는 그들의 경쟁자인 데일리 뉴스 사가 그들의 기사를 훔치는지를 증명하기 위해서 이 거짓 기사를 발행했다.

33 데일리 뉴스 사는 그 다음 날 'Swenekafew'에 대한 동일한 기사를 발행했고 그래서 훔친 것이 발각되었다.

34 데일리 뉴스 사의 사람들은 그들의 행동을 인정해야만 했고 대중들로부터 혹독한 비난을 받았다.

35 이 두 기사는 특별한 경우였지만, 매일 발행되는 '가짜' 뉴스 기사는 많이 있다.

36 독자로서, 우리는 비판적으로 읽고 그 뉴스가 진짜인지 가짜인지 판단할 필요가 있다.

37 가짜 뉴스 판별 방법!

38 출처를 고려하라

39 그것은 믿을 만한 출처에서 온 것인가?

40 우리는 그 필자를 신뢰할 수 있는가?

41 날짜를 확인하라

42 그것은 새로운 이야기인가 혹은 오래된 이야기인가?

43 그것은 현재의 사건들과 관련된 것인가?

44 기사 제목 그 이상을 읽어라

45 기사 제목이 기사 내용과 일치하는가?

46 뒷받침하는 자료를 찾아라

47 다른 관련된 이야기도 비슷한 내용을 제공하는가?

※ 다음 우리말과 일치하도록 빈칸에 알맞은 것을 골라 쓰시오.

1 Can You _____ _____ _____?

2 Every day we watch, hear, or read _____ _____.

3 However, _____ you ever seriously _____ _____ an article is really true?

4 Everyone likes an interesting news story but _____ _____ it is _____ _____ _____?

5 Fake news can be very _____ _____ _____ it can make people _____ _____ or even _____.

6 _____, there have been _____ _____ news reports _____ _____.

7 Why have some people _____ _____ _____ _____ _____?

8 _____ _____ _____ some articles _____ about _____ _____ _____ _____ them.

9 _____ DISASTER

10 Last night, an angry group of rhinoceroses _____ _____ the walls of the cage at the zoo and _____.

11 They also _____ _____ the walls of _____ _____ wild animals' cages.

12 These animals _____ _____ the streets and _____ _____ _____ people.

13 Twelve of the animals are still _____ _____ _____.

14 _____ should stay indoors _____ _____ _____.

15 Not a single act or incident _____ _____ has _____ _____.

16 At that time, those who read the article carefully _____ _____ _____.

1	당신은 가짜 뉴스임을 알아챌 수 있는가?
2	매일 우리는 흥미로운 뉴스를 보고, 듣고, 읽는다.
3	그러나 당신은 뉴스 기사가 정말로 진실인지 심각하게 고려해 본 적이 있는가?
4	모든 사람이 흥미로운 뉴스 기사를 좋아하지만, 만약 그것이 완전히 지어낸 것이라면 어떻게 할 것인가?
5	가짜 뉴스는 사람들에게 정보를 부족하게 제공하거나 사람들을 잘못 이끌 수 있다는 점에서 매우 해로울 수 있다.
6	그럼에도 불구하고, 역사를 통틀어 다양한 가짜 뉴스 보도들이 존재해 왔다.
7	왜 어떤 사람들은 그러한 거짓 정보를 써 왔던 것일까?
8	그 뒤에 숨겨진 동기를 생각하면서 몇 가지 뉴스 기사를 살펴보자.
9	끔찍한 참사
10	어젯밤, 화가 난 코뿔소 떼가 동물원 우리의 벽을 부수고 도망쳤다.
11	그들은 또한 다른 야생 동물 우리의 벽도 부수었다.
12	이 동물들은 거리를 뛰어다니며 수백 명의 사람들에게 부상을 입혔다.
13	그중 열두 마리의 동물들이 아직 잡히지 않았다.
14	시민들은 추후 안내가 있을 때까지 집 안에 머물러야 한다.
15	위에 기술된 어떤 행동이나 사건도 일어나지 않았다.
16	그 당시 이 기사를 주의 깊게 읽었던 사람들은 크게 웃었다.

17 Those who didn't read it to the end _____ _____ _____ .

18 _____ _____ the news was _____ , many people _____ .

19 _____ tried _____ _____ the city while _____ went into the parks with guns _____ _____ the animals.

20 So why did *The Herald* _____ _____ _____ _____ _____ ?

21 Later, they confessed that they _____ _____ _____ _____ _____ they _____ draw the _____ _____ _____ the unsafe conditions at the zoo.

22 SLAV _____ A FRIEND _____ _____

23 Mejk Swenekafew, a Slav worker at the Columbia Coal Mine, _____ _____ and _____ _____ _____ John Pecitello near the mining camp Thursday evening.

24 The two men _____ _____ _____ _____ _____ a meeting.

25 The argument _____ _____ a fight, and Pecitello shot Swenekafew _____ , _____ _____ _____ and leg.

26 He is now at the hospital _____ _____ _____ .

27 Pecitello _____ _____ _____ _____ _____ .

28 The police _____ _____ _____ him now and _____ _____ citizens that he is _____ _____ .

29 Is there _____ _____ about the _____ ?

30 Read the Slav's name _____ ; it spells, "we-fake-news."

31 Who _____ this and _____ ?

---

17 그것을 끝까지 읽지 않은 사람들은 정말로 걱정하였다.

18 그 기사가 거짓이라는 것을 알지 못했기 때문에 많은 사람이 겁에 질려 어쩔 줄 몰랐다.

19 어떤 사람들은 도시를 빠져나가려고 했고 다른 사람들은 그 동물들을 사냥하기 위해 총을 들고 공원으로 나갔다.

20 그렇다면 왜 헤럴드 사는 이러한 뉴스를 만들어 냈을까?

21 나중에 그들은 동물원의 안전하지 않은 상태에 대해 독자들의 주의를 끌기 위해 그 기사를 지어냈다고 고백했다.

22 슬라브인이 언쟁 중에 친구에게 총을 쏘다

23 목요일 저녁 채굴 야영지 근처에서, 컬럼비아 광산 소속의 슬라브인 노동자 Mejk Swenekafew가 John Pecitello에 의해 총상을 입어 심각하게 다쳤다.

24 그 두 사람은 회의 중에 언쟁을 벌였다.

25 언쟁이 싸움으로 번졌고, Pecitello가 Swenekafew의 가슴과 다리에 두 번 총을 쏘았다.

26 현재 그는 위독한 상태로 입원 중이다.

27 Pecitello는 총격 이후 도주했다.

28 경찰이 지금 그를 찾고 있으며, 그가 극히 위험하다고 시민들에게 경고하고 있다.

29 이 기사에 뭔가 이상한 점이 있는가?

30 그 슬라브인의 이름을 거꾸로 읽어 보아라. 그것의 철자는 "우리는 뉴스를 조작한다."가 된다.

31 누가 이것을 썼고 왜 그랬을까?

32 *The Daily Telegram* _____ this fake article _____ _____ they _____ prove _____ *The Daily News*, their competitor, was stealing _____ _____.

33 *The Daily News* published the same article about "Swenekafew" the next day and thus _____ _____ _____.

34 The people at *The Daily News* _____ _____ _____ their act and _____ _____ _____ by the public.

35 The two articles were _____ _____, but there are many "fake" news articles _____ every day.

36 _____ readers, we need to read _____ and _____ _____ the news is real _____ fake.

37 _____ _____ _____ fake news!

38 _____ the _____

39 Is it from a _____ _____?

40 Can we _____ the _____?

41 _____ the Date

42 Is it a _____ or an _____?

43 _____ it _____ events?

44 Read _____ _____ _____

45 Does the headline _____ _____ _____?

46 Find _____ _____

47 Do other _____ stories provide _____ _____?

32 데일리 텔레그램 사는 그들의 경쟁자인 데일리 뉴스 사가 그들의 기사를 훔치는지를 증명하기 위해서 이 거짓 기사를 발행했다.

33 데일리 뉴스 사는 그 다음 날 'Swenekafew'에 대한 동일한 기사를 발행했고 그래서 훔친 것이 발각되었다.

34 데일리 뉴스 사의 사람들은 그들의 행동을 인정해야만 했고 대중들로부터 혹독한 비난을 받았다.

35 이 두 기사는 특별한 경우였지만, 매일 발행되는 '가짜' 뉴스 기사는 많이 있다.

36 독자로서, 우리는 비판적으로 읽고 그 뉴스가 진짜인지 가짜인지 판단할 필요가 있다.

37 가짜 뉴스 판별 방법!

38 출처를 고려하라

39 그것은 믿을 만한 출처에서 온 것인가?

40 우리는 그 필자를 신뢰할 수 있는가?

41 날짜를 확인하라

42 그것은 새로운 이야기인가 혹은 오래된 이야기인가?

43 그것은 현재의 사건들과 관련된 것인가?

44 기사 제목 그 이상을 읽어라

45 기사 제목이 기사 내용과 일치하는가?

46 뒷받침하는 자료를 찾아라

47 다른 관련된 이야기도 비슷한 내용을 제공하는가?

※ 다음 문장을 우리말로 쓰시오.

1 Can You Spot Fake News?

➡ _____

2 Every day we watch, hear, or read interesting news.

➡ _____

3 However, have you ever seriously considered whether an article is really true?

➡ _____

4 Everyone likes an interesting news story but what if it is completely made up?

➡ _____

5 Fake news can be very harmful in that it can make people less informed or even misled.

➡ _____

6 Nevertheless, there have been various fake news reports throughout history.

➡ _____

7 Why have some people written such false information?

➡ _____

8 Let's look into some articles thinking about the hidden motives behind them.

➡ _____

9 AWFUL DISASTER

➡ _____

10 Last night, an angry group of rhinoceroses broke down the walls of the cage at the zoo and escaped.

➡ _____

11 They also broke down the walls of the other wild animals' cages.

➡ _____

12 These animals ran down the streets and injured hundreds of people.

➡ _____

13 Twelve of the animals are still on the loose.

➡ _____

14 Citizens should stay indoors until further notice.

➡ _____

15 Not a single act or incident described above has taken place.

➡ _____

16 At that time, those who read the article carefully laughed out loud.

➡ _____

17 Those who didn't read it to the end got really worried.

➡ _____

18 Not knowing the news was false, many people panicked.

➡ _____

19 Some tried to escape the city while others went into the parks with guns to hunt the animals.

➡ _____

20 So why did *The Herald* make up such news?

➡ _____

21 Later, they confessed that they made it up so that they could draw the readers' attention to the unsafe conditions at the zoo.

➡ _____

22 SLAV SHOOTS A FRIEND IN ARGUMENT

➡ _____

23 Mejk Swenekafew, a Slav worker at the Columbia Coal Mine, was shot and seriously wounded by John Pecitello near the mining camp Thursday evening.

➡ _____

  _____

24 The two men had an argument during a meeting.

➡ _____

25 The argument led to a fight, and Pecitello shot Swenekafew twice, in the chest and leg.

➡ _____

26 He is now at the hospital in critical condition.

➡ _____

27 Pecitello ran away after the shooting.

➡ _____

28 The police are searching for him now and are warning citizens that he is extremely dangerous.

➡ _____

29 Is there anything strange about the article?

➡ _____

30 Read the Slav's name backwards; it spells, "we-fake-news."

➡ _____

31 Who wrote this and why?

➡ _____

32 *The Daily Telegram* published this fake article so that they could prove if *The Daily News*, their competitor, was stealing their articles.

➡ _____

_____

33 *The Daily News* published the same article about "Swenekafew" the next day and thus got caught stealing.

➡ _____

34 The people at *The Daily News* had to admit their act and were harshly criticized by the public.

➡ _____

35 The two articles were special cases, but there are many "fake" news articles published every day.

➡ _____

36 As readers, we need to read critically and judge whether the news is real or fake.

➡ _____

37 How to spot fake news!

➡ _____

38 Consider the Source

➡ _____

39 Is it from a reliable source?

➡ _____

40 Can we trust the writer?

➡ _____

41 Check the Date

➡ _____

42 Is it a new or an old story?

➡ _____

43 Is it related to current events?

➡ _____

44 Read Beyond the Headlines

➡ _____

45 Does the headline match the content?

➡ _____

46 Find Supporting Sources

➡ _____

47 Do other related stories provide similar content?

➡ _____

※ 다음 괄호 안의 단어들을 우리말에 맞도록 바르게 배열하시오.

1 (You / Can / Fake / Spot / News?)
➡ _____

2 (day / every / watch, / we / or / hear, / read / news. / interesting)
➡ _____

3 (have / however, / ever / you / considered / seriously / an / whether / is / article / true? / really)
➡ _____

4 (likes / everyone / an / news / interesting / but / story / if / what / is / it / made / completely / up?)
➡ _____

5 (news / fake / be / can / harmful / very / that / in / can / it / people / make / less / or / informed / misled. / even)
➡ _____

6 (there / nevertheless, / been / have / fake / various / reports / news / history. / throughout)
➡ _____

7 (have / why / people / some / such / written / information? / false)
➡ _____

8 (look / let's / some / into / thinking / articles / the / about / motives / hidden / them. / behind)
➡ _____

9 (DISASTER / AWFUL)
➡ _____

10 (night, / last / angry / an / group / rhinoceroses / of / down / broke / walls / the / the / of / cage / the / at / zoo / escaped. / and)
➡ _____

11 (also / they / down / broke / walls / the / the / of / other / animals' / wild / cages.)
➡ _____

12 (animals / these / down / ran / streets / the / and / hundreds / injured / people. / of)
➡ _____

13 (of / twelve / animals / the / still / are / on / loose. / the)
➡ _____

14 (should / citizens / indoors / stay / further / until / notice.)
➡ _____

15 (a / not / act / single / or / described / incident / has / above / place. / taken)
➡ _____

16 (that / at / time, / who / those / the / read / carefully / article / out / laughed / loud.)
➡ _____

1 당신은 가짜 뉴스임을 알아챌 수 있는가?
2 매일 우리는 흥미로운 뉴스를 보고, 듣고, 읽는다.
3 그러나 당신은 뉴스 기사가 정말로 진실인지 심각하게 고려해 본 적이 있는가?
4 모든 사람이 흥미로운 뉴스 기사를 좋아하지만, 만약 그것이 완전히 지어낸 것이라면 어떻게 할 것인가?
5 가짜 뉴스는 사람들에게 정보를 부족하게 제공하거나 사람들을 잘못 이끌 수 있다는 점에서 매우 해로울 수 있다.
6 그럼에도 불구하고, 역사를 통틀어 다양한 가짜 뉴스 보도들이 존재해 왔다.
7 왜 어떤 사람들은 그러한 거짓 정보를 써 왔던 것일까?
8 그 뒤에 숨겨진 동기를 생각하면서 몇 가지 뉴스 기사를 살펴보자.
9 끔찍한 참사
10 어젯밤, 화가 난 코뿔소 떼가 동물원 우리의 벽을 부수고 도망쳤다.
11 그들은 또한 다른 야생 동물 우리의 벽도 부수었다.
12 이 동물들은 거리를 뛰어다니며 수백 명의 사람들에게 부상을 입혔다.
13 그중 열두 마리의 동물들이 아직 잡히지 않았다.
14 시민들은 추후 안내가 있을 때까지 집 안에 머물러야 한다.
15 위에 기술된 어떤 행동이나 사건도 일어나지 않았다.
16 그 당시 이 기사를 주의 깊게 읽었던 사람들은 크게 웃었다.

17 (who / those / read / didn't / to / it / end / the / got / worried. / really)
➡ _____

18 (knowing / not / news / the / false, / was / people / many / panicked.)
➡ _____

19 (tried / some / escape / to / city / the / others / while / into / went / parks / the / guns / with / hunt / to / animals. / the)
➡ _____

20 (why / so / *The* / did / make / *Herald* / up / news? / such)
➡ _____

21 (they / later, / that / confessed / made / they / up / it / that / so / could / they / the / draw / readers' / the / to / attention / conditions / unsafe / at / zoo. / the)
➡ _____

22 (SHOOTS / SLAV / FRIEND / A / ARGUMENT / IN)
➡ _____

23 (Swenekafew, / Mejk / Slave / a / worker / the / at / Columbia / Mine, / Coal / shot / was / and / wounded / seriously / by / Pecitello / John / near / mining / the / camp / evening. / Thursday)
➡ _____

24 (two / the / had / men / an / during / argument / meeting. / a)
➡ _____

25 (argument / the / to / led / fight, / a / and / shot / Pecitello / Swenekafew / twice, / the / in / chest / leg. / and)
➡ _____

26 (is / he / at / now / the / in / hospital / condition. / critical)
➡ _____

27 (Pecitello / away / ran / the / after / shooting.)
➡ _____

28 (police / the / searching / are / him / for / now / are / and / warning / that / citizens / is / he / dangerous. / extremely)
➡ _____

29 (there / is / strange / anything / about / article? / the)
➡ _____

30 (the / read / name / Slav's / backwards; / it / "we-fake-news." / spells,)
➡ _____

31 (wrote / who / why? / and / this)
➡ _____

17 그것을 끝까지 읽지 않은 사람들은 정말로 걱정하였다.

18 그 기사가 거짓이라는 것을 알지 못했기 때문에 많은 사람이 겁에 질려 어쩔 줄 몰랐다.

19 어떤 사람들은 도시를 빠져나가려고 했고 다른 사람들은 그 동물들을 사냥하기 위해 총을 들고 공원으로 나갔다.

20 그렇다면 왜 헤럴드 사는 이러한 뉴스를 만들어 냈을까?

21 나중에 그들은 동물원의 안전하지 않은 상태에 대해 독자들의 주의를 끌기 위해 그 기사를 지어냈다고 고백했다.

22 슬라브인이 언쟁 중에 친구에게 총을 쏘다

23 목요일 저녁 채굴 야영지 근처에서, 컬럼비아 광산 소속의 슬라브인 노동자 Mejk Swenekafew가 John Pecitello에 의해 총상을 입어 심각하게 다쳤다.

24 그 두 사람은 회의 중에 언쟁을 벌였다.

25 언쟁이 싸움으로 번졌고, Pecitello가 Swenekafew의 가슴과 다리에 두 번 총을 쏘았다.

26 현재 그는 위독한 상태로 입원 중이다.

27 Pecitello는 총격 이후 도주했다.

28 경찰이 지금 그를 찾고 있으며, 그가 극히 위험하다고 시민들에게 경고하고 있다.

29 이 기사에 뭔가 이상한 점이 있는가?

30 그 슬라브인의 이름을 거꾸로 읽어 보아라. 그것의 철자는 "우리는 뉴스를 조작한다."가 된다.

31 누가 이것을 썼고 왜 그랬을까?

32 (*Daily* / *The* / *Telegram* / this / published / fake / so / article / that / could / they / if / prove / *Daily* / *The* / *News*, / competitor, / their / stealing / was / articles. / their)

➡ _____

_____

33 (*Daily* / *The* / *News* / the / published / article / same / "Swenekafew" / about / next / the / day / thus / and / caught / got / stealing.)

➡ _____

_____

34 (people / the / at / *News* / *The* / *Daily* / to / had / admit / act / their / and / harshly / were / criticized / the / by / public.)

➡ _____

_____

35 (two / the / were / articles / cases, / special / there / but / many / are / news / "fake" / articles / every / published / day.)

➡ _____

_____

36 (readers, / as / need / we / read / to / and / critically / whether / judge / news / the / real / is / fake. / or)

➡ _____

_____

37 (to / how / fake / spot / news!)

➡ _____

38 (the / consider / Source)

➡ _____

39 (it / is / a / from / source? / reliable)

➡ _____

40 (we / can / the / trust / writer?)

➡ _____

41 (the / check / Date)

➡ _____

42 (it / is / new / a / or / old / an / story?)

➡ _____

43 (is / related / it / current / to / events?)

➡ _____

44 (Beyond / Read / Headlines / the)

➡ _____

45 (the / does / match / headline / content? / the)

➡ _____

46 (Supporting / Find / Sources)

➡ _____

47 (other / do / stories / related / similar / provide / content?)

➡ _____

32 데일리 텔레그램 사는 그들의 경쟁자인 데일리 뉴스 사가 그들의 기사를 훔치는지를 증명하기 위해서 이 거짓 기사를 발행했다.

33 데일리 뉴스 사는 그 다음 날 'Swenekafew'에 대한 동일한 기사를 발행했고 그래서 훔친 것이 발각되었다.

34 데일리 뉴스 사의 사람들은 그들의 행동을 인정해야만 했고 대중들로부터 혹독한 비난을 받았다.

35 이 두 기사는 특별한 경우였지만, 매일 발행되는 '가짜' 뉴스 기사는 많이 있다.

36 독자로서, 우리는 비판적으로 읽고 그 뉴스가 진짜인지 가짜인지 판단할 필요가 있다.

37 가짜 뉴스 판별 방법!

38 출처를 고려하라

39 그것은 믿을 만한 출처에서 온 것인가?

40 우리는 그 필자를 신뢰할 수 있는가?

41 날짜를 확인하라

42 그것은 새로운 이야기인가 혹은 오래된 이야기인가?

43 그것은 현재의 사건들과 관련된 것인가?

44 기사 제목 그 이상을 읽어라

45 기사 제목이 기사 내용과 일치하는가?

46 뒷받침하는 자료를 찾아라

47 다른 관련된 이야기도 비슷한 내용을 제공하는가?

※ 다음 우리말을 영어로 쓰시오.

1 당신은 가짜 뉴스임을 알아챌 수 있는가?

➡ _____

2 매일 우리는 흥미로운 뉴스를 보고, 듣고, 읽는다.

➡ _____

3 그러나 당신은 뉴스 기사가 정말로 진실인지 심각하게 고려해 본 적이 있는가?

➡ _____

4 모든 사람이 흥미로운 뉴스 기사를 좋아하지만, 만약 그것이 완전히 지어낸 것이라면 어떻게 할 것인가?

➡ _____

5 가짜 뉴스는 사람들에게 정보를 부족하게 제공하거나 사람들을 잘못 이끌 수 있다는 점에서 매우 해로울 수 있다.

➡ _____

6 그럼에도 불구하고, 역사를 통틀어 다양한 가짜 뉴스 보도들이 존재해 왔다.

➡ _____

7 왜 어떤 사람들은 그러한 거짓 정보를 써 왔던 것일까?

➡ _____

8 그 뒤에 숨겨진 동기를 생각하면서 몇 가지 뉴스 기사를 살펴보자.

➡ _____

9 끔찍한 참사

➡ _____

10 어젯밤, 화가 난 코뿔소 떼가 동물원 우리의 벽을 부수고 도망쳤다.

➡ _____

11 그들은 또한 다른 야생 동물 우리의 벽도 부수었다.

➡ _____

12 이 동물들은 거리를 뛰어다니며 수백 명의 사람들에게 부상을 입혔다.

➡ _____

13 그중 열두 마리의 동물들이 아직 잡히지 않았다.

➡ _____

14 시민들은 추후 안내가 있을 때까지 집 안에 머물러야 한다.

➡ _____

15 위에 기술된 어떤 행동이나 사건도 일어나지 않았다.

➡ _____

16 그 당시 이 기사를 주의 깊게 읽었던 사람들은 크게 웃었다.

➡ _____

17 그것을 끝까지 읽지 않은 사람들은 정말로 걱정하였다.

➡ _____

18 그 기사가 거짓이라는 것을 알지 못했기 때문에 많은 사람이 겁에 질려 어쩔 줄 몰랐다.

➡ _____

19 어떤 사람들은 도시를 빠져나가려고 했고 다른 사람들은 그 동물들을 사냥하기 위해 총을 들고 공원으로 나갔다.

➡ _____

20 그렇다면 왜 헤럴드 사는 이러한 뉴스를 만들어 냈을까?

➡ _____

21 나중에 그들은 동물원의 안전하지 않은 상태에 대해 독자들의 주의를 끌기 위해 그 기사를 지어냈다고 고백했다.

➡ _____

_____

22 슬라브인이 언쟁 중에 친구에게 총을 쏘다

➡ _____

23 목요일 저녁 채굴 야영지 근처에서, 컬럼비아 광산 소속의 슬라브인 노동자 Mejk Swenekafew가 John Pecitello에 의해 총상을 입어 심각하게 다쳤다.

➡ _____

_____

24 그 두 사람은 회의 중에 언쟁을 벌였다.

➡ _____

25 언쟁이 싸움으로 번졌고, Pecitello가 Swenekafew의 가슴과 다리에 두 번 총을 쏘았다.

➡ _____

26 현재 그는 위독한 상태로 입원 중이다.

➡ _____

27 Pecitello는 총격 이후 도주했다.

➡ _____

28 경찰이 지금 그를 찾고 있으며, 그가 극히 위험하다고 시민들에게 경고하고 있다.

➡ _____

29 이 기사에 뭔가 이상한 점이 있는가?

➡ _____

30 그 슬라브인의 이름을 거꾸로 읽어 보아라. 그것의 철자는 "우리는 뉴스를 조작한다."가 된다.

➡ _____

31 누가 이것을 썼고 왜 그랬을까?

➡ _____

32 데일리 텔레그램 사는 그들의 경쟁자인 데일리 뉴스 사가 그들의 기사를 훔치는지를 증명하기 위해서 이 거짓 기사를 발행했다.

　➡ _____

　_____

33 데일리 뉴스 사는 그 다음 날 'Swenekafew'에 대한 동일한 기사를 발행했고 그래서 훔친 것이 발각되었다.

　➡ _____

34 데일리 뉴스 사의 사람들은 그들의 행동을 인정해야만 했고 대중들로부터 혹독한 비난을 받았다.

　➡ _____

35 이 두 기사는 특별한 경우였지만, 매일 발행되는 '가짜' 뉴스 기사는 많이 있다.

　➡ _____

36 독자로서, 우리는 비판적으로 읽고 그 뉴스가 진짜인지 가짜인지 판단할 필요가 있다.

　➡ _____

37 가짜 뉴스 판별 방법!

　➡ _____

38 출처를 고려하라

　➡ _____

39 그것은 믿을 만한 출처에서 온 것인가?

　➡ _____

40 우리는 그 필자를 신뢰할 수 있는가?

　➡ _____

41 날짜를 확인하라

　➡ _____

42 그것은 새로운 이야기인가 혹은 오래된 이야기인가?

　➡ _____

43 그것은 현재의 사건들과 관련된 것인가?

　➡ _____

44 기사 제목 그 이상을 읽어라

　➡ _____

45 기사 제목이 기사 내용과 일치하는가?

　➡ _____

46 뒷받침하는 자료를 찾아라

　➡ _____

47 다른 관련된 이야기도 비슷한 내용을 제공하는가?

　➡ _____

※ 다음 우리말과 일치하도록 빈칸에 알맞은 말을 쓰시오.

Wrap Up 3

1. A: Wow! The news _____ _____ "Longer Vacation for Students." Hey, we're _____ _____ _____ _____ _____!

2. B: Wait! We _____ _____ first _____ _____ _____ _____.

3. A: _____ do you _____ _____?

4. B: Some news _____ _____ _____ _____ but _____ _____ _____ _____ a different story.

5. A: Oh, I see. I _____ _____ _____ the news title.

1. A: 와! 뉴스 제목이 "학생들을 위한 더 긴 방학"이야. 이봐, 우리 더 긴 방학을 갖나봐!
2. B: 기다려! 우리는 먼저 이게 사실인지를 확인해야 해.
3. A: 왜 그렇게 생각해?
4. B: 어떤 뉴스는 충격적인 제목을 사용하지만 그 내용은 다른 이야기를 할지도 몰라.
5. A: 오, 알았다. 뉴스 제목 너머를 읽어야 하는구나.

Read & Think After You Read B

1. Reporter: Why did *The Herald* _____ the "_____ _____" story, Mr. Right?

2. Mr. Right: They just wanted to _____ _____ _____ _____ to the _____ _____ at the zoo.

3. Reporter: _____, readers _____ _____ _____ _____ _____ that it was _____. _____ _____ "Slav Shoots a Friend in Argument?" What was the _____?

4. Mr. Right: *The Daily Telegram* _____ _____ _____ _____ *The Daily News* _____ _____ _____ _____.

1. 기자: 왜 헤럴드 사는 〈끔찍한 참사〉 이야기를 썼을까요, Right 씨?
2. Mr. Right: 그들은 단지 동물원의 안전하지 않은 상태에 대해 독자들의 주의를 끌고 싶었답니다.
3. 기자: 사실, 독자들은 그것이 가짜라는 것을 알고 매우 화가 났어요. 〈슬라브인이 언쟁 중에 친구에게 총을 쏘다〉는 어떤가요? 동기가 무엇이었나요?
4. Mr. Right: 데일리 텔레그램 사는 데일리 뉴스 사가 그들의 기사를 훔치고 있다는 것을 증명하기를 원했어요.

Read & Think After You Read C

1. A: _____ the four tips, which do you _____ _____ _____ _____ _____, and why?

2. B: I think _____ _____ _____ _____ the most important _____ I can check _____ the _____ _____ _____.

1. A: 네 가지 조언 중에서 너는 어떤 것이 가장 중요하다고 생각하며, 그 이유는 무엇이니?
2. B: 나는 뒷받침하는 자료들을 찾는 것이 가장 중요하다고 생각하는데, 그 정보가 올바른지 확인할 수 있기 때문이야.

※ 다음 우리말을 영어로 쓰시오.

Wrap Up 3

1. A: 와! 뉴스 제목이 "학생들을 위한 더 긴 방학"이야. 이봐, 우리 더 긴 방학을 갖나봐!

➡ _____

_____

2. B: 기다려! 우리는 먼저 이게 사실인지를 확인해야 해.

➡ _____

3. A: 왜 그렇게 생각해?

➡ _____

4. B: 어떤 뉴스는 충격적인 제목을 사용하지만 그 내용은 다른 이야기를 할지도 몰라.

➡ _____

5. A: 오, 알았다. 뉴스 제목 너머를 읽어야 하는구나.

➡ _____

Read & Think After You Read B

1. 기자: 왜 헤럴드 사는 〈끔찍한 참사〉 이야기를 썼을까요, Right 씨?

➡ _____

2. Mr. Right: 그들은 단지 동물원의 안전하지 않은 상태에 대해 독자들의 주의를 끌고 싶었답니다.

➡ _____

3. 기자: 사실, 독자들은 그것이 가짜라는 것을 알고 매우 화가 났어요. 〈슬라브인이 전쟁 중에 친구에게 총을 쏘다〉는 어떤가요? 동기가 무엇이었나요?

➡ _____

4. Mr. Right: 데일리 텔레그램 사는 데일리 뉴스 사가 그들의 기사를 훔치고 있다는 것을 증명하기를 원했어요.

➡ _____

Read & Think After You Read C

1. A: 네 가지 조언 중에서 너는 어떤 것이 가장 중요하다고 생각하며, 그 이유는 무엇이니?

➡ _____

2. B: 나는 뒷받침하는 자료들을 찾는 것이 가장 중요하다고 생각하는데, 그 정보가 올바른지 확인할 수 있기 때문이야.

➡ _____

_____

※ 다음 영어를 우리말로 쓰시오.

01 forever _____

02 suppose _____

03 confusing _____

04 design _____

05 exhibit _____

06 freedom _____

07 expensive _____

08 twin _____

09 priceless _____

10 comfortably _____

11 stardom _____

12 death _____

13 puzzled _____

14 wisdom _____

15 expert _____

16 matter _____

17 captain _____

18 motto _____

19 failure _____

20 express _____

21 foolish _____

22 luxurious _____

23 dwarf _____

24 hire _____

25 forest _____

26 dragon _____

27 lastly _____

28 deadline _____

29 magical _____

30 far-away _____

31 reward _____

32 situation _____

33 castle _____

34 character _____

35 fill up _____

36 bring back _____

37 lock up _____

38 pass away _____

39 run out of _____

40 be stuck on _____

41 come true _____

42 live by _____

43 look after _____

※ 다음 우리말을 영어로 쓰시오.

01 좌우명

02 한가롭게 이야기하다, 담소하다

03 전시하다

04 죽음

05 스타덤, 스타의 반열

06 사치스러운, 호화로운

07 표현하다

08 기한, 마감 일자

09 자유

10 선장

11 고용하다

12 용

13 상황, 환경

14 마술의, 마력이 있는

15 편안하게

16 영원히

17 난장이

18 어리석은, 바보 같은

19 실패

20 혼란스러운, 헷갈리는

21 대단히 귀중한, 값을 매길 수 없는

22 비싼, 돈이 많이 드는

23 당혹스러운, 어리둥절한

24 보상

25 멀리 떨어진

26 성

27 숲, 삼림, 산림

28 전문가

29 추측하다, 추정하다

30 마지막으로, 끝으로

31 쌍둥이의

32 지혜, 현명함

33 설명하다

34 설계하다

35 돌려주다

36 (신조, 원칙 등)에 따라 살다

37 투옥시키다

38 세상을 떠나다, 돌아가시다

39 ~이 없어지다, ~이 다 떨어지다

40 ~에 자리 잡다, ~에 정착하다

41 ~을 살피다, ~을 돌보다

42 잘못하다, 실수를 하다

43 이루어지다, 실현되다

※ 다음 영영풀이에 알맞은 단어를 <보기>에서 골라 쓴 후, 우리말 뜻을 쓰시오.

1 _____ : to show what you think or feel: _____

2 _____ : very comfortable and expensive: _____.

3 _____ : worth a large amount of money: _____

4 _____ : a person who is in charge of a ship or an airplane: _____

5 _____ : a person represented in a film, play, or story: _____

6 _____ : to employ them or pay them to do a particular job for you: _____

7 _____ : a professional cook, especially the most senior cook in a restaurant, hotel, etc.: _____

8 _____ : a specific time or date by which you have to do something: _____

9 _____ : a large aggressive animal with wings and a long tail, that can breathe out fire: _____

10 _____ : something given in exchange for good behavior or good work, etc.: _____

11 _____ : to show something in a public place for people to enjoy or to give them information: _____

12 _____ : a person with a high level of knowledge or skill relating to a particular subject or activity: _____

13 _____ : to make something clear or easy to understand by describing or giving information about it: _____

14 _____ : a lack of success in doing or achieving something, especially in relation to a particular activity: _____

15 _____ : the ability to use your knowledge and experience to make good decisions and judgments: _____

16 _____ : a large building usually with high, thick walls and towers that was built in the past to protect against attack: _____

보기			
explain	hire	failure	chef
wisdom	luxurious	reward	express
exhibit	character	castle	deadline
expert	priceless	dragon	captain

※ 다음 우리말과 일치하도록 빈칸에 알맞은 말을 쓰시오.

Listen & Talk 1 A

1. W: James, why are _____ _____ _____? It's 11 o'clock!

   M: I can't sleep _____ _____ _____ _____ the Bookworm Competition tomorrow.

   W: _____ _____ all of the books on the list. What do you _____ _____ _____ _____?

   M: Some of the writers' names are _____, so I'm _____ _____ I _____ _____ _____ them.

   W: _____ _____ about something _____ _____ _____ yet. You'll do fine.

   M: Thanks. I'll _____ _____ _____ _____ so much.

2. M: Sujin, what are you doing this weekend?

   W: _____ _____, why?

   M: I _____ _____ _____ _____ Busan for a family trip tomorrow but I _____ _____ _____ my dog, Lucy.

   W: Don't _____ _____ Lucy. I'll _____ _____ _____ her.

   M: Oh, thank you so much. I was so _____.

   W: I'll take her _____ _____ _____ in the park, too. The weather's _____ _____ _____ nice tomorrow.

Listen & Talk 1 B

M: Jane, you look _____. What's the _____?

W: I _____ _____ _____ _____ _____ the school musical.

M: I _____ you _____. You sound great!

W: It's just that I _____ _____ _____. I'm so _____.

M: Oh, you just need _____ _____ more _____. Don't worry about _____ _____. You can actually learn from them.

W: Thanks, Dad. I hope I do a good job.

M: You'll do great.

해석

1. W: James, 왜 아직 깨어 있니? 11시야!

   M: 내일 있을 책벌레 경연 대회가 걱정되어서 저는 잠을 잘 수가 없어요.

   W: 너는 목록에 있는 책들을 다 읽었잖아. 뭐가 걱정이니?

   M: 몇몇 작가들의 이름이 헷갈려서 그들을 기억하지 못할까봐 걱정이 돼요.

   W: 아직 일어나지 않은 일을 걱정하지 마. 너는 잘할 거야.

   M: 고마워요. 너무 걱정하지 않도록 해 볼게요.

2. M: 수진아, 이번 주말에 뭐 할 거야?

   W: 특별한 일은 없어, 왜?

   M: 내일 부산으로 가족 여행을 가야 하는데 내 개 Lucy에게 먹이를 줄 사람을 아무도 찾을 수가 없어.

   W: Lucy에 대해서는 걱정하지 마. 내가 그 개를 돌봐 줄게.

   M: 오, 정말 고마워. 나 너무 걱정했거든.

   W: 내가 그 개를 데리고 공원에서 산책도 시켜 줄게. 내일 날씨가 좋을 거래.

M: Jane, 너 걱정스러워 보이는구나. 무슨 일 있니?

W: 제가 학교 뮤지컬에서 큰 역할을 맡았어요.

M: 네가 노래하는 것을 들었어. 잘하던데!

W: 그냥 제가 자꾸만 실수하는 거예요. 저는 너무 걱정돼요.

M: 오, 너는 그저 조금만 더 연습하면 돼. 실수하는 것에 대해서는 걱정하지 마. 사실 실수로부터 배울 수 있어.

W: 고마워요, 아빠. 제가 잘하면 좋겠어요.

M: 너는 아주 잘해 낼 거야.

1. M: Caroline, _____ you _____ the book, *Tuck Everlasting*?

   W: Yeah, it is about a family that drank _____ _____ and _____ _____, right?

   M: Right. _____ _____ _____ _____ you could live _____?

   W: Well, I _____ live in _____ _____ all around the world.

   M: Really? I would collect _____ items and make a museum.

   W: Cool.

2. W: Jason, what are you reading?

   M: I'm reading a book _____ *Three Wishes*.

   W: Oh, I've _____ about it. A genie makes a boy's wishes _____ _____, right?

   M: Yeah. What would you do _____ _____ _____ _____ _____?

   W: I _____ _____ the genies _____ with me _____. Then, I could _____ _____ _____ _____ _____ _____.

   M: That's _____!

W: What are you doing, Jinho?

M: I'm _____ _____ _____ of the movie, *The Time Traveler's Wife*.

W: I saw that movie, too. It's _____ _____ my favorite romantic _____.

M: I loved it, too. Emily, _____ _____ _____ _____ time travel?

W: I _____ _____ to the 1940s and _____ World War II. _____ _____ you?

M: I _____ _____ _____ the Joseon Dynasty and _____ King Sejong. I'm a _____ _____ _____ him.

1. M: Caroline, 너 트리갭의 샘물(Tuck Everlasting)이라는 책을 읽어 봤니?

   W: 응, 그것은 마법의 물을 마시고 영원히 살게 된 한 가족에 대한 이야기잖아, 맞지?

   M: 맞아. 만약 네가 영원히 살게 된다면 너는 뭘 할 거야?

   W: 글쎄, 나는 전 세계의 다양한 도시에서 살고 싶어.

   M: 정말? 나는 흥미로운 물건들을 모아서 박물관을 만들 거야.

   W: 멋지다.

2. W: Jason, 무엇을 읽고 있니?

   M: 나는 〈세 가지 소원〉이라는 책을 읽고 있어.

   W: 오, 그것에 대해 들어 본 적 있어. 요정이 어떤 남자아이의 소원을 들어주는 거지, 그렇지?

   M: 맞아. 만약 소원 하나를 빌 수 있다면 너는 무엇을 할 거니?

   W: 나는 요정을 영원히 내 옆에 있도록 만들 거야. 그러면, 나는 나의 모든 소원들을 이룰 수 있어.

   M: 그거 똑똑한데!

W: 진호야, 무엇을 하고 있니?

M: 나는 〈시간 여행자의 아내〉라는 영화의 후기를 쓰고 있어.

W: 나도 그 영화 봤어. 그건 내가 가장 좋아하는 로맨스 영화 중 하나야.

M: 나도 너무 좋았어. Emily, 만약 네가 시간 여행을 할 수 있다면 무엇을 하겠니?

W: 나는 1940년대로 가서 제2차 세계 대전을 막고 싶어. 너는 어때?

M: 나는 조선 시대로 가서 세종대왕을 만나고 싶어. 나는 그의 엄청난 팬이야.

Communication Step A

M: _____ your online story _____, Amy?

W: Not well. The deadline is this weekend but I _____ _____ of ideas.

M: _____ _____ _____ it. I can help you.

W: That would be great. My main _____ has special powers. _____ _____ _____ _____ _____ _____ _____ able to read people's minds?

M: Well, I would _____ _____ _____ the girl I like _____ me.

W: That's a good idea. Thanks.

Wrap Up

1. M: _____ _____ _____ you're going to be in the _____ _____ next week.

   W: Yeah, it's _____ next week.

   M: You look _____. What's _____?

   W: _____ _____ _____ the topic would be _____ _____ for me.

   M: _____ _____ _____ something you can't change. Just _____ _____ _____.

   W: Thanks. I'll try.

2. M: Lisa, have you _____ the movie, *Cast Away*?

   W: No, I _____. What is it about?

   M: It's about _____ _____ _____ _____ _____ _____ _____ a _____ _____ for 4 years.

   W: It sounds interesting.

   M: Yeah, the man _____ everything to stay alive. What _____ you do _____ _____ _____ _____?

   W: To stay _____? Well, I would _____ a tree house and _____ for food.

   M: Yeah, me too. And _____ _____ _____ _____ _____ in the movie.

M: 네 온라인 이야기는 어떻게 되어 가고 있니, Amy?

W: 별로야. 마감이 이번 주말인데 아이디어가 다 떨어졌어.

M: 그건 걱정하지 마. 내가 도와줄게.

W: 그럼 정말 좋겠다. 내 주인공은 특별한 능력을 가지고 있어. 만약 네가 사람들의 생각을 읽을 수 있다면 무엇을 하겠니?

M: 음, 나는 내가 좋아하는 여자아이가 나를 좋아하는지 알아보고 싶어.

W: 그거 좋은 생각이다. 고마워.

1. M: 네가 다음 주에 글쓰기 대회에 나간다고 들었어.

   W: 맞아, 그게 벌써 다음 주야.

   M: 너 걱정스러워 보인다. 무슨 일이니?

   W: 주제가 나에게 너무 어려울까봐 걱정이야.

   M: 네가 바꿀 수 없는 것에 대해 걱정하지 마. 그저 자신을 믿어봐.

   W: 고마워. 그렇게 해 볼게.

2. M: Lisa, 영화 〈캐스트 어웨이〉 본 적 있니?

   W: 아니, 없어. 무슨 내용이야?

   M: 4년 동안 외딴섬에 갇힌 어떤 남자에 관한 영화야.

   W: 재미있게 들린다.

   M: 응, 그 남자는 살기 위해 모든 것을 시도해. 만약 네가 그 남자라면 무엇을 하겠니?

   W: 살기 위해서? 글쎄, 나는 나무로 집을 만들고 먹을 것을 사냥할 거야.

   M: 응, 나도. 그리고 그게 그 남자가 영화에서 했던 거야.

※ 다음 우리말에 맞도록 대화를 영어로 쓰시오.

Listen & Talk 1 A

1. W: _____

   M: _____
   _____

   W: _____

   M: _____

   W: _____

   M: _____

2. M: _____

   W: _____

   M: _____
   _____

   W: _____

   M: _____

   W: _____
   _____

Listen & Talk 1 B

M: _____

W: _____

M: _____

W: _____

M: _____

W: _____

M: _____

해석

1. W: James, 왜 아직 깨어 있니? 11시야!
   M: 내일 있을 책벌레 경연 대회가 걱정되어서 저는 잠을 잘 수가 없어요.
   W: 너는 목록에 있는 책들을 다 읽었잖아. 뭐가 걱정이니?
   M: 몇몇 작가들의 이름이 헷갈려서 그들을 기억하지 못할까봐 걱정이 돼요.
   W: 아직 일어나지 않은 일을 걱정하지 마. 너는 잘할 거야.
   M: 고마워요. 너무 걱정하지 않도록 해 볼게요.

2. M: 수진아, 이번 주말에 뭐 할 거야?
   W: 특별한 일은 없어, 왜?
   M: 내일 부산으로 가족 여행을 가야 하는데 내 개 Lucy에게 먹이를 줄 사람을 아무도 찾을 수가 없어.
   W: Lucy에 대해서는 걱정하지 마. 내가 그 개를 돌봐 줄게.
   M: 오, 정말 고마워. 나 너무 걱정했거든.
   W: 내가 그 개를 데리고 공원에서 산책도 시켜 줄게. 내일 날씨가 좋을 거래.

M: Jane, 너 걱정스러워 보이는구나. 무슨 일 있니?
W: 제가 학교 뮤지컬에서 큰 역할을 맡았어요.
M: 네가 노래하는 것을 들었어. 잘하던데!
W: 그냥 제가 자꾸만 실수하는 거예요. 저는 너무 걱정돼요.
M: 오, 너는 그저 조금만 더 연습하면 돼. 실수하는 것에 대해서는 걱정하지 마. 사실 실수로부터 배울 수 있어.
W: 고마워요, 아빠. 제가 잘하면 좋겠어요.
M: 너는 아주 잘해 낼 거야.

Listen & Talk 2 A

1. M: _____

   W: _____

   M: _____

   W: _____

   M: _____

   W: _____

2. W: _____

   M: _____

   W: _____

   M: _____

   W: _____
   _____

   M: _____

Listen & Talk 2 B

W: _____

M: _____

W: _____

M: _____

W: _____

M: _____

1. M: Caroline, 너 트리갭의 샘물(Tuck Everlasting)이라는 책을 읽어 봤니?

   W: 응, 그것은 마법의 물을 마시고 영원히 살게 된 한 가족에 대한 이야기잖아, 맞지?

   M: 맞아. 만약 네가 영원히 살게 된다면 너는 뭘 할 거야?

   W: 글쎄, 나는 전 세계의 다양한 도시에서 살고 싶어.

   M: 정말? 나는 흥미로운 물건들을 모아서 박물관을 만들 거야.

   W: 멋지다.

2. W: Jason, 무엇을 읽고 있니?

   M: 나는 〈세 가지 소원〉이라는 책을 읽고 있어.

   W: 오, 그것에 대해 들어 본 적 있어. 요정이 어떤 남자아이의 소원을 들어주는 거지, 그렇지?

   M: 맞아. 만약 소원 하나를 빌 수 있다면 너는 무엇을 할 거니?

   W: 나는 요정을 영원히 내 옆에 있도록 만들 거야. 그러면, 나는 나의 모든 소원들을 이룰 수 있어.

   M: 그거 똑똑한데!

W: 진호야, 무엇을 하고 있니?

M: 나는 〈시간 여행자의 아내〉라는 영화의 후기를 쓰고 있어.

W: 나도 그 영화 봤어. 그건 내가 가장 좋아하는 로맨스 영화 중 하나야.

M: 나도 너무 좋았어. Emily, 만약 네가 시간 여행을 할 수 있다면 무엇을 하겠니?

W: 나는 1940년대로 가서 제2차 세계 대전을 막고 싶어. 너는 어때?

M: 나는 조선 시대로 가서 세종대왕을 만나고 싶어. 나는 그의 엄청난 팬이야.

Communication Step A

M: _____
W: _____
M: _____
W: _____
_____
M: _____
W: _____

M: 네 온라인 이야기는 어떻게 되어 가고 있니, Amy?
W: 별로야. 마감이 이번 주말인데 아이디어가 다 떨어졌어.
M: 그건 걱정하지 마. 내가 도와줄게.
W: 그럼 정말 좋겠다. 내 주인공은 특별한 능력을 가지고 있어. 만약 네가 사람들의 생각을 읽을 수 있다면 무엇을 하겠니?
M: 음, 나는 내가 좋아하는 여자아이가 나를 좋아하는지 알아보고 싶어.
W: 그거 좋은 생각이다. 고마워.

Wrap Up

1. M: _____
   W: _____
   M: _____
   W: _____
   M: _____
   W: _____

2. M: _____
   W: _____
   M: _____
   W: _____
   M: _____
   _____
   W: _____
   M: _____

1. M: 네가 다음 주에 글쓰기 대회에 나간다고 들었어.
   W: 맞아, 그게 벌써 다음 주야.
   M: 너 걱정스러워 보인다. 무슨 일이니?
   W: 주제가 나에게 너무 어려울까봐 걱정이야.
   M: 네가 바꿀 수 없는 것에 대해 걱정하지 마. 그저 자신을 믿어봐.
   W: 고마워. 그렇게 해 볼게.

2. M: Lisa, 영화 〈캐스트 어웨이〉 본 적 있니?
   W: 아니, 없어. 무슨 내용이야?
   M: 4년 동안 외딴섬에 갇힌 어떤 남자에 관한 영화야.
   W: 재미있게 들린다.
   M: 응, 그 남자는 살기 위해 모든 것을 시도해. 만약 네가 그 남자라면 무엇을 하겠니?
   W: 살기 위해서? 글쎄, 나는 나무로 집을 만들고 먹을 것을 사냥할 거야.
   M: 응, 나도. 그리고 그게 그 남자가 영화에서 했던 거야.

※ 다음 우리말과 일치하도록 빈칸에 알맞은 것을 골라 쓰시오.

1 A _____ and _____ father _____ two _____, Puru and Puneet.

A. had   B. wise   C. sons   D. rich

2 Before he _____ _____, he called his two sons to give them some last _____ of _____.

A. away   B. words   C. passed   D. advice

3 "Listen carefully, my dear sons. _____ _____ these words _____ your _____, and you will be happy," he said.

A. throughout   B. by   C. life   D. live

4 "_____ a house in every city. Sleep _____. Enjoy your food. _____, spend money _____ a rich man... ."

A. comfortably   B. like   C. lastly   D. build

5 Before he could _____ _____, he _____ _____.

A. passed   B. explain   C. away   D. himself

6 After his _____, the two sons took their _____ of the father's _____ and _____ in different cities.

A. settled   B. death   C. share   D. wealth

7 Five years _____. Puru, who had been _____ his father's _____ carefully, had no money _____.

A. words   B. following   C. passed   D. left

8 But his brother was _____ _____ _____.

A. than   B. richer   C. ever

9 Puru was _____ about where he had gone _____, so he visited Puneet to _____ _____.

A. wrong   B. puzzled   C. out   D. find

10 Puneet _____ Puru _____ _____ _____.

A. open   B. welcomed   C. arms   D. with

11 That night, when the brothers sat _____ to _____ after dinner, Puru asked the question that had _____ on his _____ for days.

A. mind   B. chat   C. been   D. down

12 "_____ was our father's advice _____ I followed, but I am not happy. I _____ a house in _____ city.

A. every   B. that   C. built   D. it

13 But because I could not always _____ there, I hired people and _____ the house _____ _____.

A. stay   B. after   C. had   D. looked

1 부유하고 지혜로운 아버지에게 두 아들, Puru와 Puneet이 있었다.

2 아버지는 돌아가시기 전에, 마지막 충고의 말을 하기 위해 그의 두 아들을 불렀다.

3 "주의 깊게 들어라, 사랑하는 아들들아. 너희의 일생 동안 이 말대로 살면, 행복해질 것이다." 그는 말했다.

4 "모든 도시에 집을 지어라. 편하게 자거라. 음식을 즐기거라. 마지막으로, 돈을 부자처럼 쓰거라…."

5 아버지는 그 말을 설명하기도 전에 돌아가셨다.

6 그의 죽음 후에, 두 아들은 아버지의 재산 중 자신들의 몫을 가지고 다른 도시에 정착했다.

7 5년이 지났다. 아버지의 말을 신중히 따라온 Puru는 남은 돈이 없었다.

8 그러나 그의 동생은 그 어느 때보다 더 부자가 되었다.

9 Puru는 그가 어디서부터 잘못했는지 어리둥절했고, 그래서 그는 (그것을) 알아내기 위해 Puneet을 방문했다.

10 Puneet은 Puru를 두 팔 벌려 환영했다.

11 그날 밤, 형제가 저녁식사 후 이야기를 하려고 앉았을 때, Puru는 며칠간 자신의 마음에 있었던 그 질문을 했다.

12 "내가 따른 건 바로 우리 아버지의 조언이었지만, 나는 행복하지 않아. 나는 모든 도시에 집을 지었어.

13 그러나 나는 그곳에 항상 머물 수 없었으므로 사람들을 고용하여 집을 돌보게 했지.

14 Father said we should sleep _____ and enjoy our food, so I _____ my bed _____ by experts and my meals _____ by a great chef.

    A. designed   B. prepared   C. comfortably   D. had

15 He told us to _____ _____ a rich man, so I bought _____ I wanted without _____ about money.

    A. worrying   B. like   C. what   D. spend

16 But _____ _____ _____ me now! I am _____.

    A. empty-handed   B. at   C. look

17 Did you _____ _____ our _____ _____?

    A. wisdom   B. follow   C. father's   D. not

18 Tell me, brother, _____ _____ you _____ so _____?"

    A. get   B. how   C. rich   D. did

19 Puneet _____ and said, "My dear brother, I _____ _____ our father's _____.

    A. followed   B. wisdom   C. smiled   D. also

20 But I understood it _____ _____ _____.

    A. bit   B. a   C. differently

21 When he said ' _____ a house in every city,' I _____ it _____ having a place to _____ all around the world.

    A. as   B. took   C. build   D. stay

22 So I _____ _____ in every city and I _____ _____ their houses when I visited those cities.

    A. at   B. stayed   C. made   D. friends

23 Also, I slept _____ each night because I would be _____ after a hard day's _____, and it did not matter if I was sleeping on a bed or on the hard _____.

    A. tired   B. comfortably   C. work   D. floor

24 I ate _____ _____ I was _____, so even a simple meal _____ great."

    A. hungry   B. when   C. tasted   D. only

25 " _____ money _____ a _____ man?" _____ Puneet.

    A. rich   B. like   C. continued   D. spend

26 "A rich man knows _____ _____ _____ money _____.

    A. how   B. grow   C. make   D. to

27 So, I tried to spend money on something that would _____ me _____ more money _____ than on _____ things.

    A. rather   B. luxurious   C. back   D. bring

28 For me, _____ was this wisdom _____ our father uo _____."

    A. explain   B. that   C. it   D. tried

29 Now Puru realized _____ _____ he _____.

    A. foolish   B. had   C. how   D. been

30 _____ this wisdom _____ _____, Puru started a new _____.

    A. mind   B. with   C. in   D. life

14 아버지께서 우리는 편하게 자고 음식을 즐겨야 한다고 말씀하셔서 나는 내 침대를 전문가들에 의해 설계되게 했고, 내 식사는 훌륭한 요리사에 의해 준비되도록 했단다.

15 아버지는 우리에게 부자처럼 돈을 쓰라고 하셨으므로, 나는 돈 걱정을 하지 않고 내가 원하는 것을 샀지.

16 그렇지만 지금 나를 봐! 나는 빈털터리야.

17 너는 우리 아버지의 지혜를 따르지 않았니?

18 나에게 말해 보렴, 동생아, 너는 어떻게 그렇게 부유해졌니?"

19 Puneet은 웃으며 말했다. "친애하는 형님, 저 또한 우리 아버지의 지혜를 따랐습니다.

20 하지만 저는 조금 다르게 이해했지요.

21 아버지가 '모든 도시에 집을 지어라'라고 말하셨을 때, 저는 그것을 전 세계에 머물 수 있는 장소를 가지는 것으로 여겼지요.

22 그래서 저는 모든 도시에서 친구를 사귀었고 그 도시들을 방문했을 때 그들의 집에 머물렀어요.

23 또한, 저는 하루 종일 열심히 일하고 나서 피곤해지곤 했기 때문에 침대에서 자든 딱딱한 바닥에서 자든 상관없이 매일 밤 편안하게 잠을 잤지요.

24 저는 배고플 때만 먹었기 때문에 간단한 식사마저도 훌륭한 맛이 났습니다."

25 "부자처럼 돈을 쓰라고요?" Puneet은 계속했다.

26 "부자는 돈을 불리는 방법을 알고 있어요.

27 그래서 저는 사치스러운 물건에 돈을 쓰는 것보다는 저에게 더 많은 돈을 돌려줄 수 있는 것에 돈을 쓰려고 노력했지요.

28 저에게는 이게 우리의 아버지가 설명하려고 하셨던 바로 그 지혜입니다."

29 이제 Puru는 그가 얼마나 어리석었는지를 깨달았다.

30 이 지혜를 마음에 새기고, Puru는 새로운 삶을 시작했다.

Step2

※ 다음 우리말과 일치하도록 빈칸에 알맞은 것을 골라 쓰시오.

1 A _____ and _____ father _____ _____ _____, Puru and Puneet.

2 Before he _____ _____, he _____ his two sons _____ _____ _____ some _____ _____ _____ _____.

3 "_____ _____, my dear sons. _____ _____ these words _____ _____ _____, and you will be happy," he said.

4 "_____ a house in _____ _____. Sleep _____. _____ your food. _____, _____ money _____ a rich man... ."

5 Before he could _____ _____, he _____ _____.

6 After _____ _____, the two sons took _____ _____ the father's _____ and _____ _____.

7 Five years _____. Puru, _____ _____ his father's words carefully, had _____ _____ _____.

8 But his brother _____ _____ _____ _____ _____.

9 Puru _____ _____ _____ he _____, so he visited Puneet _____ _____ _____.

10 Puneet _____ Puru _____ _____ _____ _____.

11 That night, when the brothers _____ _____ _____ after dinner, Puru asked the question _____ _____ _____ _____ _____ _____.

12 "_____ our father's advice _____ I followed, but I am not happy. I built a house _____ _____ _____.

13 But because I could not _____ _____ _____, I _____ people and _____ the house _____ _____.

1 부유하고 지혜로운 아버지에게 두 아들, Puru와 Puneet이 있었다.

2 아버지는 돌아가시기 전에, 마지막 충고의 말을 하기 위해 그의 두 아들을 불렀다.

3 "주의 깊게 듣거라, 사랑하는 아들들아. 너희의 일생 동안 이 말대로 살면, 행복해질 것이다." 그는 말했다.

4 "모든 도시에 집을 지어라. 편하게 자거라. 음식을 즐기거라. 마지막으로, 돈을 부자처럼 쓰거라…."

5 아버지는 그 말을 설명하기도 전에 돌아가셨다.

6 그의 죽음 후에, 두 아들은 아버지의 재산 중 자신들의 몫을 가지고 다른 도시에 정착했다.

7 5년이 지났다. 아버지의 말을 신중히 따라온 Puru는 남은 돈이 없었다.

8 그러나 그의 동생은 그 어느 때보다 더 부자가 되었다.

9 Puru는 그가 어디서부터 잘못했는지 어리둥절했고, 그래서 그는 (그것을) 알아내기 위해 Puneet을 방문했다.

10 Puneet은 Puru를 두 팔 벌려 환영했다.

11 그날 밤, 형제가 저녁식사 후 이야기를 하려고 앉았을 때, Puru는 며칠간 자신의 마음에 있었던 그 질문을 했다.

12 "내가 따른 건 바로 우리 아버지의 조언이었지만, 나는 행복하지 않아. 나는 모든 도시에 집을 지었어.

13 그러나 나는 그곳에 항상 머물 수 없었으므로 사람들을 고용하여 집을 돌보게 했지.

14 Father said we should _____ _____ and _____ our food, so I _____ my bed _____ by experts and _____ _____ _____ _____ a great chef.

15 He _____ us _____ _____ _____ a rich man, so I bought _____ _____ _____ without _____ about money.

16 But _____ _____ _____ now! I am _____.

17 Did you _____ _____ our _____ _____?

18 Tell me, brother, _____ _____ you _____ so _____?"

19 Puneet _____ and said, "My dear brother, I _____ _____ our _____ _____.

20 But I understood _____ _____ _____ _____ _____.

21 When he said '_____ a house in every city,' I _____ _____ _____ _____ _____ _____ _____ all around the world.

22 So I _____ _____ in every city and I _____ _____ their houses when I visited _____ _____.

23 Also, I slept _____ each night _____ I would be tired after a hard day's work, and it did not matter _____ _____ _____ _____ on a bed _____ on the _____ _____.

24 I ate _____ _____ _____ _____ _____ _____, so even a simple meal _____ _____."

25 "Spend money _____ _____ _____ _____ _____?" _____ Puneet.

26 "A rich man knows _____ _____ _____ _____ _____.

27 So, I tried to spend money _____ something _____ would _____ _____ _____ more money _____ _____ _____ _____ _____.

28 For me, _____ _____ this wisdom _____ our father _____ _____ _____."

29 Now Puru realized _____ _____ _____ _____ _____.

30 _____ this wisdom _____ _____, Puru started a new life.

14 아버지께서 우리는 편하게 자고 음식을 즐겨야 한다고 말씀하셔서 나는 내 침대를 전문가들에 의해 설계되게 했고, 내 식사는 훌륭한 요리사에 의해 준비되도록 했단다.

15 아버지는 우리에게 부자처럼 돈을 쓰라고 하셨으므로, 나는 돈 걱정을 하지 않고 내가 원하는 것을 샀지.

16 그렇지만 지금 나를 봐! 나는 빈털터리야.

17 너는 우리 아버지의 지혜를 따르지 않았니?

18 나에게 말해 보렴, 동생아, 너는 어떻게 그렇게 부유해졌니?"

19 Puneet은 웃으며 말했다. "친애하는 형님, 저 또한 우리 아버지의 지혜를 따랐습니다.

20 하지만 저는 조금 다르게 이해했지요.

21 아버지가 '모든 도시에 집을 지어라'라고 말하셨을 때, 저는 그것을 전 세계에 머물 수 있는 장소를 가지는 것으로 여겼지요.

22 그래서 저는 모든 도시에서 친구를 사귀었고 그 도시들을 방문했을 때 그들의 집에 머물렀어요.

23 또한, 저는 하루 종일 열심히 일하고 나서 피곤해지곤 했기 때문에 침대에서 자든 딱딱한 바닥에서 자든 상관없이 매일 밤 편안하게 잠을 잤지요.

24 저는 배고플 때만 먹었기 때문에 간단한 식사마저도 훌륭한 맛이 났습니다."

25 "부자처럼 돈을 쓰라고요?" Puneet은 계속했다.

26 "부자는 돈을 불리는 방법을 알고 있어요.

27 그래서 저는 사치스러운 물건에 돈을 쓰는 것보다는 저에게 더 많은 돈을 돌려줄 수 있는 것에 돈을 쓰려고 노력했지요.

28 저에게는 이게 우리의 아버지가 설명하려고 하셨던 바로 그 지혜입니다."

29 이제 Puru는 그가 얼마나 어리석었는지를 깨달았다.

30 이 지혜를 마음에 새기고, Puru는 새로운 삶을 시작했다.

※ 다음 문장을 우리말로 쓰시오.

1 A rich and wise father had two sons, Puru and Puneet.

➡ _____

2 Before he passed away, he called his two sons to give them some last words of advice.

➡ _____

3 "Listen carefully, my dear sons. Live by these words throughout your life, and you will be happy," he said.

➡ _____

4 "Build a house in every city. Sleep comfortably. Enjoy your food. Lastly, spend money like a rich man... ."

➡ _____

5 Before he could explain himself, he passed away.

➡ _____

6 After his death, the two sons took their share of the father's wealth and settled in different cities.

➡ _____

7 Five years passed. Puru, who had been following his father's words carefully, had no money left.

➡ _____

8 But his brother was richer than ever.

➡ _____

9 Puru was puzzled about where he had gone wrong, so he visited Puneet to find out.

➡ _____

10 Puneet welcomed Puru with open arms.

➡ _____

11 That night, when the brothers sat down to chat after dinner, Puru asked the question that had been on his mind for days.

➡ _____

12 "It was our father's advice that I followed, but I am not happy. I built a house in every city.

➡ _____

13 But because I could not always stay there, I hired people and had the house looked after.

➡ _____

14 ▶ Father said we should sleep comfortably and enjoy our food, so I had my bed designed by experts
and my meals prepared by a great chef.
➡ _____

15 ▶ He told us to spend like a rich man, so I bought what I wanted without worrying about money.
➡ _____

16 ▶ But look at me now! I am empty-handed.
➡ _____

17 ▶ Did you not follow our father's wisdom?
➡ _____

18 ▶ Tell me, brother, how did you get so rich?"
➡ _____

19 ▶ Puneet smiled and said, "My dear brother, I also followed our father's wisdom.
➡ _____

20 ▶ But I understood it a bit differently.
➡ _____

21 ▶ When he said 'build a house in every city,' I took it as having a place to stay all around the world.
➡ _____

22 ▶ So I made friends in every city and I stayed at their houses when I visited those cities.
➡ _____

23 ▶ Also, I slept comfortably each night because I would be tired after a hard day's work, and it did
not matter if I was sleeping on a bed or on the hard floor.
➡ _____

24 ▶ I ate only when I was hungry, so even a simple meal tasted great."
➡ _____

25 ▶ "Spend money like a rich man?" continued Puneet.
➡ _____

26 ▶ "A rich man knows how to make money grow.
➡ _____

27 ▶ So, I tried to spend money on something that would bring me back more money rather than
on luxurious things.
➡ _____

28 ▶ For me, it was this wisdom that our father tried to explain."
➡ _____

29 ▶ Now Puru realized how foolish he had been.
➡ _____

30 ▶ With this wisdom in mind, Puru started a new life.
➡ _____

※ 다음 괄호 안의 단어들을 우리말에 맞도록 바르게 배열하시오.

1 (rich / a / and father / wise / two / had / sons, / Puneet. / and / Puru)
➡ _____

2 (he / before / away, / passed / called / he / two / his / give / to / sons / some / them / words / last / advice. / of)
➡ _____

3 (carefully, / "listen / dear / my / sons. // by / live / words / these / throughout / life, / your / and / will / you / happy." / be / said. / he)
➡ _____

4 (a / "build / house / every / in / city. // comfortably. / sleep // food. / enjoy / your // lastly, / money / spend / a / like / man...." / rich)
➡ _____

5 (he / before / explain / could / himself, / passed / he / away.)
➡ _____

6 (his / after / death, / two / the / took / sons / share / their / the / of / wealth / father's / and / in / settled / cities. / different)
➡ _____

7 (years / five / passed. // who / Puru, / been / had / following / father's / his / words / carefully, / no / had / left. / money)
➡ _____

8 (his / but / was / brother / than / richer / ever.)
➡ _____

9 (was / Puru / puzzled / where / about / had / he / wrong, / gone / so / he / Puneet / visited / find / to / out.)
➡ _____

10 (welcomed / Puneet / with / Puru / arms. / open)
➡ _____

11 (night, / that / the / when / sat / brothers / down / chat / to / dinner, / after / asked / Puru / the / question / had / that / on / been / mind / his / days. / for)
➡ _____

12 (was / "it / our / advice / father's / I / that / followed, / I / but / not / am / happy. // built / I / house / a / every / in / city.)
➡ _____

13 (because / but / could / I / always / not / there, / stay / hired / I / people / and / the / had / house / after. / looked)
➡ _____

1 부유하고 지혜로운 아버지에게 두 아들, Puru와 Puneet이 있었다.

2 아버지는 돌아가시기 전에, 마지막 충고의 말을 하기 위해 그의 두 아들을 불렀다.

3 "주의 깊게 듣거라, 사랑하는 아들들아. 너희의 일생 동안 이 말대로 살면, 행복해질 것이다." 그는 말했다.

4 "모든 도시에 집을 지어라. 편하게 자거라. 음식을 즐기거라. 마지막으로, 돈을 부자처럼 쓰거라…."

5 아버지는 그 말을 설명하기도 전에 돌아가셨다.

6 그의 죽음 후에, 두 아들은 아버지의 재산 중 자신들의 몫을 가지고 다른 도시에 정착했다.

7 5년이 지났다. 아버지의 말을 신중히 따라온 Puru는 남은 돈이 없었다.

8 그러나 그의 동생은 그 어느 때보다 더 부자가 되었다.

9 Puru는 그가 어디서부터 잘못했는지 어리둥절했고, 그래서 그는 (그것을) 알아내기 위해 Puneet을 방문했다.

10 Puneet은 Puru를 두 팔 벌려 환영했다.

11 그날 밤, 형제가 저녁식사 후 이야기를 하려고 앉았을 때, Puru는 며칠간 자신의 마음에 있었던 그 질문을 했다.

12 "내가 따른 건 바로 우리 아버지의 조언이었지만, 나는 행복하지 않아. 나는 모든 도시에 집을 지었어.

13 그러나 나는 그곳에 항상 머물 수 없었으므로 사람들을 고용하여 집을 돌보게 했지.

14 (said / father / should / we / comfortably / sleep / enjoy / and / food, / our / I / so / my / had / bed / my / by / designed / experts / and / meals / my / by / prepared / great / a / chef.)

➡ _____

15 (told / he / to / us / like / spend / a / man, / rich / so / bought / I / what / wanted / I / worrying / without / money. / about)

➡ _____

16 (look / but / me / at / now! // am / I / empty-handed.)

➡ _____

17 (you / did / follow / not / father's / our / wisdom?)

➡ _____

18 (me, / tell / how / brother, / did / get / you / rich?" / so)

➡ _____

19 (smiled / Puneet / said, / and / dear / "my / brother, / also / I / our / followed / wisdom. / father's)

➡ _____

20 (I / but / it / understood / bit / a / differently.)

➡ _____

21 (he / when / 'build / said / house / a / every / in / city,' / took / I / as / it / a / having / place / to / stay / around / all / world. / the)

➡ _____

22 (I / so / friends / made / every / in / city / I / and / stayed / their / at / when / houses / I / those / visited / cities.)

➡ _____

23 (I / also, / comfortably / slept / night / each / because / would / I / tired / be / a / after / day's / hard / work, / it / and / did / matter / not / if / was / I / on / sleeping / bed / a / the / on / or / floor. / hard)

➡ _____

24 (ate / I / when / only / was / I / hungry / even / so, / simple / a / tasted / meal / great."

➡ _____

25 (money / "spend / a / like / man?" / rich / Puneet. / continued)

➡ _____

26 (rich / "a / knows / man / to / how / money / make / grow.)

➡ _____

27 (I / so, / to / tried / money / spend / something / on / would / that / me / bring / back / money / more / than / rather / luxurious / on / things.)

➡ _____

28 (me, / for / was / it / wisdom / this / our / that / father / to / tried / explain.")

➡ _____

29 (Puru / now / how / realized / foolish / had / he / been.)

➡ _____

30 (this / with / in / wisdom / mind, / started / Puru / new / a / life.)

➡ _____

14 아버지께서 우리는 편하게 자고 음식을 즐겨야 한다고 말씀하셔서 나는 내 침대를 전문가들에 의해 설계되게 했고, 내 식사는 훌륭한 요리사에 의해 준비되도록 했단다.

15 아버지는 우리에게 부자처럼 돈을 쓰라고 하셨으므로, 나는 돈 걱정을 하지 않고 내가 원하는 것을 샀지.

16 그렇지만 지금 나를 봐! 나는 빈털터리야.

17 너는 우리 아버지의 지혜를 따르지 않았니?

18 나에게 말해 보렴, 동생아, 너는 어떻게 그렇게 부유해졌니?"

19 Puneet은 웃으며 말했다. "친애하는 형님, 저 또한 우리 아버지의 지혜를 따랐습니다.

20 하지만 저는 조금 다르게 이해했지요.

21 아버지가 '모든 도시에 집을 지어라'라고 말하셨을 때, 저는 그것을 전 세계에 머물 수 있는 장소를 가지는 것으로 여겼지요.

22 그래서 저는 모든 도시에서 친구를 사귀었고 그 도시들을 방문했을 때 그들의 집에 머물렀어요.

23 또한, 저는 하루 종일 열심히 일하고 나서 피곤해지곤 했기 때문에 침대에서 자든 딱딱한 바닥에서 자든 상관없이 매일 밤 편안하게 잠을 잤지요.

24 저는 배고플 때만 먹었기 때문에 간단한 식사마저도 훌륭한 맛이 났습니다."

25 "부자처럼 돈을 쓰라고요?" Puneet은 계속했다.

26 "부자는 돈을 불리는 방법을 알고 있어요.

27 그래서 저는 사치스러운 물건에 돈을 쓰는 것보다는 저에게 더 많은 돈을 돌려줄 수 있는 것에 돈을 쓰려고 노력했지요.

28 저에게는 이게 우리의 아버지가 설명하려고 하셨던 바로 그 지혜입니다."

29 이제 Puru는 그가 얼마나 어리석었는지를 깨달았다.

30 이 지혜를 마음에 새기고, Puru는 새로운 삶을 시작했다.

※ 다음 우리말을 영어로 쓰시오.

1 부유하고 지혜로운 아버지에게 두 아들, Puru와 Puneet이 있었다.

➡ _____

2 아버지는 돌아가시기 전에, 마지막 충고의 말을 하기 위해 그의 두 아들을 불렀다.

➡ _____

3 "주의 깊게 듣거라, 사랑하는 아들들아. 너희의 일생 동안 이 말대로 살면, 행복해질 것이다." 그는 말했다.

➡ _____

4 "모든 도시에 집을 지어라. 편하게 자거라. 음식을 즐기거라. 마지막으로, 돈을 부자처럼 쓰거라…."

➡ _____

5 아버지는 그 말을 설명하기도 전에 돌아가셨다.

➡ _____

6 그의 죽음 후에, 두 아들은 아버지의 재산 중 자신들의 몫을 가지고 다른 도시에 정착했다.

➡ _____

7 5년이 지났다. 아버지의 말을 신중히 따라온 Puru는 남은 돈이 없었다.

➡ _____

8 그러나 그의 동생은 그 어느 때보다 더 부자가 되었다.

➡ _____

9 Puru는 그가 어디서부터 잘못했는지 어리둥절했고, 그래서 그는 (그것을) 알아내기 위해 Puneet을 방문했다.

➡ _____

10 Puneet은 Puru를 두 팔 벌려 환영했다.

➡ _____

11 그날 밤, 형제가 저녁식사 후 이야기를 하려고 앉았을 때, Puru는 며칠간 자신의 마음에 있었던 그 질문을 했다.

➡ _____

12 "내가 따른 건 바로 우리 아버지의 조언이었지만, 나는 행복하지 않아. 나는 모든 도시에 집을 지었어.

➡ _____

13 그러나 나는 그곳에 항상 머물 수 없었으므로 사람들을 고용하여 집을 돌보게 했지.

➡ _____

14 아버지께서 우리는 편하게 자고 음식을 즐겨야 한다고 말씀하셔서 나는 내 침대를 전문가들에 의해 설계되게 했고, 내 식사는 훌륭한 요리사에 의해 준비되도록 했단다.

➡ _____

_____

15 아버지는 우리에게 부자처럼 돈을 쓰라고 하셨으므로, 나는 돈 걱정을 하지 않고 내가 원하는 것을 샀지.

➡ _____

16 그렇지만 지금 나를 봐! 나는 빈털터리야.

➡ _____

17 너는 우리 아버지의 지혜를 따르지 않았니?

➡ _____

18 나에게 말해 보렴, 동생아, 너는 어떻게 그렇게 부유해졌니?"

➡ _____

19 Puneet은 웃으며 말했다. "친애하는 형님, 저 또한 우리 아버지의 지혜를 따랐습니다.

➡ _____

20 하지만 저는 조금 다르게 이해했지요.

➡ _____

21 아버지가 '모든 도시에 집을 지어라'라고 말하셨을 때, 저는 그것을 전 세계에 머물 수 있는 장소를 가지는 것으로 여겼지요.

➡ _____

22 그래서 저는 모든 도시에서 친구를 사귀었고 그 도시들을 방문했을 때 그들의 집에 머물렀어요.

➡ _____

23 또한, 저는 하루 종일 열심히 일하고 나서 피곤해지곤 했기 때문에 침대에서 자든 딱딱한 바닥에서 자든 상관없이 매일 밤 편안하게 잠을 잤지요.

➡ _____

_____

24 저는 배고플 때만 먹었기 때문에 간단한 식사마저도 훌륭한 맛이 났습니다."

➡ _____

25 "부자처럼 돈을 쓰라고요?" Puneet은 계속했다.

➡ _____

26 "부자는 돈을 불리는 방법을 알고 있어요.

➡ _____

27 그래서 저는 사치스러운 물건에 돈을 쓰는 것보다는 저에게 더 많은 돈을 돌려줄 수 있는 것에 돈을 쓰려고 노력했지요

➡ _____

_____

28 저에게는 이게 우리의 아버지가 설명하려고 하셨던 바로 그 지혜입니다."

➡ _____

29 이제 Puru는 그가 얼마나 어리석었었는지를 깨달았다.

➡ _____

30 이 지혜를 마음에 새기고, Puru는 새로운 삶을 시작했다.

➡ _____

※ 다음 우리말과 일치하도록 빈칸에 알맞은 말을 쓰시오.

Language in Use

1. Everyone has _____ _____ _____ and _____ .

2. Can you _____ _____ _____ of the game _____ _____ _____ _____ _____ ?

1. 모든 사람들은 언론과 표현의 자유가 있다.
2. 우리가 경기를 시작하기 전에 규칙을 설명해 줄래?

Grammar in Real Life B Look and Write

1. Do you _____ _____ _____ the computer _____ ? Call the Computer Doctor.

2. _____ _____ you _____ _____ _____ _____ at Susie's Hair Studio?

3. _____ _____ _____ your pet cleaned from head to toe? Come to Happy Pet.

4. Do you want to have your party room _____ _____ _____ ? _____ _____ Mary's Flowers.

1. 컴퓨터를 고쳐야 하나요? '컴퓨터 닥터'에게 전화하세요.
2. '수지의 헤어 스튜디오'에서 머리카락을 자르는 게 어때요?
3. 당신의 애완동물을 머리부터 발끝까지 깨끗하게 하는 것은 어떨까요? '해피 펫'으로 오세요.
4. 당신의 파티 룸을 꽃으로 장식하고 싶은가요? '메리의 꽃들'을 찾아 주세요.

Think & Write C

1. _____ me _____ my motto.

2. It is "Go _____ it!"

3. It _____ "Go and do things _____ _____ because failure is also a _____ _____ ."

4. I _____ it _____ _____ _____ _____ _____ _____ _____ in the school soccer team.

5. _____ the motto, I learned that _____ the bad kicks _____ me _____ _____ _____ _____ _____ _____ _____ .

6. _____ is this motto _____ _____ _____ _____ _____ _____ !

1. 나의 좌우명을 소개하게 해 줘.
2. 그것은 "어서 해!"야
3. 그것은 "실패 또한 좋은 경험이기 때문에 두려움 없이 무언가를 해'라는 의미야.
4. 나는 학교 축구팀에서 키커였을 때, 그것을 나의 좌우명으로 삼았어.
5. 그 좌우명에서 나는 나쁜 킥들조차 결국엔 나를 더 좋은 키커로 만들어 준다는 것을 배웠지.
6. 나의 삶을 바꾼 것은 바로 이 좌우명이야!

※ 다음 우리말을 영어로 쓰시오.

Language in Use

1. 모든 사람들은 언론과 표현의 자유가 있다.

➡ _____

2. 우리가 경기를 시작하기 전에 규칙을 설명해 줄래?

➡ _____

Grammar in Real Life B Look and Write

1. 컴퓨터를 고쳐야 하나요? '컴퓨터 닥터'에게 전화하세요.

➡ _____

2. '수지의 헤어 스튜디오'에서 머리카락을 자르는 게 어때요?

➡ _____

3. 당신의 애완동물을 머리부터 발끝까지 깨끗하게 하는 것은 어떨까요? '해피 펫'으로 오세요.

➡ _____

4. 당신의 파티 룸을 꽃으로 장식하고 싶은가요? '메리의 꽃들'을 찾아 주세요.

➡ _____

Think & Write C

1. 나의 좌우명을 소개하게 해 줘.

➡ _____

2. 그것은 "어서 해!"야

➡ _____

3. 그것은 "실패 또한 좋은 경험이기 때문에 두려움 없이 무언가를 해'라는 의미야.

➡ _____

4. 나는 학교 축구팀에서 키커였을 때, 그것을 나의 좌우명으로 삼았어.

➡ _____

5. 그 좌우명에서 나는 나쁜 킥들조차 결국엔 나를 더 좋은 키커로 만들어 준다는 것을 배웠지.

➡ _____

6. 나의 삶을 바꾼 것은 바로 이 좌우명이야!

➡ _____

※ 다음 영어를 우리말로 쓰시오.

01 convenient	
02 last	
03 match	
04 compete	
05 allowance	
06 purchase	
07 release	
08 affect	
09 disappear	
10 behavior	
11 combine	
12 replace	
13 mention	
14 aboard	
15 discount	
16 encourage	
17 effect	
18 compare	
19 refund	
20 spending	
21 concept	

22 endanger	
23 complete	
24 fix	
25 striped	
26 difference	
27 immediately	
28 tight	
29 influence	
30 lack	
31 anchor	
32 billion	
33 overheated	
34 consume	
35 on display	
36 in comparison	
37 go well with	
38 just because	
39 keep track of	
40 when it comes to	
41 be likely to	
42 more than half	
43 at a glance	

※ 다음 우리말을 영어로 쓰시오.

01	용돈	_____
02	결합하다	_____
03	즉시, 바로	_____
04	효과	_____
05	편리한, 간편한	_____
06	거래	_____
07	10억	_____
08	완성하다	_____
09	~에 영향을 주다	_____
10	언급하다, 말하다	_____
11	소비하다, 소모하다	_____
12	닻; 닻을 내리다	_____
13	행동, 행위	_____
14	놓치다	_____
15	차이, 차이점	_____
16	비교하다	_____
17	부추기다, 조장하다	_____
18	경쟁하다	_____
19	위험에 빠뜨리다	_____
20	개념	_____
21	줄무늬가 있는	_____

22	환불	_____
23	출시하다, 발매하다	_____
24	~에 영향을 주다	_____
25	부족, 결핍	_____
26	사라지다	_____
27	할인; 할인하다	_____
28	어울리다	_____
29	구매하다, 구입하다	_____
30	기르다, 키우다	_____
31	바꾸다, 교체하다	_____
32	지출	_____
33	꽉 조이는, 딱 붙는	_____
34	낭비하다, 소모하다	_____
35	진열된, 전시된	_____
36	한눈에, 즉시	_____
37	비교해 보면	_____
38	~을 기록하다	_____
39	그러한 결과로	_____
40	단지 ~라는 이유로	_____
41	~와 잘 어울리다	_____
42	~에 관해서, ~에 대해 말하자면	_____
43	~할 가능성이 있다, ~하기 쉽다	_____

※ 다음 영영풀이에 알맞은 단어를 <보기>에서 골라 쓴 후, 우리말 뜻을 쓰시오.

1 _____ : without delay: _____

2 _____ : a principle or idea: _____

3 _____ : to become impossible to see: _____

4 _____ : to buy property, goods, etc.: _____

5 _____ : to make something available to the public: _____

6 _____ : to be right for a particular person, situation, or occasion: _____

7 _____ : rather small and fit closely to your body: _____

8 _____ : to join together to make a single thing or group: _____

9 _____ : to use more of something than is necessary or useful: _____

10 _____ : suitable for your purposes and needs and causing the least difficulty:

_____

11 _____ : to support an activity or make it more likely: _____

12 _____ : an amount of money that is given to someone regularly or for a particular

purpose: _____

13 _____ : to use fuel, energy, or time, especially in large amounts or to eat or drink,

especially a lot of something: _____

14 _____ : to put someone or something at risk or in danger of being harmed,

damaged, or destroyed: _____

15 _____ : a condition of not having any or enough of something, especially

something necessary or wanted: _____

16 _____ : to have an influence on someone or something, or to cause a change in

someone or something: _____

※ 다음 우리말과 일치하도록 빈칸에 알맞은 말을 쓰시오.

Listen & Talk 1 A

1. M: Hi, can I _____ you _____ anything?

   W: Yes, can I _____ _____ that cap _____ stars over there?

   M: Sure. _____ _____ _____ _____ it?

   W: The design is nice, _____ I don't think the color _____ me.
   Do you _____ it in black?

   M: Yes. I'll get _____ from the back. *(pause)* Here it is.

   W: Great. I'll _____ it.

2. M: Good morning. _____ _____ Kelly's Sporting Goods Store.

   W: Hi, _____ _____ _____ a backpack for hiking.

   M: These two are _____ _____ hikers. _____ _____
   _____ _____ them?

   W: The _____ _____ _____ _____ _____ the blue
   _____ . I'll take the _____ _____ .

   M: Great _____ .

1. M: 안녕하세요, 무엇을 도와 드릴까요?
   W: 네, 저기 별들이 그려진 모자를 써 볼 수 있나요?
   M: 그럼요. 어떠세요?
   W: 디자인은 좋은데, 색이 제게 안 어울리는 것 같아요. 이거 검은색으로 있나요?
   M: 네. 제가 안쪽에서 가져다 드릴게요. (잠시 후) 여기 있어요.
   W: 좋아요. 그걸로 할게요.

2. M: 안녕하세요. Kelly의 스포츠 용품 가게에 오신 것을 환영합니다.
   W: 안녕하세요, 저는 하이킹할 때 쓸 배낭을 찾고 있어요.
   M: 이 두 개가 하이킹하시는 분들 사이에서 인기가 있어요, 어떠세요?
   W: 초록색 배낭이 파란색 배낭보다 더 가볍네요. 더 가벼운 걸로 할게요.
   M: 탁월한 선택입니다.

Listen & Talk 1 B

W: Hi, Luke. Is that a new speaker?

M: Yes, I _____ it a _____ _____ _____ .

W: It _____ cool. _____ _____ _____ _____ _____ it?

M: It's _____ . I can take it _____ and listen to music. The sound
_____ is good, _____ .

W: Great. _____ _____ does the battery _____ ?

M: _____ 2 hours. The battery _____ _____ long.

W: That's _____ _____ .

M: Yeah, but I'm _____ _____ with it, _____ .

W: 안녕, Luke. 그거 새 스피커니?
M: 응, 몇 주 전에 샀어.
W: 멋져 보인다. 그거 어때?
M: 편리해. 나는 그것을 어디든지 가져가서 음악을 들을 수 있어. 음질도 좋아.
W: 좋다. 배터리가 얼마나 오래가니?
M: 2시간 정도야. 배터리가 그렇게 오래 가지 않아.
W: 그거 안타깝구나.
M: 응, 하지만 어쨌든 나는 꽤 만족해.

Listen & Talk 2 A

1. M: Oh, this coat is _____ _____ .

   W: Why? _____ _____ _____ _____ ?

   M: It's too _____ .

   W: Didn't _____ _____ _____ _____ _____ it?

   M: No. It was my size, _____ I just _____ it. I _____ _____ _____ it _____ .

2. W: Hey, Eric. Camilla and I _____ _____ _____ _____ a movie. Do you want _____ _____ us?

   M: I'd _____ _____ , but I can't. _____ _____ all of my _____ for this week.

   W: Didn't you just _____ _____ a few days _____ ? How did you spend it all?

   M: I'm not sure. I _____ _____ _____ _____ _____ _____ _____ .

Listen & Talk 2 B

M: Did you get a new phone, Jamie? It's just _____ _____ .

W: Yeah, I got it last weekend _____ _____ .

M: It was _____ _____ ? But it _____ _____ _____ _____ , hasn't it?

W: Right, but the store on Green Street _____ _____ a year-end _____ .

M: Oh, I bought mine _____ _____ _____ !

W: Really? That's too bad. They're _____ them _____ a 40 percent _____ .

M: I _____ _____ _____ _____ _____ _____ _____ buying mine.

1. M: 오, 이 코트는 너무 불편해.
   W: 왜? 무슨 문제가 있니?
   M: 너무 꽉 껴.
   W: 사기 전에 입어 보지 않았어?
   M: 아니. 내 사이즈여서 그냥 사 버렸어. 난 그것을 입어 봤어야 했어.

2. W: 안녕, Eric. Camilla랑 나는 영화를 보러 갈 거야. 우리랑 같이 갈래?
   M: 그러고 싶지만, 안 돼. 이번 주 용돈을 전부 써 버렸거든.
   W: 너 고작 며칠 전에 받지 않았어? 어떻게 다 써 버렸어?
   M: 잘 모르겠어. 내 지출을 기록했어야 했어.

M: 새 전화기를 샀니, Jamie? 내 것과 똑같다.
W: 응, 나는 이것을 지난주 할인할 때 샀어.
M: 그거 할인 중이었어? 하지만 그것은 막 출시되었잖아, 그렇지 않아?
W: 맞아, 하지만 Green가에 있는 가게에서 연말 할인 판매를 하더라.
M: 오, 나는 내 것을 정가를 주고 샀는데!
W: 정말? 그것 참 안됐다. 40퍼센트 할인하여 팔고 있어.
M: 내 것을 사기 전에 할인 판매를 확인했어야 했어.

Communication Step A

M: Hi, Riley. I _____ _____ _____ _____ a laptop online. _____ do you _____ it?

W: Oh, I'm _____ _____ with _____.

M: _____? _____ wrong?

W: It makes too much noise and _____ _____. I should _____ _____ more _____.

M: Oh, then you should _____ _____ your money back.

W: The online store _____ _____ _____ _____ my money because _____ _____ it for a week.

M: How about _____ the online shop and _____ your problem?

W: Yeah, I think I should _____ that.

Wrap Up

1. **M:** Good morning. May I help you?

   W: _____ _____ _____ buy a T-shirt for my sister. She's eleven years old.

   M: _____ _____ _____ _____ _____ _____ _____? This character is quite popular _____ children.

   W: Well, she doesn't like animation characters _____ much. Can I see the blue _____?

   M: You mean this blue _____ T-shirt? _____ design is simple and cool.

   W: Yes, I think my sister will like it. I'll _____ it.

2. **W:** Jake, here's a _____ for you.

   M: It's my helmet. I _____ it at an _____ _____ _____ a few days _____.

   W: Oh, open it and _____ _____ _____ it.

   M: Okay. *(pause)* Oh, this outer part _____ _____ _____ _____. The seller _____ _____ it's perfectly fine though.

   W: Didn't you check the pictures of the helmet _____ you bought it?

   M: No, _____ _____ _____ the seller. I _____ _____ _____ _____ _____ _____.

   W: You _____ _____ the seller and _____ _____ _____ _____.

M: 안녕, Riley. 네가 온라인으로 노트북을 샀다고 들었어. 그거 어때?

W: 아, 나는 별로 마음에 들지 않아.

M: 왜? 무슨 문제가 있어?

W: 소음이 너무 심하고 과열이 돼. 난 후기를 더 많이 읽어 봤어야 했어.

M: 오, 그럼 환불을 요청해 봐.

W: 내가 그것을 일주일 동안 사용했기 때문에 온라인 가게는 환불을 해 주지 않을 거야.

M: 온라인 가게에 전화해서 문제를 설명하는 건 어때?

W: 응, 그렇게 해야 할 것 같아.

1. **M:** 안녕하세요. 도와 드릴까요?

   W: 저는 여동생에게 티셔츠를 사 주고 싶어요. 그 애는 11살이에요.

   M: 이 빨간색 티셔츠는 어떠세요? 이 캐릭터는 아이들 사이에서 꽤 인기가 있어요.

   W: 글쎄요, 그 애는 만화 캐릭터를 그다지 좋아하지 않아요. 파란색 티셔츠 좀 볼 수 있을까요?

   M: 파란색 줄무늬 티셔츠 말씀이시죠? 그건 디자인이 단순하고 멋있어요.

   W: 네, 제 여동생이 좋아할 것 같아요. 그걸로 할게요.

2. **W:** Jake, 여기 네 소포가 있어.

   M: 그거 내 헬멧이야. 며칠 전에 온라인 중고 가게에서 샀어.

   W: 오, 열어서 보여 줘.

   M: 그래. (잠시 후) 아, 이 바깥 부분이 조금 깨졌어. 하지만 판매자는 이것이 완벽하게 괜찮다고 말했어.

   W: 사기 전에 헬멧 사진을 확인해 보지 않았니?

   M: 아니, 나는 그냥 판매자를 믿었어. 조금 더 확인을 했어야 했어.

   W: 너는 판매자에게 전화해서 환불을 요청해야 해.

※ 다음 우리말에 맞도록 대화를 영어로 쓰시오.

Listen & Talk 1 A

1. M: _____

   W: _____

   M: _____

   W: _____

   _____

   M: _____

   W: _____

2. M: _____

   W: _____

   M: _____

   W: _____

   M: _____

Listen & Talk 1 B

W: _____

M: _____

W: _____

M: _____

_____

W: _____

M: _____

W: _____

M: _____

1. M: 안녕하세요, 무엇을 도와 드릴까요?
   W: 네, 저기 별들이 그려진 모자를 써 볼 수 있나요?
   M: 그럼요. 어떠세요?
   W: 디자인은 좋은데, 색이 제게 안 어울리는 것 같아요. 이거 검은색으로 있나요?
   M: 네. 제가 안쪽에서 가져다 드릴게요. (잠시 후) 여기 있어요.
   W: 좋아요. 그걸로 할게요.

2. M: 안녕하세요. Kelly의 스포츠 용품 가게에 오신 것을 환영합니다.
   W: 안녕하세요, 저는 하이킹할 때 쓸 배낭을 찾고 있어요.
   M: 이 두 개가 하이킹하시는 분들 사이에서 인기가 있어요. 어떠세요?
   W: 초록색 배낭이 파란색 배낭보다 더 가볍네요. 더 가벼운 걸로 할게요.
   M: 탁월한 선택입니다.

W: 안녕, Luke. 그거 새 스피커니?
M: 응, 몇 주 전에 샀어.
W: 멋져 보인다. 그거 어때?
M: 편리해. 나는 그것을 어디든지 가져가서 음악을 들을 수 있어. 음질도 좋아.
W: 좋다. 배터리가 얼마나 오래가니?
M: 2시간 정도야. 배터리가 그렇게 오래가지 않아.
W: 그거 안타깝구나.
M: 응, 하지만 어쨌든 나는 꽤 만족해.

1. M: _____
   W: _____
   M: _____
   W: _____
   M: _____

2. W: _____
   _____
   M: _____
   W: _____
   M: _____

M: _____
W: _____
M: _____
W: _____
M: _____
W: _____
M: _____

1. M: 오, 이 코트는 너무 불편해.
   W: 왜? 무슨 문제가 있니?
   M: 너무 꽉 껴.
   W: 사기 전에 입어 보지 않았어?
   M: 아니. 내 사이즈여서 그냥 사 버
      렸어. 난 그것을 입어 봤어야 했
      어.

2. W: 안녕, Eric. Camilla랑 나는 영화
      를 보러 갈 거야. 우리랑 같이 갈
      래?
   M: 그러고 싶지만, 안 돼. 이번 주 용
      돈을 전부 써 버렸거든.
   W: 너 고작 며칠 전에 받지 않았어?
      어떻게 다 써 버렸어?
   M: 잘 모르겠어. 내 지출을 기록했어
      야 했어.

M: 새 전화기를 샀니, Jamie? 내 것과
   똑같다.
W: 응, 나는 이것을 지난주 할인할 때
   샀어.
M: 그거 할인 중이었어? 하지만 그것은
   막 출시되었잖아, 그렇지 않아?
W: 맞아, 하지만 Green가에 있는 가게
   에서 연말 할인 판매를 하더라.
M: 오, 나는 내 것을 정가를 주고 샀는
   데!
W: 정말? 그것 참 안됐다. 40퍼센트 할
   인하여 팔고 있어.
M: 내 것을 사기 전에 할인 판매를 확인
   했어야 했어.

Communication Step A

M: _____

W: _____

M: _____

W: _____

_____

M: _____

W: _____

M: _____

W: _____

M: 안녕, Riley. 네가 온라인으로 노트북을 샀다고 들었어. 그거 어때?
W: 아, 나는 별로 마음에 들지 않아.
M: 왜? 무슨 문제가 있어?
W: 소음이 너무 심하고 과열이 돼. 난 후기를 더 많이 읽어 봤어야 했어.
M: 오, 그럼 환불을 요청해 봐.
W: 내가 그것을 일주일 동안 사용했기 때문에 온라인 가게는 환불을 해 주지 않을 거야.
M: 온라인 가게에 전화해서 문제를 설명하는 건 어때?
W: 응, 그렇게 해야 할 것 같아.

Wrap Up

1. M: _____

W: _____

M: _____

_____

W: _____

_____

M: _____

W: _____

2. W: _____

M: _____

W: _____

M: _____

_____

W: _____

M: _____

W: _____

1. M: 안녕하세요. 도와 드릴까요?
   W: 저는 여동생에게 티셔츠를 사 주고 싶어요. 그 애는 11살이에요.
   M: 이 빨간색 티셔츠는 어떠세요? 이 캐릭터는 아이들 사이에서 꽤 인기가 있어요.
   W: 글쎄요, 그 애는 만화 캐릭터를 그다지 좋아하지 않아요. 파란색 티셔츠 좀 볼 수 있을까요?
   M: 파란색 줄무늬 티셔츠 말씀이시죠? 그건 디자인이 단순하고 멋있어요.
   W: 네, 제 여동생이 좋아할 것 같아요. 그걸로 할게요.

2. W: Jake, 여기 네 소포가 있어.
   M: 그거 내 헬멧이야. 며칠 전에 온라인 중고 가게에서 샀어.
   W: 오, 열어서 보여 줘.
   M: 그래. (잠시 후) 아, 이 바깥 부분이 조금 깨졌어. 하지만 판매자는 이것이 완벽하게 괜찮다고 말했어.
   W: 사기 전에 헬멧 사진을 확인해 보지 않았니?
   M: 아니, 나는 그냥 판매자를 믿었어. 조금 더 확인을 했어야 했어.
   W: 너는 판매자에게 전화해서 환불을 요청해야 해.

※ 다음 우리말과 일치하도록 빈칸에 알맞은 것을 골라 쓰시오.

1 Have you ever _____ _____ you've _____ things that you don't _____ want or need?
- A. bought
- B. wondered
- C. why
- D. even

여러분은 원하거나 필요로 하지도 않는 것들을 자신이 왜 구입했는지 궁금해 한 적이 있는가?

2 Let's consider _____ _____ us when it _____ to _____ things.
- A. affects
- B. buying
- C. what
- D. comes

물건들을 구입하는 것에 관하여 무엇이 우리에게 영향을 주는지 생각해 보자.

3 Why do I want to buy _____ _____ _____ _____?
- A. bought
- B. my
- C. what
- D. friends

나는 왜 친구들이 산 것을 사고 싶은 걸까?

4 Jeff _____ to the shopping center and sees a _____ of soccer shoes _____ _____.
- A. display
- B. goes
- C. pair
- D. on

Jeff는 쇼핑센터에 가서 진열되어 있는 축구화 한 켤레를 보게 된다.

5 He _____ the shoes at a glance _____ more than _____ of the boys on his soccer team _____ them.
- A. half
- B. recognizes
- C. wear
- D. because

그의 축구팀에 있는 소년들의 반 이상이 그 축구화를 신기 때문에 그는 그 신발을 한눈에 알아챈다.

6 _____ he already has many pairs of soccer shoes, he _____ _____ buying _____ new pair.
- A. ends
- B. although
- C. up
- D. another

이미 그에게는 축구화가 많이 있지만 결국 그는 또 다른 새 축구화를 사 버리고 만다.

7 We can use the "bandwagon _____" _____ _____ Jeff's _____.
- A. behavior
- B. effect
- C. explain
- D. to

우리는 Jeff의 행동을 설명하기 위해 '밴드왜건 효과'를 이용할 수 있다.

8 A bandwagon is a wagon in a _____ that _____ people to _____ _____ and enjoy the music.
- A. encourages
- B. aboard
- C. parade
- D. jump

밴드왜건(악대차)은 사람들이 올라타서 음악을 즐기게끔 부추기는 퍼레이드에 있는 사륜마차이다.

9 As more and more people get on the bandwagon, _____ are more _____ to _____ on or _____ it.
- A. others
- B. get
- C. follow
- D. likely

더 많은 사람들이 밴드왜건에 올라탈수록 다른 사람들이 더욱 그것에 올라타거나 그것을 따라가려 한다.

10 In this _____, people _____ to buy something _____ because other people have _____ it.
- A. bought
- B. way
- C. just
- D. tend

이런 식으로, 사람들은 단지 다른 사람들이 어떤 것을 샀다는 이유로 그것을 구매하는 경향이 있다.

11 Why do I _____ a _____ of pants and a bag _____ I have _____ a new coat?
- A. bought
- B. pair
- C. after
- D. buy

나는 왜 새 코트를 구입한 후에 바지와 가방을 사는 걸까?

12 Lisa buys a coat _____ she really loves. _____, she _____ that her pants do not _____ her new coat.

A. realizes   B. match   C. immediately   D. that

13 So, she _____ new pants that _____ _____ _____ her new coat.

A. go   B. buys   C. with   D. perfectly

14 But she _____ that _____ of her bags _____ her new _____.

A. clothes   B. none   C. match   D. sees

15 So, she buys a new bag. _____ of her money is spent _____ buying the new _____ to _____ her new look.

A. most   B. on   C. complete   D. items

16 What _____ Lisa _____ for new items immediately _____ _____ a new coat?

A. search   B. buying   C. made   D. after

17 The "Diderot effect" may _____ it. Denis Diderot, a French writer, _____ a new gown _____ a _____.

A. received   B. explain   C. gift   D. as

18 Soon after receiving the gift, he _____ that all of his _____ did not _____ well with his new gown. So, he ended up _____ most of it.

A. noticed   B. go   C. replacing   D. furniture

19 The Diderot effect, _____, is the concept that _____ a new item often _____ to more _____ purchases.

A. leads   B. therefore   C. unplanned   D. purchasing

20 Why do I buy things _____ _____ they are _____ _____?

A. sale   B. because   C. on   D. just

21 Nathan _____ _____ shopping and _____ a _____ of headphones.

A. goes   B. sees   C. pair   D. window

---

12 Lisa는 정말 마음에 드는 코트를 산다. 그녀는 그녀의 바지가 새 코트와 어울리지 않는다는 것을 즉시 알아차린다.

13 그래서 그녀는 새 코트와 완벽하게 어울리는 새 바지를 구입한다.

14 하지만 그녀는 자신의 가방 중 어느 것도 새로운 옷들과 어울리지 않는다는 것을 알게 된다.

15 그래서 그녀는 새 가방을 산다. 그녀의 돈 대부분이 그녀의 새로운 모습을 완성하기 위하여 새로운 물품을 사는 데 쓰인다.

16 무엇이 Lisa로 하여금 새 코트를 산 후 즉시 새로운 물품을 찾게 했을까?

17 '디드로 효과'가 그것을 설명해 줄지도 모른다. 프랑스 작가인 Denis Diderot는 선물로 새 가운을 받았다.

18 그 선물을 받은 후에 곧 그는 그의 모든 가구가 새로운 가운과 어울리지 않는다는 것을 알아챘다. 그래서 그는 결국 대부분의 가구를 바꾸고 말았다.

19 그러므로 디드로 효과는 새로운 물품을 구입하는 것이 흔히 계획에 없던 더 많은 구매로 이어진다는 개념이다.

20 나는 왜 단지 할인 중이라는 이유로 물건을 구입하는 걸까?

21 Nathan은 진열된 상품을 구경하러 가서 헤드폰을 하나 본다.

22 He _____ the price and_____ _____ that they are $200. He thinks that the headphones are too _____.

    A. out   B. expensive   C. checks   D. finds

23 The _____ person _____ him and says, "You can get a 20 percent _____ _____ those headphones."

    A. discount   B. sales   C. on   D. approaches

24 Even _____ the _____ price is _____ not very _____, Nathan decides to buy the headphones.

    A. low   B. discounted   C. though   D. still

25 The situation _____ _____ is an _____ of the "anchoring _____."

    A. above   B. effect   C. example   D. described

26 The price _____ first _____ our _____ of _____ mentioned afterwards.

    A. prices   B. mentioned   C. opinion   D. affects

27 For example, if we start with $200, then $160 will _____ _____ _____ _____.

    A. comparison   B. seem   C. in   D. cheap

28 _____, as the difference of the two prices _____ _____, the effect will be more _____.

    A. bigger   B. furthermore   C. powerful   D. becomes

29 _____ _____, the price mentioned first acts as an "anchor" that _____ our _____ about the price of an item.

    A. thoughts   B. such   C. fixes   D. as

30 Just _____ Jeff and his friends, we tend to buy _____ without seriously _____ why we are _____ them.

    A. considering   B. buying   C. like   D. things

31 _____ these effects have _____, many things _____ our _____.

    A. shown   B. purchases   C. as   D. influence

32 The next _____ you decide to buy something, _____ for a moment _____ why you are _____ it.

    A. think   B. about   C. time   D. buying

22 그는 가격을 확인하고 그것이 200달러임을 알게 된다. 그는 그 헤드폰이 너무 비싸다고 생각한다.

23 점원이 그에게 다가와 "이 헤드폰에 20퍼센트 할인을 받을 수 있어요."라고 말한다.

24 비록 할인된 가격이 여전히 별로 저렴하지는 않지만 Nathan은 그 헤드폰을 사기로 결심한다.

25 위에 기술된 상황은 '앵커링 효과'의 한 예이다.

26 처음에 언급된 가격이 이후에 언급되는 가격에 대한 우리의 의견에 영향을 미친다.

27 예를 들어, 만약 우리가 200달러로 시작한다면, 비교해 볼 때 160달러는 저렴해 보일 것이다.

28 그뿐만 아니라, 두 가격의 차이가 커질수록 그 효과는 더욱 강력해질 것이다.

29 이와 같이 처음에 언급된 가격이 물건의 가격에 대한 우리의 생각을 고정하는 '닻'으로서 작동한다.

30 Jeff와 그의 친구들처럼, 우리는 우리가 왜 물건들을 사는지 진지하게 고려하지 않고 그것들을 구입하는 경향이 있다.

31 이러한 효과들이 보여 주듯이, 많은 것들이 우리의 구매에 영향을 미친다.

32 다음번에 여러분이 어떤 것을 구매하려고 결정할 때에는, 자신이 그것을 왜 사려는지 잠시 동안 생각해 보아라.

※ 다음 우리말과 일치하도록 빈칸에 알맞은 것을 골라 쓰시오.

1 Have you ever wondered _____ _____ _____ _____ _____ you don't even want or need?

2 Let's consider _____ _____ _____ when it _____ _____ _____ things.

3 Why do I want to buy _____ _____ _____ _____ _____?

4 Jeff _____ to the shopping center and _____ _____ _____ _____ soccer shoes _____ _____.

5 He _____ the shoes at a glance _____ more than _____ _____ _____ _____ on his soccer team _____ them.

6 _____ he already has _____ _____ _____ soccer shoes, he _____ _____ _____ _____ new pair.

7 We can use the "_____ _____" _____ _____ Jeff's _____.

8 A bandwagon is a wagon in a parade _____ _____ people _____ _____ _____ and enjoy the music.

9 As _____ _____ _____ _____ get on the bandwagon, _____ _____ more _____ _____ _____ _____ or _____ it.

10 _____ this _____, people tend _____ _____ something _____ _____ other people _____ _____ _____.

11 Why do I _____ _____ _____ _____ _____ pants and a bag _____ I _____ _____ a new coat?

12 Lisa buys a coat _____ she really loves. _____, she _____ _____ her pants do not _____ her new coat.

13 So, she buys new pants _____ _____ perfectly _____ her new coat.

14 But she sees _____ _____ _____ _____ _____ _____ her _____ _____.

15 So, she _____ a new bag. _____ _____ _____ _____ _____ _____ spent _____ buying the new items _____ _____ _____ her _____ _____.

16 What _____ Lisa _____ immediately _____ _____ a new coat?

1 여러분은 원하거나 필요로 하지도 않는 것들을 자신이 왜 구입했는지 궁금해 한 적이 있는가?

2 물건들을 구입하는 것에 관하여 무엇이 우리에게 영향을 주는지 생각해 보자.

3 나는 왜 친구들이 산 것을 사고 싶은 걸까?

4 Jeff는 쇼핑센터에 가서 진열되어 있는 축구화 한 켤레를 보게 된다.

5 그의 축구팀에 있는 소년들의 반 이상이 그 축구화를 신기 때문에 그는 그 신발을 한눈에 알아챈다.

6 이미 그에게는 축구화가 많이 있지만 결국 그는 또 다른 새 축구화를 사 버리고 만다.

7 우리는 Jeff의 행동을 설명하기 위해 '밴드왜건 효과'를 이용할 수 있다.

8 밴드왜건(악대차)은 사람들이 올라타서 음악을 즐기게끔 부추기는 퍼레이드에 있는 사륜마차이다.

9 더 많은 사람들이 밴드왜건에 올라탈수록 다른 사람들이 더욱 그것에 올라타거나 그것을 따라가려 한다.

10 이런 식으로, 사람들은 단지 다른 사람들이 어떤 것을 샀다는 이유로 그것을 구매하는 경향이 있다.

11 나는 왜 새 코트를 구입한 후에 바지와 가방을 사는 걸까?

12 Lisa는 정말 마음에 드는 코트를 산다. 그녀는 그녀의 바지가 새 코트와 어울리지 않는다는 것을 즉시 알아차린다.

13 그래서 그녀는 새 코트와 완벽하게 어울리는 새 바지를 구입한다.

14 하지만 그녀는 자신의 가방 중 어느 것도 새로운 옷들과 어울리지 않는다는 것을 알게 된다.

15 그래서 그녀는 새 가방을 산다. 그녀의 돈 대부분이 그녀의 새로운 모습을 완성하기 위하여 새로운 물품을 사는 데 쓰인다.

16 무엇이 Lisa로 하여금 새 코트를 산 후 즉시 새로운 물품을 찾게 했을까?

17 The "Diderot _____" may _____ _____. Denis Diderot, a French writer, _____ a new gown _____ a _____.

18 Soon _____ _____ the gift, he _____ _____ all of his _____ did not _____ _____ with his new gown. So, he ended up _____ _____ _____ _____.

19 The Diderot effect, _____, is the concept _____ _____ _____ _____ _____ often _____ _____ more _____ _____.

20 Why do I buy things _____ _____ _____ _____ _____ _____?

21 Nathan _____ _____ _____ and _____ a _____ of headphones.

22 He _____ the price and _____ _____ _____ they are $200. He thinks _____ the headphones are _____ _____.

23 The sales person _____ _____ and says, "You can get a 20 percent _____ _____ those headphones."

24 _____ _____ the discounted price _____ _____ not very _____, Nathan decides _____ _____ the headphones.

25 The situation _____ _____ is an _____ of the "_____ _____."

26 The price _____ first _____ our _____ _____ _____ _____ afterwards.

27 _____ _____, if we start with $200, then $160 will _____ _____ _____ _____.

28 _____, as _____ _____ of the two prices _____ _____, the effect will _____ _____ _____.

29 _____ _____ _____, the price _____ _____ acts as an "_____" that _____ _____ _____ _____ about the price of an item.

30 _____ _____ Jeff and his friends, we tend _____ _____ things _____ seriously _____ _____ _____ _____ them.

31 _____ these effects _____ _____, many things _____ _____ _____.

32 _____ _____ _____ you _____ _____ _____ something, _____ for a moment _____ _____ _____ _____ it.

17 '디드로 효과'가 그것을 설명해 줄지도 모른다. 프랑스 작가인 Denis Diderot는 선물로 새 가운을 받았다.

18 그 선물을 받은 후에 곧 그는 그의 모든 가구가 새로운 가운과 어울리지 않는다는 것을 알아챘다. 그래서 그는 결국 대부분의 가구를 바꾸고 말았다.

19 그러므로 디드로 효과는 새로운 물품을 구입하는 것이 흔히 계획에 없던 더 많은 구매로 이어진다는 개념이다.

20 나는 왜 단지 할인 중이라는 이유로 물건을 구입하는 걸까?

21 Nathan은 진열된 상품을 구경하러 가서 헤드폰을 하나 본다.

22 그는 가격을 확인하고 그것이 200달러임을 알게 된다. 그는 그 헤드폰이 너무 비싸다고 생각한다.

23 점원이 그에게 다가와 "이 헤드폰에 20퍼센트 할인을 받을 수 있어요."라고 말한다.

24 비록 할인된 가격이 여전히 별로 저렴하지는 않지만 Nathan은 그 헤드폰을 사기로 결심한다.

25 위에 기술된 상황은 '앵커링 효과'의 한 예이다.

26 처음에 언급된 가격이 이후에 언급되는 가격에 대한 우리의 의견에 영향을 미친다.

27 예를 들어, 만약 우리가 200달러로 시작한다면, 비교해 볼 때 160달러는 저렴해 보일 것이다.

28 그뿐만 아니라, 두 가격의 차이가 커질수록 그 효과는 더욱 강력해질 것이다.

29 이와 같이 처음에 언급된 가격이 물건의 가격에 대한 우리의 생각을 고정하는 '닻'으로서 작동한다.

30 Jeff와 그의 친구들처럼, 우리는 우리가 왜 물건들을 사는지 진지하게 고려하지 않고 그것들을 구입하는 경향이 있다.

31 이러한 효과들이 보여 주듯이, 많은 것들이 우리의 구매에 영향을 미친다.

32 다음번에 여러분이 어떤 것을 구매하려고 결정할 때에는, 자신이 그것을 왜 사려는지 잠시 동안 생각해 보아라.

※ 다음 문장을 우리말로 쓰시오.

1 ▶ Have you ever wondered why you've bought things that you don't even want or need?

➡ _____

2 ▶ Let's consider what affects us when it comes to buying things.

➡ _____

3 ▶ Why do I want to buy what my friends bought?

➡ _____

4 ▶ Jeff goes to the shopping center and sees a pair of soccer shoes on display.

➡ _____

5 ▶ He recognizes the shoes at a glance because more than half of the boys on his soccer team wear them.

➡ _____

6 ▶ Although he already has many pairs of soccer shoes, he ends up buying another new pair.

➡ _____

7 ▶ We can use the "bandwagon effect" to explain Jeff's behavior.

➡ _____

8 ▶ A bandwagon is a wagon in a parade that encourages people to jump aboard and enjoy the music.

➡ _____

9 ▶ As more and more people get on the bandwagon, others are more likely to get on or follow it.

➡ _____

10 ▶ In this way, people tend to buy something just because other people have bought it.

➡ _____

11 ▶ Why do I buy a pair of pants and a bag after I have bought a new coat?

➡ _____

12 ▶ Lisa buys a coat that she really loves. Immediately, she realizes that her pants do not match her new coat.

➡ _____

13 ▶ So, she buys new pants that go perfectly with her new coat.

➡ _____

14 ▶ But she sees that none of her bags match her new clothes.

➡ _____

15 ▶ So, she buys a new bag. Most of her money is spent on buying the new items to complete her new look.

➡ _____

16 ▶ What made Lisa search for new items immediately after buying a new coat?

➡ _____

17 The "Diderot effect" may explain it. Denis Diderot, a French writer, received a new gown as a gift.
➡ _____

18 Soon after receiving the gift, he noticed that all of his furniture did not go well with his new gown. So, he ended up replacing most of it.
➡ _____
_____

19 The Diderot effect, therefore, is the concept that purchasing a new item often leads to more unplanned purchases.
➡ _____

20 Why do I buy things just because they are on sale?
➡ _____

21 Nathan goes window shopping and sees a pair of headphones.
➡ _____

22 He checks the price and finds out that they are $200. He thinks that the headphones are too expensive.
➡ _____

23 The sales person approaches him and says, "You can get a 20 percent discount on those headphones."
➡ _____

24 Even though the discounted price is still not very low, Nathan decides to buy the headphones.
➡ _____

25 The situation described above is an example of the "anchoring effect."
➡ _____

26 The price mentioned first affects our opinion of prices mentioned afterwards.
➡ _____

27 For example, if we start with $200, then $160 will seem cheap in comparison.
➡ _____

28 Furthermore, as the difference of the two prices becomes bigger, the effect will be more powerful.
➡ _____

29 As such, the price mentioned first acts as an "anchor" that fixes our thoughts about the price of an item.
➡ _____

30 Just like Jeff and his friends, we tend to buy things without seriously considering why we are buying them.
➡ _____

31 As these effects have shown, many things influence our purchases.
➡ _____

32 The next time you decide to buy something, think for a moment about why you are buying it.
➡ _____

※ 다음 괄호 안의 단어들을 우리말에 맞도록 바르게 배열하시오.

1 (you / have / wondered / ever / you've / why / things / bought / that / don't / you / want / even / need? / or)
➡ _____
_____

2 (consider / let's / affects / what / when / us / comes / it / buying / to / things.)
➡ _____

3 (do / why / want / I / buy / to / what / friends / my / thought?)
➡ _____

4 (goes / Jeff / the / to / center / shoppiing / and / a / sees / pair / soccer / of / on / shoes / display.)
➡ _____

5 (recognizes / he / shoes / the / a / at / because / glance / more / half / than / the / of / boys / his / on / soccer / wear / team / them.)
➡ _____

6 (he / although / has / already / many / of / pairs / shoes, / soccer / ends / he / buying / up / new / another / pair.)
➡ _____

7 (can / we / the / use / effect" / "bandwagon / to / Jeff's / explain / behavior.)
➡ _____

8 (bandwagon / a / is / wagon / a / in / parade / a / that / people / encourages / to / jump / and / aboard / the / enjoy / music.)
➡ _____

9 (more / as / and / people / more / on / get / bandwagon, / the / are / others / likely / more / get / to / or / on / it. / follow)
➡ _____

10 (this / in / way, / tend / people / buy / to / just / something / other / because / people / bought / have / it.)
➡ _____

11 (do / why / buy / I / pair / a / pants / of / and / bag / a / after / have / I / a / bought / coat? / new)
➡ _____

1 여러분은 원하거나 필요로 하지도 않는 것들을 자신이 왜 구입했는지 궁금해 한 적이 있는가?

2 물건들을 구입하는 것에 관하여 무엇이 우리에게 영향을 주는지 생각해 보자.

3 나는 왜 친구들이 산 것을 사고 싶은 걸까?

4 Jeff는 쇼핑센터에 가서 진열되어 있는 축구화 한 켤레를 보게 된다.

5 그의 축구팀에 있는 소년들의 반 이상이 그 축구화를 신기 때문에 그는 그 신발을 한눈에 알아챈다.

6 이미 그에게는 축구화가 많이 있지만 결국 그는 또 다른 새 축구화를 사 버리고 만다.

7 우리는 Jeff의 행동을 설명하기 위해 '밴드왜건 효과'를 이용할 수 있다.

8 밴드왜건(악대차)은 사람들이 올라타서 음악을 즐기게끔 부추기는 퍼레이드에 있는 사륜마차이다.

9 더 많은 사람들이 밴드왜건에 올라탈수록 다른 사람들이 더욱 그것에 올라타거나 그것을 따라가려 한다.

10 이런 식으로, 사람들은 단지 다른 사람들이 어떤 것을 샀다는 이유로 그것을 구매하는 경향이 있다.

11 나는 왜 새 코트를 구입한 후에 바지와 가방을 사는 걸까?

12 (buys / Lisa / coat / a / she / that / loves. / really // she / immediately, / that / realizes / her / do / pants / match / not / new / coat. / her)

➡ _____

_____

13 (she / so, / new / buys / that / pants / go / with / perfectly / her / coat. / new)

➡ _____

14 (she / but / that / sees / none / her / of / bags / her / match / clothes. / new)

➡ _____

15 (she / so, / a / buys / bag. / new // of / most / money / her / spent / is / buying / on / new / the / items / complete / to / new / her / look.)

➡ _____

_____

16 (made / what / search / Lisa / new / for / immediately / items / buying / after / new / a / coat?)

➡ _____

_____

17 ("Diderot / the / effect" / explain / may / it. // Diderot, / Denis / a / writer, / French / a / received / new / a / as / gown / gift.)

➡ _____

_____

18 (after / soon / the / receiving / gift, / noticed / he / all / that / his / of / did / furniture / not / well / go / his / with / gown. / new // so, / ended / he / up / most / replacing / it. / of)

➡ _____

_____

19 (Diderot / the / effect, / is / therefore, / concept / the / purchasing / that / new / a / often / item / to / leads / more / purchases. / unplanned)

➡ _____

_____

20 (do / why / buy / I / just / things / because / are / they / sale? / on)

➡ _____

12 Lisa는 정말 마음에 드는 코트를 산다. 그녀는 그녀의 바지가 새 코트와 어울리지 않는다는 것을 즉시 알아차린다.

13 그래서 그녀는 새 코트와 완벽하게 어울리는 새 바지를 구입한다.

14 하지만 그녀는 자신의 가방 중 어느 것도 새로운 옷들과 어울리지 않는다는 것을 알게 된다.

15 그래서 그녀는 새 가방을 산다. 그녀의 돈 대부분이 그녀의 새로운 모습을 완성하기 위하여 새로운 물품을 사는 데 쓰인다.

16 무엇이 Lisa로 하여금 새 코트를 산 후 즉시 새로운 물품을 찾게 했을까?

17 '디드로 효과'가 그것을 설명해 줄지도 모른다. 프랑스 작가인 Denis Diderot는 선물로 새 가운을 받았다.

18 그 선물을 받은 후에 곧 그는 그의 모든 가구가 새로운 가운과 어울리지 않는다는 것을 알아챘다. 그래서 그는 결국 대부분의 가구를 바꾸고 말았다.

19 그러므로 디드로 효과는 새로운 물품을 구입하는 것이 흔히 계획에 없던 더 많은 구매로 이어진다는 개념이다.

20 나는 왜 단지 할인 중이라는 이유로 물건을 구입하는 걸까?

21 (goes / Nathan / shopping / window / and / a / sees / of / pair / headphones.)

➡ _____

22 (checks / he / price / the / and / out / finds / they / that / $200. / are // thinks / he / that / headphones / the / too / are / expensive.)

➡ _____

23 (sales / the / person / him / approaches / says, / and / can / "you / a / get / percent / 20 / on / discount / headphones." / those)

➡ _____

24 (though / even / discounted / the / is / price / not / still / low, / very / decides / Nathan / buy / to / headphones. / the)

➡ _____

25 (situation / the / above / described / an / is / of / example / the / effect." / "anchoring)

➡ _____

26 (price / the / first / mentioned / affects / opinion / our / prices / of / afterwards. / mentioned)

➡ _____

27 (example, / for / we / if / with / start / $200, / $160 / then / will / cheap / seem / comparison. / in)

➡ _____

28 (as / furthermore, / the / of / difference / two / the / becomes / prices / bigger, / effect / the / will / more / be / powerful.)

➡ _____

29 (such, / as / price / the / first / mentioned / acts / an / as / that / "anchor" / our / fixes / about / thoughts / the / of / price / item. / an)

➡ _____

30 (like / just / and / Jeff / friends, / his / tend / we / buy / to / without / things / seriously / we / considering / why / buying / are / them.)

➡ _____

31 (these / as / have / effects / shown, / things / many / our / influence / purchases.)

➡ _____

32 (next / the / you / time / to / decide / something, / buy / for / think / moment / a / about / you / why / buying / are / it.)

➡ _____

21 Nathan은 진열된 상품을 구경하러 가서 헤드폰을 하나 본다.

22 그는 가격을 확인하고 그것이 200달러임을 알게 된다. 그는 그 헤드폰이 너무 비싸다고 생각한다.

23 점원이 그에게 다가와 "이 헤드폰에 20퍼센트 할인을 받을 수 있어요."라고 말한다.

24 비록 할인된 가격이 여전히 별로 저렴하지는 않지만 Nathan은 그 헤드폰을 사기로 결심한다.

25 위에 기술된 상황은 '앵커링 효과'의 한 예이다.

26 처음에 언급된 가격이 이후에 언급되는 가격에 대한 우리의 의견에 영향을 미친다.

27 예를 들어, 만약 우리가 200달러로 시작한다면, 비교해 볼 때 160달러는 저렴해 보일 것이다.

28 그뿐만 아니라, 두 가격의 차이가 커질수록 그 효과는 더욱 강력해질 것이다.

29 이와 같이 처음에 언급된 가격이 물건의 가격에 대한 우리의 생각을 고정하는 '닻'으로서 작동한다.

30 Jeff와 그의 친구들처럼, 우리는 우리가 왜 물건들을 사는지 진지하게 고려하지 않고 그것들을 구입하는 경향이 있다.

31 이러한 효과들이 보여 주듯이, 많은 것들이 우리의 구매에 영향을 미친다.

32 다음번에 여러분이 어떤 것을 구매하려고 결정할 때에는, 자신이 그것을 왜 사려는지 잠시 동안 생각해 보아라.

※ 다음 우리말을 영어로 쓰시오.

1 여러분은 원하거나 필요로 하지도 않는 것들을 자신이 왜 구입했는지 궁금해 한 적이 있는가?
➡ _____

2 물건들을 구입하는 것에 관하여 무엇이 우리에게 영향을 주는지 생각해 보자.
➡ _____

3 나는 왜 친구들이 산 것을 사고 싶은 걸까?
➡ _____

4 Jeff는 쇼핑센터에 가서 진열되어 있는 축구화 한 켤레를 보게 된다.
➡ _____

5 그의 축구팀에 있는 소년들의 반 이상이 그 축구화를 신기 때문에 그는 그 신발을 한눈에 알아챈다.
➡ _____
_____

6 이미 그에게는 축구화가 많이 있지만 결국 그는 또 다른 새 축구화를 사 버리고 만다.
➡ _____

7 우리는 Jeff의 행동을 설명하기 위해 '밴드왜건 효과'를 이용할 수 있다.
➡ _____

8 밴드왜건(악대차)은 사람들이 올라타서 음악을 즐기게끔 부추기는 퍼레이드에 있는 사륜마차이다.
➡ _____
_____

9 더 많은 사람들이 밴드왜건에 올라탈수록 다른 사람들이 더욱 그것에 올라타거나 그것을 따라가려 한다.
➡ _____

10 이런 식으로, 사람들은 단지 다른 사람들이 어떤 것을 샀다는 이유로 그것을 구매하는 경향이 있다.
➡ _____

11 나는 왜 새 코트를 구입한 후에 바지와 가방을 사는 걸까?
➡ _____

12 Lisa는 정말 마음에 드는 코트를 산다. 그녀는 그녀의 바지가 새 코트와 어울리지 않는다는 것을 즉시 알아차린다.
➡ _____
_____

13 그래서 그녀는 새 코트와 완벽하게 어울리는 새 바지를 구입한다.
➡ _____

14 하지만 그녀는 자신의 가방 중 어느 것도 새로운 옷들과 어울리지 않는다는 것을 알게 된다.
➡ _____

15 그래서 그녀는 새 가방을 산다. 그녀의 돈 대부분이 그녀의 새로운 모습을 완성하기 위하여 새로운 물품을 사는 데 쓰인다.
➡ _____
_____

16 무엇이 Lisa로 하여금 새 코트를 산 후 즉시 새로운 물품을 찾게 했을까?
➡ _____

17 '디드로 효과'가 그것을 설명해 줄지도 모른다. 프랑스 작가인 Denis Diderot는 선물로 새 가운을 받았다.

➡ _____

18 그 선물을 받은 후에 곧 그는 그의 모든 가구가 새로운 가운과 어울리지 않는다는 것을 알아챘다.
그래서 그는 결국 대부분의 가구를 바꾸고 말았다.

➡ _____

19 그러므로 디드로 효과는 새로운 물품을 구입하는 것이 흔히 계획에 없던 더 많은 구매로 이어진다는 개념이다.

➡ _____
_____

20 나는 왜 단지 할인 중이라는 이유로 물건을 구입하는 걸까?

➡ _____

21 Nathan은 진열된 상품을 구경하러 가서 헤드폰을 하나 본다.

➡ _____

22 그는 가격을 확인하고 그것이 200달러임을 알게 된다. 그는 그 헤드폰이 너무 비싸다고 생각한다.

➡ _____

23 점원이 그에게 다가와 "이 헤드폰에 20퍼센트 할인을 받을 수 있어요."라고 말한다.

➡ _____

24 비록 할인된 가격이 여전히 별로 저렴하지는 않지만 Nathan은 그 헤드폰을 사기로 결심한다.

➡ _____

25 위에 기술된 상황은 '앵커링 효과'의 한 예이다.

➡ _____

26 처음에 언급된 가격이 이후에 언급되는 가격에 대한 우리의 의견에 영향을 미친다.

➡ _____

27 예를 들어, 만약 우리가 200달러로 시작한다면, 비교해 볼 때 160달러는 저렴해 보일 것이다.

➡ _____

28 그뿐만 아니라, 두 가격의 차이가 커질수록 그 효과는 더욱 강력해질 것이다.

➡ _____
_____

29 이와 같이 처음에 언급된 가격이 물건의 가격에 대한 우리의 생각을 고정하는 '닻'으로서 작동한다.

➡ _____
_____

30 Jeff와 그의 친구들처럼, 우리는 우리가 왜 물건들을 사는지 진지하게 고려하지 않고 그것들을 구입하는
경향이 있다.

➡ _____
_____

31 이러한 효과들이 보여 주듯이, 많은 것들이 우리의 구매에 영향을 미친다.

➡ _____

32 다음번에 여러분이 어떤 것을 구매하려고 결정할 때에는, 자신이 그것을 왜 사려는지 잠시 동안 생각해
보아라.

➡ _____

※ 다음 우리말과 일치하도록 빈칸에 알맞은 말을 쓰시오.

Language in Use

1. _____ is difficult _____ _____ the results _____ _____.

2. We _____ children _____ _____ _____ _____ _____.

1. 결과를 상세히 비교하는 것은 어렵다.
2. 우리는 아이들이 스스로 생각하도록 장려한다.

Grammar in Real Life B Look and Write

1. About _____ _____ the water _____ _____ _____ _____ animals in the U.S.

2. _____ _____ _____ the world's food _____ _____ —1.3 _____ _____ every year.

3. In Somalia, _____ _____ _____ _____ the children _____ _____ _____.

4. _____ fourteen percent of all people _____ know _____ _____ _____ _____ _____ education.

1. 물의 절반 가량이 미국에서 동물을 키우기 위해 사용된다.
2. 세계 식량의 삼분의 일, 즉 매년 13억 톤이 낭비된다.
3. 소말리아에서는 단지 10퍼센트의 아이들이 학교에 다닌다.
4. 전체 인구의 약 14퍼센트는 교육의 부족으로 읽는 법을 알지 못한다.

Think & Write C

1. I _____ _____ _____ about _____.

2. First, I asked 10 students _____ _____ _____ _____ _____ _____.

3. Twenty percent of the students _____ _____ every week and _____ _____ of the students _____ _____ _____ _____ _____.

4. Second, I asked them _____ they _____ _____ _____ _____ _____.

5. _____ _____ _____ _____ is spent on clothes and _____ _____ of the allowance _____ _____ _____ _____.

6. Lastly, I asked them _____ _____ _____ that they _____ _____ _____ _____.

7. _____ _____ _____ _____ _____ _____ that they should get a higher allowance.

1. 저는 용돈에 관하여 설문 조사를 했습니다.
2. 우선, 저는 10명의 학생들에게 그들이 얼마나 자주 용돈을 받는지 물었습니다.
3. 20퍼센트의 학생들은 매주 용돈을 받고, 70퍼센트의 학생들은 매달 용돈을 받습니다.
4. 두 번째로, 저는 학생들에게 어디에 용돈의 대부분을 쓰는지 물었습니다.
5. 대부분의 용돈은 옷에 쓰이고, 용돈의 4분의 1은 간식에 쓰입니다.
6. 마지막으로, 저는 학생들에게 그들이 더 많은 용돈을 받아야 한다고 생각하는지 물었습니다.
7. 학생들의 90퍼센트는 그들이 더 많은 용돈을 받아야 한다고 생각합니다.

※ 다음 우리말을 영어로 쓰시오.

Language in Use

1. 결과를 상세히 비교하는 것은 어렵다.

➡ _____

2. 우리는 아이들이 스스로 생각하도록 장려한다.

➡ _____

Grammar in Real Life B Look and Write

1. 물의 절반 가량이 미국에서 동물을 키우기 위해 사용된다.

➡ _____

2. 세계 식량의 삼분의 일, 즉 매년 13억 톤이 낭비된다.

➡ _____

3. 소말리아에서는 단지 10퍼센트의 아이들이 학교에 다닌다.

➡ _____

4. 전체 인구의 약 14퍼센트는 교육의 부족으로 읽는 법을 알지 못한다.

➡ _____

Think & Write C

1. 저는 용돈에 관하여 설문 조사를 했습니다.

➡ _____

2. 우선, 저는 10명의 학생들에게 그들이 얼마나 자주 용돈을 받는지 물었습니다.

➡ _____

3. 20퍼센트의 학생들은 매주 용돈을 받고, 70퍼센트의 학생들은 매달 용돈을 받습니다.

➡ _____

    _____

4. 두 번째로, 저는 학생들에게 어디에 용돈의 대부분을 쓰는지 물었습니다.

➡ _____

5. 대부분의 용돈은 옷에 쓰이고, 용돈의 4분의 1은 간식에 쓰입니다.

➡ _____

6. 마지막으로, 저는 학생들에게 그들이 더 많은 용돈을 받아야 한다고 생각하는지 물었습니다.

➡ _____

7. 학생들의 90퍼센트는 그들이 더 많은 용돈을 받아야 한다고 생각합니다.

➡ _____

MEMO

영어 기출 문제집

적중100

2학기

정답 및 해설

비상 | 김진완

중 3

적중100

Lesson 5

Critical Minds

시험대비 실력평가   p.08

01 distrust   02 ④   03 ①   04 ⑤

05 ⑤

06 (1) He had been wounded in the arm.

   (2) I can't trust her anymore because she lied again.

   (3) The temperature went up to forty today.

01 주어진 관계는 반의어 관계이다. trust: 신뢰하다, distrust: 불신하다

02 '해, 손상, 고통을 초래하는 사건'을 나타내는 말은 disaster(재난)이다.

03 trust는 명사로 '신뢰', 동사로 '신뢰하다'를 의미한다.

04 mine: 광산

05 보기에 주어진 judge는 '판단하다'를 의미한다. ⑤번은 '판사'를 뜻한다.

06 wound: 상처를 입히다, trust: 신뢰하다, temperature: 온도

서술형 시험대비   p.09

01 realize

02 (1) competitors (2) condition (3) confessed

   (4) critical

03 (1) on the loose (2) think outside the box

   (3) search for (4) catch a cold (5) got caught

04 (1) Don't you think the restaurant is extremely loud?

   (2) Eating too much sugar is harmful for your teeth.

   (3) He is almost the same height as my sister.

05 (1) She admitted that she had made mistakes.

   (2) I had an argument with my boyfriend yesterday.

   (3) Adults should pay an entrance fee, but children get in free.

01 형용사에 접미사 '-ize'를 붙여 동사를 만들 수 있다. realize: 실현하다, regularize: 합법화하다

02 competitor: 경쟁자, condition: 상태, confess: 고백하다, critical: 위독한

03 catch a cold: 감기에 걸리다, got caught -ing: ~하다가 걸리다, on the loose: 잡히지 않은, search for: ~을 찾다, think outside the box: 고정관념에서 벗어나다

04 extremely: 극도로, 극히, harmful: 해로운, height: 키

05 admit: 인정하다, argument: 논쟁, entrance fee: 입장료, adult: 어른

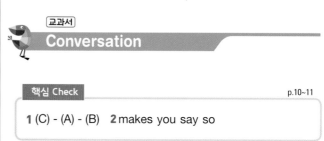

교과서
Conversation

핵심 Check   p.10~11

1 (C) - (A) - (B)   **2** makes you say so

교과서 대화문 익히기

Check(√) True or False   p.12

1 T   2 T   3 T   4 F

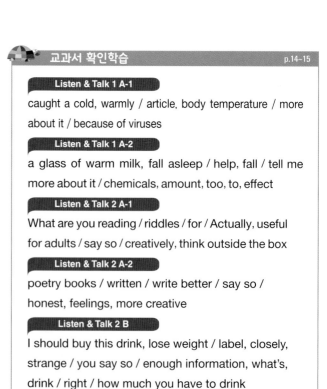

교과서 확인학습   p.14~15

Listen & Talk 1 A-1

caught a cold, warmly / article, body temperature / more about it / because of viruses

Listen & Talk 1 A-2

a glass of warm milk, fall asleep / help, fall / tell me more about it / chemicals, amount, too, to, effect

Listen & Talk 2 A-1

What are you reading / riddles / for / Actually, useful for adults / say so / creatively, think outside the box

Listen & Talk 2 A-2

poetry books / written / write better / say so / honest, feelings, more creative

Listen & Talk 2 B

I should buy this drink, lose weight / label, closely, strange / you say so / enough information, what's, drink / right / how much you have to drink

Communication

information, facts, completely wrong / examples, facts that are wrong / what / goldfish, goldfish /

recognize their owners / know that

Wrap Up 2

interesting article, where it is / between, and / What color / guess / called / dangerous

01 ⓓ → make   02 ⑤   03 ⓓ → because of
04 (A) their low body temperature   (B) viruses

01 관계대명사의 선행사가 chemicals로 복수이므로 make가 적절하다.

02 우유 한 잔에 있는 특별한 성분의 양이 너무 적어서 효과가 없다.

03 뒤에 명사가 이어지므로 because of가 알맞다.

04 기사에 따르면 사람들은 체온이 낮아서가 아니라 바이러스 때문에 감기에 걸린다.

01 ⓔ → which   02 ⑤
03 She drinks a glass of warm milk.
04 They make people sleepy.
05 It's because the amount in a glass is too small to have any effect.
06 (C) → (A) → (D) → (B) → (E)   07 ⑤
08 ⑤
09 We need to think outside the box to find the answers.
10 written   11 ⑤   12 children

01 관계대명사의 계속적 용법으로 which가 적절하다.

03 수지는 자기 전에 따뜻한 우유 한 잔을 마신다.

04 우유에 있는 화학물질이 사람들을 졸리게 만든다.

05 우유 한 잔에 들어 있는 화학물질의 양이 너무 적어 효과가 없다.

06 (C) 시집에 대한 설명 → (A) 확인 → (D) 자신의 의견 표현 → (B) 이유 질문 → (E) 이유 설명

07 사실을 알고 있는지 묻는 질문에 '무슨 말인지 알겠다.'라는 대답은 어색하다.

08 ⑤번을 제외한 나머지는 모두 이유를 묻는 표현이다.

10 어린이들에 의해 쓰여진 시로 과거분사 written이 알맞다.

11 ⑤번을 제외한 나머지는 모두 이유를 묻고 있다.

12 They는 아이들(children)을 가리킨다.

01 Can you tell me more about it
02 She thinks (that) she caught a cold because she didn't dress warmly yesterday.
03 (A) Napoleon   (B) height   (C) the French measuring system   (D) the English one
04 Why do you say so?
05 They were written by children.
06 It is because they're really honest about their feelings and much more creative than adults.

02 여자는 어제 따뜻하게 옷을 입지 않았기 때문에 감기에 걸렸다고 생각한다.

03 나폴레옹은 정말 키가 작았을까? 우리는 나폴레옹의 키에 대해 잘못 알았다. 오해는 프랑스의 측정 체계와 영국의 측정 체계와의 차이에서 비롯되었다. 그는 실제로 약 168 cm였다.

05 시집에 있는 시들은 아이들에 의해 쓰여졌다.

06 어린이들은 감정에 매우 솔직하고 어른들보다 훨씬 더 창의적이기 때문에 Sue는 어른들보다 어린이들이 시를 더 잘 쓴다고 생각한다.

1 (1) Living   (2) Listening
2 (1) that   (2) so that

01 ②
02 (1) Having   (2) Not knowing   (3) so that   (4) so that
03 ①
04 (1) Mom's face darkened looking at the report card.
    (2) We are going to the library so that we can borrow books.

01 'so that'은 '~하기 위해', '~하고자', '~하도록'의 의미로 '목적'이나 '의도'를 나타낸다.

02 (1) 접속사가 없으므로 '접속사+주어+동사'의 역할을 할 수 있는 분사구문 Having이 적절하다. (2) 분사구문의 부정은 분사

3

앞에 'not'이나 'never'를 쓴다. (3) '내 동생이 야생 동물들을 볼 수 있을지라도 동물원에 갔다'는 말은 어색하다. '목적'이나 '의도'를 나타내는 'so that'이 적절하다. (4) 'so that' 앞에 콤마(,)가 있고, '결과'의 부사절을 이끄는 '그래서, 그러므로'의 의미의 'so that'이 적절하다.

03 접속사 없이 '주어+동사'가 이어지고 있으므로 빈칸에는 '접속사+주어+동사'의 역할을 할 수 있는 분사구문이 되어야 한다.

04 (1) looking을 '접속사+주어+동사'의 역할을 하는 분사구문으로 하여 알맞게 배열한다. (2) 일반적으로 '주절+so that+주어+can/will(조동사)+동사원형 ~'의 형태로 쓰여, 'so that'은 '~하기 위해', '~하고자', '~하도록'의 의미로 '목적'이나 '의도'를 나타낸다.

01 Aaron danced on the stage listening to the music.

02 The bird practiced flying hard so as to fly up high.

03 첫 번째 빈칸에는 접속사가 없으므로 '접속사+주어+동사'의 역할을 할 수 있는 reading이 적절하다. 두 번째 빈칸에는 '~하기 위해', '~하도록'이라는 의미의 '목적'이나 '의도'를 나타내는 'so that'의 so가 적절하다.

04 (1) '~하기 위해', '~하도록'이라는 의미의 '목적'을 나타내도록 that이 적절하다. (2) '목적'을 나타내는 'so that ~ can ...'은 주절과 종속절의 주어가 같은 경우, 'so as to부정사'로 바꿔 쓸 수 있다. (3) '목적'을 나타내는 'so that ~ can ...'은 'in order

that ~ can ...'으로 바꿔 쓸 수 있다.' (4) 접속사가 없으므로 '접속사+주어+동사'의 역할을 할 수 있는 분사구문으로 써야 한다. (5) 분사구문의 뜻을 명확히 하기 위해 접속사 When을 생략하지 않고 남겨둔 경우이다. (6) 분사구문의 부정은 분사 앞에 'not'이나 'never'를 쓴다.

05 '접속사+주어+동사'의 부사절을 분사구문으로 바꾸어 쓸 수 있다. 이때, 분사구문의 뜻을 명확히 하기 위해 접속사를 생략하지 않기도 한다.

06 (A) 'so that ~ can ...'은 주절과 종속절의 주어가 같은 경우 'so as to부정사'로 바꿔 쓸 수 있다. (B) 'so+형용사[부사]+that+주어+can ...(매우 ~해서 …할 수 있는)'은 '형용사+enough to ...(…할 정도로 충분히 ~한)'로 바꿔 쓸 수 있다.

07 접속사가 없으므로 분사구문 thinking으로 만들어야 한다. 분사구문이 문장의 중간에 삽입된 형태이다.

08 'so that ~ can ...'은 'in order that ~ can ...'으로 바꿔 쓸 수 있으며, 주절과 종속절의 주어가 같은 경우 '(in order[so as]) to부정사'로 바꿔 쓸 수 있다.

09 한 문장으로 쓰면 'When you cross the street, you should be careful.'이고, 분사구문으로 바꾸면 'When you cross'를 현재분사 Crossing으로 써야 한다.

10 일반적으로 '주절+so that+주어+can/will(조동사)+동사원형 ~'의 형태로 쓰여, '~하기 위해', '~하고자', '~하도록'의 의미로 '목적'이나 '의도'를 나타낸다.

11 주어진 문장과 ②번은 '양보'를 나타낸다. ① 이유, ③ 시간, ④ 동시동작, ⑤ 조건

12 부사절에서 주어가 주절의 주어와 같을 때 '주어+be동사'를 생략할 수 있으며 이것은 분사구문으로 고쳤을 때 being을 생략하고 접속사를 남겨둔 것과 같다.

13 'so+형용사[부사]+that+주어+can't'는 '너무 ~해서 …할 수 없다'라는 의미이며, 'too+형용사[부사]+to부정사'(…하기에 너무 ~한)로 바꿔 쓸 수 있다.

14 (1) for 뒤에 절이 오므로 for를 that으로 고쳐 'in order that'으로 쓰는 것이 적절하다. (2) 'so as to+부정사' 형태나 'so that+절'의 형태로 써야 하므로 as를 삭제해야 한다. (3) 수영을 하고 있는 '진행'의 의미이므로 Swum을 Swimming으로 고치는 것이 적절하다. (4) 'As it is fine, we went out.'을 분사구문을 이용해서 쓴 문장으로 주절의 주어와 부사절의 주어가 다르므로 독립분사구문으로 써야 한다. (5) Being이 생략된 분사구문으로 '보는' 것이 아니라 '보이는' 것이므로 Seeing을 Seen으로 고쳐야 한다.

15 'Though she had heard their names, Kathryn couldn't

recognize them.'을 분사구문으로 바꾼 것이므로 'Though she had heard' 대신에 'Having heard'로 쓰는 것이 적절하다.

16 ② I was stupid enough to believe him. ③ Come early so as to have plenty of time. 또는 Come early so that you can have plenty of time.

17 'so that'은 '~하기 위해', '~하고자', '~하도록'의 의미로 '목적'이나 '의도'를 나타낸다.

서술형 시험대비
p.26~27

01 (1) Catching a bad cold, my mom couldn't get to work.
　(2) Finishing breakfast, I took a taxi to school.
　(3) Mixing blue and yellow, you get green.
　(4) Being nervous, she said it was a good experience.
　(5) Not knowing what happened, I called my friend, Sam.
　(6) If it being fine tomorrow, I will go hiking.

02 (1) Read the book carefully so that you can find hidden ideas.
　(2) Sally bought a camera so that she could take great pictures.

03 (1) Not knowing the news was false, many people panicked.
　(2) Leaving early, he was late for the meeting.
　(3) He worked so hard that he finally became a lawyer.
　(4) He got up early, so that he could catch the first bus.

04 (1) Exhausting → Exhausted
　(2) Failing → Having failed

05 (1) so that she can
　(2) in order to
　(3) so as to

06 (1) It being
　(2) Watching

07 (1) Turning to the left, you will find the house. / If you turn to the left, you will find the house.
　(2) Being sick, she was absent from school. / Because[As, Since] she was sick, she was absent from school.
　(3) Lisa bought some oranges so[in order] that her mother could make orange juice.

08 (1) Judy practices playing the piano in order that she can win the top prize.

---

　(2) I got up early so that I could go jogging. 또는 I got up early so as to go jogging.
　(3) Arriving late at the station, I saw the train leaving.

01 '접속사+주어+동사'로 이루어진 부사절의 주어가 주절의 주어와 일치할 때 접속사와 주어를 생략하고 동사를 분사(동사원형+-ing)로 만든다. (1) '이유', (2) '시간' (3) '조건' (4) '양보' (5) 분사구문의 부정은 분사 앞에 'not'이나 'never'를 쓴다. (6) 주절의 주어와 부사절의 주어가 다르므로 주어를 생략하면 안 된다.(독립분사구문)

02 so that은 '~하기 위해', '~하고자', '~하도록'의 의미로 '목적'이나 '의도'를 나타낸다. 일반적으로 '주절+so that+주어+can/will(조동사)+동사원형 ~'의 형태로 쓰인다.

03 (1), (2) 현재분사가 분사구문을 이끌도록 한다. 부정은 분사 앞에 'not'이나 'never'를 쓴다. (3) so와 that 사이에 수식어가 오면, '너무 ~해서 결국 …하다'라는 뜻이 된다. (4) 'so that'은 '결과'의 부사절을 이끌어 '그래서, 그러므로'의 의미를 갖는 접속사로 쓰이기도 하는데, 대개 앞에 쉼표(,)가 온다.

04 (1) '지친'의 뜻으로 '수동'의 의미가 되어야 하므로 Exhausting을 Exhausted로 고쳐 써야 한다. (2) 부사절의 시제가 주절보다 앞선 경우에는 완료분사구문(having+과거분사)으로 쓴다.

05 'so that ~ can …'은 'in order that ~ can …'으로 바꿔 쓸 수 있으며, 주절과 종속절의 주어가 같은 경우 '(in order[so as]) to부정사'로 바꿔 쓸 수 있다.

06 (1) 'Because it is rainy, ~'를 부사구문으로 고쳐 쓴다. 주절의 주어와 부사절의 주어가 다르므로 주어를 생략하면 안 된다.(독립분사구문) (2) 'While they are watching the rain, ~'을 부사구문으로 고쳐 쓴다.

07 (1), (2) '접속사+주어+동사'로 이루어진 부사절의 주어가 주절의 주어와 일치할 때 접속사와 주어를 생략하고 동사를 분사(동사원형+-ing)로 만들어서 분사구문으로 바꿔 쓴다. (3) so[in order] that은 '~하기 위해', '~하고자', '~하도록'의 의미로 '목적'이나 '의도'를 나타낸다. 일반적으로 '주절+so [in order] that+주어+can/will(조동사)+동사원형 ~'의 형태로 쓰인다.

08 (1), (2) 'so that ~ can …'은 'in order that ~ can …'으로 바꿔 쓸 수 있으며, 주절과 종속절의 주어가 같은 경우 '(in order[so as]) to부정사'로 바꿔 쓸 수 있다. (3) 내가 도착하는 능동의 의미이므로 현재분사를 쓰는 것이 적절하다.

📎 **확인문제** p.28

1 T 2 F 3 T 4 F

📎 **확인문제** p.29

1 T 2 F 3 T 4 F 5 T 6 F

📎 **확인문제** p.30

1 T 2 F 3 T 4 F 5 T 6 F

교과서 확인학습 A p.31~33

01 Spot Fake News
02 interesting news   03 whether
04 what if, made up
05 in that, less informed, misled
06 Nevertheless, throughout history
07 such false information
08 thinking, the hidden motives
09 AWFUL   10 broke down
11 the other   12 hundreds of   13 on the loose
14 until further notice
15 described above
16 laughed out loud
17 got really worried
18 Not knowing, panicked   19 Some, others
20 make up such news
21 made it up so that, could
22 IN ARGUMENT
23 was shot, wounded
24 had an argument
25 led to, in the chest
26 in critical condition
27 after the shooting
28 are searching for, are warning
29 anything strange   30 backwards
31 why   32 so that, could, if
33 got caught stealing
34 admit, were harshly criticized   35 published
36 As, whether, or   37 How to spot
38 Source   39 reliable   40 trust
41 Check   42 new, old
43 Is, related to current
44 Beyond the Headlines
45 match the content   46 Supporting
47 related, similar

교과서 확인학습 B p.34~36

1 Can You Spot Fake News?
2 Every day we watch, hear, or read interesting news.
3 However, have you ever seriously considered whether an article is really true?
4 Everyone likes an interesting news story but what if it is completely made up?
5 Fake news can be very harmful in that it can make people less informed or even misled.
6 Nevertheless, there have been various fake news reports throughout history.
7 Why have some people written such false information?
8 Let's look into some articles thinking about the hidden motives behind them.
9 AWFUL DISASTER
10 Last night, an angry group of rhinoceroses broke down the walls of the cage at the zoo and escaped.
11 They also broke down the walls of the other wild animals' cages.
12 These animals ran down the streets and injured hundreds of people.
13 Twelve of the animals are still on the loose.
14 Citizens should stay indoors until further notice.
15 Not a single act or incident described above has taken place.
16 At that time, those who read the article carefully laughed out loud.
17 Those who didn't read it to the end got really worried.
18 Not knowing the news was false, many people panicked.
19 Some tried to escape the city while others went into the parks with guns to hunt the animals.
20 So why did *The Herald* make up such news?
21 Later, they confessed that they made it up so that they could draw the readers' attention to the unsafe conditions at the zoo.
22 SLAV SHOOTS A FRIEND IN ARGUMENT
23 Mejk Swenekafew, a Slav worker at the Columbia Coal Mine, was shot and seriously wounded by

John Pecitello near the mining camp Thursday evening.

24 The two men had an argument during a meeting.

25 The argument led to a fight, and Pecitello shot Swenekafew twice, in the chest and leg.

26 He is now at the hospital in critical condition.

27 Pecitello ran away after the shooting.

28 The police are searching for him now and are warning citizens that he is extremely dangerous.

29 Is there anything strange about the article?

30 Read the Slav's name backwards; it spells, "we-fake-news."

31 Who wrote this and why?

32 *The Daily Telegram* published this fake article so that they could prove if *The Daily News*, their competitor, was stealing their articles.

33 *The Daily News* published the same article about "Swenekafew" the next day and thus got caught stealing.

34 The people at *The Daily News* had to admit their act and were harshly criticized by the public.

35 The two articles were special cases, but there are many "fake" news articles published every day.

36 As readers, we need to read critically and judge whether the news is real or fake.

37 How to spot fake news!

38 Consider the Source

39 Is it from a reliable source?

40 Can we trust the writer?

41 Check the Date

42 Is it a new or an old story?

43 Is it related to current events?

44 Read Beyond the Headlines

45 Does the headline match the content?

46 Find Supporting Sources

47 Do other related stories provide similar content?

01 ④   02 ③   03 ④

04 they → it   05 ②   06 ⑤   07 ②, ③, ⑤

08 ③   09 ①   10 ④

11 (A) shot   (B) are   (C) are

12 Swenekafew   13 ②

14 (A) in that   (B) misled   (C) such   15 ①, ④

16 ①   17 published   18 ④   19 ②

20 forward → backwards   21 ③, ⑤   22 ③

23 fake   24 ③, ⑤   25 some articles

26 ④   27 ⑤

28 Those who didn't read it to the end got really worried.

29 made up it → made it up

01 ④ 앞에 나오는 내용과 상반되는 내용이 뒤에 이어지므로 However가 가장 적절하다. ① 게다가, 더욱이, ② 다시 말해서, ③ 그러므로

02 주어진 문장의 Nevertheless에 주목한다. 비록 ③번 앞 문장의 내용이 사실이지만, 그럼에도 불구하고, 역사를 통틀어 다양한 가짜 뉴스 보도들이 존재해 왔다는 내용이므로 ③번이 적절하다.

03 가짜 뉴스는 사람들에게 정보를 '부족하게' 제공할 수 있다. well-informed: 사정에 정통한, 박식한, ① day after day: 매일, ③ damaging: 손해를 끼치는, 해로운

04 news는 단수로 취급하기 때문에, they를 it으로 고치는 것이 적절하다.

05 ⓐ on the loose 잡히지 않은, 탈주 중인, ⓑ until: ~까지(계속), by: ~까지는(완료)

06 ⑤ 그 중 열두 마리의 동물들이 아직 잡히지 않았다. on the loose 잡히지 않은, 탈주 중인

07 happen = occur = arise: (사고·일·문제 등이) 발생하다, 일어나다, be held = be hosted: 개최되다

08 ⓐ와 ②, ⑤: 이유, ①, ④: 양보, ③: 조건

09 ⓑ와 ①: (이야기 등을) 지어내다, 만들어 내다, ② (잃어버린 것) ~을 대신하다; ~에 대해 보상하다, ③ (~와) 화해하다, ④ (각 부분이) ~을 구성[형성]하다, ⑤ 화장하다, 분장하다

10 이 글은 '동물원의 안전하지 않은 상태에 대해 독자들의 주의를 끌기 위해 헤럴드사가 기사를 지어냈다는 것이므로, 주제로는 ④번 '독자들의 주의를 끌기 위한 거짓 뉴스'가 적절하다.

11 (A) '총상을 입었다'고 해야 하므로 shot이 적절하다. shoot-shot-shot: (총 등을) 쏘다, shut-shut-shut: (문 등을[이]) 닫다[닫히다], (눈을) 감다, (B) 'The police'는 복수 취급하므로 are가 적절하다. (C) 'The police'가 주어이므로 are가 적절하다.

12 'Swenekafew'를 가리킨다.

13 그가 왜 John Pecitello와 언쟁을 벌였는지는 알 수 없다. ① He worked at the Columbia Coal Mine. ③ He was shot on Thursday evening. ④ He was shot twice. ⑤ He is now at the hospital.

14 (A) '가짜 뉴스는 사람들을 잘못 이끌 수 있다는 점에서 매우 해로울 수 있다'고 해야 하므로 in that이 적절하다. in that: ~이

므로, ~라는 점에서, (B) 목적어인 people이 '잘못 이끌어질 수 있다'는 수동의 의미이므로, 과거분사 misled가 적절하다. (C) such+(a)+형용사+명사

15 ⓐ와 ①, ④: 경험 용법, ② 결과 용법, ③ 계속 용법, ⑤ 완료 용법

16 '매일 우리가 얼마나 많은 흥미로운 뉴스를 보거나 듣고, 읽는지'는 대답할 수 없다. ② Everyone likes an interesting news story. ③ Yes. ④ Yes. ⑤ Yes.

17 앞에 나온 명사 articles를 수식하도록 과거분사 published로 쓰는 것이 적절하다.

18 ⓑ와 ④: 현재의, the current year: 올해, ① 통용되는, ② (물·공기의) 흐름, 해류(명사), ③ 전류(명사), direct current: 직류, ⑤ 때의 흐름(course), 경향, 풍조(명사), swim against the current: 세상 풍조[천하대세]에 거스르다

19 가짜 뉴스 판별 방법 중의 하나인 'Read Beyond the Headlines(기사 제목 그 이상을 읽어라)'는 단순히 기사 제목만 읽고 뉴스의 내용을 짐작하여 판단하지 말고 그 기사의 내용까지 모두 읽으라는 의미이므로, ②번의 '제목으로 내용을 짐작하기'는 가짜 뉴스 판별 방법에 해당하지 않는다.

20 그 슬라브인의 이름을 '거꾸로' 읽어 보라고 하는 것이 적절하다. forward: 앞으로

21 ⓑ와 ③, ⑤: ~인지 아닌지, ①, ②, ④: (가정적 조건을 나타내어) (만약) ~라면

22 ③ 그 다음 날 'Swenekafew'에 대한 동일한 기사를 발행한 것은 '데일리 뉴스 사'이다.

23 fake: 가짜의, 거짓된, genuine: 진짜의, 진품의

24 nevertheless: 그럼에도 불구하고(부사), even so, still, nonetheless 등과 바꿔 쓸 수 있다. ① despite ~: ~에도 불구하고(전치사), ② therefore: 그러므로(부사) ④ otherwise: (만약) 그렇지 않으면[않았다면](부사)

25 '몇 가지 뉴스 기사'를 가리킨다.

26 이 글은 '가짜 뉴스는 매우 해로울 수 있지만, 역사를 통틀어 다양한 가짜 뉴스 보도들이 존재해 왔다'는 내용의 글이므로, 제목으로는 ④번 '해로운 그러나 계속되는 가짜 뉴스 보도들'이 적절하다. continuous: 계속되는, 지속적인, ⑤ faithful: 충실한, from now on: 이제부터

27 '어떤 사람들은', '다른 사람들은'이라고 해야 하므로, Some, others가 적절하다. some: 처음 지칭하는 어떤 것[사람]들, others: 다른 것[사람]들, ① one: 2개 이상의 대상 중 불특정한 한 개를 처음으로 지칭할 때 사용하는 대명사, the other: 2개 중 나머지 한 개, ② the others: 앞에 지칭한 것들을 제외한 나머지 전부들, ③ another: 3개 이상의 대상에서 두 번째로 불특

정한 한 개를 지칭할 때 사용하는 대명사, ④ the first: 전자, the second: 후자

28 주격 관계대명사절 'who didn't read it to the end'가 선행사 those를 수식하도록 쓰는 것이 적절하다.

29 구동사의 목적어가 인칭대명사이므로 부사의 앞에 목적어를 쓰는 것이 적절하다

서술형 시험대비
p.42~43

01 (A) if   (B) harmful   (C) informed
02 Why have some people written such false information?
03 while we think about the hidden motives behind them
04 on the loose
05 has been taken place → has taken place
06 (A) No   (B) escape
07 in order that[so that], could[might]
08 such news
09 ②번 near from → near
10 (A) had an argument   (B) critical
11 Whether
12 *The Daily News* published the same article about "Swenekafew" the next day

01 (A) '만약 그것이 완전히 지어낸 것이라면 어떻게 할 것인가?'라고 해야 하므로 if가 적절하다. What if ~?: ~라면 어떻게 될까? (B) '가짜 뉴스는 사람들을 잘못 이끌 수 있다는 점에서 매우 해로울 수 있다'고 해야 하므로 harmful이 적절하다. harmless: 해가 없는, 무해한, (C) 목적어인 people이 '정보를 부족하게 제공받거나'라고 수동의 의미이므로, 과거분사 informed가 적절하다.

02 현재완료 시제의 의문문은 'Have+주어+p.p.'의 순서로 쓰는 것이 적절하다. such+(a)+형용사+명사

03 위 글의 밑줄 친 ⓑ는 동시동작을 나타내는 분사구문으로, '~하는 동안에'라는 의미의 접속사 while을 사용하여 부사절로 고치는 것이 적절하다.

04 on the loose: 잡히지 않은; 탈주 중인

05 take place는 '(사고·일·문제 등이) 발생하다, 일어나다'라는 뜻으로 수동태로 쓸 수 없다.

06 실제로는 어젯밤 동물들이 동물원에서 '도망치지' 않았기 때문에, 동물원에서 탈출한 동물들에 의해 '아무도' 다치지 않았다.

07 목적을 나타내는 부사적 용법의 to부정사는 복문으로 전환할 때 'in order that[so that]+주어+can[may]+동사원형'으로 고

치는 것이 적절하다.

08 '이러한 뉴스'를 가리킨다.

09 전치사 near 뒤에 바로 목적어를 쓰는 것이 적절하다. ① by+수동태의 행위자, ③ be shot in the ~: ~에 총을 맞다, ④ in critical condition: 위독한 상태로, ⑤ search for: ~를 찾다

10 Mejk Swenekafew는 John Pecitello와 회의 중에 '언쟁을 벌였고', Pecitello가 Swenekafew에게 총을 쏘았다. Swenekafew는 지금 입원 중이고, 그의 상태는 '위독하다.'

11 if는 '~인지 아닌지'라는 의미의 명사절을 이끄는 접속사로 whether와 바꾸어 쓸 수 있으며, if가 이끄는 명사절이 동사 prove의 목적어이다.

12 '데일리 뉴스사가 그 다음 날 'Swenekafew'에 대한 동일한 기사를 발행한 것'을 가리킨다.

영역별 핵심문제

p.45~49

01 misunderstand 02 ②

03 (1) reliable (2) riddle (3) seriously (4) shoot
  (5) source 04 ① 05 ⑤

06 (1) break down (2) According to (3) made up

07 (1) She described what happened last night.
  (2) This is one of the worst natural disasters.
  (3) A lion escaped from the zoo an hour ago.

08 (C) → (D) → (B) → (E) → (A) 09 ①

10 ⑤

11 It's because they help adults think more creatively.

12 We need to think outside the box.

13 ⑤ 14 ⑤

15 (1) Linda was stupid enough to make a big
    mistake.
  (2) Bill is too poor to buy the house.

16 ① 17 ⑤

18 (1) Though[Although] the two articles were special
    cases
  (2) and[while] he smiled brightly
  (3) Because[As, Since] I was tired from the work

19 ② 20 ② 21 ⑤ 22 ⑤

23 ③ 24 ④

25 (A) the other (B) further (C) described

26 Twelve of the animals are still on the loose.

27 John Pecitello 28 ② 29 ④

30 ⓐ To draw the readers' attention to the unsafe
    conditions at the zoo.
  ⓑ To prove that *The Daily News* was stealing
    their articles.

---

01 접두사 'mis'는 '잘못된, 나쁜'을 의미한다. misunderstand: 오해하다, 잘못 이해하다

02 nevertheless: 그럼에도 불구하고

03 riddle: 수수께끼, seriously: 심하게, 진지하게, reliable: 믿을 만한, source: 출처, shoot: 쏘다

04 '갑자기 너무 걱정이 되어서 이성적일 수 없다고 느끼다'를 가리키는 말은 panic이다.

05 보기에 주어진 current는 '현재의'를 뜻한다. ⑤번은 '흐름, 해류'를 의미한다.

06 break down: 부수다, 무너뜨리다, according to: ~에 따르면, make up: 지어내다, 만들다

07 describe: 기술하다, disaster: 재난, escape: 탈출하다

08 (C) TV 뉴스를 보는 이유 질문 → (D) 이유 설명 → (B) TV가 가장 유용하다고 생각하는 이유 질문 → (E) 이유 설명 → (A) 반응 및 이해 표현

09 위 대화에서 Sandy는 '주의 깊은, 신중한' 성격임을 알 수 있다.

10 Sandy에 따르면 음료수가 무엇으로 만들어졌는지에 대한 정보가 없다.

11 John은 수수께끼 책들이 어른들이 좀 더 창의적으로 생각하도록 도와주기 때문에 유익하다고 생각한다.

12 수수께끼의 답을 찾기 위해 고정관념에서 벗어날 필요가 있다.

13 ⑤번을 제외한 나머지는 모두 자세한 설명을 요청하는 표현이다.

14 여자는 체온이 낮아서 감기에 걸렸다는 설명은 대화의 내용과 일치하지 않는다.

15 (1) 'so+형용사[부사]+that+주어+can …'은 '형용사+enough to …'로 바꿔 쓸 수 있다. (2) 'so+형용사[부사]+that+주어+can't …'은 'too+형용사[부사]+to부정사'로 바꿔 쓸 수 있다.

16 'so that ~ can …'은 'in order that ~ can …'으로 바꿔 쓸 수 있다.

17 As she didn't hand out the report, she is responsible for the result.를 분사구문으로 쓴 것이므로 handing을 'having handed'로 고쳐야 한다.

18 (1) 내용상 '양보'가 적절하고, 주어가 다른 독립분사구문이므로 다른 주어를 써 주고, having been이 있으므로 한 시제 앞선 양보의 부사절로 쓴다. (2) 내용상 '동시동작'이나 '시간'의 부사절이 적절하다. (3) 내용상 '이유'의 부사절이 적절하다.

19 전치사 with는 '~한 채'의 뜻으로 부대 상황을 나타낸다.

20 앞에 나오는 내용과 상반되는 내용이 뒤에 이어지므로 Nevertheless가 가장 적절하다. ① 뿐만 아니라, 더욱이, ③ 똑같이, 비슷하게, ④ 즉[말하자면], ⑤ 따라서, 그러므로

21 ① every day = each day: 매일, ② whether = if: ~인지

아닌지, ③ what if는 회화에서 자주 쓰이는 줄임말로, 본래 표현은 'what would happen if'이며 '~한다면 어쩌지?'라는 뜻으로 사용된다. ④ in the sense that: ~라는 점에서, ⑤ motive: 동기, 이유, theme: 주제, 테마

22 look into: ~을 조사하다

23 문장 끝에서 '왜 어떤 사람들은 그러한 거짓 정보를 써 왔던 것일까? 그 뒤에 숨겨진 동기를 생각하면서 몇 가지 뉴스 기사를 살펴보자.'라고 했으므로, 뒤에 올 내용으로는 '그 뒤에 숨겨진 동기에 대해 생각할 수 있는 몇 가지 가짜 뉴스 기사'가 적절하다.

24 ⓐ와 ④: 부수다, ① 실패하다, 결렬되다, ②와 ⑤: (기계·차량이) 고장 나다, ③ 아주 나빠지다

25 (A) 뒤에 복수 명사가 이어지므로 the other가 적절하다. another+단수 명사, (B) '추후 안내가 있을 때까지'라고 해야 하므로 further가 적절하다. farther: (공간, 시간상으로) 더 멀리, further: 더 이상의, 추가의, (C) '위에 기술된 어떤 행동이나 사건도'라고 해야 하므로 described가 적절하다.

26 on the loose: 잡히지 않은, 탈주 중인

27 Mejk Swenekafew에게 총을 쏜 John Pecitello를 가리킨다.

28 주어진 문장의 The argument에 주목한다. ②번 앞 문장의 an argument를 받고 있으므로 ②번이 적절하다.

29 위 글은 '인터뷰'이다. ① (신문·잡지의) 글, 기사, ② 수필, ③ (책·연극·영화 등에 대한) 논평[비평], 감상문, ⑤ 요약, 개요

30 ⓐ: 동물원의 안전하지 않은 상태에 대해 독자들의 주의를 끌기 위해서. ⓑ: 데일리 뉴스 사가 그들의 기사를 훔치고 있다는 것을 증명하기 위해서

단원별 예상문제
p.50~53

01 ⑤
02 Can you give me more information about it?
03 ⑤　　**04** ②　　**05** ④　　**06** riddle
07 ⑤　　**08** ⓐ → where it is　　**09** ⑤
10 ③
11 (1) As[Because, Since] I was driving my car, I couldn't reply to your text message.
(2) While[When, As] I was walking down the street, I met my friend.
(3) Although[Though] there was no work to do, he remained at his office until late.
12 playing the guitar　　**13** ④　　**14** ②, ④
15 ②, ③, ⑤　**16** ⑤　　**17** panicked
18 Because[As/Since] they didn't know the news was false　　**19** ④
20 ⑤

21 (A) *The Daily Telegram*
(B) The people at *The Daily News*
22 the public harshly criticized the people at *The Daily News*

01 '알맞은 순서로 문자를 가지고 단어를 형성하다'를 가리키는 말은 spell이다.

03 수지가 잠을 잘 자기 위해 몇 잔의 우유를 마셔야 하는지는 대화를 통해 알 수 없다.

04 주어진 문장은 기사에 대한 구체적인 설명을 요청하므로 (B)에 들어가는 것이 적절하다.

05 왜 프랑스의 1인치가 영국과 달랐는지는 대화를 통해 알 수 없다.

06 '이해하기 힘든 질문으로 놀라운 답을 갖고 있고 게임으로 다른 사람에게 묻는 질문'을 가리키는 것은 riddle(수수께끼)이다.

07 think outside the box: 고정관념에서 벗어나다

08 간접의문문으로 '의문사+주어+동사'의 순서가 적절하다.

10 ③ She was too tired to think straight. 'so+형용사[부사]+that+주어+can't ...'는 '너무 ~해서 …할 수 없다'라는 의미이며, 'too+형용사[부사]+to부정사'(…하기에 너무 ~한)로 바꿔 쓸 수 있다.

11 (1), (2) 분사구문의 분사(동사원형+-ing)를 의미에 맞게 '접속사+주어+동사'로 이루어진 부사절로 만든다. (3) 분사구문의 주어가 주절의 주어와 일치하지 않으므로 부사절의 주어를 따로 써 주어야 한다.

12 '접속사+주어+동사'로 이루어진 부사절의 주어가 주절의 주어와 일치할 때 접속사와 주어를 생략하고 동사를 분사(동사원형+-ing)로 만든다.

13 Don't waste water in order to prevent water shortages.

14 ⓐ와 ②, ④: (신문·잡지 따위의) 기사, ①, ⑤: (종류가 같은 것의) 한 개, 한 가지(item), ③ 관사, a definite article: 정관사(the)

15 ⓑ와 ②, ③, ⑤: 현재분사, ①, ④: 동명사

16 이 글은 '가짜 뉴스는 매우 해로울 수 있지만, 역사를 통틀어 다양한 가짜 뉴스 보도들이 존재해 왔다'는 내용의 글이므로, 주제로는 ⑤번 '해로운 영향들에도 불구하고, 다양한 가짜 뉴스 보도들이 존재해 왔다'가 적절하다. ④ faithfully: (내용이 틀리지 않게) 충실히, 정확히

17 'panic'의 과거형은 끝에 '-ked'를 붙이는 것이 적절하다. 'paniced'로 쓰지 않도록 주의해야 한다. panic 겁에 질려 어쩔 줄 모르다

18 '이유'를 나타내는 부사절로 고치는 것이 적절하다.

19 헤럴드 사는 사람들에게 '겁주기 위하여' 이러한 뉴스를 만들어 낸 것이 아니라, '동물원의 안전하지 않은 상태에 대해 독자들의 주의를 끌기 위해' 그 기사를 지어냈다.

20 앞의 내용의 결과가 나오고 있으므로 thus가 가장 적절하다. ① 게다가, ② 그 대신에, 그렇지 않으면(둘째 대안을 소개할 때 씀), ③ 다른 한편으로는, 반면에, ④ 게다가, 더욱이

21 (A) 데일리 텔레그램 사, The Daily Telegram과 같이 특정 회사를 지칭할 때는 그 회사를 이루는 구성원 전체를 받아 they 로 복수 취급하기도 한다. (B) 데일리 뉴스 사의 사람들을 가리킨다.

22 the public을 주어로 해서 능동태로 고치는 것이 적절하다.

01 It says that Napoleon was actually fairly tall.
02 A French doctor wrote it down according to the French measuring system.
03 An inch in France was longer than an inch in England.
04 (1) Because[As, Since] Jenny won the first prize, she was so happy.
  (2) If you walk with Wing Walker, you burn more calories and get slimmer.
  (3) Using the hidden board technology, they strengthen leg muscles.
  (4) She studied very hard, passing the exam.
05 (1) in order that   (2) in[so] order[as] to
  (3) enough to   (4) too hot, to
06 that → whether[if]
07 what if it is completely made up?
08 (A) fake news   (B) fake news
09 the article
10 (in order/so as) to draw the readers' attention to the unsafe conditions at the zoo
11 (A) escape the city   (B) went into the parks

01 기사에 따르면 나폴레옹은 꽤 키가 컸다.
02 프랑스 의사가 나폴레옹의 키를 적었고 프랑스 측정 체계에 따라 적었다.
03 프랑스의 1인치는 영국의 1인치보다 더 길었다.
04 (1) 의미상 '이유'를 나타내는 분사구문이다. (2) 의미상 '조건'을 나타내는 분사구문이다. (3) 의미상 '이유'를 나타내는 분사구문으로 바꾼다. (4) 의미상 '연속상황'을 나타내는 분사구문으로 바꾼다.

05 (1), (2) 'so that ~ can ...'은 'in order that ~ can ...'으로 바꿔 쓸 수 있으며, 주절과 종속절의 주어가 같은 경우 '(in order[so as]) to부정사'로 바꿔 쓸 수 있다. (3), (4) 'so+형용사[부사]+that+주어+can ...'은 '형용사+enough to ...'로 바꿔 쓸 수 있으며, 'so+형용사[부사]+that+주어+can't ...'는 'too+형용사[부사]+to부정사'로 바꿔 쓸 수 있다. (4)번의 경우 주절과 종속절의 주어가 다르지만 일반인이 주어이므로 따로 밝혀 쓰지 않아도 된다.

06 '뉴스 기사가 정말로 진실인지 심각하게 고려해 본 적이 있는가?' 라고 해야 하므로, that을 whether로 고치는 것이 적절하다. that을 쓰면, '뉴스 기사가 정말로 진실이라는 것을 심각하게 고려해 본 적이 있는가?'라는 뜻이 되어 어색하다.

07 what if: ~라면 어떻게 될까?, make up 지어내다, 만들어 내다

08 '가짜 뉴스' 때문에 사람들에게 정보가 부족하게 제공되거나 사람들이 잘못 이끌릴 수 있지만, 역사를 통틀어 다양한 '가짜 뉴스' 보도들이 존재해 왔다.

09 '그 기사'를 가리킨다.

10 so that+주어+can+동사원형 = (in order/so as) to+동사원형: ~하기 위하여(목적)

11 어떤 사람들은 '도시를 빠져나가려고 했고' 다른 사람들은 그 동물들을 사냥하기 위해 총을 들고 '공원으로 나갔다.'

|모범답안|
01 (A) I drunk a glass of warm milk
  (B) a glass of warm milk doesn't actually help me fall asleep
  (C) make people sleepy
  (D) amount
02 (A) the walking shoes, Wing Walker
  (B) burn more calories and get slimmer
  (C) the hidden board technology
  (D) scientifically proven
  (E) what materials

01 최근에 나는 잠을 잘 잘 수 없어서 잠들기 전에 따뜻한 우유를 한 잔 마셨다. 하지만 효과가 없었다. 나는 이에 대해 민수에게 이야기했다. 그는 한 잔의 따뜻한 우유가 실제로는 잠을 잘 자는 데 도움이 되지 않는다고 설명했다. 의사에 따르면 우유에는 사람들을 졸리게 만드는 특별한 화학물질이 있지만 우유 한 잔에 있는 양은 너무 적었다. 나는 잠을 잘 자기 위해 다른 방법을 찾아야겠다고 생각했다.

01 (D) → (C) → (A) → (B)

02 (1) awful   (2) chemicals   (3) chest   (4) citizen

03 (1) poems   (2) prove   (3) public   (4) published
    (5) recognize

04 ③   05 ④   06 ⑤

07 She reads the label of the drink closely.

08 It's because the label on the drink looks a bit strange.

09 What's in the drink and how much one has to drink to lose weight are not shown.   10 ②

11 ⑤

12 (1) Think critically and don't believe everything (that) they tell you.
    (2) Do not criticize or make fun of your classmates.
    (3) Is this your current address?
    (4) It's difficult to judge whether it's true or not.

13 (1) Sam saved some money so that he could buy a new backpack. 또는 Sam saved some money so as to buy a new backpack.
    (2) You must follow the rules in order for everyone to enjoy the experience. 또는 You must follow the rules in order that everyone may[can] enjoy the experience.
    (3) She saw Thomas entering[enter] the classroom.
    (4) Very embarrassed, she didn't tell us that news.

14 (1) Having no work to do, he goes fishing.
    (2) Susan spoke quietly so that other people couldn't hear her voice.

15 ③   16 ①, ③, ④

17 (1) 해석: Jinho는 외국인과 영어로 말할 수 있도록 영어를 열심히 공부했다.
    차이: so that은 '~하기 위해', '~하고자', '~하도록'의 의미로 '목적'이나 '의도'를 나타낸다. 일반적으로 '주절+so that+주어+can/will(조동사)+동사원형 ~'의 형태로 쓰인다.
    (2) 해석: Jinho는 영어를 열심히 공부해서 외국인과 영어로 말할 수 있었다.
    차이: so와 that 사이에 형용사나 부사가 오면, '너무 ~해서 결국 …하다'라는 뜻이 된다.

18 ①   19 an interesting news story

20 ③   21 ③   22 ④   23 ⑤

24 The two men had an argument during a meeting.

25 ③   26 ④

---

01 (D) 감기에 걸린 것 같다며 이유 설명 → (C) 기사 내용 설명 → (A) 구체적인 설명 요청 → (B) 감기에 걸리는 이유에 대해

구체적인 설명

02 awful: 끔찍한, 지독한, chemical: 화학 물질, chest: 흉부, 가슴, citizen: 시민

03 public: 대중, recognize: 알아보다, publish: 출판하다, prove: 증명하다, poem: 시

04 mine은 명사로 '광산', 동사로 '채굴하다', 대명사로 '나의 것'을 의미한다.

05 주어진 문장은 금붕어가 사실은 똑똑하다는 말 앞에 오는 것이 자연스러우므로 (D)가 적절하다.

06 위 대화를 통해 금붕어가 어떻게 주인을 알아보는지 알 수 없다.

07 Sandy는 음료의 라벨을 자세히 읽는다.

08 음료수의 라벨이 조금 이상해 보이기 때문에 Sandy는 David가 음료수를 사지 말아야 한다고 생각한다.

09 음료수에 무엇이 있는지 살을 빼기 위해 얼마나 마셔야 하는지 볼 수 없다.

10 (A) useful: 유용한, useless: 무익한, (B) ordinarily: 평범하게, creatively: 창의적으로, (C) think outside the box: 고정관념에서 벗어나다

11 위 대화를 통해 John의 상자 밖에 무엇이 있는지 알 수 없다.

12 critically: 비판적으로, criticize: 비판하다, current: 현재의, judge: 판단하다

13 (1) 'so that+절' 또는 'so as to부정사'가 되어야 한다. (2) 'for everyone to enjoy'로 의미상의 주어를 쓰거나 'in order that+절'이 되어야 한다. (3) entered를 entering[enter]로 바꾸어 목적보어로 만든다. (4) 주어가 embarrassed되는 수동의 관계이므로 being이 생략된 과거분사 embarrassed로 시작하는 문장으로 바꾼다.

14 (1) 분사구문을 이용하고 'no work to do'를 분사 Having의 목적어로 이용한다. (2) 일반적으로 '주절+so that+주어+can/will(조동사)+동사원형 ~'의 형태로 so that은 '목적'이나 '의도'를 나타낸다.

15 Wear a swimming cap in order for the pool to be kept clean. 주절과 부사절의 주어가 다른 경우 서로 다른 주어를 나타내야 하는데 to부정사의 경우 'for+목적격'으로 쓴다.

16 ② Pass → Passing ⑤ Feeling not → Not feeling ⑥ Meeting → Having met

17 'so that+주어+can ...'과 'so+형용사[부사]+that+주어+can ...'의 차이를 구별한다.

18 ⓑ와 ③: 계속 용법, ①: 결과 용법, ②, ④: 완료 용법, ⑤: 경험 용법

19 '흥미로운 뉴스 기사'를 가리킨다.

20 ⓐ to the end: 끝까지, ⓑ draw one's attention to ~: ~에 대해 …의 주의를 끌다

21 ③ 잠깐, 잠시(명사), ③을 제외한 나머지: [반대·비교·대조를 나타내어] 그런데, 한편(접속사)

22 주어진 문장의 such news에 주목한다. ④번 앞 단락에서 말한 '거짓 뉴스'를 가리키므로 ④번이 적절하다.

23 이 글은 '컬럼비아 광산 소속의 슬라브인 노동자 두 명이 언쟁을 벌이다가 한 명이 총상을 입어 심각하게 다쳤다'는 내용의 글이므로, 제목으로는 ⑤번 '슬라브인이 언쟁 중에 친구를 쏘다'가 적절하다. ④ criminal: 범인

24 had an argument: 언쟁을 벌였다

25 run away: 도망치다

26 경찰이 찾고 있는 것은 'Pecitello'이다.

Words of Wisdom

시험대비 실력평가
p.66

01 ④	02 ③	03 ②	04 failure
05 ②	06 ①	07 ⑤	

01 ④ novel(새로운)은 뒤에 ty를 붙여 novelty(새로움)를 만들 수 있다. ④ 이외의 보기에는 접미사 dom을 붙여 명사를 만들 수 있다. ① wise+dom → wisdom 지혜 ② free+dom → freedom 자유 ③ bore+dom → boredom 지루함, 따분함 ⑤ fan+dom → fandom 팬덤, 팬층

02 priceless: 대단히 귀중한, 값을 매길 수 없는 / 그는 주변 사람들이 편안함을 느끼게 만드는 귀중한 능력을 가진 사람이다. ① 가치가 없는, 하찮은 ② 가치 없는 ③ 귀중한 ④ 경제적인 ⑤ 비싼

03 (A) settle in: ~에 자리 잡다, 정착하다. 그는 몇 년 동안 여행을 한 후에, 뉴욕에 정착했다. (B) get stuck on: ~에 갇히다. 만약 네가 어려운 단어에 막히면, 도움을 청해라.

04 fail: 실패하다 failure: 실패 / 그의 새 영화는 완전한 실패였다.

05 ① character: 등장인물 / 그는 이 영화에서 가장 재미있는 등장인물이다. ② express: 표현하다 / 나는 나의 친구 지나에게 고마움을 표현하고 싶다. ③ reward: 보상 / 그들은 그가 열심히 일한 것에 대한 보상을 주었다. ④ situation: 상황, 환경 / 지금은 어려운 상황이고 나는 무엇을 해야 할지 모르겠다. ⑤ far-away: 멀리 떨어진 / 우리 할머니는 멀리 떨어진 산에서 사셨다.

06 hire: 고용하다 / 당신을 위해 특정한 일을 하도록 어떤 사람에게 일을 주거나 그에게 돈을 지불하다

07 make friends: 친구를 사귀다 / 나는 여름 캠프에서 많은 친구들을 사귀었다. make a wish: 소원을 빌다 / 그들은 유성이 떨어지는 것을 보면서 소원을 빌었다.

서술형 시험대비
p.67

01 (b)ring back

02 (1) After a hard day's work (2) explain myself

03 (t)ake care of

04 ran

05 (1) You have so much to learn throughout your life.

   (2) The price is supposed to go down this week.

   (3) All the students were puzzled by the question.

---

(4) This situation matters a lot.

(5) That's a philosophy I could live by.

06 with open arms

01 단어의 관계는 동의어이다. hire: 고용하다 employ: 고용하다 return: 돌려주다, 반납하다 bring back: 돌려주다

02 (1) after a hard day's work: 하루 종일 열심히 일하고 나서 (2) explain oneself: 자기 생각을 밝히다, 심중을 털어놓다

03 look after ~: ~을 살피다, 돌보다 take care of ~ :~을 돌보다. 당신이 없을 때 아이들은 누가 돌볼 것인가요?

04 run out of: ~이 없어지다, 다 떨어지다 / 나는 그 시험을 끝내지 못했다. 나는 시간을 다 썼다. run: 달리다 / 나는 가능한 한 빨리 학교로 달려갔다.

05 (1) throughout one's life: 일생을 통해 (2) suppose: 추측하다, 추정하다 (3) puzzled: 당혹스러운, 어리둥절한 (4) matter: 중요하다 situation: 상황, 환경 (5) live by: (신조, 원칙 등)에 따라 살다

06 with open arms: 두 팔을 벌리고 / 이모는 나를 두 팔을 벌려 환영했다.

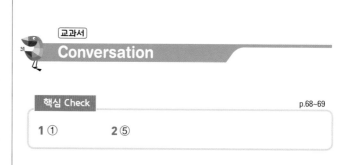

교과서 Conversation

핵심 Check
p.68~69

1 ①	2 ⑤

교과서 대화문 익히기

Check(√) True or False
p.70

1 T 2 F 3 F 4 T

Check(√) True or False
p.71

5 F 6 T 7 T 8 T

교과서 확인학습
p.73~75

Listen & Speak 1 A

1. you still up / because I'm worried about / You've read, have to worry about / confusing, worried that / that hasn't happened / try not to worry

2. Nothing special / have to go to, can't find anyone / worry about / worried / supposed to be

Listen & Talk 1 B

worried / got a big part in / keep making mistakes / practice / making mistakes

Listen & Talk 2 A

1. lived forever / What would you do if / would / interesting

2. called / heard, come true / if you could make one wish / would make, stay, make all my wishes come true

Listen & Talk 2 B

one of, movies / what would you do if you could / prevent / would go to, meet

Communication Step A

How's / ran out / Don't worry about / character, What would you do if you were / find out if

Wrap Up

1. I've heard that / worried / I'm worried that, too difficult / Don't worry about, believe in yourself

2. watched / a man who was stuck on / tries, would, if you were him / alive / that's what the man did

시험대비 기본평가 p.76

01 ④   02 ①

01 'What would you do if you+과거시제 ~?'에 대한 대답으로 '나는 ~할 거야.'라는 의미로 'I would 동사원형 ~.' 형태의 가정법 과거를 사용하여 대답한다.

02 빈칸 다음의 남자가 'I'll try not to worry so much.(너무 걱정하지 않도록 해 볼게요.)'라고 말하는 것으로 보아 여자가 걱정하지 말라고 말하면서 상대방을 안심시켰을 것이다.

시험대비 실력평가 p.77~78

01 ②   02 ③   03 ①   04 ④
05 ②   06 ③   07 ③
08 I'll try not to worry so much. 09 ④   10 ⑤
11 ②

01 상대방을 안심시키는 표현으로는 'Don't worry about ~.'이라는 말을 쓸 수 있다. 위의 대화에서 마감이 이번 주말인데 아이디어가 다 떨어진 여자아이에게 남자가 안심시키는 것이 어울리므로 ②가 적절하다.

02 '마감이 이번 주말이다.'와 '아이디어가 다 떨어졌다.'는 역접의 접속사 'but(하지만)'이 들어가야 적절하다.

03 현재 사실과 반대되는 상황이나 일에 대해 가정하거나 현재 사실에 대한 후회나 아쉬움을 강조할 때, 가정법 과거를 쓴다. 즉, 현재 사실과 반대이므로 과거 시제를 쓴다. 조건절은 'if 주어+동사 과거형'으로, 주절은 '주어+would+동사원형 ~'을 쓴다. 이때 해석은 '~라면 …할 텐데.'라고 해석한다.

04 패션모델이라면 무엇을 할 것인지 묻는 말에, '나는 키가 클 수 있다.'라는 대답은 어울리지 않는다.

05 'What would you do if you+동사의 과거형 ~?'은 '네가 만약 ~한다면, 너는 무엇을 할 거니?'라는 의미의 가정법 과거로 현재 사실과 반대되는 것을 상상하여 말할 때 쓰인다. 그리고 책의 내용이 마법의 물을 마시고 영원히 살게 되게 된 한 가족에 대한 이야기이므로, 내용상 영원히 살게 되면 무엇을 할지 질문하는 것이 어울린다.

06 영원히 살게 된다면 여자아이는 전 세계의 다양한 도시에서 살고 싶다고 말했다.

07 주어진 문장은 '뭐가 걱정이니?'의 의미로 걱정에 대한 구체적인 내용을 묻고 있는 질문이다. 이에 대한 대답으로 'Some of the writers' names are confusing, so I'm worried that I might not remember them.(몇몇 작가들의 이름이 헷갈려서 그들을 기억하지 못할까봐 걱정이 돼요.)'이 어울리므로 ③이 적절하다.

08 to worry는 try의 목적어이다. to부정사를 부정하기 위해서 앞에 not을 쓴다. 'try to 동사원형'은 '~하기 위해 노력하다'라는 의미이므로, 'try not to 동사원형'은 '~하지 않기 위해 노력하다'로 해석할 수 있다.

09 빈칸에서 them은 the writers' names를 의미하는 것이고, 내용상 작가들의 이름이 헷갈려서 그 이름을 기억하지 못하는 것에 대한 걱정을 표현하는 것이 알맞으므로 ④가 적절하다.

10 주어진 문장에서 them은 mistakes를 가리키는 말이다. 더 연습을 하라고 말하면서, 실수하는 것에 대해 걱정하지 말고, 실수로부터 배울 수 있다고 말할 수 있으므로 ⑤가 어울린다.

11 아빠가 'Don't worry about making mistakes.(실수하는 것에 대해서는 걱정하지 마.)'라고 말하는 것으로 보아 Jane은 실수하는 것에 대해 걱정하고 있다.

서술형 시험대비 p.79

01 called   02 make
03 about   04 confusing
05 What would you do if you could live forever?
06 made → make

01 called는 과거분사로 '~라는 이름의, ~라고 불리는'의 의미로 앞에 있는 명사 a book을 수식하고 있다.

02 (A), (C), (D) make는 '~에게 …하게 하다'라는 의미를 가지는 사역동사로, 목적격보어로 동사원형을 쓴다. (B) make a wish: 소원을 빌다

03 'I'm worried about ~.'은 '나는 ~에 대해 걱정한다.'의 의미로 걱정을 나타낼 때 사용하는 표현이다.

04 감정을 나타내는 동사의 경우 현재분사는 '~하게 하는'의 뜻으로 감정을 유발하는 대상에 쓰인다. confuse: 혼란시키다, confusing: 혼란스러운

05 '만약 ~라면 어떻게 하겠니?'라고 실제가 아닌 상황이나 사실을 가정하여 물어볼 때는 가정법 과거를 이용하여 'What would you do if you+과거시제 ~?'로 표현한다. forever: 영원히

06 흥미로운 물건들을 모아서 박물관을 만들 거라는 의미로 collect와 make가 접속사 and에 의해 병렬로 연결되어 있다.

Grammar 교과서

핵심 Check
p.80~81

1 (1) It　(2) that
2 (1) finish　(2) broken　(3) to sing

시험대비 기본평가
p.82

01 ④　　　　02 ⑤
03 (1) repair　(2) stolen　(3) It　(4) who
04 (1) It was Minji that ate the pizza.
　　(2) It is the school that Prince William went to.
　　(3) Della was surprised that Jim had his leg broken.

01 'It ~ that ...' 강조 구문은 'It is/was ~ that ...'의 형태로, 강조하고자 하는 부분을 'It is/was'와 that 사이에 넣고, 나머지 부분을 that 뒤에 써서 주어, 목적어인 명사, 부사(구/절) 등을 강조한다. that이나 who가 들어가는 것이 적절하다.

02 의자가 고쳐지는 것(목적어가 목적격 보어의 동작을 당하는 대상)으로 수동의 의미이므로 과거분사를 써야 한다.

03 (1) 목적어가 목적격 보어의 동작을 하는 주체이므로 동사원형이 적절하다. (2) 돈이 도둑맞는 것(목적어가 목적격 보어의 동작을 당하는 대상)으로 수동의 의미이므로 과거분사가 적절하다. (3) 'It+is/was+강조어(구)+that ...'의 형태로 특정 부분을 강조하여 나타낼 때 사용한다. That이 아닌 It이 적절하다. (4)

강조되는 어구가 사람일 때는 that 대신에 who를 쓸 수 있다.

04 (1) 'It ~ that ...' 강조 구문은 'It is/was ~ that ...'의 형태로, 강조하고자 하는 부분을 'It is/was'와 that 사이에 넣고, 나머지 부분을 that 뒤에 쓴다. '바로 민지'라고 주어를 강조하고 있으므로 Minji를 'It is/was'와 that 사이에 넣고 나머지를 that 뒤에 쓴다. (2) '바로 그 학교'라고 전치사 to의 목적어를 강조하고 있으므로 the school을 'It is/was'와 that 사이에 넣고 나머지를 that 뒤에 쓴다. (3) 다리가 부러졌다는 것으로 수동의 의미이므로 'have+목적어+과거분사'로 쓴다.

시험대비 실력평가
p.83~85

01 ③　　　02 ②　　　03 ①
04 (1) painted　(2) wash　(3) to bring　(4) who　(5) when
　　(6) where
05 ④　　　06 ②　　　07 ③　　　08 ⑤
09 ①　　　10 ④　　　11 ②
12 Mary had her table made by her brother.
13 ①　　　14 buy, repaired　　　15 ③
16 (1) The writer had his book printed at his own expense.
　　(2) How can I get him to dress better?
　　(3) I found out that it was the price that[which] frightened me.
　　(4) It was when they are heated that metals expand.
　　(5) It was at the theater that I met Jack last weekend.　　　17 ⑤

01 'It ~ that ...' 강조 구문은 동사를 강조할 수 없다.

02 목적어가 목적격 보어의 동작을 하는 주체이므로 동사원형이 적절하다. How did you have him pose for this picture?

03 첫 번째 빈칸에는 'It ~ that ...' 강조 구문으로 that이나 which가 적절하다. 두 번째 빈칸에는 목적어가 목적격 보어의 동작을 당하는 대상으로 수동의 의미이므로 과거분사 checked가 적절하다.

04 (1) 얼굴에 칠해지는 것이므로 과거분사가 적절하다. (2) 그가 설거지하는 것이므로 동사원형이 적절하다. (3) get 동사는 'get+목적어+to부정사'의 형태로 쓰인다. (4) 강조하는 것이 the princess로 사람이므로 who가 적절하다. (5) 강조하는 것이 시간을 나타내는 부사구 last night이므로 when이 적절하다. (6) 강조하는 것이 장소를 나타내는 부사구 'at the festival'이므로 where가 적절하다.

05 컴퓨터가 수리되는 것으로 목적어가 목적격 보어의 동작을 당하는 대상으로 수동의 의미이므로 과거분사 fixed가 적절하다.

06 (A)에는 'It ~ that ...' 강조 구문으로 that이 적절하고, (B)에는 우유가 배달되는 것이므로 과거분사가 적절하다.

07 <보기>와 ③번은 강조 용법의 that이다. ① 지시대명사 [앞서 말한 명사의 반복을 피하기 위해] (~의) 그것. 코브라의 독은 방울뱀의 그 것보다 더 치명적이다. ② 지시부사. [수량·정도를 나타내는 말을 한 정하여] 그만큼, 그렇게, 그 정도로. 정말 그녀가 그렇게 젊다는 거 냐? ③ 급소를 찌른 것은 바로 그 질문이었다. ④ 지시형용사. 그, 저; 또 다른. 우리는 그 일에 대하여 이렇게도 저렇게도 논의했다. ⑤ 접속사. [판단의 표준] ~이라니, ~하다니. 그런 짓을 하다니 미쳤나?

08 신발이 닦이는 것(목적어가 목적격 보어의 동작을 당하는 대상 으로 수동의 의미)이므로 ⓒ의 clean은 과거분사 cleaned로 고치는 것이 적절하다.

09 'It ~ that ...' 강조 구문은 강조하고자 하는 부분을 'It is/was' 와 that 사이에 넣고, 나머지 부분을 that 뒤에 쓴다.

10 get이 'get+목적어+과거분사'의 형태로 쓰여 have와 같은 의미 를 갖는다.

11 'It ~ that ...' 강조 구문에서 강조하는 대상이 사람인 경우 that 대 신에 who(주어)나 whom(목적어)을 쓸 수 있다.

12 탁자가 만들어지는 것(목적어가 목적격 보어의 동작을 당하는 대상으로 수동의 의미)이므로 make를 made로 고치는 것이 적절하다.

13 ①번은 'It: 가주어, that절: 진주어'이고 나머지는 모두 'It ~ that ...' 강조 구문으로 쓰였다.

14 '컴퓨터를 사도록 요청했다'는 말을 '컴퓨터를 사도록 시켰다'는 말로 쓸 수 있고, '컴퓨터를 고치도록 요청했다'는 말은 '컴퓨터가 고쳐지도록 했다'는 말로 쓸 수 있다. 보통 'have+사람+동사원 형', 'have[get]+사물+과거분사'의 형태로 쓰인다.

15 ③번은 과거완료에 쓰인 과거분사이지만 <보기>와 나머지는 모 두 'have+목적어+목적격보어'에서 수동의 의미로 쓰인 과거분 사이다.

16 (1) 책이 인쇄되는 것이므로 과거분사가 적절하다. (2) get이 'get+목적어+to부정사'나 'get+목적어+과거분사'의 형태로 쓰 여 have와 같은 의미를 가지므로 'dress'를 'to dress'로 고치 는 것이 적절하다. (3) 강조하는 것이 'the price'이므로 who 를 that이나 which로 고치는 것이 적절하다. (4) 강조하는 것이 'when they are heated'이므로 which를 that으로 고치는 것이 적절하다. (5) that 다음에 완전한 절이 나오므로 'the theater' 를 강조하는 것이 아니라 'at the theater'로 장소의 부사구를 강 조하는 것으로 고치는 것이 적절하다.

17 강조하는 것이 '별똥별'이므로 'a shooting star'를 'It was'와 'that' 사이에 넣고 'Jenny saw at the park yesterday'를 that 뒤에 쓴다. 강조하는 것이 사물이므로 that 대신에 which를 쓸 수 있다.

01 (1) have the food prepared
　　(2) got Harry to hand in his report
　　(3) forced Nick to repair

02 (1) It was at the party that Romeo first met Juliet.
　　(2) It was his notebook which I borrowed.
　　(3) Jim was surprised that Della had her hair cut.
　　(4) She needs to have the car washed.

03 (1) Tom made his son have his eyes checked.
　　(2) He got his brother to do his homework for him.
　　(3) It was pizza that[which] Jake ate at a cafe.
　　(4) It is at the restaurant that I'll have dinner with you this evening.
　　(5) He read the letter more carefully again.

04 (1) had the dragon take
　　(2) It was Steve Jobs who

05 (1) designed by Zaha Hadid
　　(2) have them delivered to their homes

06 (1) It was Matthew who met Jake at the park last weekend.
　　(2) Matthew did meet Jake at the park last weekend.
　　(3) It was Jake who[whom] Matthew met at the park last weekend.
　　(4) It was at the park where Matthew met Jake last weekend.
　　(5) It was last weekend when Matthew met Jake at the park.

07 (1) It was last week that[when] they started a swimming class.
　　(2) It was Mary and Mike that[who] danced hard to be a mascot.
　　(3) It was the vase that[which] Robin broke yesterday.
　　(4) Was it him that[who/whom] his sister taught how to play the guitar?

01 'have+목적어+목적격보어'의 형태로 목적어가 목적격 보어의 동작을 당하는 대상(주로 사물)이면 과거분사를 사용하고, 목적 어가 목적격 보어의 동작을 하는 주체(주로 사람)면 동사원형을 사용한다. get이 'get+목적어+to부정사'나 'get+목적어+과거 분사'의 형태로 쓰여 have와 같은 의미를 갖는다. (1) 'have+ 목적어+과거분사', (2) 'get+목적어+to부정사', (3) 'force+목 적어+to부정사'를 쓰는 것이 적절하다.

02 (1) 장소(at the party)를 강조하는 'It ~ that ...' 강조 구문을 이 용한다. (2) 사물(his notebook)을 강조하는 'It ~ that ...' 강조 구문을 이용한다. (3) 머리카락이 잘리는 것이므로 과거분사로 나

17

타낸다. (4) 차가 세차되는 것이므로 과거분사로 나타낸다.

03 (1) 눈이 검사하는 것이 아니라 검사를 받는 것이므로(목적어가 목적격 보어의 동작을 당하는 대상) 과거분사가 적절하다. (2) get이 'get+목적어+to부정사'나 'get+목적어+과거분사'의 형태로 쓰여 have와 같은 의미를 갖는다. 목적어가 목적격 보어의 동작을 하는 주체일 경우 to부정사를 쓴다. (3) 강조하는 것이 'pizza'이므로 who를 that이나 which로 고치는 것이 적절하다. (4) that 뒤에 완전한 절이 이어지므로 'the restaurant'을 강조하는 것이 아니라 'at the restaurant'으로 장소의 부사구를 강조하는 것으로 고치는 것이 적절하다. (5) 'It ~ that …' 강조 구문은 동사나 양태부사를 강조하는 데 쓰이지 않는다.

04 (1) 용이 공주를 태워 날고 있으므로(목적어가 목적격 보어의 동작을 하는 주체) 'have+목적어+동사원형'을 이용한다. (2) 주어 'Steve Jobs'를 강조하는 'It ~ that …' 강조 용법을 이용한다. 강조 대상이 사람이므로 who를 사용할 수 있다.

05 'have+목적어+목적격보어'의 형태로 목적어가 목적격 보어의 동작을 당하는 대상(주로 사물)이므로 과거분사를 사용한다.

06 과거시제이므로 강조하고자 하는 부분을 It was와 that 사이에 넣고, 나머지 부분을 that 뒤에 쓴다. 이때 that을 사용하지 말라고 하였으므로, that 대신에 강조하고자 하는 것이 사람이면 who(주격/목적격) 또는 whom(목적격), 사물이면 which, 장소일 경우 where, 시간일 경우 when을 사용한다. 또한 'It is[was] ~ that …' 구문은 동사를 강조할 수 없으므로 동사는 동사 앞에 do/does/did를 사용하여 강조한다.

07 'It ~ that …' 강조 구문은 강조하고자 하는 부분을 'It is/was'와 that 사이에 넣고, 나머지 부분을 that 뒤에 쓴다. (4)번은 평서문으로 고친 후 강조 용법으로 쓰고 그것을 다시 의문문으로 바꾸면 쉽다.

교과서 Reading

확인문제 p.88

1 T 2 F 3 F 4 F

확인문제 p.89

1 T 2 F 3 T 4 F 5 T

교과서 확인학습 A   p.90~91

01 had two sons
02 passed away, called, to give them, last words of advice
03 Listen carefully, Live by, throughout your life
04 Build, every city, comfortably. Enjoy, Lastly, like
05 explain himself, passed away
06 his death, their share of, wealth, settled in
07 who had been following, no money left
08 was richer than ever
09 was puzzled about where, had gone wrong, to find out
10 welcomed, with open arms
11 sat down to chat, that had been on his mind
12 It was, that, in every city
13 always stay there, had, looked after
14 sleep comfortably, enjoy, had, designed, my meals prepared by
15 told, to spend like, what I wanted, worrying
16 look at me, empty-handed
17 not follow, father's wisdom
18 how did, get, rich
19 smiled, also followed, father's wisdom
20 it a bit differently
21 build, took it as having a place to stay
22 made friends, stayed at, those cities
23 comfortably, because, if I was sleeping, or
24 only when I was hungry, tasted great
25 like a rich man, continued
26 how to make money grow
27 on, that, bring me back, rather than on
28 it was, that, tried to explain
29 how foolish he had been
30 With, in mind

교과서 확인학습 B   p.92~93

1 A rich and wise father had two sons, Puru and Puneet.
2 Before he passed away, he called his two sons to give them some last words of advice.
3 "Listen carefully, my dear sons. Live by these words throughout your life, and you will be happy," he said.
4 "Build a house in every city. Sleep comfortably. Enjoy your food. Lastly, spend money like a rich man... ."

5 Before he could explain himself, he passed away.

6 After his death, the two sons took their share of the father's wealth and settled in different cities.

7 Five years passed. Puru, who had been following his father's words carefully, had no money left.

8 But his brother was richer than ever.

9 Puru was puzzled about where he had gone wrong, so he visited Puneet to find out.

10 Puneet welcomed Puru with open arms.

11 That night, when the brothers sat down to chat after dinner, Puru asked the question that had been on his mind for days.

12 "It was our father's advice that I followed, but I am not happy. I built a house in every city.

13 But because I could not always stay there, I hired people and had the house looked after.

14 Father said we should sleep comfortably and enjoy our food, so I had my bed designed by experts and my meals prepared by a great chef.

15 He told us to spend like a rich man, so I bought what I wanted without worrying about money.

16 But look at me now! I am empty-handed.

17 Did you not follow our father's wisdom?

18 Tell me, brother, how did you get so rich?"

19 Puneet smiled and said, "My dear brother, I also followed our father's wisdom.

20 But I understood it a bit differently.

21 When he said 'build a house in every city,' I took it as having a place to stay all around the world.

22 So I made friends in every city and I stayed at their houses when I visited those cities.

23 Also, I slept comfortably each night because I would be tired after a hard day's work, and it did not matter if I was sleeping on a bed or on the hard floor.

24 I ate only when I was hungry, so even a simple meal tasted great."

25 "Spend money like a rich man?" continued Puneet.

26 "A rich man knows how to make money grow.

27 So, I tried to spend money on something that would bring me back more money rather than on luxurious things.

28 For me, it was this wisdom that our father tried to explain."

29 Now Puru realized how foolish he had been.

30 With this wisdom in mind, Puru started a new life.

01 ③　　　　02 death

03 They were Puru and Puneet.　　　04 ⑤

05 He followed his father's advice.

06 ④　　　07 ④　　　08 ⑤　　　09 ③

10 ③

11 Because he ate only when he was hungry.

12 He stayed at his friends' houses when he visited cities all around the world.

13 ④　　　　14 ③

15 He had no money left.　16 ②

17 prepared　18 ⑤

19 He built a house in every city.

20 ③　　　21 ②　　　22 ②　　　23 ④

24 differently　25 ③

01 (A)에는 전치사 by가 들어간다. ① take part in: ~에 참여하다 ② consist of: ~으로 구성되다 ③ go by: (시간이) 흐르다 ④ be different from: ~와 다르다 ⑤ similar to: ~와 비슷한

02 '삶의 끝'은 '죽음(death)'을 의미한다.

03 두 아들의 이름은 Puru와 Puneet이라고 하였다.

04 부유하고 지혜로운 아버지는 죽어가고 있을 때 두 아들에게 마지막 충고의 말을 남겼다.

05 Puru는 아버지의 조언을 따랐지만 행복하지 않다고 하였다.

06 위 글에 따르면 아버지의 조언은 '모든 도시에 집을 짓는 것, 편안하게 자는 것, 음식을 즐기는 것, 부자처럼 돈을 쓰라는 것'이므로 ④번이 아버지의 조언에 해당한다. take pleasure in: ~을 즐기다, 좋아하다

07 집은 돌보아지는 대상이므로 목적어와 수동의 관계에 있다. 따라서 과거분사 'looked after'라고 쓰는 것이 적절하다.

08 Puru는 돈 걱정을 하지 않고 원하는 것을 샀다.

09 부자들은 돈을 불리는 방법을 알고 있으므로 사치스러운 물건에 돈을 쓰는 것보다는 자신에게 더 많은 돈을 돌려줄 수 있는 것에 돈을 쓰려고 노력했다는 말이 들어가는 것이 적절하다.

10 '게다가, 또한'이라는 의미이므로 ③번이 가장 적절하다.

11 Puneet은 배고플 때만 먹었기 때문에 소박한 식사마저도 훌륭한 맛이 났다고 하였다.

12 Puneet은 모든 도시에서 친구를 사귀었고 그 도시들을 방문했을 때 그들의 집에 머물렀다고 하였다.

13 Puru가 당황한 이유는 자신에게는 남은 돈이 없었던 반면 그의 동생은 그 어느 때보다 더 부자가 되어 있었기 때문이었다. 따라서 ④번에 들어가는 것이 가장 적절하다.

19

14 Puru에게는 남은 돈이 없었지만 Puneet은 그 어느 때보다 더 부자가 되었다는 말에 그는 자신의 동생을 방문했다는 말로 끝나고 있으므로 ③번이 가장 적절하다. stop by: ~에 들르다

15 5년 후 Puru에게 남은 돈이 없었다.

16 밑줄 친 (A)는 재귀대명사의 재귀 용법으로, 주어와 목적어가 같을 때 쓰인다. 모두 재귀 용법으로 쓰였지만 ②번은 강조 용법으로 쓰인 재귀대명사이다.

17 사역동사 have의 목적격보어 자리로, 목적어 my meals와 수동의 관계에 있으므로 과거분사를 쓰는 것이 적절하다.

18 Puneet은 Puru를 두 팔 벌려 환영했다는 의미이므로 ⑤번이 가장 적절하다. reluctantly: 마지못해서

19 Puru는 모든 도시에 집을 지었다고 하였다.

20 Puru는 자신이 아버지의 조언을 따랐지만 빈털터리가 되었다고 말하며 동생 Puneet에게 어떻게 그렇게 부자가 되었느냐고 묻고 있으므로 이어질 내용으로는 ③번이 가장 적절하다.

21 on something과 병렬 연결이 이루어져야 하므로 ②번이 적절하다. spend+시간/돈+on A: A에 시간이나 돈을 쓰다

22 밑줄 친 내용으로 미루어 보아 두 형제의 아버지는 편안하게 잠자라는 말을 남겼음을 유추할 수 있다.

23 동생의 말을 들은 Puru는 그의 지혜를 마음에 새기고 새로운 삶을 시작했다고 하였다.

24 Puru와 달리 Puneet은 아버지의 지혜를 조금 다르게 이해했다고 하였다.

25 Puneet은 '모든 도시에 집을 지어라'라는 아버지의 말씀을 전 세계에 머물 수 있는 장소를 가지라는 말로 이해하여 모든 도시에서 친구를 사귀고 그 도시들을 방문할 때 그들의 집에 머물렀다고 하였다.

서술형 시험대비 p.98~99

01 It was because he wanted to give them some last words of advice.

02 He had been following his father's words carefully.

03 If you live by these words throughout your life, you will be happy.

04 Puru, Puneet

05 The two sons took their share of the father's wealth and settled in different cities.

06 knows how to make money grow

07 A simple meal tasted great to him because he ate only when he was hungry.

08 He tried to spend money on something that would bring him back more money rather than on luxurious things.

09 brother → father, poor → rich

10 It was because he worked hard all day.

11 He realized how foolish he had been.

12 Puru가 모든 도시에 지은 집에서

13 had the house looked after

14 Their father told them to spend like a rich man.

15 (A) Although   (B) unhappy   (C) broke

01 아버지는 죽기 전에 그의 두 아들을 부른 이유는 그들에게 마지막 충고의 말을 하기 위해서였다.

02 Puru는 아버지가 돌아가신 이후로 아버지의 말을 신중히 따랐다고 하였다.

03 '명령문, and ...'는 '~해라. 그러면 …'이라는 의미이므로 명령문을 'If 조건절'로 바꾸고 and를 생략하여 같은 의미의 문장을 쓸 수 있다.

04 Puru와 달리 Puneet은 그 어느 때보다 더 부자가 되었다고 하였다.

05 아버지가 돌아가신 후, 두 아들은 아버지의 재산 중 자신들의 몫을 가지고 다른 도시에 정착했다.

06 사역동사 make는 목적격보어로 동사원형을 취하며, '의문사+to부정사'는 명사구 역할을 한다.

07 Puneet은 배고플 때만 먹었기 때문에 소박한 식사마저도 훌륭한 맛이 났다고 하였다.

08 Puneet는 사치스러운 물건에 돈을 쓰는 것보다는 자신에게 더 많은 돈을 돌려줄 수 있는 것에 돈을 쓰려고 노력했다.

09 글의 내용에 따르면 형제에게 조언의 말을 남긴 사람은 그들의 아버지이며, Puneet은 아버지의 말을 그의 형과 달리 해석하여 부자가 되었다.

10 Puneet이 잠자리를 가리지 않은 이유는 하루 종일 열심히 일했기 때문이었다.

11 Puru는 자신이 얼마나 어리석었었는지를 깨달았다고 하였다.

12 Puru는 아버지의 조언대로 모든 도시에 집을 지었지만 그곳에 항상 머물 수 없었다는 의미이다.

13 집은 돌보아지는 대상이므로 사역동사 have의 목적격보어로 과거분사 looked after를 쓰는 것에 유의한다.

14 형제의 아버지는 그들에게 부자처럼 돈을 쓰라고 말하였다

15 해석: Puru는 아버지의 조언을 따랐지만, 그는 불행한 삶을 살았고 무일푼이 되었다.

영역별 핵심문제 p.101~105

01 ①   02 deserted   03 ③   04 ④

05 ④   06 ②   07 ⑤

08 what would you do if you could time travel?

09 ②   10 character   11 ⑤   12 ②

13 ⑤   14 ④

15 at the cafe where Jane is reading

16 ⓐ, ⓓ, ⓖ

17 Tom had Rene pick up his mom at the airport for him.

18 ①, ②   19 ①

20 have the writing contest held

21 ⑤   22 ①   23 luxurious

24 It did not matter if he was sleeping on a bed or on the hard floor.

25 It is because failure is also a good experience.

26 ③   27 (C)–(B)–(A)   28 ②

29 ④   30 ③

01 priceless: 대단히 귀중한, 값을 매길 수 없는

02 deserted island: 무인도 / 그는 10년 동안 혼자서 이 무인도에 살았다.

03 run out of: ~이 없어지다, 다 떨어지다 / 우리 종이가 다 떨어져 간다. 오늘 쓸 만큼은 충분히 있는 것 같습니까?

04 pass away: 세상을 떠나다, 돌아가시다

05 주어진 문장에서 it은 <시간 여행자의 아내>라는 영화이다. too는 '역시'이므로 여자가 그 영화를 가장 좋아하는 로맨스 영화 중 하나라고 말한 것에 대해 자신도 또한 아주 좋아했다는 말이 들어가야 알맞다.

06 review: 후기, 보고서

07 <시간 여행자의 아내>라는 영화에 대해서 가장 좋아하는 로맨스 영화 중 하나라고 언급하였지 어떤 종류의 영화를 좋아하는지에 대해서는 말하지 않았다.

08 '만약 ~라면 어떻게 하겠니?'라고 실제가 아닌 상황이나 사실을 가정하여 물어볼 때는 가정법 과거를 이용하여 'What would you do if you+과거시제 ~?'로 표현한다.

09 ⓐ How ⓑ ran, run out of: ~이 없어지다, 다 떨어지다 ⓒ were, 'What would you do if you+과거시제 ~?: 만약 ~라면 어떻게 하겠니?(실제가 아닌 상황이나 사실을 가정) ⓓ read ⓔ if, if: ~인지 아닌지

10 character:등장인물 / 영화나 연극 혹은 이야기 속에 나오는 사람

11 ① 사람들의 생각을 읽을 수 있다. ② 마감이 다가오는데 아이디어가 다 떨어졌다. ③ 도와준다. ④ 이야기의 마감은 이번 주말이다. ⑤ 남자가 사람들의 마음을 읽을 수 있다면 좋아하는 여자아이가 나를 좋아하는지 알아보고 싶다고 말했다.

12 (B) 남자가 여자에게 <트리갭의 샘물>이라는 책을 읽어봤는지를 물어보자 (C) 읽어봤다고 대답하며 그 책의 내용에 대해 말한다. (A) 여자가 말한 책의 내용이 맞다고 대답하면서, 영원히 살게 된다면 무엇을 할지 질문을 하자 (D) 전 세계의 다양한 도시에서 살고 싶다고 대답한다.

13 'It ~ that ...' 강조 구문에서 강조하는 대상이 장소의 부사(구/절)일 경우, that 대신에 where로 바꿔 쓸 수 있다.

14 Dad had me return home as it was very late at night. 내가 돌아오는 '능동'의 의미이므로 동사원형으로 써야 한다.

15 The cafe is the place which Jane is reading a comic book at.을 'at the cafe'를 강조하며 쓰면 It is at the cafe where Jane is reading a comic book.이 된다.

16 ⓑ plant → planted ⓒ come → to come ⓔ when → that[where], steal → stolen ⓕ which → that[where]

17 Rene가 모셔오는(pick up) 것이므로 'have+목적어+동사원형'을 이용하여 영작한다.

18 ① I had my bed designed by experts and my meals prepared by a great chef. ② It was on the stage that BTS performed their first show.

19 'It ~ that ...' 강조 구문은 강조하고자 하는 부분을 'It is [was]'와 that 사이에 넣고, 나머지 부분을 that 뒤에 쓴다.

20 the writing contest가 개최되는(수동) 것이므로 'have+목적어+과거분사'를 이용한다.

21 사역동사 make는 동사원형을 목적격보어로 취한다. 따라서 grow라고 쓰는 것이 적절하다.

22 With this wisdom in mind: 이 지혜를 명심하고

23 특히 아주 비싼 것을 포함하여 매우 편안하거나 우아한 것은 '사치스러운, 호화스러운(luxurious)'이다.

24 Puneet은 하루 종일 열심히 일하고 나서 피곤해지곤 했기 때문에 침대에서 자든 딱딱한 바닥에서 자든 상관없었다고 하였다.

25 실패 역시 좋은 경험이기 때문에 글쓴이는 두려움 없이 무언가를 하려고 한다.

26 글쓴이는 나쁜 킥조차도 자신을 더 좋은 키커로 만들어 주었다는 것을 배웠다고 하였다.

27 (C) 아버지의 조언을 따라 모든 도시에 집을 지음. (B) 그곳에 항상 머물 수 없기 때문에 사람을 고용함. (A) 아버지의 또 다른 조언을 지켰지만 지금 빈털터리가 되었음을 말하며 Puneet이 어떻게 부자가 되었는지 물어봄.

28 동생 Puneet에게 어떻게 그렇게 부자가 되었는지를 묻는 말로 끝나고 있으므로 ②번이 가장 적절하다.

29 Puru는 모든 도시에 집을 지었다고 하였으므로 그의 집은 모든 도시에서 발견될 수 있었다고 말하는 것이 적절하다.

30 밑줄 친 ⓑ는 전치사 without의 목적어로 쓰인 동명사이다. 모두 동명사이지만 ③번은 진행 시제를 나타내는 현재분사이다.

01 ex   02 (r)eward

03 ③   04 ④   05 ③   06 would

07 ④   08 ①

09 would go to the Joseon Dynasty and meet King Sejong

10 in

11 Don't worry about something you can't change.

12 ④   13 ④   14 ②

15 (1) My dad has his car washed once a month.

(2) Mom had a robot vacuum cleaner clean the floor.

(3) Jane got Richard to guess her age when she first met him.

(4) It was at the restaurant that[where] Angelina had dinner with her friends.

(5) It was a knife that[which] I forgot to bring to the cooking class.

16 that[who] had the table decorated   17 ②

18 Puneet was richer than Puru.   19 ⑤

20 He felt puzzled.   21 ③

22 our father's wisdom   23 ④   23 ②

---

01 특정 어근 앞에 'ex-'를 붙이면 '밖으로'라는 의미를 더한다. ex-+plain → explain 설명하다 ex-+hibit → exhibit 전시하다 ex-+press→ express 표현하다

02 '좋은 행동이나 업적 등의 대가로 주어지는 어떤 것'은 보상 (reward)이다. 그들은 그가 열심히 일한 것에 대한 보상을 주었다.

03 (A) from head to toe: 머리에서 발끝까지 / 추워서 이불을 머리부터 발까지 담요를 뒤집어쓰고 잤다. (B) look after: ~을 살피다, 돌보다 / 하루 종일 3명의 아이들을 돌보는 것은 힘든 일이다.

04 lastly: 마지막으로, 끝으로 / 끝으로, 당신의 미래 계획에 대해 묻고 싶습니다.

05 ⓒ lives→lived, that은 주격 관계대명사이고, that 이하가 a family를 수식하고 있다. drank와 lived는 접속사 and로 연결되어 병렬 구문을 이루고 있다.

06 '만약 ~라면 어떻게 하겠니?'라고 실제가 아닌 상황이나 사실을 가정하여 물어볼 때는 가정법 과거를 이용하여 'What would you do if you+과거시제 ~?'로 표현한다. 대답으로는 '나는 '할 거야.'라는 의미로 'I would 동사원형 ~.'형태의 가정법 과거를 사용하여 대답한다.

07 현재 사실과 반대되는 상황이나 일에 대해 가정하거나 현재 사실에 대한 후회나 아쉬움을 강조할 때, 가정법 과거를 쓴다. 즉,

현재 사실과 반대이므로, 과거 시제를 쓴다. 조건절은 'if 주어+동사의 과거형'으로, 주절은 '주어+would+동사원형 ~'을 쓴다. 이때 해석은 '~라면 …할 텐데.' 라고 해석한다.

08 prevent: 예방하다 ② 표현하다 ③ 허락하다 ④ 얻다, 획득하다 ⑤ 전시하다

09 'What would you do if you+과거시제 ~?'에 대한 대답으로 '나는 '할 거야.'라는 의미로 'I would 동사원형 ~.'형태의 가정법 과거를 사용하여 대답한다.

10 believe in 사람: ~을[~의 능력을] 믿다

11 상대방을 안심시키는 표현으로는 'Don't worry about ~.(~에 대해 걱정하지 마.)'이라는 말을 쓸 수 있다. something과 you can't change 사이에 목적격 관계대명사 that이 생략되어 있다.

12 have+목적어+동사원형: 목적어가 ~하게 만들다

13 It was at the amusement park that Minsu rode the roller coaster.

14 첫 번째 문장에서는 저녁이 준비되는 것이므로 과거분사 prepared가 적절하다. 두 번째 문장에서는 'It ~ that ...' 강조 구문에서 강조하는 대상이 시간의 부사 yesterday이므로 that이나 when이 적절하다.

15 (1) 'have+목적어+목적격보어'의 형태로 목적어가 목적격보어의 동작을 당하는 대상(주로 사물)이면 과거분사를 사용한다. (2) 'have+목적어+목적격보어'의 형태로 목적어가 목적격보어의 동작을 하는 주체(주로 사람)면 동사원형을 사용한다. (3) get이 'get+목적어+to부정사'나 'get+목적어+과거분사'의 형태로 쓰여 have와 같은 의미를 갖는다. (4) that 뒤에 완전한 절이 나오므로 'at the restaurant'을 강조하는 것이 되어야 한다. which를 that이나 where로 써야 한다. (5) 강조하는 것이 'a knife'이므로 that이나 which로 써야 한다.

16 'It ~ that ...' 강조 구문에서 강조하는 대상이 the princess로 사람이므로 that이나 who를 쓰고, the table이 장식되는(수동) 것이므로 'have+목적어+과거분사'를 이용한다.

17 live on은 '~을 먹고 살다'라는 의미이다. live by: (신조, 원칙 등)에 따라 살다

18 5년 후 Puneet이 Puru보다 더 부자가 되어 있었다.

19 Puru는 아버지의 말을 신중히 따랐다고 하였으므로 ⑤번이 글의 내용과 일치한다. stick to: 굳게 고수하다

20 Puru는 자신과 달리 동생이 부자가 되었음을 알고 당황하였다.

21 주어진 문장은 ③번 앞 문장의 결과이므로 ③번에 들어가는 것이 가장 적절하다.

22 앞 문장의 '우리 아버지의 지혜'를 가리키는 말이다.

23 밑줄 친 (B)는 to부정사의 형용사적 용법으로, 앞선 명사 a place를 수식하고 있다. ① 부사적 용법 중 목적 ② 명사적 용법 중 목적격보어 ③ 명사적 용법 중 진주어 ④ 형용사적 용법 ⑤ 부사적 용법 중 감정의 원인

24 밑줄 친 (C)는 '이 지혜를 마음에 새기고'라는 의미이다. bear in mind: 명심하다, 마음에 새기다

서술형 실전문제 p.110~111

01 What would you do if you were him?

02 ③ easy → difficult

03 look

04 (1) Why don't you have the groceries delivered to your home?

(2) The students got their classroom painted.

(3) It was Matt that[who] had coffee at the office this morning.

05 They sat down to chat after dinner.

06 He took it as making many friends living in different places.

07 (1) built a house / made friends

(2) my bed designed by / tired, a hard day's work

(3) my meals prepared / I was hungry

08 He told us to spend money like a rich man

09 introduce

10 It means "Go and do things without fear because failure is also a good experience."

01 '만약 ~라면 어떻게 하겠니?'라고 실제가 아닌 상황이나 사실을 가정하여 물어볼 때는 가정법 과거를 이용하여 'What would you do if you+과거시제 ~?'로 표현한다.

02 be worried (that) 주어+동사'는 '(주어)가 ~인 것이 걱정이다.'라는 의미로 걱정을 표현할 때 사용하는 표현이다. 글쓰기 대회의 주제가 나에게 너무 쉬울까봐 걱정이라는 말은 어색하다.

03 take care of = look after: ~을 돌보다

04 (1) 'have+목적어+목적격보어'의 형태로 목적어가 목적격보어의 동작을 당하는 대상(주로 사물)이면 과거분사를 사용한다. (2) get은 'get+목적어+과거분사'의 형태로 쓰여 have와 같은 의미를 갖는다. (3) 'It ~ that ...' 강조 구문에서 강조하고자 하는 것이 'Matt'로 사람이므로 which를 that이나 who로 고치는 것이 적절하다.

05 저녁 식사 후 두 형제는 이야기를 하려고 앉았다고 하였다.

06 Puneet은 모든 도시에 집을 지으라는 아버지의 조언을 여러 도

시에 살고 있는 많은 친구를 만들라는 말로 받아들였다.

07 모든 도시에 집을 지으라는 아버지의 유언에 Puru는 말 그대로 모든 도시에 집을 지었고, Puneet은 모든 도시에 친구들을 만들었다. 편안하게 잠을 자라는 아버지의 유언에 Puru는 전문가가 자신의 침대를 설계하게 하였고, Puneet은 하루 종일 열심히 일하고 나서 피곤해졌기 때문에 매일 밤 편안아히 잠을 잤다. 마지막으로 Puru는 훌륭한 요리사가 음식을 준비하게 하여 음식을 즐겼지만, Puneet은 배가 고플 때만 음식을 먹었다고 하였다.

08 tell은 목적격보어로 to부정사를 취하는 동사이다.

09 사역동사 let은 목적격보어로 동사원형을 취한다.

10 "Go for it!"은 "실패도 역시 좋은 경험이므로 두려움 없이 해라"라는 의미라고 하였다.

창의사고력 서술형 문제 p.112

|모범답안|

01 A: would catch criminals and bring them to the police. / I would go to the food court and eat rare food.

02 (1) She had her ears checked.

(2) They had the Opera House in Sydney designed by Jørn Utzon.
They had Jørn Utzon design the Opera House in Sydney.

(3) Mom had me play a computer game after dinner.
Mom had a computer game played by me after dinner.

03 No Pain, No Gain! Without hard work, you can get nothing as a reward., I was a kicker in the school soccer team, even the bad kicks made me a better kicker at the end

02 'have+목적어+목적격보어'의 형태로 목적어가 목적격보어의 동작을 당하는 대상(주로 사물)이면 과거분사를 사용하고, 목적어가 목적격보어의 동작을 하는 주체(주로 사람)면 동사원형을 사용한다.

단원별 모의고사 p.113~116

01 ①   02 ④   03 take

04 (l)uxurious   05 ⑤

06 Don't worry about making mistakes.

07 What would you do if you had a magic carpet?

08 (A) that   (B) character   (C) if   (D) yourself

09 (1) Don't worry about it.　(2) Don't let it bother you.

10 ③　　　　11 ①　　　　12 take care　13 ⑤

14 ①, ③, ④, ⑥

15 (1) It was many bugs that[which] were in the bottle.

　　(2) It was at the concert that[where] I saw her.

　　(3) This morning I had my watch that I had bought last month repaired.

　　(4) I'll help you so that you can have your homework finished before the movie starts.

16 have it returned　　　　17 ③　　　　18 ⑤

19 ④

20 He had his meals prepared by a great chef in order to enjoy his food.　21 ③

22 ②　　　　　23 ④

24 Because he wanted to find out where he had gone wrong.

25 They took their share of the father's wealth and settled in different cities.

26 ⑤

---

01 ①은 동의어, 나머지 보기들은 반의어 관계이다. ① puzzled: 당혹스러운, 어리둥절한 confused: 혼란스러운 ② hire: 고용하다 fire: 해고하다 ③ priceless: 대단히 귀중한, 값을 매길 수 없는 worthless: 가치 없는, 보잘 것 없는 ④ death: 죽음 life: 삶, 인생, 생명 ⑤ lastly: 마지막으로, 끝으로 firstly: 첫째로

02 believe in 사람: ~을[~의 능력을] 믿다

03 take ~ for a walk: ~를 산책하러 데리고 가다 / 나는 개를 산책하러 데리고 나갈 것이다. take care of: 돌보다 / 그는 스스로를 돌볼 만큼 나이가 들었다. take one's share: 자기 몫을 취하다, 차지하다 / 그는 단지 그의 몫을 차지하려고 했었다.

04 luxurious: 사치스러운, 호화로운 / 매우 편안하고 비용이 많이 드는

05 ⓐ worried ⓑ got ⓒ singing ⓓ making ⓔ learn

06 상대방을 안심시키는 표현으로는 'Don't worry about ~.(~에 대해 걱정하지 마.)'이라는 말을 쓸 수 있다. make a mistake: 실수하다

07 '만약 ~라면 어떻게 하겠니?'라고 실제가 아닌 상황이나 사실을 가정하여 물어볼 때는 가정법 과거를 이용하여 'What would you do if you+과거시제 ~?'로 표현한다.

08 (A) be worried (that) 주어+동사'는 '(주어)가 ~인 것이 걱정이다.'라는 의미로 걱정을 표현할 때 사용하는 표현이다. (B) character: 등장인물 (C) 실제로는 일어나기 어려운 상황을 가정하거나 상상하여 물을 때 'If you+동사의 과거형 ~, what

---

would you+동사원형 ~?'의 형태인 가정법 과거를 사용하여 현재 사실과 반대되는 것을 말할 수 있다. (D) 주어와 목적어가 같을 경우에 재귀대명사를 사용해야 하므로 yourself가 들어가야 적절하다

09 상대방을 안심시키는 표현으로는 'Don't worry about ~.'이라는 말을 쓸 수 있다. 이와 같은 표현으로는 'Don't let ~ bother you.(~에 대해 너무 신경 쓰지 마.)'가 있다.

10 부산으로 여행을 가야 하는데 Lucy에게 먹이를 줄 사람을 찾을 수 없다는 남자의 말에, 여자가 걱정하지 말라고 말하면서 개를 돌봐 준다고 말하는 것이 어울린다.

11 여행을 가지만 Lucy에게 먹이를 줄 사람을 아무도 찾을 수가 없다는 말이 어울리므로 '하지만'의 의미를 가지고 있는 접속사 but이 적절하다.

12 take care of: ~을 돌보다

13 suppose: 추측하다, 추정하다

14 ② How about having your pet cleaned from head to toe? ⑤ It was in the street that[where] I saw Jane this morning. ⑦ It was a cat that[which] went to save the princess.

15 (1) 'many bugs'를 강조하므로 where가 아니라 that이나 which를 써야 한다. (2) 접속사 없이 동사가 2개가 나온 형태이므로 'It ~ that ...' 강조 구문의 that이나 where를 넣어 주는 것이 적절하다. (3) 시계가 수리되는 것이므로 과거분사로 쓰는 것이 적절하다. (4) 숙제가 무엇인가를 끝내는 것이 아니라 끝내지는 것이므로 과거분사로 쓰는 것이 적절하다.

16 'have+목적어+목적격보어'의 형태로 목적어가 목적격보어의 동작을 당하는 대상(주로 사물)이면 과거분사를 사용한다.

17 It was at the park that[where] I met Tim last Sunday. that 뒤에 나오는 절이 완전하므로 'at the park'를 강조하는 문장으로 쓴다.

18 빈칸 (A)에는 관계대명사 what이 들어간다. ①, ③, ④ 명사절 접속사 that, ② 관계대명사 that, ⑤ 관계대명사 what

19 ④ 부자처럼 돈을 쓰라는 말에 '돈 걱정을 하지 않고' 돈을 썼다고 말하는 것이 자연스럽다. 따라서 without이라고 쓰는 것이 적절하다.

20 Puru는 음식을 즐기기 위해 훌륭한 요리사에 의해 자신의 식사가 준비되도록 하였다.

21 Puru가 전문가를 고용한 이유는 자신의 침대를 설계하기 위해서였다.

22 'explain oneself'는 '심중을 털어놓다'는 의미로, 아버지가 자

신이 전해준 조언의 말들이 실제로 어떤 의미가 있는지를 말해준다는 의미이다.

23 아버지의 마지막 조언의 말은 두 아들들이 행복한 삶을 사는 데에 도움이 되는 말이었지만 두 형제는 대조되는 삶을 살았다.

24 Puru는 자신과 달리 동생이 부자가 되었음을 알고, 자신이 어디서 잘못했는지를 알아내기 위해 Puneet을 방문하였다.

25 아버지의 죽음 이후 두 형제는 아버지의 재산 중 자신들의 몫을 가지고 다른 도시에 정착하였다.

26 ⑤번의 he는 Puru를 가리키지만 나머지는 모두 A rich and wise father를 가리킨다.

Spend Wisely

01 ②   02 ①   03 When it comes to

04 ⑤   05 ④   06 ④   07 ③

01 ②에서 en은 '안에'라는 'in'의 의미이다. en(= in)+close(닫다). 안에 넣고 닫다 → 둘러싸다, 동봉하다 ① en-+large → enlarge: 확대하다, 확장하다 ③ en-+able → enable: 가능케 하다 ④ en-+force → enforce: 집행하다, 강요하다 ⑤ en-+rich → enrich: 풍부하게 하다

02 replace: 바꾸다, 교체하다 / 우리는 이 양탄자를 곧 바꿔야 한다. ② 수리하다 ③ 제거하다 ④ 영향을 주다, 충격을 주다 ⑤ 지키다, 보호하다

03 when it comes to: ~에 관해서, ~에 대해 말하자면

04 consume: 소비하다, 소모하다 / 연료, 에너지, 혹은 시간을 특히 많은 양으로 쓰다, 또는 특히 어떤 것을 많이 먹고 마시다 ① 포함하다 ② 요구하다 ③ 유지하다 ④ 추정하다

05 <보기>는 동의어 관계이다. quality: 질, 품질, 특성, 자질 characteristic: 특질, 특징 ⓐ tight: 꽉 조이는 loose: 헐거운 ⓑ endanger: 위험에 빠뜨리다 save: 구하다 ⓒ effect: 결과, 효과 result: 결과, 성과 ⓓ replace: 바꾸다, 교체하다 substitute: 대신하다 ⓔ encourage: 부추기다, 조장하다 discourage: 낙담시키다

06 ① 그의 말은 위로하는 효과를 가지고 있었다. ② 아름다움의 개념을 정의하기는 어렵다. ③ 너의 의견은 많은 사람에게 영향을 줄 것이다. ④ allowance: 용돈 / 나는 부모님에게서 용돈을 받는다. ⑤ 그녀가 버스에 탔을 때, 그 버스는 거의 비어 있었다.

07 furthermore: 그뿐만 아니라, 더욱이 / 그 셔츠는 예쁠 뿐만 아니라 싸다. ① 따라서, 그러므로 ② 그럼에도 불구하고 ④ 그러므로 ⑤ 똑같이, 비슷하게

01 com

02 (1) spending   (2) next time   (3) even though

     (4) go window shopping

03 on

04 (1) with   (2) In   (3) for   (4) at   (5) As

05 (1) mention   (2) compare   (3) combine

     (4) endangered

01 특정 어근 앞에 com-을 붙이면 '함께'라는 의미를 더한다. com-+parison → comparison: 비교 com-+promise → compromise: 타협(하다) com-+pose → compose: 구성하다

02 (1) record: 기록하다 spending: 지출, 소비 (2) the next time+주어+동사: 다음번에 ~할 때에 (3) even though: 비록 ~이지만 (4) go window shopping: 진열된 상품을 구경하고 다니다

03 on display: 진열된, 전시된 / 그림은 현재 뉴욕에 전시 중이다. on sale: 판매 중인 / 표는 매표소에서 판매하고 있다.

04 (1) go well with: ~와 잘 어울리다 / 나는 이 블라우스가 네가 입고 있는 치마와 잘 어울린다고 생각한다. (2) in comparison: 비교해 보면 / 그녀의 문제와 비교해 보면, 내 문제들은 사소해 보인다. (3) for a moment: 잠깐 / 너는 잠시 동안 숨을 참아야 한다. (4) at a glance: 한눈에, 즉시 / 나는 무슨 일이 일어났는지 한눈에 알아챘다. (5) as such: 그렇게, 이와 같이 / 이와 같이 그는 인내력이 있는 인물이었다.

05 (1) mention: 언급하다, 말하다 / 내가 다음 달에 캐나다로 이사 간다고 말했니? (2) compare: 비교하다 / 너는 물건을 사기 전에 가격을 비교해야 한다. (3) combine: 결합하다 / 그는 일과 즐거움을 결합하고 싶어 한다. (4) endanger: 위험에 빠뜨리다 / 불은 숲 속에 있는 동물들을 위험에 빠뜨렸다.

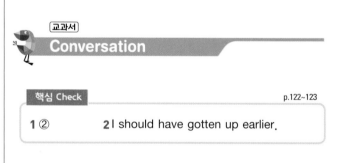

교과서

Conversation

1 ②   2 I should have gotten up earlier.

교과서 대화문 익히기

1 T   2 F   3 F   4 F

5 T   6 F   7 F   8 T

Listen & Talk 1 A

1. help / try on / How do you like / but, suits, have / one

2. to / I'm looking for / popular among, How do you like / green one is lighter than, one

Listen & Talk 1 B

bought, ago / looks, How do you like / convenient, anywhere, quality / How long, last / doesn't last / too bad / pretty happy

Listen & Talk 2 A

1. too uncomfortable / What's wrong with it / tight / you try it on before buying / so, should have tried, on

2. are going to watch / I've spent, allowance / get it / should have kept track of my spending

Listen & Talk 2 B

on sale / on sale, has just been released / is having / at full price / at, discount / should have checked the sales before

Communication Step A

heard that you bought / not happy, it / Why, What's / gets overheated, have read / for / won't give me back, I've used / calling, explaining / do

Wrap Up

1. I'd like to / How do you like this red one / that, one / striped, Its / take

2. online used store / let me see / is a little broken, said that / before / I just trusted, should have checked a bit more / should call, ask for a refund

01 ②　　　　02 ⑤　　　　03 ①

01 여자가 별들이 그려진 모자를 써 볼 수 있는지 질문하자 남자가 된다고 대답한다. 그리고 이어진 질문에 여자가 써 본 모자와 색깔에 대해서 말하고 있으므로, 상대방의 의견 혹은 만족 여부를 물을 때 사용하는 'How do you like ~?'을 이용한 ②번이 적절하다.

02 (C) 코트가 불편하다는 말에 (D) 상대방은 이유를 물어본다. (B) 너무 꽉 껴서 불편하다고 대답한다. (A) 사기 전에 입어 보지 않았냐고 질문하고 자신의 사이즈여서 그냥 사버렸다는 얘기를 하면서, 미리 입어 보지 않은 것에 후회를 나타낸다.

03 'should have p.p. ~.'는 어떤 일을 했어야 했다고, 또는 하지 말았어야 했다고 후회할 때 사용한다. try on: (옷 등을 시험 삼아) 입어 보다

01 ②, ④, ⑤　　02 (A) ⓔ　(B) ⓑ

03 I should have tried it on.　04 ③　　　05 ⑤

06 ④　　　　07 ④　　　　08 ③　　　　09 ②

01 'I love them. They are very comfortable.'은 '좋아요, 매우 편안해요.'의 의미로 빈칸에 어울리는 질문은 them에 해당하는 것에 대한 상대방의 만족이나 불만족을 물어보는 질문이 어울린다. 'How do you like ~?'는 '~는 어때?'의 의미이며, 'Are you satisfied[happy] with ~?', 'How is ~?', 'Are you enjoying ~?' 등으로 바꿔 쓸 수 있다.

02 (A) 코트가 불편하다는 말에, 여자가 왜 그런지 질문을 하는 말에 이어, 'What's wrong with it?(무슨 문제가 있니?)'이라고 했을 때 옷이 꽉 낀다고 말하는 것이 어울린다. (B) 'No. It was my size, so I just bought it.(아니. 내 사이즈여서 그냥 사 버렸어.)' 이라고 대답하는 것으로 볼 때 옷을 살 때 안 입어봤는지 질문하는 것이 적절하다.

03 'should have p.p. ~.'는 어떤 일을 했어야 했다고, 후회할 때 사용한다. 'try it on'의 어순에 주의한다. try on: (옷 등을 시험 삼아) 입어 보다

04 온라인에서 산 아이스티가 만족스럽지 않다는 말에, 이유를 물어보니 너무 설탕이 많이 들어 있다고 대답한다. 빈칸에는 영양 분석을 확인했어야 했다고 말하는 것이 어울린다. nutrition fact: 영양 분석

05 일요일에 본 영화에 대해 만족을 묻는 말인 'How did you like it?'에 Yes나 No로 대답할 수 없다.

06 주어진 문장 'That's too bad.'는 '그것 참 안됐다.'라는 뜻으로 상대방의 실망에 대해 위로하는 표현이다. 정가를 주고 샀다는 남자아이의 말에 여자아이가 위로하는 것이 어울리므로 ④가 적절하다.

07 (A) release: 출시하다, 발매하다. it이 가리키는 것은 a new phone을 의미하는 것이므로 수동태가 들어가야 한다. just는 '방금'이라는 뜻으로 'have p.p.'인 현재완료 중에서 '완료'의 의미로 사용하였다. (B) 'should have p.p. ~'는 '~했어야 했는데 (사실은 하지 않았다)'라는 뜻으로 과거 사실에 대한 유감을 나타내는 표현이다. 내용상 할인 판매를 확인했어야 했다는 내용이 들어가야 하므로 'should have p.p. ~'가 어울린다.

08 'How do you like ~?'는 '~는 어때?'라는 의미로 상대방에게 어떤 것에 대한 만족 또는 불만족을 묻는 표현이다.

09 Luke가 무엇을 위해 새 스피커를 사용할 것인지는 대화를 통해 알 수 없다. ① 새 스피커의 음질은 어떠한가? The sound quality is good. ③ Luke는 언제 새 스피커를 샀는가? He bought it a few weeks ago. ④ Luke는 새 스피커에 만족하는

27

가? He is pretty happy with it. ⑤ 배터리는 얼마나 지속되는 가? About 2 hours.

p.133

서술형 시험대비

01 should have worn a warm jacket
02 How do you like it?
03 explaining
04 I should have read more reviews.
05 (A) on   (B) at
06 I should have checked the sales before buying mine.

01 'should have p.p. ~'는 '~했어야 했는데 (사실은 하지 않았다)'라는 뜻으로 과거 사실에 대한 유감을 나타내는 표현이다.

02 'Oh, I'm not happy with it.(아, 나는 별로 마음에 들지 않아.)'은 여자가 온라인으로 산 노트북에 대해 불만족을 표현하는 말이다. 그러므로 빈칸에는 어떤 것에 만족하거나 불만이 있는지 묻는 'How do you like it?'이 어울린다.

03 'How about ~?'은 '~하는 게 어때?'라는 뜻으로 상대방에게 권유할 때 사용하는 표현이고, about은 전치사이기 때문에 뒤에 명사나 동명사가 올 수 있다. explaining은 calling과 접속사 and로 연결되어 있다.

04 과거 사실에 대해 후회나 유감을 나타낼 때 '~했어야 했다'라는 의미로 'should have p.p. ~'를 쓴다. review: 후기

05 (A) on sale: 할인 중인 (B) at full price: 정가에, 제값에

06 대화의 흐름상 '사기 전에 할인 판매를 확인했어야 했다'라는 내용이 어울리므로, 'should have p.p. ~'를 이용해서 문장을 완성한다. 여기서 before는 전치사이므로 뒤에 동명사형이 온다.

교과서

Grammar

핵심 Check

p.134~135

1 ④
2 (1) is   (2) are   (3) are

시험대비 기본평가

p.136

01 ④   02 ③   03 ①   04 ②
05 I love you as time goes by.

01 ④는 보어절을 이끄는 접속사 that이 적절하다.

02 부분을 나타내는 말은 뒤에 오는 명사의 수에 따라 그 수가 결정되는데, Half of 다음에 the money라고 단수 명사가 나오므로 ③번이 적절하다.

03 '~함에 따라'로 해석되는 '비례, 추이'를 나타내는 as가 적절하다.

04 ②번에는 부사절과 주절의 내용이 서로 상반되므로 양보의 접속사 Though[Although]가 적절하다. 나머지는 모두 as가 들어갈 수 있다. 각각 ① '시간' ③ '방식, 양태' ④ '비례, 추이' ⑤ '이유'를 나타낸다.

05 '비례, 추이(~함에 따라서, ~에 비례하여)'를 나타내는 as를 이용하여 영작한다.

시험대비 실력평가

p.137~139

01 ⑤   02 ②   03 ③   04 ⑤
05 ④   06 likes → like 07 ②   08 ①
09 ④   10 ③   11 ①   12 ⑤
13 ④   14 ②   15 ①
16 Strange as it may seem

01 ⑤는 '~으로, ~로서'라는 뜻으로 전치사로 쓰였다. 나머지는 모두 접속사 as로 사용되었다.

02 ②는 '~하기 때문에'라는 뜻이다. 나머지는 모두 '~함에 따라, ~할수록'이라는 비례의 의미를 나타낸다.

03 문맥상 '~하듯이, ~하는 것처럼'이라는 뜻의 접속사 As를 쓰는 것이 가장 적절하다.

04 '부분을 나타내는 명사+of' 다음에 명사가 올 때 동사의 수를 명사의 수에 일치시킨다. 모두 복수 명사가 이어지고 있으므로 복수 동사 were가 적절하다.

05 부분을 나타내는 말은 뒤에 오는 명사의 수에 따라 그 수가 결정되는데, 'About one third of' 다음에 all the students라고 복수 명사가 나오므로 wear가 적절하다.

06 '부분을 나타내는 말+단수 명사: 단수 동사', '부분을 나타내는 말+복수 명사: 복수 동사' the students로 복수 명사가 이어지고 있으므로 복수 동사 like가 적절하다.

07 (1) '비례, 추이'를 나타내는 접속사 (2) '이유'를 나타내는 접속사 (3) '~으로, ~처럼'의 뜻으로 쓰인 전치사

08 '비례, 추이(~함에 따라서, ~에 비례하여)'를 나타내는 접속사 as를 이용하는 것이 가장 적절하다.

09 'a number of+복수 명사+복수 동사' (많은= many), 'the number of+복수 명사+단수 동사' (~의 수). a great deal of = much

10 ① being 이하가 분사구문으로 쓰여서 as를 접속사로도 전치사로도 쓸 수 없다.(As → 삭제) ② as가 아니라 명사절을 이끄는 접속사가 필요하다.(as → that) ④ 내용상 know의 목적어 역할을 할 수 있는 '의문사+to부정사'가 적절하다. (as → what) ⑤ '부사구(In addition)'이 앞에 나온 완전한 절이므로, as는 접속사로도 전치사로도 쓸 수 없다.(as → 삭제)

11 부분을 나타내는 말이 있는 어구가 주어로 쓰일 때 뒤에 단수 명사가 나오면 단수 동사를 쓰고, 복수 명사가 나오면 복수 동사를 쓴다. ①은 is[was], 나머지는 모두 are[were]이다.

12 주어진 문장과 ⑤의 as는 '~함에 따라, ~할수록'이라는 뜻으로서 '비례, 추이'를 나타낸다. 나머지는 각각 ① 비록 ~할지라도, ~이지만(양보) ② ~ 때문에(이유) ③ ~하는 것처럼, ~하는 대로 (방식, 양태) ④ ~할 때(시간) 등이다.

13 서울에서 한국 음식을 먹어 봤고, 삼겹살을 먹어 봤으므로 '먹어 본 것 중의 하나'가 삼겹살이라고 쓸 수 있다. 'one of+복수 명사'가 주어일 경우 핵심이 되는 주어가 one이므로 동사는 단수로 쓴다.

14 ②는 '금반지를 껴도 원숭이는 원숭이다.'라는 뜻이다. 의미상 as를 양보의 접속사 though나 although 등으로 바꾸는 것이 적절하다.

15 주절의 동사가 과거시제인 경우 종속절의 시제는 과거나 과거완료가 나오지만 종속절이 불변의 진리, 격언, 현재의 습관, 과학적 사실 등을 나타내면 현재시제를 쓴다. 남편이 매일 아침 커피를 마시는 것은 '현재의 습관'이므로 현재시제로 나타낸다.

16 접속사 as가 '양보'의 의미로 쓰일 때는 '형용사/부사/무관사 명사'를 as 앞에 둔다.

서술형 시험대비 p.140~141

01 (1) Do as the Romans do when you are in Rome.
   (2) As the song became more popular, he was known to more people.
   (3) About half of the water is used to raise animals in the U.S.
   (4) About 14 percent of all people don't know how to read due to lack of education.
02 (1) I caught him just as he was leaving the building.
   (2) Brave as he was, he could not help weeping at the sight.
   (3) Each blind student was paired with a sighted student.
   (4) Jeff buys soccer shoes because more than half of the boys on his team wear them.
   (5) Most of the allowance is spent on clothes and one fourth of the allowance is spent on snacks.
03 (1) As you give more love, you will receive more love.
   (2) As you exercise harder, you become healthier.
04 is sitting
05 As you eat more
06 (1) like (2) are (3) knows (4) goes (5) decreases
   (6) ended
07 (1) About two thirds of the books Sophie wrote were read by Steve.
   (2) Some of the food that Mom made was thrown away by Mike.
   (3) One of Dominic's hobbies is basketball.

01 (1) ~하듯이, ~하는 대로(방식)의 접속사 as를 이용한다. (2) ~함에 따라서, ~에 비례하여(비례, 추이)의 접속사 as를 이용한다. (3), (4) 부분을 나타내는 말이 있는 어구가 주어로 쓰일 때 뒤에 단수 명사가 나오면 단수 동사를 쓰고, 복수 명사가 나오면 복수 동사를 쓴다.

02 (1) just though → just as (2) 문맥상 양보의 의미가 적절하므로 '형용사+as+주어+동사 ~'의 어순이 적절하다. (3) each 다음에는 단수 명사와 단수 동사가 이어진다. (4) 'half of' 다음에 'the boys on his team'라는 복수 명사가 나오므로 복수 동사 wear가 적절하다. (5) 'Most of'와 'one fourth of' 다음에 'the allowance'라는 단수 명사가 나오므로 단수 동사 is가 적절하다.

03 'the 비교급 …, the 비교급 ~' 구문을 '비례, 추이'를 나타내는 as를 이용하여 바꿔 쓸 수 있다.

04 'one of+복수 명사'가 주어일 경우 핵심이 되는 주어가 one이므로 동사는 단수로 쓴다.

05 '비례, 추이(~함에 따라서, ~에 비례하여)'의 부사절을 이끄는 as를 이용한다.

06 (1), (2) 부분을 나타내는 말 뒤에 오는 명사가 단수이면 단수 동사를 쓰고 복수이면 복수 동사를 쓴다. (3) 'none of+명사+동사'에서 명사가 단수일 경우, 동사의 수는 명사에 일치시켜 단수 동사로 쓴다. 명사가 복수일 경우에는 복수 동사나 단수 동사를 모두 쓸 수 있다. (4) 주절의 시제가 과거일지라도 종속절이 불변의 진리, 격언, 현재의 습관, 과학적 사실 등을 나타내면 현재시제를 쓴다. (5) the number of+단수[복수] 명사+단수 동사 (6) 역사적인 사실은 주절의 시제와 상관없이 과거시제를 쓴다.

07 부분을 나타내는 말은 뒤에 오는 명사의 수에 따라 그 수가 결정된다. (1) 'two thirds of the books'에서 'the books'로 복수이므로 were를 써야 한다. (2) 'Some of the food'에서 'the

food'로 단수이므로 was를 써야 한다. (3) 'one of' 다음에는 복수 명사가 나오며 핵심 주어가 one이므로 단수 동사로 받는다.

Reading

p.142

확인문제

1 T 2 F

확인문제

p.143

1 F 2 T 3 F

교과서 확인학습 A
p.144~146

01 why you've bought things that
02 what affects us, buying
03 what my friends bought
04 goes, sees a pair of, on display
05 recognizes, because, half of the boys, wear
06 Although, many pairs of, ends up buying
07 bandwagon effect, to explain
08 that encourages, to jump aboard
09 more and more people, others are, likely to get on
10 to buy, just because, have bought it
11 buy a pair of, after, have bought
12 that, realizes that, match
13 that go, with
14 that none of her bags match
15 buys, Most of her money is, on, to complete
16 made, search for, after buying
17 explain it, received, as
18 after receiving, noticed that, furniture, go well, replacing most of it
19 therefore, that purchasing a new item, leads to, unplanned
20 they are on sale
21 goes window shopping, sees
22 checks, finds out that, that, too expensive
23 approaches him, discount on
24 Even though, is still, low, to buy
25 described above, anchoring effect
26 mentioned, affects, opinion of prices
27 For example, seem cheap in comparison
28 Furthermore, becomes bigger, be more powerful

29 As such, mentioned first, anchor, fixes our thoughts
30 Just like, to buy, considering why we are buying
31 As, have shown, influence
32 The next time, think, about why you are buying

교과서 확인학습 B
p.146~147

1 Have you ever wondered why you've bought things that you don't even want or need?
2 Let's consider what affects us when it comes to buying things.
3 Why do I want to buy what my friends bought?
4 Jeff goes to the shopping center and sees a pair of soccer shoes on display.
5 He recognizes the shoes at a glance because more than half of the boys on his soccer team wear them.
6 Although he already has many pairs of soccer shoes, he ends up buying another new pair.
7 We can use the "bandwagon effect" to explain Jeff's behavior.
8 A bandwagon is a wagon in a parade that encourages people to jump aboard and enjoy the music.
9 As more and more people get on the bandwagon, others are more likely to get on or follow it.
10 In this way, people tend to buy something just because other people have bought it.
11 Why do I buy a pair of pants and a bag after I have bought a new coat?
12 Lisa buys a coat that she really loves. Immediately, she realizes that her pants do not match her new coat.
13 So, she buys new pants that go perfectly with her new coat.
14 But she sees that none of her bags match her new clothes.
15 So, she buys a new bag. Most of her money is spent on buying the new items to complete her new look.
16 What made Lisa search for new items immediately after buying a new coat?
17 The "Diderot effect" may explain it. Denis Diderot, a French writer, received a new gown as a gift.
18 Soon after receiving the gift, he noticed that all of his furniture did not go well with his new gown.

19 The Diderot effect, therefore, is the concept that purchasing a new item often leads to more unplanned purchases.

20 Why do I buy things just because they are on sale?

21 Nathan goes window shopping and sees a pair of headphones.

22 He checks the price and finds out that they are $200. He thinks that the headphones are too expensive.

23 The sales person approaches him and says, "You can get a 20 percent discount on those headphones."

24 Even though the discounted price is still not very low, Nathan decides to buy the headphones.

25 The situation described above is an example of the "anchoring effect."

26 "The price mentioned first affects our opinion of prices mentioned afterwards.

27 For example, if we start with $200, then $160 will seem cheap in comparison.

28 Furthermore, as the difference of the two prices becomes bigger, the effect will be more powerful.

29 As such, the price mentioned first acts as an "anchor" that fixes our thoughts about the price of an item.

30 Just like Jeff and his friends, we tend to buy things without seriously considering why we are buying them.

31 As these effects have shown, many things influence our purchases.

32 The next time you decide to buy something, think for a moment about why you are buying it.

시험대비 실력평가
p.148~151

01 ②　　　　02 He goes to the shopping center.

03 behavior　04 ③　　　05 ④

06 ①, ④　　07 ⑤

08 She bought a new bag.　09 ④　　　10 ③

11 ②　　　12 It is 200 dollars.

13 He says that Nathan can get a 20 percent discount on those headphones.

14 ③　　　15 ②

16 He sees a pair of soccer shoes on display.

17 ④

18 We can use the "bandwagon effect."

19 after I have bought a new coat

20 ⑤　　　21 his furniture　　　22 ③

23 ③　　　24 ②

25 They have shown that many things influence our purchases.

01 글의 내용은 다른 사람들이 어떤 것을 샀다는 이유로 그것을 구매하는 경향에 관한 것이므로 ②번이 가장 적절하다.

03 사람이나 동물이 하는 것은 '행동(behavior)'이다.

04 Jeff는 진열되어 있는 축구화 한 켤레를 보고 결국 사 버리고 말았다.

05 주어진 문장의 it은 Lisa로 하여금 새 코트를 산 후 즉시 새로운 물품을 찾게 하는 것을 가리킨다. 따라서 ④번에 들어가는 것이 가장 자연스럽다.

06 Lisa는 새 코트를 산 후 잇따라 바지와 가방을 샀다.

07 Lisa는 그녀의 새로운 모습을 완성하기 위하여 새로운 물품을 사는 데 돈의 대부분을 썼다고 하였다.

08 새로운 옷들을 산 후 Lisa는 새 가방을 샀다.

09 앵커링 효과는 처음에 언급된 가격이 이후에 언급되는 가격에 대한 우리의 의견에 영향을 미친다는 것이다. 처음에 언급된 가격이 물건의 가격에 대한 우리의 생각을 고정하는 닻으로서 작동하기 때문이다. 따라서 afterwards라고 쓰는 것이 적절하다.

10 예시를 들어 앞선 진술을 명확히 설명하고 있으므로 ③번이 가장 적절하다.

11 위 글은 "앵커링 효과"에 관한 글로, 단지 할인 중이라는 이유로 물건을 구입하는 이유에 관하여 설명하고 있다. 따라서 ②번이 가장 적절하다.

12 헤드폰의 가격에 대해 Nathan이 갖는 생각을 고정시키는 '닻' 역할을 하는 가격은 200달러이다.

13 점원은 Nathan에게 다가와 헤드폰에 20퍼센트 할인을 받을 수 있다고 말한다.

14 (C) Jeff는 쇼핑센터에서 축구팀에 있는 소년들의 반 이상이 신고 있는 축구화가 진열된 것을 봄 (A) 그에게 이미 축구화가 많이 있지만 결국 그것을 삼 (D) Jeff의 행동은 : '밴드왜건 효과'로 설명할 수 있는데, 밴드왜건에 사람들이 올라타서 음악을 즐기게 부추김 (B) 더 많은 사람들이 밴드왜건에 올라탈수록 다른 사람들도 그것을 따르려 함

15 when it comes to Ving: V에 대해서 말하자면

16 쇼핑센터에 간 Jeff는 진열되어 있는 축구화 한 켤레를 보게 된다고 하였다.

17 위 글은 원하거나 필요하지 않는 것들을 사는 이유에 대해 설명하는 글이다. 따라서 ④번 '우리가 돈을 쓰도록 만드는 것은 무엇인가?'가 가장 적절하다.

So, he ended up replacing most of it.

18 Jeff의 행동은 "밴드왜건 효과"로 설명할 수 있다.

19 위 글은 새 코트를 산 후 연이어 바지와 가방을 산 사례와 그 이유를 설명하는 내용이다.

20 빈칸 (B)에는 전치사 on이 들어간다. ① break down: 고장나다 ② stand for: 상징하다 ③ bring up: ~을 양육하다 ④ put off: ~을 미루다 ⑤ live on: ~을 먹고 살다

21 Diderot는 선물로 받은 새 가운과 자신의 모든 가구가 어울리지 않는 것을 알아채고 결국 대부분의 가구를 바꾸었다.

22 밑줄 친 (D)는 완전한 절을 이끄는 명사절 접속사이다. ③번은 불완전한 절을 이끄는 관계대명사이다.

23 approach는 타동사이므로 전치사 없이 목적어를 취한다. 따라서 'approaches him'이라고 쓰는 것이 적절하다.

24 글의 내용은 우리가 왜 물건들을 사는지 진지하게 고려하지 않고 구매한다는 것이다. 따라서 다음에 어떤 것을 구매하려고 결정할 때 자신이 그것을 왜 사려는지 잠시 동안 생각해 보라는 말이 들어가는 것이 적절하다.

25 이러한 효과들은 많은 것들이 우리의 구매에 영향을 미친다는 것을 보여주고 있다.

서술형 시험대비   p.152~153

01 what affects us when it comes to buying things
02 wear
03 a bandwagon
04 As more and more people get on the bandwagon, others are more likely to get on or follow it.
05 It's because other people have bought it.
06 She buys a coat (that she really loves).
07 She realizes (that) her pants do not match her new coat.
08 It was because he noticed that all of his furniture did not go well with his new gown.
09 planned → unplanned
10 He sees a pair of headphones.
11 He finds out that the headphones are 200 dollars.
12 anchor
13 The writer suggests that we should think for a moment about why we are buying it.

01 동사 consider의 목적어로 간접의문문을 쓰는 것에 유의한다.
    when it comes to Ving: V에 관하여
02 'half of+명사'는 명사에 수의 일치를 한다. 따라서 the boys에 맞추어 복수동사 wear를 쓴다.
03 퍼레이드에 있는 사륜마차인 밴드왜건을 가리키는 말이다.

04 더 많은 사람들이 밴드왜건에 올라탈수록 다른 사람들이 더욱 그것에 올라타거나 그것을 따라가려 한다.

05 '밴드왜건 효과'는 단지 다른 사람들이 어떤 것을 샀다는 이유로 그것을 구매하는 현상을 의미한다.

06 Lisa가 처음에 산 것은 코트이다.

07 새 코트를 산 후 Lisa는 그녀의 바지가 새 코트와 어울리지 않는다는 것을 즉시 알아차린다.

08 새 가운을 선물로 받은 Diderot는 그의 모든 가구가 새로운 가운과 어울리지 않는다는 것을 알아채고는 결국 대부분의 가구를 바꾸고야 말았다.

09 디드로 효과는 새로운 물품을 구입하는 것이 흔히 계획에 없던 더 많은 구매로 이어지는 개념이라고 하였다.

10 Nathan은 진열된 상품을 구경하러 가서 헤드폰을 하나 본다고 하였다.

11 헤드폰의 가격을 확인했을 때, Nathan은 가격이 200달러라는 것을 알게 된다.

12 배가 움직이지 않도록 물 속에 떨어뜨리는 것은 '닻(anchor)'이다.

13 글쓴이는 다음번에 우리가 어떤 것을 구매하려고 결정할 때, 자신이 그것을 왜 사려는지 잠시 동안 생각해 보라고 하였다.

영역별 핵심문제   p.155~159

01 ⑤   02 ①   03 encourages
04 More   05 ④
06 I should have kept track of my spending.
07 ⑤   08 ④   09 ④   10 like
11 (1) How do you like them?
    (2) Are you satisfied with them?   12 ②
13 ③   14 ②, ⑤   15 ⑤   16 ④
17 ①
18 (1) One third of the students are here.
    (2) Much of the house was ruined by the heavy rain.
    (3) Ten percent of the girls want to learn Spanish.
    (4) None of the furniture in our house is made of wood.
    (5) Last night she said that she takes a shower every day.
19 (1) as → though[although]
    (2) as → unless

(3) like → as

20 enjoys → enjoy 　　　　21 ⑤

22 ④번 → enjoy 　　　　23 no other → other

24 ② 　　　　25 ③

26 She buys (a pair of) new pants and a new bag.

27 He ended up replacing most of it. 　　　28 ④

29 ⑤

30 Most of the allowance is spent on clothes.

01 affect: ~에 영향을 주다 influence: ~에 영향을 주다 / 어린 사람들은 그들의 동료 그룹에 의해 크게 영향을 받는 경향이 있다. ① 발명하다 ② 조절하다 ③ 향상시키다 ④ 발생하다 *tend to: ~하는 경향이 있다 *peer: 동료

02 저 재킷은 너의 치마와 완벽하게 어울린다. ① 어울리다 ② 소비하다 ③ 오래가다, (기능이) 지속되다 ④ 교체하다 ⑤ 맞추다, 조정하다

03 courage: 용기 encourage: 부추기다, 조장하다 / 새 선생님은 학생들이 창의적인 생각을 하도록 부추긴다.

04 more and more: 점점 더 많은 / 점점 더 많은 사람들이 인터넷을 이용하고 있다. more than half: 반 이상의 / 길은 30분 이상 동안 폐쇄되었다.

05 주어진 문장에서 it은 용돈을 의미한다. 용돈을 어떻게 다 써버렸는지에 대한 대답으로 'I'm not sure.(잘 모르겠어.)'가 어울리므로 ④가 적절하다.

06 과거 사실에 대해 후회나 유감을 나타낼 때 '~했어야 했다'는 의미로 'should have p.p. ~'를 쓴다. keep track of: ~을 기록하다 spending: 지출

07 (A) 'I heard that ~.'은 '~에 대해 들었다'의 뜻으로 알고 있거나 들은 것에 대해 말할 때 쓰는 표현이다. 접속사 that 뒤에는 절이 오며 'I've heard that ~'으로 바꿔 쓸 수 있다. (B) 'What's wrong?'은 상대방이 뭔가에 불만족하거나 실망하고 있는 것을 보고 그 원인을 물을 때 사용하는 표현이므로 빈칸에는 not happy가 어울린다. (C) 'should have p.p. ~.'는 어떤 일을 했어야 했다고 후회할 때 사용한다.

08 'How do you like ~?'는 '~는 어떠니?'라는 뜻으로 어떤 것에 대한 의견을 물을 때 쓰인다. 바꿔 쓸 수 있는 표현으로 'Are you satisfied[happy] with ~?', 'How is ~?', 'Are you enjoying ~?', 'Do you like ~?' 등이 있다.

09 캐릭터 티셔츠를 추천한 직원에게 여동생이 만화 캐릭터를 안 좋아한다고 얘기하면서 'Can I see the blue one?(파란 티셔츠 좀 볼 수 있을까요?)'이라고 물어본다.

10 (A) 'How do you like ~?'는 '~는 어떠니?'라는 뜻으로 어떤 것에 대한 의견을 물을 때 쓰인다. (B) like: 좋아하다

11 'How do you like ~?'는 상대방의 의견 혹은 만족 여부를 물

을 때 사용한다. 비슷한 표현인 'Are you satisfied[happy] with ~?'로 직접적으로 만족이나 불만족 여부를 물을 수 있다.

12 ⓐ 초록색 가방과 파란색 가방 중 무엇을 샀는가? (초록색 가방을 샀다.) ⓑ 초록색 가방과 파란색 가방 중 무엇이 더 가벼운가? (초록색 가방이 더 가볍다.) ⓒ 무슨 용도로 가방을 쓸 것인가? (하이킹할 때 사용할 것이다.) ⓓ 어떤 가방이 더 인기 있는가? (알 수 없다.)

13 각각 ①, ② '비례' ④ '시간' ⑤ '이유'이다. ③ as는 가정법의 if 대신 사용할 수 없다.

14 ① One of the highlights was seeing the Taj Mahal. ③ The number of employees was reduced from 40 to 25. ④ The rest of the money is used to run other government programs.

15 'Jane은 그가 건물을 나설 때 만났다.'는 내용으로서 so as는 어법상 어색하다. 'so as'를 'just as'로 바꾸는 것이 적절하다.

16 'a few of+복수 명사' 주어는 복수 동사로 받는다. Last weekend로 시제가 과거로 표시되어야 함에 주의한다.

17 주어진 문장과 ①의 접속사 As는 '~함에 따라'(비례)를 나타낸다. ② ~하는 동안(시간) ③ ~하는 대로(방식) ④ ~만큼(비교) ⑤ ~해서, ~ 때문에(이유)

18 (1), (3) 부분을 나타내는 말의 뒤에 단수 명사가 나오면 단수 동사를 쓰고 복수 명사가 나오면 복수 동사를 쓴다. (2) 'much of+단수 명사' 주어는 단수 동사로 받는다. (4) 'none of +명사+동사'에서는 명사가 단수일 경우 단수 동사를 쓰고 명사가 복수일 경우 복수 동사나 단수 동사를 모두 쓸 수 있다. (5) 주절의 시제가 과거일지라도 종속절이 불변의 진리, 격언, 현재의 습관, 과학적 사실 등을 나타내면 현재시제를 쓴다.

19 (1) 앞과 뒤의 절의 내용이 상반되므로 as가 아니라 though[although]가 적절하다. (2) 내용상 '정말로 춥지 않다면 창문을 열어 놓고 잠을 잔다.'고 하는 것이 자연스럽다. as를 unless로 고치는 것이 적절하다. (3) like는 전치사로 '~ 같은'이라는 뜻이고 as는 전치사로 '~로서'라는 뜻이다. 또한 'regard A as B'는 'A를 B로 여기다'라는 뜻이다.

20 부분을 나타내는 말은 뒤에 오는 명사의 수에 따라 그 수가 결정되는데, percent of 다음에 students라고 복수 명사가 나오므로 enjoy가 적절하다.

21 글의 내용은 '밴드왜건 효과'에 관한 것이므로 Jeff는 축구팀에 있는 소년들이 신는 축구화라는 이유로 결국 그 축구화를 사버리고 만다는 내용이 적절하다.

22 밴드왜건은 사람들이 올라타서 음악을 즐기게끔 부추기는 퍼레이드에 있는 사륜마차라는 의미이다. 따라서 to jump에 병렬 연결되도록 enjoy라고 쓰는 것이 적절하다.

23 다른 사람들이 어떤 것을 샀다는 이유로 그것을 구매하는 경향

이므로 부정어 no가 없어야 한다.

24 진열되어 있는 축구화 한 켤레를 본 Jeff는 그 신발을 한눈에 알아챘다고 하였다.

25 디드로 효과가 무엇인지를 설명한 후 한 문장으로 정리하여 진술하고 있으므로 결과를 이끄는 therefore가 적절하다.

26 Lisa는 새 코트를 산 후 새 바지와 새 가방을 샀다.

27 Diderot는 결국 대부분의 가구를 바꾸었다.

28 Lisa는 원래 마음에 드는 코트를 사려고 했지만 자신의 새로운 모습을 완성하기 위하여 계획에 없던 물건을 사고 있다.

29 이어지는 글의 내용으로 보아 용돈을 얼마나 자주 받는지 물어봤음을 알 수 있다.

30 대부분의 용돈은 옷에 쓰인다고 하였다.

단원별 예상문제　　　　　　　　　p.160~163

01 (1) (p)urchase　(2) (t)ight　02 difference
03 ③
04 (a)ffect　(c)ombine　(c)oncept
　　(1) concept　(2) affects　(3) combine
05 (D) → (B) → (C) → (A)
06 (A) ⓓ　(B) ⓑ　(C) ⓔ
07 suit　　　　08 ②　　　　09 for
10 ②
11 call the online shop and explain my problem
12 ①　　　　13 ④　　　　14 was → were
15 As people eat more junk food, they may gain more weight.
16 ②
17 As you run more, you become stronger.
18 ③　　　19 anchor, lower　　　20 ⑤
21 The price mentioned first affects our opinion of prices mentioned afterwards.
22 ⑤
23 They think (that) they should get a higher allowance.　　　　24 ②

01 (1) 두 단어의 관계는 동의어 관계이다. immediately: 즉시, 바로 at once: 즉시 buy: 사다 purchase: 사다, 구입하다 (2) 두 단어의 관계는 반의어 관계이다. waste: 낭비하다, 소모하다 save: 낭비를 막다, 절약하다 loose: 헐거운, 느슨한 tight: 꽉 조이는, 딱 붙는

02 differ: 다르다 difference: 차이, 차이점 / 이 두 컴퓨터의 차이점이 무엇인가요?

03 (A) spend A on 동사ing: A를 ~하는 데 쓰다 / 우리는 예전보다 음식에 더 많은 돈을 쓰고 있는 중이다. (B) keep track of: ~을 기록하다 / 우리는 비용을 기록하는 시스템이 필요하다.

(C) lead to: ~로 이어지다 / 스트레스가 신체적인 병으로 이어질 수 있다는 것에는 의심의 여지가 없다.

04 (1) concept: 개념. 어떤 원리나 생각 / 우리는 지금 새로운 개념을 생각해 내야 할 필요가 있다. (2) affect: ~에 영향을 주다. 어떤 사람이나 사물에 영향을 미치다, 혹은 어떤 사람이나 사물에 변화를 야기하다 / 네가 하는 모든 선택은 너의 삶에 영향을 준다. (3) combine: 결합하다. 하나 하나의 혹은 집단으로 만들기 위해 합치다 / 그는 일과 즐거움을 결합하고 싶어 한다.

05 새로운 스피커인지 물어보는 질문에 (D) 맞다고 대답하면서 몇 주 전에 샀다고 말한다. (B) 새로운 스피커에 대한 의견을 물어본다. (C) 편리하고, 어디든지 가져가서 음악을 들을 수 있고, 음질도 좋다고 말한다. (A) 배터리는 얼마나 오래가는지 질문하자 2시간 정도라고 대답한다.

06 (A) '무엇을 도와드릴까요?'라고 묻는 질문에 별들이 그려진 모자를 써 볼 수 있는지 묻는 것이 어울린다. (B) 별들이 그려진 모자에 대해 의견을 물어보고, 디자인은 좋은데 색깔은 어울리지 않는다고 대답하는 것이 어울린다. (C) 같은 모양의 검은색이 있는지 질문을 하고 안쪽에서 가져다 드리겠다고 말하는 것이 어울린다.

07 suit: 어울리다 / 어떤 특정한 사람이나 상황, 경우에 알맞다

08 노트북이 마음에 들지 않는다는 여자의 말에 무슨 문제가 있는지 물어보고, 그 말에 소음이 심하고 과열이 된다고 대답을 해 주는 것이 어울린다.

09 ask for: 요청하다

10 일주일 동안 사용했기 때문에 온라인 가게는 환불을 해 주지 않을 거라고 말하는 것이 어울리므로 이유의 접속사 because가 알맞다.

11 온라인 가게에 전화해 문제를 설명하라고 충고하는 말에 '그렇게 해야 할 것 같다'라고 말하고 있으므로 'do that'은 '온라인 가게에 전화해 문제를 설명하는 것'을 가리킨다.

12 버스를 또 놓쳤다고 말하고 있으므로 빈칸에는 일찍 일어나지 않았던 것에 대해 유감을 표현하는 말이 들어가는 것이 적절하다. 'should have p.p. ~'는 '~했어야 했는데 (사실은 하지 않았다)'의 뜻으로 과거 사실에 대한 유감을 나타내는 표현이다.

13 ④번의 as는 전치사이고, 나머지는 모두 접속사이다.

14 부분을 나타내는 말은 뒤에 오는 명사의 수에 따라 그 수가 결정되는데, part of 다음에 the expenses라고 복수 명사가 나오므로 were가 적절하다.

15 '~함에 따라, ~할수록'이라는 비례의 의미를 갖는 접속사 as를 이용한다.

16 ②에는 부분을 나타내는 말(Some of)의 뒤에 단수 명사(the pie)가 나왔으므로 단수 동사 is가 적절하다. 나머지는 모두 are가 적절하다.

17 'the 비교급 …, the 비교급 ~' 구문을 '비례, 추이'를 나타내는 as를 이용하여 바꿔 쓸 수 있다.

18 (A) on sale: 할인 중인, for sale: 판매를 위한 (B) 종속절이 주절의 이유라기보다는 양보절을 이끄는 것이 더 적절하다. (C) "닻"은 우리의 생각을 고정하는 역할을 한다.

19 처음에 언급된 가격은 '닻'으로서 작용한다. 만약 나중에 언급된 가격이 처음의 가격보다 더 낮으면 당신은 그 상품이 싸다고 생각할 것이다.

20 Nathan은 헤드폰이 여전히 별로 저렴하지 않다고 생각했지만 "앵커링 효과"에 영향을 받아 결국 헤드폰을 산다.

21 처음에 언급된 가격이 이후에 언급되는 가격에 대한 우리의 의견에 영향을 미친다고 하였다.

22 '~인지 아닌지'를 물어보았다는 표현이 적절하므로 that이 아니라 if나 whether를 써야 한다. 명사절 접속사 that은 확정적인 내용의 절을, if나 whether는 확정적이지 않은 내용의 절을 이끈다.

23 설문 조사에 참여한 10명의 학생 중 90퍼센트에 해당하는 9명의 학생들은 자신이 용돈을 더 많이 받아야 한다고 생각한다.

24 설문 조사를 받은 학생의 수는 10명이다.

서술형 실전문제 p.164~165

01 should have brought an umbrella
02 (1) Are you enjoying this dress?
   (2) Are you satisfied with this dress?
   (3) Are you happy with this dress?
03 I should have tried it on.
04 (1) was spent (2) is (3) died (4) has
05 (1) Jason came up to me as I was speaking.
   (2) Young as he was, he was very wise.
   (3) As these effects have shown, many things influence our purchases.
   (4) One third of the world's food is wasted.
06 Because more than half of the boys on his soccer team wear them.
07 It is a wagon in a parade that encourages people to jump aboard and enjoy the music.
08 Because she wants to complete her new look.
09 The "Diderot effect" may explain it.
10 It is the concept that purchasing a new item often leads to more unplanned purchases.

01 'should have p.p. ~'는 '~했어야 했는데 (사실은 하지 않았다)'의 뜻으로 과거 사실에 대한 유감을 나타내는 표현이다.
02 어떤 것에 만족하거나 불만이 있는지 물어보는 표현으로 'How

do you like ~?', 'Are you satisfied[happy] with ~?', 'Are you enjoying ~?' 등을 쓸 수 있다.

03 사기 전에 입어 보지 않았느냐는 질문에, 자신의 사이즈여서 그냥 사 버렸다고 말하고 있으므로 빈칸에는 입어 보지 않은 것에 대해 후회를 하는 말이 어울린다. try on: (옷 등을 시험 삼아) 입어 보다

04 (1) 부분을 나타내는 말 뒤에 오는 명사가 단수이면 단수 동사를 쓰고 복수이면 복수 동사를 쓴다. the money가 주어이므로 수동태로 써야 함에 주의한다. (2) 학문 이름은 단수 취급한다. (3) 역사적인 사실은 주절의 시제와 상관없이 과거시제를 쓴다. (4) the number of+단수(복수) 명사+단수 동사

05 (1) as가 '시간'을 나타내는 부사절을 이끌도록 쓴다. (2) 접속사 as가 '양보'의 의미로 쓰일 때는 '형용사/부사/무관사 명사를 as 앞에 둔다. (3) as가 '방식'을 나타내는 부사절을 이끌도록 쓴다. (4) 부분을 나타내는 말 뒤에 오는 명사가 단수이면 단수 동사를 쓰고 복수이면 복수 동사를 쓴다.

06 위 글의 내용에 따르면, Jeff가 축구화를 산 이유는 그의 축구팀에 있는 소년들의 반 이상이 그 축구화를 신기 때문에 그는 그 축구화를 산다.

07 밴드왜건(악대차)은 사람들이 올라타서 음악을 즐기게끔 부추기는 퍼레이드에 있는 사륜마차라고 하였다.

08 Lisa는 그녀의 새로운 모습을 완성하기 위하여 대부분의 돈을 쓴다고 하였다.

09 Lisa의 소비는 '디드로 효과'가 설명해 줄지도 모른다고 하였다.

10 디드로 효과는 새로운 물품을 구입하는 것이 흔히 계획에 없던 더 많은 구매로 이어진다는 개념이다

창의사고력 서술형 문제 p.166

|모범답안|
01 should have stayed at home / should have not gone to school
02 (1) I respected her more
   (2) I was so hungry
   (3) I need more money
   (4) he becomes more curious about the world
03 how often they get an allowance, Twenty, every week, seventy percent of the students get an allowance every month, spent on clothes, one fourth of the allowance, whether[if] they think that they should get a higher allowance, Ninety percent of the students think that they should get a higher allowance

p.167~170

01 어제 아픈데도 불구하고 학교 간 것에 대해 후회를 하는 말이 어울리므로, 학교를 가지 않았어야 했는데 간 것에 대해 후회하는 표현이 어울린다.

단원별 모의고사

01 go
02 (1) are likely to be (2) comfortable
  (3) (s)oon, (a)fter (4) at a glance
03 (1) When (2) because (3) Although
04 comparison   **05** ③
06 How do you like this red one[T-shirt]?
07 I regret not checking the sales before buying mine.
  I wish I had checked the sales before buying mine.
08 ③
09 (A) should (B) should (C) won't (D) should
10 ⑤
11 (A) used (B) see (C) broken   **12** ④
13 ③
14 As we cut more trees to make land, more forests disappear on Earth.
15 One third of the power (that[which]) your body consumes comes from the food (that[which]) you eat.
16 ①, ②, ⑤   **17** It is $160.
18 It is the price mentioned first.
19 ④   **20** ③   **21**
22 (B)-(A)-(C) 23 ②

01 go well with: ~와 잘 어울리다 / 어떤 신발이 이 옷에 가장 잘 어울리니? go window shopping: 진열된 상품을 구경하고 다니다 / 나는 다음 주말에 친구와 진열된 상품을 구경하고 다닐 것이다.

02 (1) be likely to: ~할 가능성이 있다, ~하기 쉽다 (2) comfortable: 편안한 tight: 꽉 조이는, 딱 붙는 (3) soon after: 직후 (4) at a glance: 한눈에, 즉시

03 (1) when it comes to: ~에 관해서, ~에 대해 말하자면 / 요리에 관해서라면, 그가 나보다 낫다. (2) just because: 단지 ~라는 이유로 / 단지 내가 불평을 안 하니까 사람들은 내가 만족해하는 줄 안다. (3) although: 비록 ~이지만 / 비록 해가 비치고 있긴 했지만, 날이 별로 따뜻하지는 않았다.

04 compare: 비교하다 in comparison: 비교해 보면 / 이에 비해

05 여자가 파란 줄무늬 티셔츠를 선택한 것으로 보아, 여동생이 만화 캐릭터를 별로 좋아하지 않는다는 것을 유추할 수 있다.

06 'How do you like ~?'는 상대방의 의견 혹은 만족 여부를 물을 때 사용한다.

07 과거 사실에 대해 후회나 유감을 나타낼 때 '~했어야 했다'라는 의미로 'should have p.p. ~'를 쓴다. 이때 조동사 should 뒤에는 과거의 일을 의미하므로 동사원형 대신 'have+p.p.'를 써야 한다. 이외에도 'I regret -ing.', 'I wish I had p.p. ~' 등으로 쓸 수 있다.

08 남자는 할인 판매를 확인하지 않았던 것에 대해 후회하고 있다.

09 (A) 과거 사실에 대해 후회나 유감을 나타낼 때 '~했어야 했다'는 의미로 'should have p.p. ~'를 쓴다. (B), (D) should: ~해야 한다 (C) '일주일 동안 사용해서 환불을 해 주지 않을 것이다'라는 내용으로 will not의 줄임말인 won't가 어울린다.

10 Riley는 일주일 동안 노트북을 사용해서 환불을 해주지 않을 것이라고 말한다.

11 (A) used: 중고의 (B) let은 '~에게 …하게 하다'라는 의미를 가지는 사역동사로, 목적격보어로 동사원형을 쓴다. (C) 바깥 부분이 부서진 것이므로 수동태인 'be broken'을 사용한다.

12 ⓓ must → should, 'should have p.p. ~.'는 어떤 일을 했어야 했다고 후회할 때 사용한다.

13 각 부분은, '~할수록', '~하는 대로', '~로서' 등으로 접속사와 전치사로 모두 쓸 수 있는 것은 as이다.

14 '~함에 따라, ~할수록'이라는 '비례'의 의미를 갖는 as를 이용하여 영작한다.

15 '부분을 나타내는 명사+of' 다음에 명사가 올 때 동사의 수를 명사의 수에 일치시킨다.

16 글의 내용으로 미루어 보아 Nathan은 헤드폰의 가격이 비싸다고 생각했음을 유추할 수 있다. *bargain: 헐값의

17 할인된 헤드폰의 가격은 160달러라고 하였다.

18 물건의 가격에 대한 우리의 생각을 고정하는 '닻'으로서 작용하는 것은 먼저 언급된 가격이다.

19 "앵커링 효과"는 나중에 언급된 가격이 먼저 언급된 가격을 더 비싸 보이게 만든다.

20 밴드왜건에 올라타 함께 음악을 즐긴다고 하였으므로 '그것에 올라타거나 그것을 따라가려고 한다'는 것이 가장 적절하다.

21 밴드왜건 효과는 다른 사람들이 어떤 것을 샀다는 이유로 그것을 구매하는 경향이므로, 친구들이 노트북을 샀기 때문에 자신도 노트북을 샀다고 말한 Ethan이 밴드왜건 효과의 영향을 받

았다고 말할 수 있다.

22 (B)의 it이 주어진 문장의 'Lisa가 새 코트를 산 후 즉시 새로운 물품을 찾은 것'을 가리킴 (A) the gift는 (B)에서 나온 새 가운임 (C) 새 가운이 자신의 모든 가구와 어울리지 않는다는 사실을 알아챈 결과로 대부분의 가구를 교체함.

23 해석: 디드로 효과에 따르면, 하나의 새로운 물건 때문에 예상치 못한 지출이 있을 수 있다.

교과서 파헤치기

Lesson 5

1 shoot, (총 등을) 쏘다   2 fake, 거짓의   3 citizen, 시민
4 disaster, 참사, 재난   5 describe, 기술하다
6 panic, 겁에 질려 어쩔 줄 모르다   7 chest, 가슴, 흉부
8 spell, 철자를 말하다, 쓰다   9 criticize, 비난하다
10 source, 출처, 자료   11 wound, 상처를 입히다
12 incident, 사건   13 publish, 발행하다, 출판하다
14 trust, 신뢰하다   15 prove, 입증하다
16 argument, 논쟁, 언쟁

01 진지하게, 심각하게   02 인정하다, 자백하다
03 비판적으로   04 끔찍한, 지독한   05 극도로, 극히
06 가짜의, 거짓의   07 고백하다, 인정하다
08 위험한, 위독한   09 해로운, 유해한   10 시민
11 잘못 이끌다, 오해하게 하다   12 키, 신장
13 강하게 하다, 더 튼튼하게 하다   14 성인, 어른
15 논쟁, 언쟁   16 발행하다, 출판하다, 게재하다
17 알아보다   18 사건   19 비난하다
20 입증하다, 증명하다   21 현재의, 지금의
22 참사, 재난   23 달아나다, 탈출하다, 벗어나다
24 판단하다   25 기술하다
26 그럼에도 불구하고 27 믿을 만한, 신뢰할 만한
28 상처를 입히다   29 근육
30 (사실임을) 입증하다, 뒷받침하다   31 광산; 채굴하다
32 측정하다, 재다   33 출처, 자료   34 가슴, 흉부
35 ~와 연관되다   36 조사하다, 들여다보다
37 지어내다, 만들어 내다
38 ~을 부수다, ~을 무너뜨리다   39 ~에 따르면
40 ~의 관심을 …로 끌다
41 고정관념에서 벗어나다   42 ~에게 유용하다
43 잡히지 않은, 탈주 중인

01 admit   02 muscle   03 nevertheless
04 competitor   05 seriously   06 adult
07 mislead   08 mine   09 criticize
10 prove   11 critically   12 disaster
13 escape   14 public   15 strengthen
16 fake   17 confess   18 extremely
19 harmful   20 incident   21 argument
22 reliable   23 awful   24 citizen
25 judge   26 measure   27 current
28 publish   29 critical   30 recognize
31 source   32 describe   33 support
34 wound   35 look into   36 search for
37 be related to   38 draw one's attention to
39 fall asleep   40 break down   41 according to
42 be useful for   43 make up

Listen & Talk 1 A-1

caught a cold, because, dress warmly / article, cold, body temperature, low / more about it / because of viruses

Listen & Talk 1 A-2

a glass of warm milk, fall asleep / help, fall asleep / tell me more about it / chemicals, make, sleepy, amount, too, to, effect

Listen & Talk 2 A-1

What are you reading / riddles / for / Actually, useful for adults / say so / help, think, creatively, think outside the box to find

Listen & Talk 2 A-2

poetry books / written by / write better pomes / say so / honest, feelings, more creative than adults

Listen & Talk 2 B

I should buy this drink, help, lose weight / Let me read, label, closely, strange / you say so / enough information, what's, drink / right / how much you have to drink to lose weight

Communication

pieces of information, facts, completely wrong / there were, examples, facts that are wrong / what / goldfish, goldfish, actually smart / tell, more / recognize their owners / know that

Wrap Up 2

interesting article, where it is / between, and, right / What color, it is / guess / called, tell moe more / because, dangerous

Listen & Talk 1 A-1

W: I think I caught a cold because I didn't dress warmly yesterday.

M: Well, I've read an article saying that you don't catch a cold because your body temperature is low.

W: Really? Can you tell me more about it?

M: The article said that people catch colds because of viruses.

Listen & Talk 1 A-2

W: I usually drink a glass of warm milk before I go to bed, but it doesn't help me fall asleep.

M: I saw a show on TV, and a doctor said that a glass of warm milk doesn't actually help you fall asleep.

W: Oh, it doesn't? Can you tell me more about it?

M: Milk has special chemicals that make people sleepy. But the amount in a glass is too small to have any effect.

Listen & Talk 2 A-1

W: What are you reading, John?

M: I'm reading a book of riddles.

W: Riddles? Aren't they for children?

M: Actually, no. Books of riddles are really useful for adults.

W: Really? Why do you say so?

M: They help us think more creatively. We need to think outside the box to find the answers.

Listen & Talk 2 A-2

M: Are these all poetry books?

W: Yeah. These are all poems written by children.

M: By children?

W: Yeah. I think children write better poems than adults.

M: Why do you say so?

W: They're really honest about their feelings and much more creative than adults.

Listen & Talk 2 B

M: Hey, Sandy. Do you think I should buy this drink? It is said that it can help me lose weight.

W: Let me read the label more closely. Hmm, it looks a bit strange to me, David.

M: Why do you say so?

W: There isn't enough information about what's in the drink.

M: Oh, you're right.

W: Also, it doesn't tell you how much you have to drink to lose weight.

Communication

W: There are so many pieces of information we call "facts" that are completely wrong.

M: Why do you say so?

W: I read a book, and there were a lot of examples of these facts that are wrong.

M: Like what?

W: Well, most people think goldfish are not smart. But, goldfish are actually smart.

M: Really? Can you tell me more about that?

W: They can recognize their owners.

M: Oh, I didn't know that

Wrap Up 2

W: I read an interesting article about the Black Sea. Do you know where it is?

M: Yes. It's between Eastern Europe and Western Asia, right?

W: Right. What color do you think it is?

M: Well, black, I guess.

W: No, it isn't. It's blue.

M: Really? Then why is it called the Black Sea? Can you tell me more about it?

W: People call it the Black Sea because it is very dangerous.

본문 TEST Step 1   p.09~11

01 Spot Fake News
02 watch, hear, interesting news
03 seriously considered whether, article
04 what if, made up
05 harmful, less informed, misled
06 Nevertheless, various, throughout history
07 written such false information
08 thinking, hidden motives behind
09 AWFUL DISATER
10 broke down, cage, escaped
11 broke down, other, cages
12 ran dawn, injured hundreds
13 still on the loose
14 stay, until further notice
15 incident described, taken place
16 article, laughed out loud
17 Those, got really worried
18 Not knowing, false, panicked
19 Some, escape, others, hunt
20 make up such news
21 confessed, up, attention, unsafe
22 SLAV SHOOTS, IN ARGUMENT
23 shot, wounded, near, mining

24 had, argument during

25 led, shot, twice, chest

26 in critical condition

27 ran away after, shooting

28 searching, warning citizens, dangerous

29 there anything strange, article

30 Read, backwards, spells

31 Who wrote, why

32 so that, competitor, stealing

33 published, article, caught stealing

34 admit, harshly criticized, public

35 special cases, articles published

36 critically, judge whether, fake   37 How to spot

38 Consider, Source

39 from, reliable source

40 Can, trust, writer   41 Check, Date

42 new, old story

43 Is, related to current

44 Beyond the Headlines

45 headline match, content

46 Supporting Sources

47 related, provide similar content

23 was shot, seriously wounded by

24 had an argument during

25 led to, twice, in the chest

26 in critical condition

27 ran away after the shooting

28 are searching for, are warning, extremely dangerous

29 anything strange, article   30 backwards

31 wrote, why

32 pubilshed, so that, could, if, their articles

33 got caught stealing

34 had to admit, were harshly criticized

35 special cases, published

36 As, critically, judge whether, or 37 How to spot

38 Consider, Source

39 reliable source   40 trust, writer

41 Check   42 new, old story

43 Is, related to current

44 Beyond the Headlines

45 match the content

46 Supporting Sources

47 related, similar content

01 Spot Fake News

02 interesting news

03 have, considered whether

04 what if, completely made up

05 harmful in that, less informed, misled

06 Nevertheless, various fake, throughout history

07 written such false information

08 Let's look into, thinking, the hidden motives behind

09 AWFUL

10 broke down, escaped

11 broke down, the other

12 ran down, injured hundreds of   13 on the loose

14 Citizens, until further notice

15 described above, taken place

16 laughed out loud

17 got really worried

18 Not knowing, false, panicked

19 Some, to escape, others, to hunt

20 make up such news

21 made it up so that, could, readers' attention to

22 SHOOTS, IN ARGUMENT

1 당신은 가짜 뉴스임을 알아챌 수 있는가?

2 매일 우리는 흥미로운 뉴스를 보고, 듣고, 읽는다.

3 그러나 당신은 뉴스 기사가 정말로 진실인지 심각하게 고려해 본 적이 있는가?

4 모든 사람이 흥미로운 뉴스 기사를 좋아하지만, 만약 그것이 완전히 지어낸 것이라면 어떻게 할 것인가?

5 가짜 뉴스는 사람들에게 정보를 부족하게 제공하거나 사람들을 잘못 이끌 수 있다는 점에서 매우 해로울 수 있다.

6 그럼에도 불구하고, 역사를 통틀어 다양한 가짜 뉴스 보도들이 존재해 왔다.

7 왜 어떤 사람들은 그러한 거짓 정보를 써 왔던 것일까?

8 그 뒤에 숨겨진 동기를 생각하면서 몇 가지 뉴스 기사를 살펴보자.

9 끔찍한 참사

10 어젯밤, 화가 난 코뿔소 떼가 동물원 우리의 벽을 부수고 도망쳤다.

11 그들은 또한 다른 야생 동물 우리의 벽도 부수었다.

12 이 동물들은 거리를 뛰어다니며 수백 명의 사람들에게 부상을 입혔다.

13 그중 열두 마리의 동물들이 아직 잡히지 않았다.

14 시민들은 추후 안내가 있을 때까지 집 안에 머물러야 한다.

15 위에 기술된 어떤 행동이나 사건도 일어나지 않았다.

16 그 당시 이 기사를 주의 깊게 읽었던 사람들은 크게 웃었다.

17 그것을 끝까지 읽지 않은 사람들은 정말로 걱정하였다.

18 그 기사가 거짓이라는 것을 알지 못했기 때문에 많은 사람이 겁에 질려 어쩔 줄 몰랐다.

19 어떤 사람들은 도시를 빠져나가려고 했고 다른 사람들은 그 동물들을 사냥하기 위해 총을 들고 공원으로 나갔다.

20 그렇다면 왜 헤럴드 사는 이러한 뉴스를 만들어 냈을까?

21 나중에 그들은 동물원의 안전하지 않은 상태에 대해 독자들의 주의를 끌기 위해 그 기사를 지어냈다고 고백했다.

22 슬라브인이 언쟁 중에 친구에게 총을 쏘다

23 목요일 저녁 채굴 야영지 근처에서, 컬럼비아 광산 소속의 슬라브인 노동자 Mejk Swenekafew가 John Pecitello 에 의해 총상을 입어 심각하게 다쳤다.

24 그 두 사람은 회의 중에 언쟁을 벌였다.

25 언쟁이 싸움으로 번졌고, Pecitello가 Swenekafew의 가슴과 다리에 두 번 총을 쏘았다.

26 현재 그는 위독한 상태로 입원 중이다.

27 Pecitello는 총격 이후 도주했다.

28 경찰이 지금 그를 찾고 있으며, 그가 극히 위험하다고 시민들에게 경고하고 있다.

29 이 기사에 뭔가 이상한 점이 있는가?

30 그 슬라브인의 이름을 거꾸로 읽어 보아라. 그것의 철자는 " 우리는 뉴스를 조작한다."가 된다.

31 누가 이것을 썼고 왜 그랬을까?

32 데일리 텔레그램 사는 그들의 경쟁자인 데일리 뉴스 사가 그들의 기사를 훔치는지를 증명하기 위해서 이 거짓 기사를 발행했다.

33 데일리 뉴스 사는 그 다음 날 'Swenekafew'에 대한 동일한 기사를 발행했고 그래서 훔친 것이 발각되었다.

34 데일리 뉴스 사의 사람들은 그들의 행동을 인정해야만 했고 대중들로부터 혹독한 비난을 받았다.

35 이 두 기사는 특별한 경우였지만, 매일 발행되는 '가짜' 뉴스 기사는 많이 있다.

36 독자로서, 우리는 비판적으로 읽고 그 뉴스가 진짜인지 가짜인지 판단할 필요가 있다.

37 가짜 뉴스 판별 방법!

38 출처를 고려하라

39 그것은 믿을 만한 출처에서 온 것인가?

40 우리는 그 필자를 신뢰할 수 있는가?

41 날짜를 확인하라

42 그것은 새로운 이야기인가 혹은 오래된 이야기인가?

43 그것은 현재의 사건들과 관련된 것인가?

44 기사 제목 그 이상을 읽어라

45 기사 제목이 기사 내용과 일치하는가?

46 뒷받침하는 자료를 찾아라

47 다른 관련된 이야기도 비슷한 내용을 제공하는가?

1 Can You Spot Fake News?

2 Every day we watch, hear, or read interesting news.

3 However, have you ever seriously considered whether an article is really true?

4 Everyone likes an interesting news story but what if it is completely made up?

5 Fake news can be very harmful in that it can make people less informed or even misled.

6 Nevertheless, there have been various fake news reports throughout history.

7 Why have some people written such false information?

8 Let's look into some articles thinking about the hidden motives behind them.

9 AWFUL DISASTER

10 Last night, an angry group of rhinoceroses broke down the walls of the cage at the zoo and escaped.

11 They also broke down the walls of the other wild animals' cages.

12 These animals ran down the streets and injured hundreds of people.

13 Twelve of the animals are still on the loose.

14 Citizens should stay indoors until further notice.

15 Not a single act or incident described above has taken place.

16 At that time, those who read the article carefully laughed out loud.

17 Those who didn't read it to the end got really worried.

18 Not knowing the news was false, many people panicked.

19 Some tried to escape the city while others went into the parks with guns to hunt the animals.

20 So why did *The Herald* make up such news?

21 Later, they confessed that they made it up so that they could draw the readers' attention to the unsafe conditions at the zoo.

22 SLAV SHOOTS A FRIEND IN ARGUMENT

23 Mejk Swenekafew, a Slav worker at the Columbia Coal Mine, was shot and seriously wounded by John Pecitello near the mining camp Thursday evening.

24 The two men had an argument during a meeting.

25 The argument led to a fight, and Pecitello shot Swenekafew twice, in the chest and leg.

26 He is now at the hospital in critical condition.

27 Pecitello ran away after the shooting.

28 The police are searching for him now and are warning citizens that he is extremely dangerous.

29 Is there anything strange about the article?

30 Read the Slav's name backwards; it spells, "we-fake-news."

31 Who wrote this and why?

32 *The Daily Telegram* published this fake article so that they could prove if *The Daily News*, their competitor, was stealing their articles.

33 *The Daily News* published the same article about "Swenekafew" the next day and thus got caught stealing.

34 The people at *The Daily News* had to admit their act and were harshly criticized by the public.

35 The two articles were special cases, but there are many "fake" news articles published every day.

36 As readers, we need to read critically and judge whether the news is real or fake.

37 How to spot fake news!

38 Consider the Source

39 Is it from a reliable source?

40 Can we trust the writer?

41 Check the Date

42 Is it a new or an old story?

43 Is it related to current events?

44 Read Beyond the Headlines

45 Does the headline match the content?

46 Find Supporting Sources

47 Do other related stories provide similar content?

Wrap Up 3

1. title says, going to have a longer vacation

2. should check, if it is true

3. Why, say so

4. uses a shocking title, its content may tell

5. should read beyond

Read & Think After You Read B

1. write, Awful Disaster

2. draw the readers' attention, unsafe conditions

3. Actually, were very upset to find, false. How about, motive

4. wanted to prove that, was stealing their articles

Read & Think After You Read C

1. Among, think is the most important

2. finding supporting sources is, because, if, information is correct

---

Wrap Up 3

1. A: Wow! The news title says "Longer Vacation for Students." Hey, we're going to have a longer vacation!

2. B: Wait! We should check first if it is true.

3. A: Why do you say so?

4. B: Some news uses a shocking title but its content may tell a different story.

5. A: Oh, I see. I should read beyond the news title.

Read & Think After You Read B

1. Reporter: Why did *The Herald* write the "Awful Disaster" story, Mr. Right?

2. Mr. Right: They just wanted to draw the readers' attention to the unsafe conditions at the zoo.

3. Reporter: Actually, readers were very upset to find that it was false. How about "Slav Shoots a Friend in Argument?" What was the motive?

4. Mr. Right: *The Daily Telegram* wanted to prove that *The Daily News* was stealing their articles.

Read & Think After You Read C

1. A: Among the four tips, which do you think is the most important, and why?

2. B: I think finding supporting sources is the most important because I can check if the information is correct.

단어 TEST Step 1 p.26

01 영원히	02 추측하다, 추정하다
03 혼란스러운, 헷갈리는	04 설계하다
05 전시하다	06 자유	07 비싼, 돈이 많이 드는
08 쌍둥이의	09 대단히 귀중한, 값을 매길 수 없는
10 편안하게	11 스타덤, 스타의 반열
12 죽음	13 당혹스러운, 어리둥절한
14 지혜, 현명함	15 전문가	16 중요하다
17 선장	18 좌우명	19 실패
20 표현하다	21 어리석은, 바보 같은
22 사치스러운, 호화로운	23 난장이
24 고용하다	25 숲, 삼림, 산림	26 용
27 마지막으로, 끝으로	28 기한, 마감 일자
29 마술의, 마력이 있는	30 멀리 떨어진
31 보상	32 상황, 환경	33 성
34 등장인물	35 채우다	36 돌려주다
37 투옥시키다	38 세상을 떠나다, 돌아가시다
39 ~이 없어지다, ~이 다 떨어지다	40 ~에 갇히다
41 이루어지다, 실현되다	
42 (신조, 원칙 등)에 따라 살다	
43 ~을 살피다, ~을 돌보다	

단어 TEST Step 2 p.27

01 motto	02 chat	03 exhibit
04 death	05 stardom	06 luxurious
07 express	08 deadline	09 freedom
10 captain	11 hire	12 dragon
13 situation	14 magical	15 comfortably
16 forever	17 dwarf	18 foolish
19 failure	20 confusing	21 priceless
22 expensive	23 puzzled	24 reward
25 far-away	26 castle	27 forest
28 expert	29 suppose	30 lastly
31 twin	32 wisdom	33 explain
34 design	35 bring back	36 live by
37 lock up	38 pass away	39 run out of
40 settle in	41 look after	42 go wrong
43 come true		

단어 TEST Step 3 p.28

1 express, 표현하다 2 luxurious, 사치스러운, 호화로운

3 priceless, 대단히 귀중한, 값을 매길 수 없는

4 captain, 선장 5 character, 등장인물 6 hire, 고용하다

7 chef, 요리사 8 deadline, 기한, 마감 일자

9 dragon, 용 10 reward, 보상 11 exhibit, 전시하다

12 expert, 전문가 13 explain, 설명하다

14 failure, 실패 15 wisdom, 지혜, 현명함 16 castle, 성

대화문 TEST Step 1 p.29~31

Listen & Talk 1 A

1 you still up / because I'm worried about / You've read, have to worry about / confusing, worried that, might not remember/ Don't worry, that hasn't happened / try not to worry

2 Nothing special / have to go to, can't find anyone to feed / worry about, take care of / worried / for a walk, supposed to be

Listen & Talk 1 B

worried, matter / got a big part in / heard, singing / keep making mistakes, worried / a little, practice / making mistakes

Listen & Talk 2 A

1 have, read / magical water, lived forever / What would you do if, forever / would, different cities / interesting

2 called / heard, come true / if you could make one wish / would make, stay, forever, make all my wishes come true / smart

Listen & Talk 2 B

writing a review / one of, movies / what would you do if you could / would travel, prevent, How about / would go to, meet, big fan of

Communication Step A

How's, going / ran out / Don't worry about / character, What would you do if you were / find out if, likes

Wrap Up

1 I've heard that, writing contest / already / worried, wrong / I'm worried that, too difficult / Don't worry about, believe in yourself

2 watched, haven't / a man who was stuck on, deserted island / tries, would, if you were him / alive, build, hunt / that's what the man did

대화문 TEST Step 2 p.32~34

Listen & Talk 1 A

1 W: James, why are you still up? It's 11 o'clock!

M: I can't sleep because I'm worried about the Bookworm Competition tomorrow.

W: You've read all of the books on the list. What do

you have to worry about?

M: Some of the writers' names are confusing, so I'm worried that I might not remember them.

W: Don't worry about something that hasn't happened yet. You'll do fine.

M: Thanks. I'll try not to worry so much.

2 M: Sujin, what are you doing this weekend?

W: Nothing special, why?

M: I have to go to Busan for a family trip tomorrow but I can't find anyone to feed my dog, Lucy.

W: Don't worry about Lucy. I'll take care of her.

M: Oh, thank you so much. I was so worried.

W: I'll take her for a walk in the park, too. The weather's supposed to be nice tomorrow.

Listen & Talk 1 B

M: Jane, you look worried. What's the matter?

W: I got a big part in the school musical.

M: I heard you singing. You sound great!

W: It's just that I keep making mistakes. I'm so worried.

M: Oh, you just need a little more practice. Don't worry about making mistakes. You can actually learn from them.

W: Thanks, Dad. I hope I do a good job.

M: You'll do great.

Listen & Talk 2 A

1 M: Caroline, have you read the book, *Tuck Everlasting*?

W: Yeah, it is about a family that drank magical water and lived forever, right?

M: Right. What would you do if you could live forever?

W: Well, I would live in different cities all around the world.

M: Really? I would collect interesting items and make a museum.

W: Cool.

2 W: Jason, what are you reading?

M: I'm reading a book called *Three Wishes*.

W: Oh, I've heard about it. A genie makes a boy's wishes come true, right?

M: Yeah. What would you do if you could make one wish?

W: I would make the genies stay with me forever. Then, I could make all my wishes come true.

M: That's smart!

Listen & Talk 2 B

W: What are you doing, Jinho?

M: I'm writing a review of the movie, *The Time Traveler's Wife*.

W: I saw that movie, too. It's one of my favorite romantic movies.

M: I loved it, too. Emily, what would you do if you could time travel?

W: I would travel to the 1940s and prevent World War II. How about you?

M: I would go to the Joseon Dynasty and meet King Sejong. I'm a big fan of him.

Communication Step A

M: How's your online story going, Amy?

W: Not well. The deadline is this weekend but I ran out of ideas.

M: Don't worry about it. I can help you.

W: That would be great. My main character has special powers. What would you do if you were able to read people's minds?

M: Well, I would find out if the girl I like likes me.

W: That's a good idea. Thanks.

Wrap Up

1 M: I've heard that you're going to be in the writing contest next week.

W: Yeah, it's already next week.

M: You look worried. What's wrong?

W: I'm worried that the topic would be too difficult for me.

M: Don't worry about something you can't change. Just believe in yourself.

W: Thanks. I'll try.

2 M: Lisa, have you watched the movie, Cast Away?

W: No, I haven't. What is it about?

M: It's about a man who was stuck on a deserted island for 4 years.

W: It sounds interesting.

M: Yeah, the man tries everything to stay alive. What would you do if you were him?

W: To stay alive? Well, I would build a tree house and hunt for food.

M: Yeah, me too. And that's what the man did in the movie.

본문 TEST Step 1   p.35~36

01 rich, wise, had, sons

02 passed away, words, advice

03 Live by, throughout, life

04 Build, comfortably, Lastly, like
05 explain himself, passed away
06 death, share, wealth, settled
07 passed, following, words, left
08 richer than ever
09 puzzled, wrong, find out
10 welcomed, with open arms
11 down, chat, been, mind
12 It, that, built, every
13 stay, had, looked after
14 comfortably, had, designed, prepared
15 spend like, what, worrying
16 look at, empty-handed
17 not follow, father's wisdom
18 how did, get, rich
19 smiled, also followed, wisdom
20 a bit differently
21 build, took, as, stay
22 made friends, stayed at
23 comfortably, tired, work, floor
24 only when, hungry, tasted
25 Spend, like, rich, continued
26 how to make, grow
27 bring, back, rather, luxurious
28 it, that, tried, explain
29 how foolish, had been
30 With, in mind, life

13 always stay there, hired, had, looked after
14 sleep comfortably, enjoy, had, designed, my meals prepared by
15 told, to spend like, what I wanted, worrying
16 look at me, empty-handed
17 not follow, father's wisdom
18 how did, get, rich
19 smiled, also followed, father's wisdom
20 it a bit differently
21 build, took it as having a place to stay
22 made friends, stayed at, those cities
23 comfortably, because, if I was sleeping, or, hard floor
24 only when I was hungry, tasted great
25 like a rich man, continued
26 how to make money grow
27 on, that, bring me back, rather than on luxurious things
28 it was, that, tried to explain
29 how foolish he had been
30 With, in mind

01 rich, wise, had two sons
02 passed away, called, to give them, last words of advice
03 Listen carefully, Live by, throughout your life
04 Build, every city, comfortably. Enjoy, Lastly, spend, like
05 explain himself, passed away
06 his death, their share of, wealth, settled in different cities
07 passed, who had been following, no money left
08 was richer than ever
09 was puzzled about where, had gone wrong, to find out
10 welcomed, with open arms
11 sat down to chat, that had been on his mind for days
12 It was, that, in every city

1 부유하고 지혜로운 아버지에게 두 아들, Puru와 Puneet이 있었다.

2 아버지는 돌아가시기 전에, 마지막 충고의 말을 하기 위해 그의 두 아들을 불렀다.

3 "주의 깊게 듣거라, 사랑하는 아들아. 너희의 일생 동안 이 말대로 살면, 행복해질 것이다." 그는 말했다.

4 "모든 도시에 집을 지어라. 편하게 자거라. 음식을 즐기거라. 마지막으로, 돈을 부자처럼 쓰거라…."

5 아버지는 그 말을 설명하기도 전에 돌아가셨다.

6 그의 죽음 후에, 두 아들은 아버지의 재산 중 자신들의 몫을 가지고 다른 도시에 정착했다.

7 5년이 지났다. 아버지의 말을 신중히 따라온 Puru는 남은 돈이 없었다.

8 그러나 그의 동생은 그 어느 때보다 더 부자가 되었다.

9 Puru는 그가 어디서부터 잘못했는지 어리둥절했고, 그래서 그는 (그것을) 알아내기 위해 Puneet을 방문했다.

10 Puneet은 Puru를 두 팔 벌려 환영했다.

11 그날 밤, 형제가 저녁식사 후 이야기를 하려고 앉았을 때, Puru는 며칠간 자신의 마음에 있었던 그 질문을 했다.

12 "내가 따른 건 바로 우리 아버지의 조언이었지만, 나는 행복하지 않아. 나는 모든 도시에 집을 지었어.

13 그러나 나는 그곳에 항상 머물 수 없었으므로 사람들을 고용하여 집을 돌보게 했지.

14 아버지께서 우리는 편하게 자고 음식을 즐겨야 한다고 말씀하셔서 나는 내 침대를 전문가들에 의해 설계되게 했고, 내 식사는 훌륭한 요리사에 의해 준비되도록 했단다.

15 아버지는 우리에게 부자처럼 돈을 쓰라고 하셨으므로, 나는 돈 걱정을 하지 않고 내가 원하는 것을 샀지.

16 그렇지만 지금 나를 봐! 나는 빈털터리야.

17 너는 우리 아버지의 지혜를 따르지 않았니?

18 나에게 말해 보렴, 동생아, 너는 어떻게 그렇게 부유해졌으니?"

19 Puneet은 웃으며 말했다. "친애하는 형님, 저 또한 우리 아버지의 지혜를 따랐습니다.

20 하지만 저는 조금 다르게 이해했지요.

21 아버지가 '모든 도시에 집을 지어라'라고 말하셨을 때, 저는 그것을 전 세계에 머물 수 있는 장소를 가지는 것으로 여겼지요.

22 그래서 저는 모든 도시에서 친구를 사귀었고 그 도시들을 방문했을 때 그들의 집에 머물렀어요.

23 또한, 저는 하루 종일 열심히 일하고 나서 피곤해지곤 했기 때문에 침대에서 자든 딱딱한 바닥에서 자든 상관없이 매일 밤 편안하게 잠을 잤지요.

24 저는 배고플 때만 먹었기 때문에 간단한 식사마저도 훌륭한 맛이 났습니다."

25 "부자처럼 돈을 쓰라고요?" Puneet은 계속했다.

26 "부자는 돈을 불리는 방법을 알고 있어요.

27 그래서 저는 사치스러운 물건에 돈을 쓰는 것보다는 저에게 더 많은 돈을 돌려줄 수 있는 것에 돈을 쓰려고 노력했지요.

28 저에게는 이게 우리의 아버지가 설명하려고 하셨던 바로 그 지혜입니다."

29 이제 Puru는 그가 얼마나 어리석었었는지를 깨달았다.

30 이 지혜를 마음에 새기고, Puru는 새로운 삶을 시작했다.

본문 TEST Step 4 - Step 5   p.41~44

1 A rich and wise father had two sons, Puru and Puneet.

2 Before he passed away, he called his two sons to give them some last words of advice.

3 "Listen carefully, my dear sons. Live by these words throughout your life, and you will be happy," he said.

4 "Build a house in every city. Sleep comfortably. Enjoy your food. Lastly, spend money like a rich man... ."

5 Before he could explain himself, he passed away.

6 After his death, the two sons took their share of the father's wealth and settled in different cities.

7 Five years passed. Puru, who had been following his father's words carefully, had no money left.

8 But his brother was richer than ever.

9 Puru was puzzled about where he had gone wrong, so he visited Puneet to find out.

10 Puneet welcomed Puru with open arms.

11 That night, when the brothers sat down to chat after dinner, Puru asked the question that had been on his mind for days.

12 "It was our father's advice that I followed, but I am not happy. I built a house in every city.

13 But because I could not always stay there, I hired people and had the house looked after.

14 Father said we should sleep comfortably and enjoy our food, so I had my bed designed by experts and my meals prepared by a great chef.

15 He told us to spend like a rich man, so I bought what I wanted without worrying about money.

16 But look at me now! I am empty-handed.

17 Did you not follow our father's wisdom?

18 Tell me, brother, how did you get so rich?"

19 Puneet smiled and said, "My dear brother, I also followed our father's wisdom.

20 But I understood it a bit differently.

21 When he said 'build a house in every city,' I took it as having a place to stay all around the world.

22 So I made friends in every city and I stayed at their houses when I visited those cities.

23 Also, I slept comfortably each night because I would be tired after a hard day's work, and it did not matter if I was sleeping on a bed or on the hard floor.

24 I ate only when I was hungry, so even a simple meal tasted great."

25 "Spend money like a rich man?" continued Puneet.

26 "A rich man knows how to make money grow.

27 So, I tried to spend money on something that would bring me back more money rather than on luxurious things.

28 For me, it was this wisdom that our father tried to explain."

29 Now Puru realized how foolish he had been.

30 With this wisdom in mind, Puru started a new life.

Language in Use

1. freedom of speech, expression
2. explain the rules, before we start playing at

Grammar in Real Life B Look and Write

1. need to have, fixed
2. Why don't, have your hair cut
3. How about having
4. decorated with flowers, Look for

Think & Write C

1. Let, introduce
2. for
3. means, without fear, good experience
4. made, my motto when I was a kicker
5. From, even, made, a better kicker at the end
6. It, that changed my life

Language in Use

1. Everyone has freedom of speech and expression.
2. Can you explain the rules of the game before we start playing at?

Grammar in Real Life B Look and Write

1. Do you need to have the computer fixed? Call the Computer Doctor.
2. Why don't you have your hair cut at Susie's Hair Studio?
3. How about having your pet cleaned from head to toe? Come to Happy Pet.
4. Do you want to have your party room decorated with flowers? Look for Mary's Flowers.

Think & Write C

1. Let me introduce my motto.
2. It is "Go for it!"
3. It means "Go and do things without fear because failure is also a good experience."
4. I made it my motto when I was a kicker in the school soccer team.
5. From the motto, I learned that even the bad kicks made me a better kicker at the end.
6. It is this motto that changed my life!

01 편리한, 간편한	02 오래가다, (기능이) 지속되다
03 어울리다	04 경쟁하다 05 용돈
06 구매하다, 구입하다	07 출시하다, 발매하다
08 ~에 영향을 주다 09 사라지다	10 행동, 행위
11 결합하다 12 바꾸다, 교체하다	13 언급하다, 말하다
14 ~에 탑승하고, ~에 타서	15 할인; 할인하다
16 부추기다, 조장하다	17 효과
18 비교하다   19 환불   20 지출
21 개념   22 위험에 빠뜨리다   23 완성하다
24 고정하다   25 줄무늬가 있는   26 차이, 차이점
27 즉시, 바로   28 꽉 조이는, 딱 붙는   29 ~에 영향을 주다
30 부족, 결핍   31 닻; 닻을 내리다   32 10억
33 지나치게 뜨거운, 과열된   34 소비하다, 소모하다
35 진열된, 전시된   36 비교해 보면   37 ~와 잘 어울리다
38 단지 ~라는 이유로   39 ~을 기록하다
40 ~에 관해서, ~에 대해 말하자면
41 ~할 가능성이 있다, ~하기 쉽다   42 반 이상의
43 한눈에, 즉시

01 allowance	02 combine	03 immediately
04 effect	05 convenient	06 deal
07 billion	08 complete	09 affect
10 mention	11 consume	12 anchor
13 behavior	14 miss	15 difference
16 compare	17 encourage	18 compete
19 endanger	20 concept	21 striped
22 refund	23 release	24 influence
25 lack	26 disappear	27 discount
28 match	29 purchase	30 raise
31 replace	32 spending	33 tight
34 waste	35 on display	36 at a glance
37 in comparison	38 keep track of	39 as such
40 just because	41 go well with	
42 when it comes to		43 be likely to

1 immediately, 즉시, 바로   2 concept, 개념
3 disappear, 사라지다   4 purchase, 구입하다, 구매하다
5 release, 출시하다   6 suit, 어울리다
7 tight, 꽉 조이는, 딱 붙는   8 combine, 결합하다
9 waste, 낭비하다, 소모하다

10 convenient, 편리한, 간편한

11 encourage, 부추기다, 조장하다

12 allowance, 용돈　13 consume, 소비하다, 소모하다

14 endanger, 위험에 빠뜨리다　15 lack, 부족, 결핍

16 affect, ~에 영향을 주다

대화문 TEST Step 1

p.50~52

Listen & Talk 1 A

1 help, with / try on, with / How do you like / but, suits, have / one / take

2 Welcome to / I'm looking for / popular among, How do you like / green one is lighter than, one, lighter one / choice

Listen & Talk 1 B

bought, few weeks ago / looks, How do you like / convenient, anywhere, quality, too / How long, last / About, doesn't last / too bad / pretty happy, anyway

Listen & Talk 2 A

1 too uncomfortable / What's wrong with it / tight / you try it on before buying / so, bought, should have tried, on

2 are going to watch / to join / love to, I've spent, allowance / get it, ago / should have kept track of my spending

Listen & Talk 2 B

like mine / on sale / on sale, has just been released / is having, sale / at full price / selling, at, discount / should have checked the sales before

Communication Step A

heard that you bought, How, like / not happy, it / Why, What's / gets overheated, have read, reviews / ask for / won't give me back, I've used / calling, explaining / do

Wrap Up

1 I'd like to / How do you like this red one, among / that, one / striped, Its / take

2 package / bought, online used store, ago / let me see / is a little broken, said that / before / I just trusted, should have checked a bit more / should call, ask for a refund

대화문 TEST Step 2

p.53~55

Listen & Talk 1 A

1 M: Hi, can I help you with anything?

W: Yes, can I try on that cap with stars over there?

M: Sure. How do you like it?

W: The design is nice, but I don't think the color suits me. Do you have it in black?

M: Yes. I'll get one from the back. (pause) Here it is.

W: Great. I'll take it.

2 M: Good morning. Welcome to Kelly's Sporting Goods Store.

W: Hi, I'm looking for a backpack for hiking.

M: These two are popular among hikers. How do you like them?

W: The green one is lighter than the blue one. I'll take the lighter one.

M: Great choice.

Listen & Talk 1 B

W: Hi, Luke. Is that a new speaker?

M: Yes, I bought it a few weeks ago.

W: It looks cool. How do you like it?

M: It's convenient. I can take it anywhere and listen to music. The sound quality is good, too.

W: Great. How long does the battery last?

M: About 2 hours. The battery doesn't last long.

W: That's too bad.

M: Yeah, but I'm pretty happy with it, anyway

Listen & Talk 2 A

1 M: Oh, this coat is too uncomfortable.

W: Why? What's wrong with it?

M: It's too tight.

W: Didn't you try it on before buying it?

M: No. It was my size, so I just bought it. I should have tried it on.

2 W: Hey, Eric. Camilla and I are going to watch a movie. Do you want to join us?

M: I'd love to, but I can't. I've spent all of my allowance for this week.

W: Didn't you just get it a few days ago? How did you spend it all?

M: I'm not sure. I should have kept track of my spending.

Listen & Talk 2 B

M: Did you get a new phone, Jamie? It's just like mine.

W: Yeah, I got it last weekend on sale.

M: It was on sale? But it has just been released, hasn't it?

W: Right, but the store on Green Street is having a year-end sale.

M: Oh, I bought mine at full price!

W: Really? That's too bad. They're selling them at a 40 percent discount.

M: I should have checked the sales before buying mine.

Communication Step A

M: Hi, Riley. I heard that you bought a laptop online. How do you like it?

W: Oh, I'm not happy with it.

M: Why ? What's wrong?

W: It makes too much noise and gets overheated. I should have read more reviews.

M: Oh, then you should ask for your money back.

W: The online store won't give me back my money because I've used it for a week.

M: How about calling the online shop and explaining your problem?

W: Yeah, I think I should do that.

Wrap Up

1 M: Good morning. May I help you?

W: I'd like to buy a T-shirt for my sister. She's eleven years old.

M: How do you like this red one? This character is quite popular among children.

W: Well, she doesn't like animation characters that much. Can I see the blue one?

M: You mean this blue striped T-shirt? Its design is simple and cool.

W: Yes, I think my sister will like it. I'll take it.

2 W: Jake, here's a package for you.

M: It's my helmet. I bought it at an online used store a few days ago.

W: Oh, open it and let me see it.

M: Okay. (*pause*) Oh, this outer part is a little broken. The seller said that it's perfectly fine though.

W: Didn't you check the pictures of the helmet before you bought it?

M: No, I just trusted the seller. I should have checked a bit more.

W: You should call the seller and ask for a refund.

본문 TEST Step 1　　　　　　　　p.56~58

01 wondered why, bought, even
02 what affects, comes, buying
03 what my friends bought
04 goes, pair, on display

---

05 recognizes, because, half, wear
06 Although, ends up, another
07 effect, to explain, behavior
08 parade, encourages, jump aboard
09 others, likely get, follow
10 way, tend, just, bought
11 buy, pair, after, bought
12 that, Immediately, realizes, match
13 buys, go perfectly with
14 sees, none, match, clothes
15 Most, on, items, complete
16 made, search, after buying
17 explain, received, as, gift
18 noticed, furniture, go, replacing
19 therefore, purchasing, leads, unplanned
20 just because, on sale
21 goes window, sees, pair
22 checks, finds out, expensive
23 sales, approaches, discount on
24 though, discounted, still, low
25 described above, example, effect
26 mentioned, affects, opinion, prices
27 seem cheap in comparison
28 Furthermore, becomes bigger, powerful
29 As such, fixes, thoughts
30 like, things, considering, buying
31 As, shown, influence, purchases
32 time, think, about, buying

본문 TEST Step 2　　　　　　　　p.59~60

01 why you've bought things that
02 what affects us, comes to buying
03 what my friends bought
04 goes, sees a pair of, on display
05 recognizes, because, half of the boys, wear
06 Although, many pairs of, ends up buying another
07 bandwagon effect, to explain, behavior
08 that encourages, to jump aboard
09 more and more people, others are, likely to get on, follow
10 In, way, to buy, just because, have bought it
11 buy a pair of, after, have bought
12 that, Immediately, realizes that, match
13 that go, with
14 that none of her bags match, new clothes
15 buys, Most of her money is, on, to complete, new look

49

16 made, search for new items, after buying

17 effect, explain it, received, as, gift

18 after receiving, noticed that, furniture, go well, replacing most of it

19 therefore, that purchasing a new item, leads to, unplanned purchases

20 just because they are on sale

21 goes window shopping, sees, pair

22 checks, finds out that, that, too expensive

23 approaches him, discount on

24 Even though, is still, low, to buy

25 described above, example, anchoring effect

26 mentioned, affects, opinion of prices mentioned

27 For example, seem cheap in comparison

28 Furthermore, the difference, becomes bigger, be more powerful

29 As such, mentioned first, anchor, fixes our thoughts

30 Just like, to buy, without, considering why we are buying

31 As, have shown, influence our purchases

32 The next time, decide to buy, think, about why you are buying

---

본문 TEST Step 3　　　　　　　　　　　　　　p.61~62

1 여러분은 원하거나 필요로 하지도 않는 것들을 자신이 왜 구입했는지 궁금해 한 적이 있는가?

2 물건들을 구입하는 것에 관하여 무엇이 우리에게 영향을 주는지 생각해 보자.

3 나는 왜 친구들이 산 것을 사고 싶은 걸까?

4 Jeff는 쇼핑센터에 가서 진열되어 있는 축구화 한 컬레를 보게 된다.

5 그의 축구팀에 있는 소년들의 반 이상이 그 축구화를 신기 때문에 그는 그 신발을 한눈에 알아챈다.

6 이미 그에게는 축구화가 많이 있지만 결국 그는 또 다른 새 축구화를 사 버리고 만다.

7 우리는 Jeff의 행동을 설명하기 위해 '밴드왜건 효과'를 이용할 수 있다.

8 밴드왜건(악대차)은 사람들이 올라타서 음악을 즐기게끔 부추기는 퍼레이드에 있는 사륜마차이다.

9 더 많은 사람들이 밴드왜건에 올라탈수록 다른 사람들이 더욱 그것에 올라타거나 그것을 따라가려 한다.

10 이런 식으로, 사람들은 단지 다른 사람들이 어떤 것을 샀다는 이유로 그것을 구매하는 경향이 있다.

11 나는 왜 새 코트를 구입한 후에 바지와 가방을 사는 걸까?

12 Lisa는 정말 마음에 드는 코트를 산다. 그녀는 그녀의 바지가

새 코트와 어울리지 않는다는 것을 즉시 알아차린다.

13 그래서 그녀는 새 코트와 완벽하게 어울리는 새 바지를 구입한다.

14 하지만 그녀는 자신의 가방 중 어느 것도 새로운 옷들과 어울리지 않는다는 것을 알게 된다.

15 그래서 그녀는 새 가방을 산다. 그녀의 돈 대부분이 그녀의 새로운 모습을 완성하기 위하여 새로운 물품을 사는 데 쓰인다.

16 무엇이 Lisa로 하여금 새 코트를 산 후 즉시 새로운 물품을 찾게 했을까?

17 '디드로 효과'가 그것을 설명해 줄지도 모른다. 프랑스 작가인 Denis Diderot는 선물로 새 가운을 받았다.

18 그 선물을 받은 후에 곧 그는 그의 모든 가구가 새로운 가운과 어울리지 않는다는 것을 알아챘다. 그래서 그는 결국 대부분의 가구를 바꾸고 말았다.

19 그러므로 디드로 효과는 새로운 물품을 구입하는 것이 흔히 계획에 없던 더 많은 구매로 이어진다는 개념이다.

20 나는 왜 단지 할인 중이라는 이유로 물건을 구입하는 걸까?

21 Nathan은 진열된 상품을 구경하러 가서 헤드폰을 하나 본다.

22 그는 가격을 확인하고 그것이 200달러임을 알게 된다. 그는 그 헤드폰이 너무 비싸다고 생각한다.

23 점원이 그에게 다가와 "이 헤드폰에 20퍼센트 할인을 받을 수 있어요."라고 말한다.

24 비록 할인된 가격이 여전히 별로 저렴하지는 않지만 Nathan은 그 헤드폰을 사기로 결심한다.

25 위에 기술된 상황은 '앵커링 효과'의 한 예이다.

26 처음에 언급된 가격이 이후에 언급되는 가격에 대한 우리의 의견에 영향을 미친다.

27 예를 들어, 만약 우리가 200달러로 시작한다면, 비교해 볼 때 160달러는 저렴해 보일 것이다.

28 그뿐만 아니라, 두 가격의 차이가 커질수록 그 효과는 더욱 강력해질 것이다.

29 이와 같이 처음에 언급된 가격이 물건의 가격에 대한 우리의 생각을 고정하는 '닻'으로서 작동한다.

30 Jeff와 그의 친구들처럼, 우리는 우리가 왜 물건들을 사는지 진지하게 고려하지 않고 그것들을 구입하는 경향이 있다.

31 이러한 효과들이 보여 주듯이, 많은 것들이 우리의 구매에 영향을 미친다.

32 다음번에 여러분이 어떤 것을 구매하려고 결정할 때에는, 자신이 그것을 왜 사려는지 잠시 동안 생각해 보아라.

본문 TEST Step 4 - Step 5　　　　　　　　　p.63~67

1 Have you ever wondered why you've bought things that you don't even want or need?

2 Let's consider what affects us when it comes to buying things.

3 Why do I want to buy what my friends bought?

4 Jeff goes to the shopping center and sees a pair of soccer shoes on display.

5 He recognizes the shoes at a glance because more than half of the boys on his soccer team wear them.

6 Although he already has many pairs of soccer shoes, he ends up buying another new pair.

7 We can use the "bandwagon effect" to explain Jeff's behavior.

8 A bandwagon is a wagon in a parade that encourages people to jump aboard and enjoy the music.

9 As more and more people get on the bandwagon, others are more likely to get on or follow it.

10 In this way, people tend to buy something just because other people have bought it.

11 Why do I buy a pair of pants and a bag after I have bought a new coat?

12 Lisa buys a coat that she really loves. Immediately, she realizes that her pants do not match her new coat.

13 So, she buys new pants that go perfectly with her new coat.

14 But she sees that none of her bags match her new clothes.

15 So, she buys a new bag. Most of her money is spent on buying the new items to complete her new look.

16 What made Lisa search for new items immediately after buying a new coat?

17 The "Diderot effect" may explain it. Denis Diderot, a French writer, received a new gown as a gift.

18 Soon after receiving the gift, he noticed that all of his furniture did not go well with his new gown. So, he ended up replacing most of it.

19 The Diderot effect, therefore, is the concept that purchasing a new item often leads to more unplanned purchases.

20 Why do I buy things just because they are on sale?

21 Nathan goes window shopping and sees a pair of headphones.

22 He checks the price and finds out that they are $200. He thinks that the headphones are too expensive.

23 The sales person approaches him and says, "You can get a 20 percent discount on those headphones."

24 Even though the discounted price is still not very

low, Nathan decides to buy the headphones.

25 The situation described above is an example of the "anchoring effect."

26 The price mentioned first affects our opinion of prices mentioned afterwards.

27 For example, if we start with $200, then $160 will seem cheap in comparison.

28 Furthermore, as the difference of the two prices becomes bigger, the effect will be more powerful.

29 As such, the price mentioned first acts as an "anchor" that fixes our thoughts about the price of an item.

30 Just like Jeff and his friends, we tend to buy things without seriously considering why we are buying them.

31 As these effects have shown, many things influence our purchases.

32 The next time you decide to buy something, think for a moment about why you are buying it.

구석구석지문 TEST Step 1 p.68

Language in Use

1. It, to compare, in detail
2. encourage, to think for themselves

Grammar in Real Life B Look and Write

1. half of, is used to raise
2. One third of, is wasted, billion tons
3. only ten percent of, go to school
4. About, don't, how to read due to lack of

Think & Write C

1. did a survey, allowance
2. how often they get an allowance
3. get an allowance, seventy percent, get an allowance every month
4. what, spend most of their allowance on
5. Most of the allowance, one fourth, is spent on snacks
6. whether they think, should get a higher allowance
7. Ninety percent of the students think

구석구석지문 TEST Step 2 p.69

Language in Use

1. It is difficult to compare the results in detail.
2. We encourage children to think for themselves.

Grammar in Real Life B Look and Write

1. About half of the water is used to raise animals in the U.S.

2. One third of the world's food is wasted—1.3 billion tons every year.

3. In Somalia, only ten percent of the children go to school.

4. About fourteen percent of all people don't know how to read due to lack of education.

Think & Write C

1. I did a survey about allowance.

2. First, I asked 10 students how often they get an allowance.

3. Twenty percent of the students get an allowance every week and seventy percent of the students get an allowance every month.

4. Second, I asked them what they spend most of their allowance on.

5. Most of the allowance is spent on clothes and one fourth of the allowance is spent on snacks.

6. Lastly, I asked them whether they think that they should get a higher allowance.

7. Ninety percent of the students think that they should get a higher allowance.

적중100

영어 기출 문제집

정답 및 해설

비상 | 김진완